From *Grassroots: The Writer's Workbook,* Twelfth Edition
by Susan Fawcett

Personal Error Patterns Chart

Error Type & Symbol	Specific Error	Correction	Rule or Reminder	Assignment & Number of Errors

From *Grassroots: The Writer's Workbook,* **Twelfth Edition**
by Susan Fawcett

Proofreading Strategies

Many writers have found that the proofreading strategies described below help them see their own writing with a fresh eye. You will learn more strategies throughout *Grassroots.* Try a number of methods and see which ones work best for you.

Proofreading Strategy: Allow enough time to proofread.

Many students don't proofread at all, or they skim their paper for grammatical errors two minutes before class. This just doesn't work. Set aside enough time to proofread slowly and carefully, searching for errors and hunting especially for your personal error patterns.

Proofreading Strategy: Work from a paper copy.

People who proofread on computers tend to miss more errors. If you write on a computer, do not proofread on the monitor. Instead, print a copy of your paper, perhaps enlarging the type to 14 point. Switching to a paper copy seems to help the brain see more clearly.

Proofreading Strategy: Read your words aloud.

Reading silently makes it easier to skip over small errors or mentally fill in missing details, whereas listening closely is a great way to hear mistakes. Listen and follow along on your printed copy, marking errors as you hear them.

    a.   Read your paper aloud to *yourself.* Be sure to read *exactly* what's on the page, and read with enthusiasm.

    b.   Ask a *friend* or *writing tutor* to read your paper out loud to you. Tell the reader you just want to hear your words and that you don't want any other suggestions right now.

Proofreading Strategy: Read "bottom up," from the end to the beginning.

One way to fool the brain into taking a fresh look at something you've written is to proofread the last sentence first. Read slowly, word by word. Then read the second-to-last sentence, and so on, all the way back to the first sentence.

Proofreading Strategy: Isolate your sentences.

If you write on a computer, spotting errors is often easier if you reformat so that each sentence appears isolated, on its own line. Double-space between sentences. This visual change can help the brain focus clearly on one sentence at a time.

Proofreading Strategy: Check for one error at a time.

If you make many mistakes, proofread separately all the way through your paper for each error pattern. Although this process takes time, you will catch many more errors this way and make real progress. You will begin to eliminate some errors altogether as you get better at spotting and fixing them.

Grassroots
WITH READINGS

The Writer's Workbook

TWELFTH EDITION

Susan Fawcett

Australia • Brazil • Mexico • Singapore • United Kingdom • United States

Grassroots with Readings: The Writer's Workbook, **Twelfth Edition**
Susan Fawcett

Product Team Manager: Laura Ross

Associate Product Manager: Nancy Tran

Content Developer: Rachel Kerns

Product Assistant: Jaime Manz

Associate Marketing Manager: Nathaniel Pires

Senior Content Project Manager: Margaret Park Bridges

Manufacturing Planner: Fola Orekoya

IP Analyst: Amber Hill

Senior IP Project Manager: Kathryn Kucharek

Production Service: SPi Global

Compositor: SPi Global

Senior Designer: Diana Graham

Text Designer: Lachina

Cover Designer: Diana Graham

Cover Images: iStockPhoto.com/cat_arch_angel (ID:600165986); iStockPhoto.com/cat_arch_angel (ID:600166520); Flas100/Shutterstock.com

For product information and technology assistance, contact us at
Cengage Customer & Sales Support, 1-800-354-9706

For permission to use material from this text or product, submit all requests online at **www.cengage.com/permissions**
Further permissions questions can be emailed to
permissionrequest@cengage.com

Student Edition:
ISBN: 978-1-337-61431-3
Loose-leaf Edition:
ISBN: 978-1-337-61433-7

Cengage
20 Channel Center Street
Boston, MA 02210
USA

Cengage is a leading provider of customized learning solutions with employees residing in nearly 40 different countries and sales in more than 125 countries around the world. Find your local representative at **www.cengage.com**.

Cengage products are represented in Canada by Nelson Education, Ltd.

To learn more about Cengage platforms and services, visit **www.cengage.com**
Purchase any of our products at your local college store or at our preferred online store **www.cengagebrain.com**.

Printed in the United States of America
Print Number: 01   Print Year: 2017

Brief Contents

Contents

v

UNIT 5 Choosing the Right Noun, Pronoun, Adjective, Adverb, or Preposition 284

Follow the MAP to Better Reading and Writing:

David G. Myers and Ed Diener 285

UNIT 6 Revising for Consistency and Parallelism 342

Follow the MAP to Better Reading and Writing:

Julia Alvarez 343

UNIT 7 Mastering Mechanics 366

Follow the MAP to Better Reading and Writing:

Adam Gopnik 367

UNIT 8 Improving Your Spelling 414

Follow the MAP to Better Reading and Writing:
Dr. Karen Castellucci Cox 415

UNIT 9 Reading Selections 442

Preface

Grassroots with Readings grew out of my experience teaching English and directing the writing lab at Bronx Community College of the City University of New York. Existing texts labeled correct forms, the way handbooks do, but failed to teach my basic writing students how to write correctly. I began creating my own lessons, with clear, minimal instruction and lots of practice. Students loved these "sheets," which grew into the first edition of *Grassroots*. I designed *Grassroots* for a range of students—native and non-native speakers diverse in age, ethnicity, and background—who have not yet mastered the basic writing skills so crucial for success in college and most careers. The hallmarks of *Grassroots'* successful pedagogy are its clear, inductive lessons in writing and grammar; modular organization; inspiring student and professional models; numerous engaging practices and writing assignments; focus on critical thinking; top-quality reading selections; and ESL coverage that is carefully integrated throughout the text. I am proud that *Grassroots* has remained the leading basic writing text through eleven editions and has won peer-juried awards for excellence.

In planning this important Twelfth Edition, my publisher and I consulted instructors across the country to learn how *Grassroots* might better serve their needs and those of their students in this high-pressure time of course redesign and constrained budgets. They told us that while they wanted *Grassroots* to remain a writing text, they would like more coverage of reading strategies, a broader range of professional reading selections, some vocabulary work, and of course, many grammar-in-context practices on current topics. Their thoughtful comments inspired the changes in this edition: more focus on reading tools and strategies; many new professional readings, with a wider variety of nonfiction for students to analyze; new material on vocabulary building; and many fresh practices, thinking tasks, and writing assignments to keep students engaged. My goal in this edition is to help instructors prepare students more quickly for the academic and work challenges they will face, while still maintaining the clear, user-friendly approach that has helped millions of *Grassroots* students learn.

IMPORTANT NEW FEATURES OF *GRASSROOTS* *12th* EDITION

New! Expanded focus on reading for writers

- Redesigned unit openers highlight *Grassroots'* read-think-write pedagogy, sometimes called the Fawcett MAP. Throughout the book, students learn by reading a written MODEL, ANALYZING it, and then PRACTICING what they have learned, usually by writing.

- New Chapter 1, Part A: The Reading and Writing Connection, describes active reading, introduces the Fawcett MAP method, explains the positive influence of reading on writing, and introduces six useful reading strategies.

- Reading Tools for Writers, the new introduction to Unit 9, Reading Selections, includes a section on Active Reading, expanded Reading Strategies for Writers (emphasizing textbook chapters, essays, and longer pieces of writing), an Annotated Model Essay, and a section titled Connecting Your Reading and Writing that concludes with a colorful *Checklist for the Reader & Checklist for the Writer.*

New! Nine professional reading selections

- *Grassroots'* diverse and powerful array of 19 nonfiction selections, many by top authors, now includes nine fresh articles, textbook excerpts, and essays: Andrew Lam on American wastefulness, Constance Staley on single-tasking as the premiere skill for college success, comedian Kunal Nayyar on his first college job, Christine Porath on incivility at work, Karen Castellucci Cox on video games that foster four types of learning, Esther Cepeda on the right to dislike tamales, James Campbell on our fading connection to nature, Angela Johnston on the ethics of carebots, and Rebecca Sutton on the power of secrets. Student and instructor favorites from the previous edition—by authors like Sherman Alexie, Maya Angelou, Leonard Pitts, and Diane Sawyer—have been retained to round out this thought-provoking collection. Each reading is accompanied by a headnote, language-awareness and vocabulary questions, discussion questions, and writing assignments.

- *Grassroots* offers the strongest collection of readings anywhere. And for instructors who want even more professional selections to supplement their courses, Questia, a bank of digital readings, is available through *Grassroots'* MindTap.

Reorganized. Paragraph patterns newly configured in 3 chapters

The nine rhetorical modes have been reorganized into three, not two, chapters. Instructors requested this far more logical and easy-to-use division:

Chapter 5—illustration, narration, description
Chapter 6—process, comparison, contrast
Chapter 7—definition, cause and effect, persuasion

New! Language Awareness and Vocabulary Feature

- The questions accompanying each reading selection in Unit 9 now include two Language Awareness Questions, which focus on vocabulary building or language in context.

New! Thirty-two new high-interest practice exercises that teach grammar in context

- *Grassroots'* hundreds of carefully crafted practices on current topics set it apart from competitors. Not only does *Grassroots* offer more grammar in context than any other text, but it includes many more engaging paragraph- and essay-length practices relevant to students' lives, education, and cultural literacy. Engagement with the text leads to persistence, and persistence is key to success in this course.

- Fresh subjects chosen to make students *want* to keep reading include 3-D printing • career skills taught on TV's *Shark Tank* • urban farmer Will Allen • the opioid epidemic • successful Latina businesswomen • Utah's canyons • the career of a medical sonographer • NBA and community star Kevin Durant • the effects of more female police officers on communities • San Diego Comic-Con • the drone debate • Lin-Manuel Miranda and the creation of *Hamilton* • the fastest-growing job in America • Paralympian Melissa Stockwell • Facebook pros and cons • NASA mathematician Katherine Johnson

- In addition, 42 more practices, like that on CTE brain damage in NFL players, have been updated with current research, thus modeling the research skills we hope to instill in our students.

Improved. Visual Program with 42 new images

The rich visual-image program that students so enjoy has been refreshed with 42 new photographs, graphs, public-service announcements, paintings, and cartoons. Reflecting the author's belief that today's students need critical viewing skills and deserve exposure to high-quality images as well as fine written models and readings, all visuals are chosen to engage students and augment the instruction at hand.

THE BEST OF GRASSROOTS

Grassroots with Readings, Twelfth Edition, retains the features that have made it the most popular first-level developmental writing text in the country:

- Clear, step-by-step lessons
- Hundreds of thought-provoking practices that teach grammar in context and keep students involved
- Provocative activities, writing assignments, and reading selections
- Critical thinking and viewing opportunities integrated throughout
- Modular organization and flexible flow of chapters
- Dynamic, clear design that supports basic readers and writers
- Numerous quality photos, paintings, cartoons, and graphics
- Integrated ESL coverage, with typical problems anticipated in the text
- "Exploring Online" web links for self-initiated practice and mini-research
- Unit openers, *Follow the MAP to Better Reading and Writing,* showcasing professional paragraphs
- Unit closers, collaborative Writers' Workshops, featuring student writing for guided peer review and writing
- Instructor's Annotated Edition that includes answers and the author's Teaching Tips and ESL Tips to guide new instructors or adjuncts and inspire even seasoned instructors

- Extensive, updated Test Bank
- Student answer key for faculty who want students to self-check

DIGITAL RESOURCES FOR *GRASSROOTS*

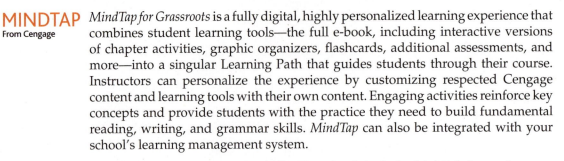

MindTap for Grassroots is a fully digital, highly personalized learning experience that combines student learning tools—the full e-book, including interactive versions of chapter activities, graphic organizers, flashcards, additional assessments, and more—into a singular Learning Path that guides students through their course. Instructors can personalize the experience by customizing respected Cengage content and learning tools with their own content. Engaging activities reinforce key concepts and provide students with the practice they need to build fundamental reading, writing, and grammar skills. *MindTap* can also be integrated with your school's learning management system.

- **Promotes students' study skills:** The e-book includes highlighting and note-taking tools that allow students to annotate and engage with the content and a Study Hub app that lets students create their own study guides.

- **Provides interactive exercises and activities to engage students:** Interactive activities and *Aplia* problem sets provide engaging exercises that challenge students and offer them a variety of ways to learn and connect with the content. Instant feedback reinforces key concepts.

- **Addresses students' busy lives:** Students can listen to chapters via the ReadSpeaker app while on the go. The *MindTap* mobile app also allows students to digest and interact with course content to stay on top of all assignments and class activities. The *MindTap* app features the e-book, flashcards, practice quizzes, notifications, reminders, and more.

- **Offers the option of Write Experience:** *Write Experience* encourages students to learn how to write well in order to communicate effectively and think critically. *Write Experience* provides students with additional writing practice without adding to an instructor's workload. Utilizing artificial intelligence to score student writing instantly and accurately, it provides students with detailed revision goals and feedback on their writing to help them constantly improve. *Write Experience* is powered by e-Write IntelliMetric Within—the gold standard for automated scoring of writing—used to score the Graduate Management Admissions Test (GMAT) analytical writing assessment. Visit **www.cengage.com/training/mindtap** and check "WriteExperience" under "MindApps" to learn more.

- **Includes free access to Questia:** *Questia* is an online research tool containing more than 78,000 online books from reputable commercial and academic presses and more than nine million quality journal, newspaper, and magazine articles. *Questia* also guides students through the entire research and writing process, from selecting topics and finding sources to creating and organizing notes, building paper outlines, and formatting proper citations. In addition, *Questia* allows instructors to select and assign additional readings in *MindTap*.

Aplia for Grassroots. Through diagnostic tests, succinct instruction, and engaging assignments, *Aplia* for *Grassroots* reinforces concepts and provides students with the practice they need to build fundamental reading, writing, and grammar skills.

- Diagnostic tests provide an overall picture of a class's performance, allowing instructors to instantly see where students are succeeding and where they need additional help.

- Assignments include immediate and constructive feedback, reinforcing important ideas and motivating students to improve their reading and writing skills.

- Grades are automatically recorded in the *Aplia* gradebook, keeping students accountable while minimizing time spent grading.

- **The Individualized Study Path (ISP).** An ISP course generates a personalized list of assignments for each student that is tailored to his or her specific strengths and weaknesses. ISP assignments are randomized, auto-graded problems that correspond to skills and concepts for a specific topic. Students get as much help and practice as they require on topics where they are weak. Conversely, if there are topics they understand well, no remediation is necessary and no additional assignments will be present.

On the *Grassroots* **Instructor Companion Website**, find everything you need for your course in one place. This collection of book-specific tools is available online via **cengage.com/login**.

- The **Instructor's Manual** offers suggestions for the new instructor looking for support or the more experienced teacher looking for ideas. Advice about instructional methods, assignments, and uses of the book's features are based on the author's many years of classroom teaching experience. Chapter-by-chapter notes provide an overview of concepts and skills addressed in each chapter, along with specific teaching suggestions.

- A robust and revised **Test Bank**, including hundreds of diagnostic and mastery tests, chapter tests, and unit tests, offers instructors a wide array of supplementary assessments that can be used as additional practice or as a way to monitor students' progress.

- **PowerPoint® lecture slides** are available for each chapter in the text.

ACKNOWLEDGMENTS

I wish to thank these astute reviewers and colleagues whose thoughtful comments and suggestions in both written reviews and focus group interviews helped strengthen this Twelfth Edition:

Silvia Babcock, *Tidewater Community College*

Lynette Bowen, *South Plains College*

Arta Clark, *Kellogg Community College*

Patricia Colella, *Bunker Hill Community College*

Sarah Condiff, *Elizabethtown Community and Technical College*

Patricia Dungan, *Austin Community College*

Mackinzee Escamilla, *South Plains College*

Susan Farmer, *Dakota County Technical College*

Susan Hester, *Florida SouthWestern State College*

Stacey Higdon, *Houston Community College*

Travis Holt, *Liberty University*

Shayla Loree, *Dakota County Technical College*

Rose McNeil, *Southwest Tennessee Community College*

Mary Ogburn, *Scott Community College*

William Ruleman, *Tennessee Wesleyan University*

Jennifer Skop, *Cuyahoga Community College*

Matilda Staudt, *Palo Alto College*

Marie Teitgen, *Kellogg Community College*

Myrna Valdez, *San Jacinto College*

Jenny Walter, *Liberty University*

Heather Wilson, *Ivy Tech Community College*

I am indebted to the team at Cengage, who worked hard to bring this revision of *Grassroots* to fruition: My thanks to Nancy Tran, Associate Product Manager, who good-naturedly kept us on mission, despite the unique challenges facing developmental education and publishing now; Rachel Kerns, Content Developer, for sharing this journey with me, problem-solving, finding our way over and through obstacles to reach the goal—this strong new edition of *Grassroots*; Ann Hoffman and Amber Hill, Intellectual Property Analysts; Kathryn Kucharek, Senior Intellectual Property Project Manager; Kristine Janssens, Text Researcher; and Nisha Bhanu Beegum, Image Researcher, Lumina Datamatics for securing rights for the high-quality text excerpts and images that help make *Grassroots* shine; Margaret Bridges, Senior Content Project Manager; Hannah Whitcher of SPi Global for helping turn our manuscript into a beautiful book; and Nathaniel Pires, Associate Marketing Manager, for getting this book to colleges and dedicated instructors across the country.

Special thanks to Dr. Karen Cox of San Francisco City College, my friend across the miles and one of the finest teachers I've known, for her advice and contributions to this book, including the fascinating classification essay she wrote exclusively for *Grassroots*. I am grateful to my friend and colleague Dr. Emmy Smith Ready, who jumped in to help when the time crush got crazy, drafted practices, commented on new material, and proofread when we needed a pair of sharp eyes. Poet and University of Miami professor Holly Iglesias read new anthology selections and drafted some of the headnotes and questions. Finally, thank you to Lauren Murphy of Cengage for believing in me and my commitment to students.

My love and profound gratitude to the friends and family who supported me during this arduous year—especially Maggie Smith, Colleen Huff, Elaine Unkeless, and my talented brother and brother-in-law, David Fawcett and Eddie Brown. I dedicate this Twelfth Edition to Dr. Richard Donovan—my husband, keenest reader, and best friend. My deepest wish, now more than ever, is that this book will achieve the goal of teaching and uplifting those students whose aspirations and determination to succeed are a force of nature.

Writing Effective Paragraphs

The goal of Grassroots is to make you a better writer, and Unit 1 is key to your success. In this unit, you will

- Follow the MAP to better reading and writing
- Learn the importance of subject, audience, and purpose
- Learn the parts of a good paragraph
- Practice the paragraph-writing process
- Learn how to revise and improve your paragraphs
- Apply these skills to exam questions and short essays
- Learn proofreading strategies to find and correct your own errors

© V.J. Matthews/Shutterstock.com

Follow the MAP to Better Reading and Writing

MODEL

Read, aloud if possible, this model paragraph, in which writer Alice Walker recalls her mother's extraordinary talent.

My mother adorned with flowers whatever shabby house we were forced to live in, and not just your typical straggly country stand of zinnias, either. She planted ambitious gardens—and still does—with over fifty different varieties of plants that bloom profusely from early March until late November. Before she left home for the fields, she watered her flowers, chopped up the grass, and laid out new beds. When she returned from the fields, she might divide clumps of bulbs, dig a cold pit, uproot and replant roses, or prune branches from her taller bushes or trees—until night came and it was too dark to see.

Alice Walker, "In Search of Our Mothers' Gardens"

ANALYSIS

- Ms. Walker's well-written paragraph brings to life her mother's passion for flowers. Are any words and details especially vivid? Why do you think Walker's mother worked so hard on her gardening?

- Good writing can make us remember, see, feel, or think in certain ways. Unit 1 will guide you through the steps of writing well and give you tools to improve your writing.

PRACTICE

- Write about an activity that you or someone close to you passionately enjoys.

- Write about someone who inspires you with her or his ambition or creativity.

Exploring the Writing Process

Did you know that the most successful students and employees are people who read and write well? In fact, many good jobs today require excellent writing and communication skills in fields as varied as computer technology, health sciences, education, and social services. According to the National Association of Colleges and Employers, 73.4 percent of all employers want job candidates with strong written communication skills.

The goal of this book is to help you become a better and more confident writer. You will realize that the ability to write well is not a magical talent that some people possess and others don't but rather a life skill that can be learned. I invite you to make a decision now to excel in this course. It will be one of the best investments you could ever make in yourself, your education, and your future. Let *Grassroots* be your guide, and enjoy the journey.

A. The Reading and Writing Connection

Reading and writing go hand in hand; practice in one improves the other. Often, people who loved to read as children become strong writers as well. They learn what good writing is through the books and magazines they read. But many others arrive in college without solid reading and writing habits; if you belong to the latter group, this course is an ideal opportunity for you to develop these skills. Your effort will pay off.

Reading and writing both require that you think critically. You can visualize the **reading, writing, thinking** process as a circle:

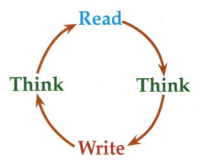

I have built the *reading-thinking-writing* process into every lesson in *Grassroots*. Instruction follows this simple three-step MAP to better English skills: (1) You will read a written MODEL (a sentence, paragraph, or longer piece of writing). (2) You will ANALYZE the model with the help of questions. (3) You will PRACTICE what you just learned, usually by writing. My publisher calls this the **Fawcett MAP**.

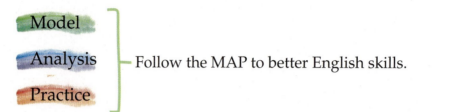

Model

Analysis   — Follow the MAP to better English skills.

Practice

Model

Here's a sample of the kind of *model* paragraph, bulleted questions for *analysis*, and *practice* that will guide you through this book:

> In 2016, Stanford University researchers released the alarming results of a year-long study of how well American middle school, high school, and college students could evaluate information they read in articles, tweets, and comments online. Even the researchers were shocked by how easily and how often students were fooled. They tested 7,800 students in 12 states, and the poor results were consistent. In exercise after exercise, students could not tell the difference between a paid advertisement, an opinion piece, and a factual news article. Eighty percent of middle school students thought "sponsored content" was real news. At every level, most students had no idea that they need to check to see whether the news or information is factual and real or not—especially if they received that information through social media like Facebook and Twitter—and most didn't know *how* to check a source. The Stanford study itself became concerning national news.

Analysis

- What is the main idea of this paragraph? _____

  _____

- What facts and details are used to support the main idea? Did you find any details especially surprising or convincing? Which ones and why?

Practice

PRACTICE 1

Small group discussion: How serious, in your view, is the study's finding that most students don't know how to evaluate information online or tell facts from fiction? What, if anything, should be done about this problem? Take notes for a possible paper on this subject.

Caution: Reading on the Internet

Reading books, reputable newspapers, and magazines will improve your writing skills because these publications model good research and writing. You will find that analyzing good writing teaches you ways to develop and organize ideas and entice the reader with well-chosen details. On the Internet, however, be very cautious because many websites have no professional editors and researchers to review stories, fact-check, or correct grammar. Social media has revolutionized the way we connect with friends and the world, but valuable tools like Facebook and Twitter also have helped promote the viral spread of rumors and stories that are not factual. Because social media users trust their friendship circles, they rarely check the source or truth of information and "news" forwarded by friends.

Groups that write and send out false information are usually trying to sell something, make money with "click bait" headlines, or promote their own cause. They know that people often click on a shocking headline or "news" that supports their prejudices and quickly forward the story without thinking critically about it or checking the facts. So be wary when you read on the Web, especially on social media. Get your college and work information from government or university websites that post research-based, factual information and your news from respected organizations like the *Wall Street Journal* and the *Washington Post* that do solid research and reporting.

Active Reading Strategies for Writers

In Practice 1, you experienced **active reading**, as you will each time you complete a lesson or chapter in this book. The active reader doesn't just move his or her eyes down the page or screen, but is actively engaged—thinking, asking and answering questions, and marking the reading selection in ways that help him or her understand and remember. If you are reading celebrity gossip or a brochure from the supermarket, you will no doubt skim it and set it aside. But in order to master college textbook chapters, works of literature, and increasingly, to evaluate material on the Internet, you will need to become an *active reader*, armed with tools and strategies to help you understand and retain what you read.

In Unit 9, Reading Selections, you will find 19 provocative professional essays and articles, many by America's most respected authors. Unit 9 opens with tools and strategies to help you become a better reader, especially of longer material. For now, try out these six specific strategies to help you become a more active and effective reader:

1. Focus. Find a quiet, pleasant place to read or work on an assignment, in the library, for instance. Mute and put away your electronic devices. Distraction is a major barrier to college and work success.*

2. Preview the reading selection. This strategy is important for longer, more difficult reading assignments like textbook chapters. Before you read, scan the title, the article, and any subtitles to get an idea of what the piece is about. Look for the main idea and supporting ideas.

3. Read and Annotate. Now carefully read the piece through, thinking about its meaning. What is the main point the author is making? What details support this main idea? As you read, **annotate** the book or online text to help you follow and understand. For example, underline or highlight the most important or striking points. Write down notes or questions you have. Jotting as you read will help you remember.

4. Build Vocabulary. As you read and annotate, mark any words you don't know, so you can look up their meanings in your print or online dictionary. Keep a list of new words, and practice using them in your writing.

---

*"Zoom In and Focus" by college success expert Constance Staley, in Unit 9, explains why this step is a key to both college and work success.

5. Reread. Now read the piece again. You'll be surprised how much more you understand the second time.

6. Review and Retell. Before you discuss the material in class or are tested on it, be sure to review: go over your annotations, underlinings, questions to refresh your memory. A helpful tool for many people is to retell out loud the main points of the reading or chapter—what it is about. This refreshes your memory and helps prepare you to share your thoughts with more confidence.

PRACTICE 2

SELF-ASSESSMENT AS A READER

Think about something you read recently for college or work and about how you approached that task. In your journal or notebook, answer these questions: How would I describe myself as a reader? How many of the six strategies do I use when reading? Which ones sound most helpful? What one change would most improve my reading skills?

PRACTICE 3

Choose three careers you might wish to pursue and imagine what reading and writing tasks you might need to take on in each career. On a separate piece of paper, list them.

B. The Writing Process

The rest of this chapter will give you an overview of the writing process, as well as some tips on how to approach your writing assignments in college. Many people have the mistaken idea that good writers just sit down and write a perfect paper or assignment from start to finish. In fact, experienced writers go through a **process** consisting of steps like these:

1 Prewriting
- Thinking about possible subjects
- Freely jotting down ideas on paper or computer
- Narrowing the subject and writing it as one sentence
- Deciding which ideas to include
- Arranging ideas in a plan or outline

2 Writing
- Writing a first draft

3 Rewriting
- Rethinking, rearranging, and revising as necessary
- Writing one or more new drafts
- Proofreading for grammar and spelling errors

Writing is a personal and often messy process. Writers don't all perform these steps in the same order, and they may have to go through some steps more than once. However, most writers **prewrite**, **write**, **rewrite**—and **proofread**.

It is important that you set aside enough time to complete every step in the writing process. A technique called **backward planning** helps many students manage their writing time. Begin with the assignment's due date and plan to complete each step on a different day. Using the calendar below, one student first wrote down the Friday deadline for her paragraph assignment. Then, working backward, she decided to proofread on Thursday and again Friday morning, to revise her paragraph on Wednesday, write her first draft on Tuesday, and start jotting and organizing her ideas on Monday.

SUNDAY	MONDAY	TUESDAY	WEDNESDAY	THURSDAY	FRIDAY	SATURDAY
1	2 Jot down and organize ideas for paragraph.	3 Write first draft of paragraph.	4 Revise paragraph.	5 Proofread.	6 Proofread again. Final draft due!	7

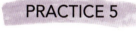

PRACTICE 4   SELF-ASSESSMENT AS A WRITER

Choose something that you wrote recently for a class or for work and think about the *process* you followed in writing it. With a group of three or four classmates, or in your notebook, answer these questions:

1. Did I do any planning or prewriting—or did I just start writing the assignment?
2. How much time did I spend improving and revising my work?
3. Was I able to spot and correct my own grammar and spelling errors?
4. What ideas or beliefs do I have about writing? (Examples: *In my field, I won't need to write*, or *English teachers make a bigger deal about errors than anyone else*.) Do any of my beliefs get in the way of my progress?
5. What one change in my writing process would most improve my writing? Spending more time for prewriting? Spending more time revising? Improving my proofreading skills?

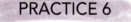

PRACTICE 5

Bring in some help-wanted ads from a newspaper or print some from career sites such as www.indeed.com or www.careerbuilder.com. Study the ads in career fields that interest you. Next, count the number of ads that stress writing and communication skills. Be prepared to present your findings to the class.

PRACTICE 6

Using a calendar, employ the *backward planning technique* to plan the steps needed to complete your next writing assignment.

C. Subject, Audience, and Purpose

As you begin a writing assignment, give some thought to your **subject**, **audience**, and **purpose**.

When your instructor assigns a broad **subject**, try to focus on one aspect that interests you. For example, suppose the broad subject is *music*, and you play the conga drums. You might focus on why you play them rather than some other instrument or on what drumming means to you. Whenever possible, choose subjects you know and care about: observing your neighborhood come to life in the morning, riding a dirt bike, helping a child become more confident, learning more about your computer. Your answers to questions like those listed below will suggest promising writing ideas. Keep a list of the best ones.

To find or focus your subject, ask

- What special experience or knowledge do I have?

- What angers, saddens, or inspires me?

- What campus, job, or community problem do I have ideas about solving?

- What story in the news affected me recently?

How you approach your subject will depend on your **audience**, your readers. Are you writing for classmates, a professor, people who know about your subject, or people who do not? For instance, if you are writing about weight training, and your readers have never been inside a gym, you will approach your subject in a simple and basic way, perhaps stressing the benefits of weightlifting. An audience of bodybuilders, however, already knows these things; for bodybuilders, you would write in more depth, perhaps focusing on how to develop one muscle group.

To focus on your audience, ask

- For whom am I writing? Who will read this?

- Are they beginners or experts? How much do they know about the subject?

- Do I think they will agree or disagree with my ideas?

Finally, keeping your **purpose** in mind helps you know what to write. Do you want to *explain* something to your readers, *convince* them that a certain point of view is correct, *describe* something, or just *tell a good story*? If your purpose is to persuade parents to support having school uniforms, you can explain that uniforms lower clothing costs and may reduce student crime. However, if your purpose is to convince students that uniforms are a good idea, you might approach the subject differently, emphasizing how stylish the uniforms look or why students from other schools feel that uniforms improve their school atmosphere.

PRACTICE 7   List five subjects you might like to write about. Consider your audience and purpose. For whom are you writing? What do you want them to know about your subject? For ideas, reread the boxed questions.

	Subject	Audience	Purpose
EXAMPLE:	how to make a Greek salad	inexperienced cooks	to show how easy it is to make a great Greek salad

	Subject	Audience	Purpose
1.			
2.			
3.			
4.			
5.			

PRACTICE 8

With a group of three or four classmates, or on your own, jot down ideas for the following two writing tasks. Notice how your points and details differ depending on your audience and purpose. (If you are not employed, write about a job with which you are familiar.)

1. For a new co-worker, you plan to write a description of a typical day on your job. Your purpose is to help train this person, who will perform the same duties you do. Your supervisor will need to approve what you write.

2. For one of your closest friends, you plan to write a description of a typical day on your job. Your purpose is to make your friend laugh because he or she has been feeling down recently.

PRACTICE 9

CRITICAL VIEWING AND WRITING

Study the advertisement shown below and then answer these questions: What *subject* is the ad addressing? Who do you think is the target *audience*? What is the ad's intended *purpose*? In your view, how successful is the ad in achieving its purpose? Explain.

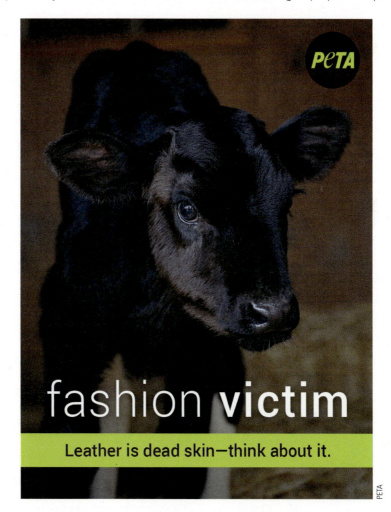

PRACTICE 10

Read the following classified ads from real city newspapers around the country, if possible in a group with three or four classmates. The *subject* of each ad is a product or service that is for sale, the *audience* is the potential customer, and the *purpose* is to convince that customer to buy the product or service. How does each ad writer undercut his or her purpose? How would you revise each ad so that it better achieves its intended purpose?

1. Do you need a dramatic new look? Visit our plastered surgeons.

2. We do not tear your clothing with machinery. We do it carefully by hand.

3. Now is your chance to have your ears pierced and get an extra pair to take home free.

4. Tired of cleaning yourself? Let me do it.

5. Auto repair service. Try us once, and you'll never go anywhere again.

D. Guidelines for Submitting Written Work

Learn your instructor's requirements for submitting written work, as these may vary from class to class. Here are some general guidelines. Write in any special instructions.

1. Choose sturdy, white, 8 ½-by-11-inch paper, plain if you use a computer, lined if you write by hand.

2. Type or clearly write your name, the date, and any other required information, using the format requested by your instructor.

3. Double-space if you write on a computer. Some instructors also want handwriting double-spaced.

4. If you write by hand, do so neatly in black or dark blue ink.

5. Write on only one side of the paper.

6. Leave margins of at least one inch on all sides.

7. Number each page of your assignment, starting with page 2. Place the numbers at the top of each page, either centered or in the top right corner. (Your instructor may prefer your paper to be formatted differently.)

Other guidelines: _____

_____

_____

_____

_____

_____

Chapter Highlights

Tips for Succeeding in this Course

- Remember that writing is a process: prewriting, writing, rewriting, and proofreading.

- Before you write, always be clear about your subject, audience, and purpose.

- Follow your instructor's guidelines for submitting written work.

- Practice in reading will improve your writing and vice versa.

- Online, get your information and news only from respected sources until you learn to evaluate media stories yourself.

- Practice the six reading strategies.

EXPLORING ONLINE

Throughout this text, the Exploring Online feature will suggest ways that you can use the Internet to improve your writing and grammar skills. You will find that if you need extra writing help, online writing centers (called OWLs) can be a great resource. Many provide extra review or practice in areas in which you might need assistance. You will want to do some searching to find the best sites for your needs, but here are two excellent OWL sites to explore:

owl.english.purdue.edu/owl/section/1
Purdue University

grammar.ccc.commnet.edu/grammar
Capital Community College

Visit **MindTap** for *Grassroots* to access this chapter's ebook, flashcards, additional practice and quizzes, and more!

CHAPTER 2

Prewriting to Generate Ideas

A: Freewriting

B: Brainstorming

C: Clustering

D: Keeping a Journal

The author of this book used to teach ice skating. On the first day of class, her students practiced falling. Once they knew how to fall without fear, they were free to learn to skate.

Writing is much like ice skating: the more you practice, the better you get. If you are free to make mistakes, you'll want to practice, and you'll look forward to new writing challenges.

The problem is that many people avoid writing. Faced with an English composition or a report at work, they put it off and then scribble something at the last minute. Other people sit staring at the blank page or computer screen—writing a sentence, crossing it out, unable to get started. In this chapter, you will learn four useful prewriting techniques that will help you jump-start your writing process and generate lots of ideas: **freewriting**, **brainstorming**, **clustering**, and **keeping a journal**.

A. Freewriting

Freewriting is a method many writers use to warm up and get ideas. Here are the guidelines: For five or ten full minutes, write without stopping. Don't worry about grammar or about writing complete sentences; just set a timer and go. If you get stuck, repeat or rhyme the last word you wrote, but keep writing nonstop until the timer sounds. Afterward, read what you have written, and underline any parts you like.

Freewriting is a wonderful way to let your ideas pour out without getting stuck by worrying too soon about correctness or "good writing." Sometimes freewriting produces nonsense, but often it provides interesting ideas for further thinking and writing. **Focused freewriting** can help you find subjects to write about.

Focused Freewriting

In *focused freewriting*, you try to focus your thoughts on one subject as you freewrite. The subject can be one assigned by your instructor, one you choose, or one you discover in unfocused freewriting.

Here is one student's focused freewriting on the topic *someone who strongly influenced me*:

> Thin, thinner, weak, weaker. You stopped cooking for yourself—forced yourself to choke down cans of nutrition. Your chest caved in; your bones stuck out. You never asked, Why me? With a weak laugh you asked, Why not me? I had a wonderful life, a great job, a good marriage while it lasted. Have beautiful kids. Your wife divorced you—couldn't stand to watch you die, couldn't stand to have her life fall apart the way your body was falling apart. I watched you stumble, trip over your own feet, sink, fall down. I held you up. Now I wonder which one of us was holding the other one up. I saw you shiver in your summer jacket because you didn't have the strength to put on your heavy coat. Bought you a feather-light winter jacket, saw your eyes fill with tears of pleasure and gratitude. You said they would find you at the bottom of the stairs. When they called to tell me we'd lost you, the news wasn't unexpected, but the pain came in huge waves. Heart gave out, they said. Your daughter found you crumpled at the foot of the stairs. How did you know? What else did you guess?
>
> *Daniel Corteau, Student*

- This student later used his freewriting as the basis for an excellent paragraph.
- Underline any words or lines that you find especially striking or powerful. Be prepared to discuss your choices.
- How was the writer influenced by the man he describes?

PRACTICE 1

1. Set a timer for ten minutes, or have someone time you. Freewrite without stopping for the full ten minutes. Repeat or rhyme words if you get stuck, but keep writing! Don't let your pen or pencil leave the page or your fingers leave the keyboard.

2. When you finish, write down one or two words that describe how you felt while freewriting. _____

3. Now read your freewriting. Underline any words or lines you like—anything that strikes you as powerful, moving, funny, or important. If nothing strikes you, that's okay.

PRACTICE 2

Now choose one word or idea from your freewriting or from the following list. Focus your thoughts on it, and do a ten-minute focused freewriting. Try to stick to the topic, but don't worry too much about it. Just keep writing! When you finish, read and underline any striking lines or ideas.

1. home
2. a good student
3. the biggest lie
4. a dream
5. someone who influenced you
6. your experiences with writing
7. the smell of _____
8. strength

PRACTICE 3

Try two more focused freewritings at home, each one ten minutes long. Do them at different times of the day when you have a few quiet moments. If possible, use a timer: set it for ten minutes, and then write fast until it rings. Later, read your freewritings, and underline any ideas or passages you might like to write more about.

B. Brainstorming

Brainstorming means freely jotting down ideas about a topic on paper or on a computer. As in freewriting, the purpose of brainstorming is to get as many ideas down as possible so that you will have something to work with later. Just write down everything that comes to mind about a topic—words and phrases, ideas, details, examples, little stories. Once you have brainstormed, read over your list, underlining any ideas you might want to develop further.

Here is one student's brainstorming list on *an interesting job*:

> midtown messenger
>
> frustrating but free
>
> I know the city backward and forward
>
> good bike needed
>
> fast, ever-changing, dangerous
>
> drivers hate messengers—we dart in and out of traffic
>
> old clothes don't get respect
>
> I wear the best Descente racing gear, a Giro helmet
>
> people respect you more
>
> I got tipped $100 for carrying a crystal vase from the showroom to Wall Street in 15 minutes
>
> other times I get stiffed
>
> lessons I've learned—controlling my temper
>
> having dignity
>
> staying calm no matter what—insane drivers, deadlines, rudeness
>
> weirdly, I like my job

As he brainstormed, this writer produced many interesting facts and details about his job as a bicycle messenger, all in just a few minutes. He might want to underline the ideas that most interest him—perhaps the time he was tipped $100—and then brainstorm again for more details.

PRACTICE 4

Choose one of the following topics that interests you, and write it at the top of your page. Then brainstorm! Write anything that comes into your head about the topic. Let your ideas flow.

1. a singer or a musician
2. the future
3. an intriguing job
4. a story in the news
5. the best/worst class I've ever had
6. making a difference
7. a place to which I never want to return
8. a community problem

After you fill a page with your list, read it over, underlining the most interesting ideas. Draw arrows to connect related ideas. Do you find one idea that might be the subject of a paper?

C. Clustering

Some writers find *clustering* or mapping an effective way to get ideas onto paper. To begin clustering, write one idea or topic—usually one word—in the center of your paper. Then let your mind make associations, and write those ideas down, branching out from the center. When one idea suggests other ideas, details, or examples, jot down those around it in a cluster, like this:

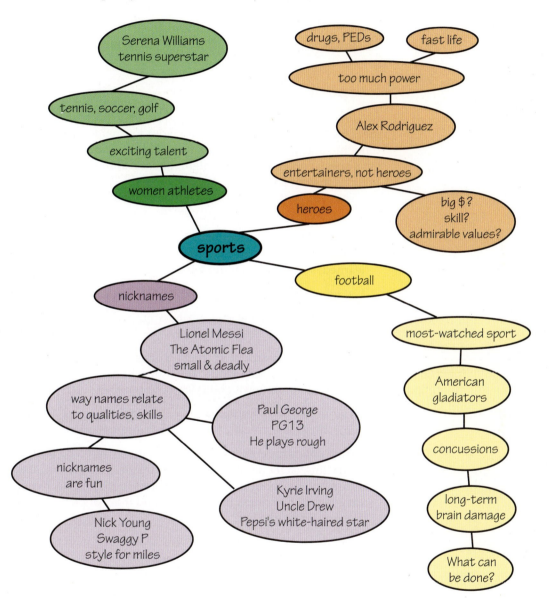

Once this student filled a page with clustered ideas about the word *sports*, his next step was choosing the cluster that most interested him and writing further. He might even have wanted to freewrite for more ideas.

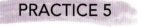

PRACTICE 5

Read over the clustering map above. If you were giving advice to the writer, which cluster or branch do you think would make the most interesting paper? Why?

PRACTICE 6

Choose one of these topics or another topic that interests you. Write it in the center of a piece of paper and then try clustering. Keep writing down associations until you have filled the page.

1. movies
2. voting
3. a lesson
4. sports

5. my hometown
6. self-esteem
7. a relative
8. someone I don't understand

D. Keeping a Journal

Keeping a journal is an excellent way to practice your writing skills and to discover ideas for future writing. Most of all, your journal is a place to record your private thoughts and important experiences. Open a journal file on your computer, or get a special notebook. Every night, or several times a week, write for at least ten minutes in your journal.

What you write about will be limited only by your imagination. Here are some ideas:

● Write in detail about things that matter to you—family relationships, falling in (or out of) love, an experience at school or work, something important you just learned, something you did well.

● List your personal goals, and brainstorm possible steps toward achieving them.

● Write about problems you are having, and "think on paper" about ways to solve them.

● Comment on classroom instruction or assignments, and evaluate your learning progress. What needs work? What questions do you need to ask? Write out a study plan for yourself and refer to it regularly.

● Write down your responses to your reading—class assignments, newspaper items, magazine articles, websites that impress or anger you.

● Search online for great or famous quotations until you find one that strikes you. Or try this list if you wish: **www.goodreads.com/quotes**. Then copy it into your journal, think about it, and write. For example, Agnes Repplier says, "It is not easy to find happiness in ourselves, and it is not possible to find it elsewhere." Do you agree with her?

● Be alert to interesting writing topics all around you. If possible, carry a notebook during the day for "fast sketches." Jot down moving or funny moments, people, or things that catch your attention—an overworked waitress in a restaurant, a scene at the day-care center where you leave your child, a man trying to persuade an officer not to give him a parking ticket.

You will soon find that ideas for writing will occur to you all day long. Before they slip away, capture them in words. Writing is like ice skating. You have to practice.

PRACTICE 7

Write in your journal for at least ten minutes three times a week.

At the end of each week, read what you have written. Underline striking passages, and mark interesting topics and ideas that you would like to explore further.

As you complete the exercises in this book and work on the writing assignments, try all four techniques—freewriting, brainstorming, clustering, and keeping a journal—and see which ones work best for you.

PRACTICE 8

From your journal, choose one or two passages that you might want to rewrite and allow others to read. Put a check beside each of those passages or mark them with sticky notes so that you can find them easily later. Underline the parts you like best. Can you already see ways you might rewrite and improve the writing?

Chapter Highlights

To get started and to discover your ideas, try these techniques.

- **Focused freewriting:** freewriting for five or ten minutes about one topic

- **Brainstorming:** freely jotting down many ideas about a topic

- **Clustering:** making word associations on paper

- **Keeping a journal:** writing regularly about things that interest and move you

EXPLORING ONLINE

owl.english.purdue.edu/owl/resource/673/1

If you still feel stuck when you start to write, try these techniques from Purdue University's OWL (Online Writing Lab).

wvde.state.wv.us/strategybank/GraphicOrganizersforWriting.html

If you like clustering, click this list to view other ways to graph your ideas visually.

Visit **MindTap** for *Grassroots* to access this chapter's ebook, flashcards, additional practice and quizzes, and more!

CHAPTER 3

Developing Effective Paragraphs

The paragraph is the basic unit of writing. This chapter will guide you through the process of writing paragraphs.

A. Defining the Paragraph and the Topic Sentence

A *paragraph* is a group of related sentences that develop one main idea. Although a paragraph has no definite length, it is often four to twelve sentences long. A paragraph usually appears with other paragraphs in a longer piece of writing—an essay, a letter, or an article, for example.

A paragraph looks like this on the page:

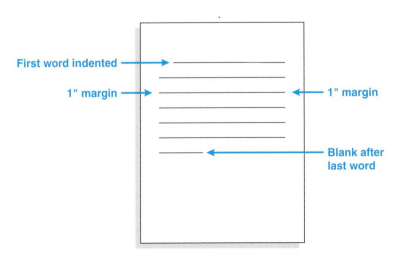

- Clearly **indent** the first word of every paragraph about 1 inch (or one tab on the computer).

- Extend every line of a paragraph as close to the right-hand margin as possible.

- If the last word of the paragraph comes before the end of the line, however, leave the rest of the line blank.

Topic Sentence and Body

Most paragraphs contain one main idea to which all the sentences relate. The **topic sentence** states this main idea. The **body** of the paragraph supports this main idea with specific details, facts, and examples.

> When I was growing up, my older brother Joe was the greatest person in my world. If anyone teased me about my braces or buckteeth, he fiercely defended me. When one boy insisted on calling me "Fang," Joe threatened to knock his teeth out. It worked—no more teasing. My brother always chose me to play on his baseball teams though I was a terrible hitter. Even after he got his driver's license, he didn't abandon me. Instead, every Sunday, the two of us went for a drive. We might stop for cheeseburgers, go to a computer showroom, drive past some girl's house, or just laugh and talk. It was one of childhood's mysteries that such a wonderful brother loved me.
>
> *Jeremiah Woolrich, Student*

- The first sentence of this paragraph is the *topic sentence*. It states in a general way the main idea of the paragraph: that *Joe was the greatest person in my world.* Although the topic sentence can appear anywhere in the paragraph, it is often the first sentence.

- The rest of the paragraph, the *body*, fully explains this statement with details about braces and buckteeth, baseball teams, Sunday drives, cheeseburgers, and so forth.

- Note that the final sentence provides a brief conclusion so that the paragraph *feels* finished.

PRACTICE 1

Read this paragraph and answer the questions.

Millions of people play video games as a way to relax and have fun. Yet because video game addiction is a growing problem, gamers and their loved ones should know the warning signs. One warning sign of video game addiction is abandoning former interests. A gamer who stops participating in activities or social events he or she once enjoyed to play video games may be in the grip of a harmful addiction. Another indication of possible addiction is constantly thinking or talking about a game even while doing other things. If thoughts about the next gaming session prevent someone from paying attention to commitments, coursework, or other people, that player could be in trouble. A final warning sign is fighting with or lying to loved ones about the amount of time spent gaming. Neglecting relationships with family and friends is a classic sign of addiction. As with gambling and other addictive behavior, people close to the addict often spot these signs first while the addict vigorously denies having a problem.

1. Is the topic sentence of this paragraph sentence 1 or 2? Which of these best states the main idea explained by the rest of the paragraph?

   _____

2. How many supporting points does this writer provide?

   _____

3. What words help introduce each of the three warning signs of gaming addiction?

   _____

PRACTICE 2 Each group of sentences below can be arranged and written as a paragraph. Circle the letter of the sentence that would be the best topic sentence. REMEMBER: The topic sentence states the main idea of the entire paragraph and includes all the other ideas.

EXAMPLE: a. Speed-walking three times a week is part of my routine.
  (b.) Staying healthy and fit is important to me.
   c. Every night, I get at least seven hours of sleep.
   d. I eat as many fresh fruits and vegetables as possible.

(Sentence b is more general than the other sentences; it would be the best topic sentence.)

1. a. Runners, hikers, and bicyclists sometimes use smartphone apps as personal trainers that plan a route and then provide maps, distances, and time goals.
   b. Many colleges are using smartphones to deliver instructional material, complete with course materials, music clips, and video.
   c. Smartphones are not just for calling or texting people, but can be used in many creative and innovative ways.
   d. Smartphone users can search for their soul mates, using dating apps to view multimedia profiles of available singles.

2. a. Each prisoner in the program receives a puppy, which he feeds, cares for, and trains to be a service dog for a combat veteran.
   b. The convicted felons often feel, many for the first time, a sense of responsibility, compassion for other creatures, and the power of unconditional love.
   c. The successful Puppies Behind Bars program improves the lives of both inmates and disabled war veterans.
   d. When a dog "graduates," each trainer presents his dog to a vet who returned from Iraq or Afghanistan with brain or bodily injuries.
   e. The disabled soldiers say that the dogs not only open doors, turn on lights, and dial 911 on special phones but greatly ease their anxiety and depression.

3. a. After meeting at band camp while in middle school in Virginia, Williams and his friend Chad Hugo began performing together.
   b. After releasing successful albums with his group N*E*R*D, Williams debuted his first solo album in 2006.
   c. Williams is now a Grammy-winning musician, producer, and TV star with fans all over the world.
   d. In 2013, Williams wrote and performed in three smash hits, Robin Thicke's "Blurred Lines," Daft Punk's "Get Lucky," and his own global hit, "Happy."
   e. An early love of music and performance launched Pharrell Williams on the path to stardom.

    f. In high school, the two friends formed a producing duo, The Neptunes, later breaking through with stars Jay-Z, Britney Spears, and Usher in the early 2000s.

4.   a. Physical courage allows soldiers or athletes to endure bodily pain or danger.

    b. Those with social courage dare to expose their deep feelings in order to build close relationships.

    c. Those rare people who stand up for their beliefs despite public pressure possess moral courage.

    d. Inventors and artists show creative courage when they break out of old ways of seeing and doing things.

    e. Psychologist Rollo May claimed that there are four different types of courage.

5.   a. In middle school, she devoured books about detective Nancy Drew, a strong female role model of courage and character.

    b. Born to Puerto Rican parents in the Bronx, NY, Sotomayor fell in love with comics like *Archie*, *Spider-Man*, and *Batman* in elementary school.

    c. Sonia Sotomayor, the first Hispanic U.S. Supreme Court Justice, says that books were her "rocket ship out of the projects" and into a meaningful life.

    d. When she was weighing job offers, great novels like George Orwell's *1984* opened her eyes to the dangers of too much government and the right use of the law.

    e. When teenaged Sotomayor saw *West Side Story*, a modern *Romeo and Juliet* about rival gangs, a lightbulb came on—that great books dealing with human emotion are always relevant.

6.   a. Many old toys and household objects are now collectors' items.

    b. A 1959 Barbie doll still in its original box recently sold for $3,552 on the eBay auction website.

    c. Many collectors now hunt for Fiesta dinnerware, made in the 1930s, in garage sales and resale shops.

    d. *Star Wars* action figures and vintage baseball cards are among the 10 most wanted collectibles.

7.   a. In our increasingly global economy, employees who can communicate with non-English-speaking customers and overseas colleagues are in demand at many American companies.

    b. People who can speak and write two languages fluently possess a valuable professional, social, and mental asset.

    c. Studies confirm that bilingualism boosts brain power because adults who grew up speaking two languages stay sharper and quicker later in life.

    d. Bilingualism brings personal rewards, such as the ability to bridge cultural boundaries and broaden one's social network to include people of other nationalities and ethnic groups.

8.   a. You should read the ingredients list on every package of food you buy.

    b. Children should not eat mandelona, which is made from peanuts soaked in almond flavoring.

    c. Avoid buying food from bins that do not list ingredients.

    d. If your child is allergic to peanuts, you need to be constantly on the alert.

    e. In a restaurant, tongs may have been used to pick up items containing peanuts.

B. Narrowing the Topic and Writing the Topic Sentence

The rest of this chapter will guide you through the process of writing paragraphs of your own. Here are the steps we will discuss:

1. Narrowing the topic and writing the topic sentence
2. Generating ideas for the body
3. Selecting and dropping ideas
4. Grouping ideas in a plan
5. Writing and revising the paragraph
6. Writing the final draft and proofreading

Narrowing the Topic

Often your first step as a writer will be **narrowing** a broad topic—one assigned by your instructor, one you have thought of yourself, or one suggested by a particular writing task, like a letter. That is, you must cut the topic down to size and choose one aspect that interests you.

Assume, for example, that you are asked to write a paragraph describing a person you know. The trick is to choose someone you would *like* to write about, someone who interests you and would probably also interest your audience of readers.

At this point, many writers find it helpful to think on paper by *brainstorming**, *freewriting*, or *clustering*. As you jot down or freely write ideas, ask yourself questions. Whom do I love, hate, or admire? Who is the funniest or most unusual person I know? Is there a family member or friend about whom others might like to read?

Suppose you choose to write about your friend Beverly. *Beverly* is too broad a topic for one paragraph. Therefore, you should limit your topic further, choosing just one of her qualities or acts. What is unusual about her? What might interest others? Perhaps what stands out in your mind is that Beverly is a determined person who doesn't let difficulties defeat her. You have now *narrowed* your broad topic to *Beverly's determination*.

You might visualize the process like this:

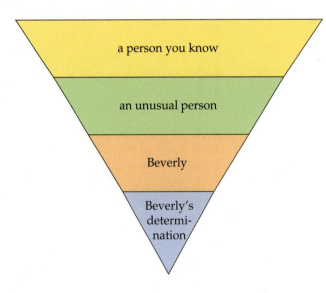

a person you know

an unusual person

Beverly

Beverly's determination

---

* Brainstorming is discussed further in Part C. Also see Chapter 2 for more information about prewriting.

PRACTICE 3   Good writers need a clear understanding of general and specific—that is, which ideas are general and which are specific. Number the items in each group below, with 1 being the most specific and limited, 2 being the second most specific, and the highest number being the most general.

1. ___ chairs
   ___ furniture
   ___ Grandma's oak rocking chair
   ___ household contents

2. ___ Malian singer Habib Koité
   ___ music
   ___ African music
   ___ music of Mali, West Africa
   ___ sound

3. ___ rose
   ___ flowering plants
   ___ living things
   ___ plants
   ___ the Betty Boop rose

4. ___ *Union-Tribune* sports writer Jim Jackson
   ___ California
   ___ North America
   ___ *San Diego Union-Tribune* office building
   ___ Earth

5. ___ athletes
   ___ Crosby's passing ability
   ___ hockey players
   ___ centers
   ___ Pittsburgh Penguins captain Sidney Crosby

6. ___ actresses
   ___ movie stars
   ___ Helen Mirren
   ___ successful older actresses
   ___ human beings

Writing the Topic Sentence

The next step is to write your **topic sentence**, which clearly states, in sentence form, your narrowed topic and a point about that topic. This step helps you further focus your topic by forcing you to make a statement about it. That statement sets forth one main idea that the rest of your paragraph will support and explain. A topic sentence can be very simple (*Beverly is very determined*), or, better yet, it can state your attitude or point of view about the topic (*Beverly's determination inspires admiration*).

Think of the topic sentence as having two parts: a **topic** and a **controlling idea**. The controlling idea states the writer's attitude, angle, or point of view about the topic.

	topic	controlling idea

Topic sentence: Beverly's determination inspires admiration.

All topics can have many possible topic sentences, depending on the writer's interests and point of view. The controlling idea helps you focus on just one aspect. Here are three possible topic sentences about the topic *attending college*:

> (1) Attending college has revolutionized my career plans.
>
> (2) Attending college has put me in debt.
>
> (3) Attending college is exhausting but rewarding.

- These topic sentences all explore the same topic—attending college—but each controlling idea is different. The controlling idea in topic sentence (1) is *has revolutionized my career plans*.

- What is the controlling idea in topic sentence (2)?

  _____

- What is the controlling idea in topic sentence (3)?

  _____

- Notice the way each controlling idea lets the reader know what that paragraph will be about. By choosing different key words, a writer can angle any topic in different directions. If you were assigned the topic *attending college*, what would your topic sentence be?

  _____

  _____

PRACTICE 4 Read each topic sentence below. Circle the topic and underline the controlling idea.

EXAMPLE: (Computer games) improved my study skills.

1. Hybrid cars offer monetary advantages over gasoline vehicles.

2. White-water rafting increased my self-confidence.

3. Ed Bradley achieved many firsts as a television journalist.

4. Immigrants frequently are stereotyped by some native-born Americans.

5. A course in financial planning should be required of all college freshmen.

Writing Limited and Complete Topic Sentences

Check to make sure your topic sentence is *limited* and *complete*. Your topic sentence should be **limited**. It should make a point that is neither too broad nor too narrow to be supported in a paragraph. As a rule, the more specific and well defined the topic sentence, the better the paragraph. Which of these topic sentences do you think will produce the best paragraph?

> (1) My recent trip to Colorado was really bad.
>
> (2) My recent trip to Colorado was disappointing because the weather ruined my camping plans.

- Topic sentence (1) is so broad that the paragraph could include almost anything.

- Topic sentence (2), on the other hand, is *limited* enough to provide the main idea for a good paragraph: how terrible weather ruined the writer's camping plans.

> (3) The Each-One-Reach-One tutoring program encourages academic excellence at Chester Elementary School.
>
> (4) Tutoring programs can be found all over the country.

- Topic sentence (3) is limited enough to provide the main idea for a good paragraph. Reading this topic sentence, what do you expect the paragraph to include?

  _____

  _____

- Topic sentence (4) lacks a limited point. Reading this sentence, someone cannot guess what the paragraph will be about.

In addition, the topic sentence must be a **complete sentence**; it must contain a subject and a verb and express a complete thought.* Do not confuse a topic with a topic sentence. For example, *the heroism of Captain "Sully" Sullenberger* cannot be a topic sentence because it is not a complete sentence. Here is one possible topic sentence: *Because Captain "Sully" Sullenberger landed a packed airplane on the Hudson River and saved 155 lives, he is a true hero.*

For now, it is best to place your topic sentence at the beginning of the paragraph. After you have mastered this pattern, you can try variations. Placed first, the topic sentence clearly establishes the focus of your paragraph and helps grab the reader's attention. Wherever the topic sentence appears, all other sentences must relate to it and support it with specific details, facts, examples, arguments, and explanations. If necessary, you can revise the topic sentence later to make it more accurately match the paragraph you have written.

Caution: Do not begin a topic sentence with *This paragraph will be about . . .* or *I am going to write about . . . .* These extra words contribute nothing. Instead, make your point directly. Make every word in the topic sentence count.

PRACTICE 5

Put a check beside each topic sentence that is limited enough to be the topic sentence of a good paragraph. If you think a topic sentence is too broad, limit the topic according to your own interests; then write a new, specific topic sentence.

EXAMPLES:

✔ Texting has changed my life in three ways.

  Rewrite: _____

  I am going to write about cell phones.

  Rewrite: *Talking on a cell phone can distract drivers to the point of causing accidents.*

_____

* For more work on writing complete sentences, see Chapters 10 and 11.

1. Working in the complaint department taught me tolerance.

   Rewrite: _____

   _____

2. A subject I want to write about is money.

   Rewrite: _____

   _____

3. This paragraph will discuss food.

   Rewrite: _____

   _____

4. Some things about college have been great.

   Rewrite: _____

   _____

5. Living in a one-room apartment forces a person to be organized.

   Rewrite: _____

   _____

PRACTICE 6

Here is a list of topics. Choose one that interests you from this list or from your own list in Chapter 1, Practice 7. Narrow the topic, and write a topic sentence limited enough to provide the main idea for a good paragraph. Make sure that your topic sentence is a complete sentence.

A talented musician	An act of courage
Why get an education?	Advertising con jobs
AIDS	Clothing styles on campus

Narrowed topic: _____

Topic sentence: _____

_____

C. Generating Ideas for the Body of the Paragraph

Rich supporting detail is one key to effective writing. A good way to generate ideas for the body of a paragraph is by *brainstorming*, freely jotting down ideas. This important step may take just a few minutes, but it gets your ideas on paper and may pull ideas out of you that you didn't even know you had.

Freely jot down anything that might relate to your topic—details, examples, little stories. Don't worry at this point if some ideas don't seem to belong. For now, just keep jotting them down.

Here is a possible brainstorming list for the topic sentence *Beverly inspires admiration because she is so determined*.

1. saved enough money for college
2. worked days, went to school nights
3. has beautiful brown eyes
4. nervous about learning to drive but didn't give up
5. failed road test twice—passed eventually
6. her favorite color—wine red
7. received degree in accounting
8. she is really admirable
9. with lots of willpower, quit smoking
10. used to be a heavy smoker
11. married to Virgil
12. I like Virgil too
13. now a good driver
14. never got a ticket
15. hasn't touched another cigarette

As you saw in Part B, some writers brainstorm or use other prewriting techniques *before* they write the topic sentence. Do what works best for you.

PRACTICE 7

Now choose the topic from Practice 5 or Practice 6 that most interests you. Write your limited topic sentence here.

Topic sentence: _____

_____

Next, brainstorm, freewrite, or cluster for specific ideas to develop a paragraph. On paper or on a computer, write anything that comes to you about your topic sentence. Just let ideas pour out—details, memories, facts. Try to fill at least one page.

PRACTICE 8

Many writers adjust the topic sentence after they have finished drafting the paragraph. In a group of three or four classmates, if possible, study the body of each of the following paragraphs. Then, working together, write the most exact and interesting topic sentence you can.

1. Topic sentence: _____

_____

One challenge is a lack of knowledge about how to apply, register for classes, and obtain financial aid. Students who are first in their families to attend college often lack an experienced guide to help them navigate these procedures. After they do enroll, first-generation college students may also find that their high school classes did not adequately prepare them for the academic demands of college work. Consequently, they may have to take courses to strengthen their reading, writing, or math skills. Even as they improve academically and progress through their studies, students whose relatives and friends never attended college must deal with a range of difficult emotions. They may feel anxious about pleasing proud relatives with high hopes for their success. They may fear losing old friends who undercut or even mock their college goals. They may experience stress from the constant struggle to find enough time to study. When they finally receive their college degrees, however, they always swell with pride, knowing that their accomplishment is worth every obstacle they have overcome.

Inocencia Colón, Student

2. Topic sentence: _____

_____

Despite his pressured schedule, he always found time to play with my sisters and me, tell us stories, and make us feel loved. From his example, I learned that men can be loving and show affection. In addition, he often sat with me and discussed the responsibilities of being a man. He instilled in me principles and morals that I would not have learned from the guys on the corner. My hero felt that a man should be the provider for his family. He demonstrated this by working two jobs, seven days a week. After many years, my father saved enough money to make a down payment on a three-bedroom house next to a park. He accomplished all this with only a sixth-grade education. The values on which I now base my life were given to me by my hero, an unknown man who deserves to be famous.

Robert Fields, Student

3. Topic sentence: _____

_____

Frigid air would hit us in the eyes when we stepped out the door to catch the school bus. Even though our faces were wrapped in scarves and our heads covered with wool caps, the cold snatched our breath away. A thin layer of snow crunched loudly under our boots as we ran gasping out to the road. I knew that the famous Minnesota windchill was pulling temperatures well below zero, but I tried not to think about that. Instead, I liked to see how everything in the yard was frozen motionless, even the blades of grass that shone like little glass knives.

Ari Henson, Student

D. Selecting and Dropping Ideas

This may be the easiest step in paragraph writing because all you have to do is select those ideas that best support your topic sentence and drop those that do not. Also drop ideas that just repeat the topic sentence and add nothing new to the paragraph.

Here is the brainstorming list for the topic sentence *Beverly inspires admiration because she is so determined.* Which ideas would you drop? Why?

1. saved enough money for college
2. worked days, went to school nights

3. has beautiful brown eyes

4. nervous about learning to drive but didn't give up

5. failed road test twice—passed eventually

6. her favorite color—wine red

7. received degree in accounting

8. she is really admirable

9. with lots of willpower, quit smoking

10. used to be a heavy smoker

11. married to Virgil

12. I like Virgil too

13. now a good driver

14. never got a ticket

15. hasn't touched another cigarette

You probably dropped ideas 3, 6, 11, and 12 because they do not relate to the topic. You also should have dropped idea 8 because it merely repeats the topic sentence.

PRACTICE 9   Read through your own brainstorming list in Practice 7. Select the ideas that best support your topic sentence, and cross out those that do not. In addition, drop ideas that merely repeat the topic sentence. You should be able to give good reasons for keeping or dropping each idea in the list.

E. Arranging Ideas in a Plan or an Outline

Next, choose an **order** in which to arrange your ideas. First, group together ideas that have something in common, that are related or alike in some way. Then decide which ideas should come first, which second, and so on. Many writers do this by numbering the ideas on their list.

Here is a plan for a paragraph about Beverly's determination.

Topic sentence: Beverly inspires admiration because she is so determined.

worked days, went to school nights

saved enough money for college

received degree in accounting

nervous about learning to drive but didn't give up

failed road test twice—passed eventually

now a good driver

never got a ticket

used to be a heavy smoker

with lots of willpower, quit smoking

hasn't touched another cigarette

- How are the ideas in each group related? _____

_____

- Does it make sense to discuss college first, driving second, and smoking last?

Why? _____

_____

Keep in mind that there is more than one way to arrange ideas. As you group your own brainstorming list, think of what you want to say; then arrange your ideas accordingly.*

PRACTICE 10

On paper or on a computer, make a plan or outline from your brainstormed list of ideas. First, group together related ideas. Then decide which ideas will come first, which second, and so on.

F. Writing and Revising the Paragraph

Writing the First Draft

By now, you should have a clear plan or outline from which to write the first draft of your paragraph. The **first draft** should contain all the ideas you have decided to use, in the order in which you have chosen to present them. Writing on every other line will leave room for later changes.

Explain your ideas fully, including details that will interest or amuse the reader. If you are unsure about something, put a check in the margin and come back to it later, but avoid getting stuck on any one word, sentence, or idea. If possible, set the paper aside for several hours or several days; this step will help you read it later with a fresh eye.

PRACTICE 11

On paper or on a computer, write a first draft of the paragraph you have been working on.

Revising

Whether you are a beginning writer or a professional, you must **revise**—that is, rewrite what you have written in order to improve it. You might cross out and rewrite words or entire sentences. You might add, drop, or rearrange details.

As you revise, keep the reader in mind. Ask yourself these questions:

- Is my topic sentence clear?
- Can the reader easily follow my ideas?
- Is the order of ideas logical?
- Will this paragraph keep the reader interested?

In addition, revise your paragraph for *support* and for *unity*.

---

* For more work on choosing an order, see Chapter 4, Part A.

Revising for Support

Make sure your paragraph contains excellent **support**—that is, specific details, facts, and examples that fully explain your topic sentence.

Avoid simply repeating the same idea in different words, especially the idea in the topic sentence. Repeated ideas are just padding, a sign that you need to brainstorm or freewrite again for new ideas. Which of the following two paragraphs contains the best and most interesting support?

> A.   Every Saturday morning, Fourteenth Street is alive with activity. From one end of the street to the other, people are out doing everything imaginable. Vendors sell many different items on the street, and storekeepers will do just about anything to get customers into their stores. They will use signs, and they will use music. There is a tremendous amount of activity on Fourteenth Street, and just watching it is enjoyable.
>
> B.   Every Saturday morning, Fourteenth Street is alive with activity. Vendors line the sidewalks, selling everything from DVD players to wigs. Trying to lure customers inside, the shops blast pop music into the street or hang brightly colored banners announcing "Grand Opening Sale" or "Everything Must Go." Shoppers jam the sidewalks, both serious bargain hunters and families just out for a stroll, munching chili dogs as they survey the merchandise. Here and there, a panhandler hustles for handouts, taking advantage of the Saturday crowd.

- The body of *paragraph A* contains vague and general statements, so the reader gets no clear picture of the activity on Fourteenth Street.

- The body of *paragraph B*, however, includes many specific *details* that clearly explain the topic sentence: *vendors selling everything from DVD players to wigs, shops blasting pop music, brightly colored banners.*

- What other details in *paragraph B* help you see just how Fourteenth Street is alive with activity?

_____

_____

_____

_____

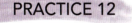 **PRACTICE 12**   Check the following paragraphs for strong, specific support. Mark places that need more details or explanation, and cross out any weak or repeated words. Then revise and rewrite each paragraph *as if you had written it*, inventing and adding support when you need to.

Paragraph A: Aunt Alethia was one of the most important people in my life. She had a strong influence on me. No matter how busy she was, she always had time for me. She paid attention to small things about me that no one else seemed to notice. When I was successful, she praised me. When I was feeling down, she gave me pep talks. She was truly wise and shared her wisdom with me. My aunt was a great person who had a major influence on my life.

Paragraph B: Just getting to school safely can be a challenge for many young people. Young as he is, my son has been robbed once and bullied on several occasions. The robbery was very frightening, for it involved a weapon. What was taken was a small thing, but it meant a lot to my son. It angers me that just getting to school is so dangerous. Something needs to be done.

Revising for Unity

While writing, you may sometimes drift away from your topic and include information that does not belong in the paragraph. It is important, therefore, to revise your paragraph for **unity**—that is, to drop any ideas or sentences that do not relate to the topic sentence.

This paragraph lacks unity:

> (1) Franklin Mars, a Minnesota candy maker, created many popular candy snacks. (2) Milky Way, his first bar, was an instant hit. (3) Snickers, which he introduced in 1930, also sold very well. (4) Milton Hershey developed the very first candy bar in 1894. (5) M&M's were a later Mars creation, supposedly designed so that soldiers could enjoy a sugar boost without getting sticky trigger fingers.

- What is the topic sentence in this paragraph?   _____

- Which sentence does *not* relate to the topic sentence?   _____

- Sentence (4) has nothing to do with the main idea, that *Franklin Mars created many popular candy snacks*. Therefore, sentence (4) should be dropped.

PRACTICE 13

Check the following paragraphs for unity. If a paragraph is unified, write U in the blank. If it is not, write the number of the sentence that does not belong in the paragraph.

1. ____   (1) Families who nourish their children with words as well as food at dinnertime produce better future readers. (2) Researchers at Harvard University studied the dinner conversations of 68 families. (3) What they found was that parents who use a few new words in conversation with their three- and four-year-olds each night quickly build the children's vocabularies and their later reading skills. (4) The researchers point out that children can learn from 8 to 28 new words a day, so they need to be "fed" new words. (5) Excellent "big words" for preschoolers include *parachute*, *emerald*, *instrument*, and *education*, the researchers say.

2. ____   (1) 3D printing may soon revolutionize the way many products are made and delivered. (2) A three-dimensional printer can layer ground plastic, metal, or other material, turning a plan into a physical product. (3) For example, Nike, Adidas, and Under Armour already are testing ways to print perfectly-fitted custom shoes for each customer right in the store. (4) Automobile manufacturers have begun to print lightweight aluminum car parts that no longer must be made from heavy metal and shipped from other countries. (5) Artificial intelligence will also transform the future. (6) Perhaps most exciting, medical researchers will be able to print custom human

JEFF PACHOUD/Staff/AFP/Getty Images

A French boy born with a deformed hand receives his new 3D printed hand.

organs from the patient's own cells. (6) This will save lives and end long waits for a liver, heart, or lung.

3. ___   (1) Swimming is excellent exercise. (2) Swimming vigorously for just twelve minutes provides aerobic benefits to the heart. (3) Unlike jogging and many other aerobic sports, however, swimming does not jolt the bones and muscles with sudden pressure. (4) Furthermore, the motions of swimming, such as reaching out in the crawl, stretch the muscles in a healthy, natural way. (5) Some swimmers wear goggles to keep chlorine or salt out of their eyes whereas others do not.

Peer Feedback for Revising

You may wish to show your first draft or read it aloud to a respected friend or classmate. Ask this person to give an honest reader response, not to rewrite your work. Having another pair of eyes inspect your writing can alert you to issues you missed and help you think like a reader. To elicit useful responses, ask specific questions of your own, or use the Peer Feedback Sheet.

PRACTICE 14   Now read the first draft of your paragraph with a critical eye. Revise and rewrite it, checking especially for a clear topic sentence, strong support, and unity.

PRACTICE 15   Exchange *revised* paragraphs with a classmate. Ask specific questions or use the Peer Feedback Sheet that follows.

   When you *give* feedback, try to be as honest and specific as possible; saying a paper is "good," "nice," or "bad" doesn't really help the writer. When you *receive* feedback, think over your classmate's responses. Do they ring true?

   Now revise a second time, with the aim of writing a fine paragraph.

PEER FEEDBACK SHEET

To _____ From _____ Date _____

1. What I like about this piece of writing is _____

   _____

   _____

2. Your main point seems to be _____

   _____

   _____

3. These particular words or lines struck me as powerful.

   Words or lines: I like them because

   _____   _____

   _____   _____

   _____   _____

   _____   _____

4. Some things aren't clear to me. These lines or parts could be improved (meaning not clear; supporting points missing; order mixed up; writing not lively):

   Lines or parts: Need improving because

   _____   _____

   _____   _____

   _____   _____

   _____   _____

5. The one change you could make that would most improve this piece of writing is

   _____

   _____

   _____

G. Writing the Final Draft and Proofreading

When you are satisfied with your revisions, retype or recopy your paper. Be sure to include all your corrections. If you must write by hand, write neatly and legibly—a carelessly scribbled paper seems to say that you don't care about your work.

The first draft of the paragraph about Beverly, with the writer's changes, and the revised final draft follow. Compare them.

First Draft with Revisions

(1) Beverly inspires admiration because she is so determined. (2) Although she could not afford to attend college right after high school, she *worked* to save money. (3) It took a *long time*, but she got her degree. (4) She is now a good driver.

doing what? add details

How long?! Better support needed–show her hard work!

(5) At first, she was very nervous about getting behind the wheel and even failed the road test twice, but she didn't quit. (6) She passed ~~eventually~~. (7) *Her husband, Virgil, loves to drive; he races cars on the weekend.* (8) Anyway, Beverly has never gotten a ticket. (9) A year ago, Beverly quit smoking. (10) For *a while*, she had a *rough time*, but she hasn't touched a cigarette. (11) Now she says that the urge to smoke has faded away. (12) She doesn't let *difficulties* defeat her.

The third time,

Drop Virgil—he doesn't belong

how long?

too general—add details here

better conclusion needed

> *Guide the reader better from point to point! Choppy—*

Final Draft

(1) Beverly inspires admiration because she is so determined. (2) Although she could not afford to attend college right after high school, she worked as a cashier to save money for tuition. (3) It took her five years working days and going to school nights, but she recently received a BS in accounting. (4) Thanks to this same determination, Beverly is now a good driver. (5) At first, she was very nervous about getting behind the wheel and even failed the road test twice, but she didn't give up. (6) The third time, she passed, and she has never gotten a ticket. (7) A year ago, Beverly quit smoking. (8) For a month or more, she chewed her nails and endless packs of gum, but she hasn't touched a cigarette. (9) Now she says that the urge to smoke has faded away. (10) When Beverly sets a goal for herself, she doesn't let difficulties defeat her.

- This paragraph provides good support for the topic sentence. The writer has made sentences (2) and (3) more specific by adding *as a cashier*, *for tuition*, *five years working days and going to school nights*, and *recently received a BS in accounting*.

- What other revisions did the writer make? How do these revisions improve

  the paragraph? _____

  _____

  _____

  _____

- *Transitional expressions* are words and phrases that guide the reader smoothly from point to point. In sentence (5) of the final draft, *at first* is a transitional expression showing time. What other transitional expressions of time are used?

  _____

  _____

- What phrase provides a transition from sentence (3) to (4)?

  _____

- Note that the last sentence now provides a brief *conclusion* so that the paragraph *feels* finished.

Proofreading

Finally, carefully **proofread** your paper for grammatical and spelling errors, consulting your dictionary and this book as necessary. Errors in your writing will lower your grades in most college courses, and they may also limit your job opportunities. The more writing errors you tend to make, the more you need to proofread.

Chapter 9 of this book will teach you tools and proofreading strategies to help you find and correct your own errors. Then Units 2 through 8 will help you improve your grammar, punctuation, and spelling skills and proofread for specific errors.

Meanwhile, allow yourself enough time to proofread; read your work slowly, word by word. Some students find it useful to point to each word and read it aloud softly; others place a blank index card or ruler under the line they are reading. These methods help them catch mistakes as well as "hear" any words they might have left out as they wrote, especially little words like *and*, *at*, and *of*.

In which of these sentences have words been omitted?

(1) Texting while driving is an easy way cause accident.

(2) Plans for the new gym were on display the library.

(3) Mr. Sampson winked at his reflection in the bathroom mirror.

- Words are missing in sentences (1) and (2).
- Sentence (1) requires *to* before *cause* and *an* before *accident*.

- What word is omitted in sentence (2)? _____
- Where should this word be placed? _____

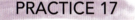
PRACTICE 16

Proofread these sentences for omitted words. Add the necessary words above the lines. Some sentences may already be correct.

> EXAMPLE: Many people listen ^*to* music at work.

1. Headphones and earbuds are a common sight many offices.

2. Yet recent study found that music almost always makes people less productive.

3. Quite simply, words and melodies distract the brain from its task.

4. Therefore, learning any new material should done with no music at all.

5. Students reading a textbook or studying for test remember far less with a soundtrack.

6. Music can, however, relax person before work or before class.

7. Playing a favorite artist a great way to calm nerves and get ready to focus.

8. But when work starts, turn off the tunes.

9. Researchers found one case when music improves performance.

10. A well-practiced expert a surgeon might focus better during surgery when music plays.

PRACTICE 17

Proofread the final draft of your paragraph, checking for grammar or spelling errors and omitted words.

PRACTICE 18

CRITICAL VIEWING AND WRITING

Look closely at the photo that follows, if possible with several classmates. It shows James Blake Miller, a marine in Fallujah, Iraq, 2004. Take notes or choose a group member to take notes. What *general impression* does this photo convey? Craft a topic sentence that states this general impression. Brainstorm five to ten details from the picture that support this general impression. Now, choose the best details and write a paragraph that captures this iconic image for readers who have never seen it. Group members should each write on their own. Conclude the paragraph; don't just stop.

Photo by Luis Sinco. Copyright © 2007. *Los Angeles Times.* Reprinted with permission.

This U.S. soldier, photographed in Iraq, became famous as the "Marlboro Marine." See Practice 18.

PRACTICE 19   WRITING AND REVISING PARAGRAPHS

The assignments that follow will give you practice in writing and revising basic paragraphs. In each assignment, aim for (1) a clear topic sentence and (2) sentences that fully support and explain the topic sentence. As you write, refer to the checklist in the Chapter Highlights at the end of this chapter.

Paragraph 1: Describe a public place. Reread paragraph B in part F. Then choose a place in your neighborhood that is "alive with activity"—a park, street, restaurant, or club. In your topic sentence, name the place and say when it is most active; for example, "Every Saturday night, the Blue Dog Café is alive with activity." Begin by freewriting or by jotting down as many details about the scene as possible. Then describe the scene. Arrange your observations in a logical order. Revise for support, making sure that your details are so lively and interesting that your readers will see the place as clearly as you do.

Paragraph 2: Evaluate your strengths as a writer. In writing as in life, it helps to know your true strengths as well as your weaknesses. You may not realize it, but you probably already possess several skills and personality traits that can nourish good writing. These include being observant and paying attention to details, imagining, feeling deep emotions, wanting to learn the truth, knowing how and where to find the answers to questions, thinking creatively, being well organized, and being persistent. Which of these abilities do you already possess? Do you possess other skills or traits that might help your writing? Describe three of your strengths as a writer. As you revise, make sure your ideas follow a logical order. Proofread carefully.

Paragraph 3: Choose your time of day. Many people have a favorite time of day—the freshness of early morning, 5 P.M. when work ends, late at night when the children are asleep. In your topic sentence, name your favorite time of day. Then develop the paragraph by explaining why you look forward to this time and exactly how you spend it. Check your work for any omitted words.

Chapter Highlights

Checklist for Writing an Effective Paragraph

- Narrow the topic: Cut the topic down to one aspect that interests you and will probably interest your readers.

- Write the topic sentence. (You may wish to brainstorm or freewrite first.)

- Brainstorm, freewrite, or cluster ideas for the body: Write down anything and everything that might relate to your topic.

- Select and drop ideas: Select those ideas that relate to your topic, and drop those that do not.

- Group together ideas that have something in common; then arrange the ideas in a plan.

- Write your first draft.

- Read what you have written, making any necessary corrections and additions. Revise for support and unity.

- Write the final draft of your paragraph neatly and legibly or print a fresh copy, using the format preferred by your instructor.

- Proofread for grammar, punctuation, spelling, and omitted words. Make neat corrections in ink.

EXPLORING ONLINE

grammar.ccc.commnet.edu/grammar/paragraphs.htm
Review paragraph unity and topic sentences at this excellent OWL.

owl.english.purdue.edu/owl/resource/606/01
A review of paragraph writing from the Purdue University OWL.

Visit **MindTap** for *Grassroots* to access this chapter's ebook, flashcards, additional practice and quizzes, and more!

CHAPTER 4

Improving Your Paragraphs

A: More Work on Organizing Ideas: Coherence

B: More Work on Revising: Exact and Concise Language

C: Turning Assignments into Paragraphs

In Chapter 3, you practiced the steps of the paragraph-writing process. This chapter builds on that work. It explains several skills that can greatly improve your writing: achieving coherence; choosing exact, concise language; and turning assignments into paragraphs.

A. More Work on Organizing Ideas: Coherence

Every paragraph should have **coherence**. A paragraph *coheres*—holds together— when its ideas are arranged in a clear and logical order.

Sometimes the order of ideas flows logically from your topic. However, three basic ways to organize ideas are **time order**, **space order**, and **order of importance**.

Time Order

Time order means arranging ideas chronologically, from present to past or from past to present. Careful use of time order helps avoid such confusing writing as *Oops, I forgot to mention before that . . .*

Most instructions, histories, processes, and stories follow the logical order of time.

Mary Pope Osborne's lifelong zest for travel and reading inspires her best-selling children's books. From ages 4 to 15, Mary bounced with her family from one army base to another, in Europe and the States. Unlike many military kids, she loved these adventures, and upon returning to North Carolina she took imaginary trips through books and community theater. After graduating from the University of North Carolina, Chapel Hill, she took off traveling the world, finally settling in New York. In 1976, she married Will Osborne, a writer of children's plays. Over the next four years, she started writing children's stories that explored other cultures or time periods: ancient Egyptian mummies, Amazon rain forests, Greek myths, mermaid tales from around the world, and endangered animals. In 1992, she wrote her first Magic Treehouse book about 8-year-old Jack and his 7-year-old sister Annie, who time travel back to the dinosaurs. More Magic Treehouse books followed, and children around the world loved them. By 2013, Mary Pope Osborne had written 45 books and sold 45 million copies in 30 countries. Parents and teachers praised her work. Refreshingly, she refuses to license Magic Treehouse toys, clothing, and games, explaining that her only goal is to ignite in children the joy of reading.

- The paragraph moves in time from Mary Pope Osborne's travel in a military family to her hugely successful writing career.

- Note how some transitional expressions—for example, *from ages 4 to 15*, *after graduating…*, *over the next four years*, *in 1992*, and *by 2013*—show time and connect the events in the paragraph.

Transitional Expressions to Show Time
first, second, third
then, next, finally
before, during, after
soon, the following month, the next year

PRACTICE 1 Arrange each set of sentences in time order, numbering them 1, 2, 3, and so on. Be prepared to explain your choices.

1. In 80 years, the T-shirt rose from simple underwear to fashion statement.
   ____ During World War II, women factory workers started wearing T-shirts on the job.
   ____ Hippies in the 1960s tie-dyed their T-shirts and wore them printed with messages.
   ____ Now, five billion T-shirts are sold worldwide each year.
   ____ The first American T-shirts were cotton underwear, worn home by soldiers returning from France after World War I.

2. The short life of Sadako Sasaki has inspired millions to value peace.
   ____ Sadako was just two years old in 1945 when the atom bomb destroyed her city, Hiroshima.
   ____ From her sickbed, Sadako set out to make 1,000 paper cranes, birds that, in Japan, symbolize long life and hope.
   ____ Although she died before making 1,000, classmates finished her project and published a book of her letters.
   ____ At age eleven, already a talented runner, she was crushed to learn that she had leukemia, caused by radiation from the bomb.
   ____ Now, every year, the Folded Crane Club places 1,000 cranes at the foot of a statue of Sadako, honoring her wish that all children might enjoy peace and a long life.

3. Scientists who study the body's daily rhythms can suggest the ideal time of day for different activities.
   ____ Taking vitamins with breakfast helps the body absorb them.
   ____ Allergy medication should be taken just before bedtime to combat early-morning hay fever—usually the worst of the day.

_____ The best time to work out is 3 P.M. to 5 P.M., when strength, flexibility, and body temperature are greatest.

_____ Ideal naptime is 1 P.M. to 3 P.M., when body temperature falls, making sleep easier.

PRACTICE 2   **WRITING ASSIGNMENT**

Have you ever been through something that lasted only a few moments but was unforgettable—for example, a sports victory, an accident, or a kiss? Write a paragraph telling about such an event. As you prewrite, pick the highlights of the experience and arrange them in time order. As you write, try to capture the drama of what happened. Use transitional expressions of time to make the story flow smoothly.

Space Order

Space order means describing a person, a place, or a thing from top to bottom, from left to right, from foreground to background, and so on.

Space order is most often used in descriptions because it moves from detail to detail, like a camera's eye.

> When the city presses in on me, I return in my mind to my hometown in St. Mary, Jamaica. I am alone, high in the mango tree on our property on the hilltop. The wind is blowing hard as usual, making a scared noise as it passes through the lush vegetation. I look down at the coconut growth with its green flooring of banana plants. Beyond that is a wide valley and then the round hills. Farther out lies the sea, and I count the ships as they pass to and from the harbor while I relax on my special branch and eat mangoes.
>
> *Daniel Dawes, Student*

- The writer describes this scene from his vantage point high in a tree. His description follows space order, moving from the plants below him, farther out to the valley and the hills, and then even farther, to the sea.

- Notice how *transitional expressions* indicating space—*beyond that*, *then*, and *farther out*—help the reader follow and "see" the details.

Transitional Expressions to Show Space Order
to the left, in the center, to the right
behind, beside, in front of
next, beyond that, farther out

PRACTICE 3   Arrange each set of details according to space order, numbering them 1, 2, 3, and so on. Be prepared to explain your choices.

1. The house was prepared for the Chinese New Year celebration.

    _____ table with bowls of oranges and red envelopes on the back wall

    _____ firecrackers stacked on the floor inside the front door

_____ red lanterns hanging from center ceiling fixture

_____ paper cutouts for luck on the glass panes of the front door

2. The nurse quietly strode into my aunt's hospital room.

_____ black and silver stethoscope draped around his neck

_____ crisp, white cotton pants and short-sleeved tunic

_____ reassuring smile

_____ blue paper covers on his shoes

_____ kind, dark brown eyes

3. The taxicab crawled through rush-hour traffic in the rain-drenched city.

_____ fare meter on the dashboard ticking relentlessly

_____ headlights barely piercing the stormy, gray dusk

_____ windshield wipers losing their battle with the latest cloudburst

_____ backseat passengers frantically checking their watches

_____ driver wishing hopelessly that he could be home watching the news

PRACTICE 4   WRITING ASSIGNMENT

Study this portrait of Dr. Mae Jemison, who in 1992 became the first woman of color ever to soar into space. Notice her facial expression, posture, clothing, equipment, and other details. Then describe the photograph to someone who has never seen it. In your topic sentence, state one feeling, impression, or message this picture conveys and then choose details that support this idea. Arrange these details in space order—from left to right, top to bottom, and so on. As you revise, make sure that your sentences flow clearly and smoothly.

To learn more about Dr. Jemison's remarkable life, view this video: **www.biography .com/people/mae-c-jemison-9542378**

Astronaut
Mae Jemison

JSC Digital Image Collection/NASA

Gehry's Disney Concert Hall in Los Angeles

Order of Importance

Order of importance means arranging your ideas from most to least important—or vice versa.

Frank Gehry is one of the greatest living architects. There are at least three reasons for his worldwide influence. Most important, Gehry has created new shapes for buildings, literally moving outside the boxes in which we often live and work. He has found ways to build walls that look like mountains, sails, and wings. In addition, Gehry uses new materials—or old materials in new ways. Going beyond plaster and wood, Gehry's buildings have rounded metal walls, curves made of glass, and stone in strange places. Third, because of its striking looks, a Gehry building can bring tourist dollars and international attention to a town or city. This happened when Gehry designed the now-famous Guggenheim Museum building in the little town of Bilbao, Spain. And like the latest blockbuster movie, the Disney Concert Hall in Los Angeles opened to rave reviews.

- The three reasons in this paragraph are discussed from the most important reason to the least important.
- Note that the words *most important*, *in addition*, and *third* help the reader move from one reason to another.

You might visualize order of importance like this:

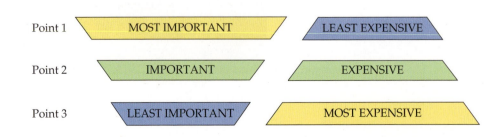

Sometimes you may wish to begin with the least important idea and build toward a climax at the end of the paragraph. Paragraphs arranged from the least important idea to the most important idea can have dramatic power.

> Although my 14-year-old daughter learned a great deal from living with a Pennsylvania Amish family last summer, adjusting to their strict lifestyle was difficult for her. Kay admitted that the fresh food served on the farm was great, but she missed her diet colas. More difficult was the fact that she had to wear long dresses—no more jeans and bomber jackets. Still worse in her view were the hours. A suburban girl and self-confessed night person, my daughter had to get up at 5 A.M. to milk cows! By far the most difficult adjustment concerned boys. If an Amish woman is not married, she cannot spend time with males, and this rule now applied to Kay. Yes, she suffered and complained, but by summer's end, she was a different girl—more open-minded and proud of the fact that all these deprivations put her more in touch with herself.
>
> *Lucy Auletta, Student*

- The adjustment difficulties this writer's daughter had are arranged from least to most important. How many difficulties are discussed? _____

- Note how the words *more difficult*, *still worse*, and *by far the most difficult adjustment* help the reader move from one idea to the next.

Transitional Expressions to Show Importance
first, next, finally
more, most
less, least

PRACTICE 5

Arrange the ideas that develop each topic sentence in order of importance, numbering them 1, 2, and 3. Begin with the most important idea, or reverse the order if you think that a paragraph would be more effective if it began with the least important idea. Be prepared to explain your choices. Then, on a separate sheet of paper, write the ideas in a paragraph.

1. Sixty-eight percent of things Americans throw in the trash should be recycled or composted.

   _____ Twenty-nine percent of all garbage in landfills is recyclable paper like newspapers and product packaging.

   _____ Plastic bottles, bags, and packaging make up 12 percent of landfill waste.

   _____ Twenty-seven percent of the trash in landfills is food scraps, leaves, grass clippings, and yard waste that could go into compost piles.

2. Stays in the hospital can expose patients to serious health risks.

   _____ Mistakes like miscommunication or an incorrect ID bracelet can result in a surgery on the wrong eye, the wrong leg, or one performed on the wrong patient.

   _____ Human or system errors in hospitals are now the third leading cause of death in the United States, after heart disease and cancer.

   _____ Hospitals are famously germ-filled places where patients and visitors can easily catch colds, the flu, or more serious infections.

3. Undiagnosed or untreated diabetes can cause serious problems.

    ____ The diabetic's craving for sweets can be difficult to control.

    ____ If diabetes is not properly managed, blindness and other serious health problems, such as ulcers and gangrene, can result.

    ____ Ignoring a diabetes diagnosis can result in premature death.

    ____ Untreated diabetes often causes dry, itchy skin and intense thirst.

PRACTICE 6   WRITING ASSIGNMENT

Write a paragraph to persuade a certain group of people to do something they don't do now. For example, you could write to convince couch potatoes to begin exercising, senior citizens to take a free class at your college, or nonvoters to register and cast a ballot. Discuss the three most important reasons why your readers should follow your advice, and arrange these reasons in order of importance—least to most important or most to least important, whichever you think would make a better paragraph. Don't forget to use transitional expressions. If you wish, use humor to win over your audience.

B. More Work on Revising: Exact and Concise Language

Good writers do not settle for the first words that spill onto their paper or computer screen. Instead, they revise what they have written, replacing vague words with exact language and repetitious words with concise language.

Exact Language

As a rule, the more specific, detailed, and exact the language is, the better the writing. Which sentence in each of the following pairs contains the more vivid and exact language?

> (1) The office was noisy.
> (2) In the office, phones jangled, printers whirred, and copy machines hummed.
>
> (3) What my tutor said made me feel good.
> (4) When my tutor whispered, "Fine job," I felt like singing.

- Sentence (2) is more exact than sentence (1) because *phones jangled, printers whirred, and copy machines hummed* provide more vivid information than the general word *noisy*.

- What *exact* words does sentence (4) use to replace the general words *said* and *made me feel good*? _____

You do not need a large vocabulary to write exactly and well, but you do need to work at finding the right words to fit each sentence.

PRACTICE 7

These sentences contain vague language. Revise each one, using vivid and exact language wherever possible.

> **EXAMPLE:** A man went through the crowd.
> Revise: _A man in a blue leather jacket pushed through the crowd._

1. An automobile went down the street.

   Revise: _____

   _____

2. This apartment has problems.

   Revise: _____

   _____

3. My job is fun.

   Revise: _____

   _____

4. This magazine is interesting.

   Revise: _____

   _____

5. The expression on his face made me feel comfortable.

   Revise: _____

   _____

6. When Allison comes home, her pet greets her.

   Revise: _____

   _____

7. There was a big storm here last week.

   Revise: _____

   _____

8. The emergency room has a lot of people in it.

   Revise: _____

   _____

Concise Language

Concise writing never uses five or six words when two or three will do. It avoids repetitious and unnecessary words that add nothing to the meaning of a sentence. As you revise your writing, cross out unnecessary words and phrases.

Which sentence in each of the following pairs is more concise?

(1) Because of the fact that Larissa owns an antiques shop, she is always poking around in dusty attics.
(2) Because Larissa owns an antiques shop, she is always poking around in dusty attics.

(3) Mr. Tibbs entered a large, dark blue room.
(4) Mr. Tibbs entered a room that was large in size and dark blue in color.

● Sentences (2) and (3) are concise; sentences (1) and (4) are wordy.

● In sentence (1), *because of the fact that* is a wordy way of saying *because*.

● In sentence (4), *in size* and *in color* just repeat which ideas?

_____

Of course, conciseness does not mean writing short, choppy sentences. It does mean dropping unnecessary words and phrases.

PRACTICE 8

The following sentences are wordy. If possible, in a group with two or three others, make each sentence more concise by deleting unnecessary words, rewording slightly as necessary. Write your revised sentences on the lines provided, making sure not to change the meaning of the original.

EXAMPLE: Many people wonder what life will be like in the future in years to come.

Revise: *Many people wonder what life will be like in the future.*

_____

1. Experts make the prediction that by 2050 some people will live to a ripe old age of 130 or even 150 years old.

   Revise: _____

   _____

2. The reason why we will be healthier is because replacement organs and parts of the human body will be grown if needed.

   Revise: _____

   _____

3. Tiny earbud computers in our ears will make us smarter and more intelligent, translating languages and linking to large, enormous databases.

   Revise: _____

   _____

4. Most of our food that we eat will come from high-rise farms rising many stories straight up to the sky.

   Revise: _____

   _____

Sophisticated robots, already in use, will be part of everyday life in 2050.

R-Type / Alamy

5. Computers will monitor our homes that we own, feed our animals and pets, and project any video game, recipe, or art on a table or wall.

   Revise: _____

   _____

6. Three-dimensional TV and computer images will seem real, with odors to smell, textures to touch, and tastes.

   Revise: _____

   _____

7. Friendly robot nannies will care for children who are still young and the elderly who are getting on in years.

   Revise: _____

   _____

8. Experts also give a warning of future dangers like extreme, severe weather and new ethical challenges that people will think about and face.

   Revise: _____

   _____

9. Because of the fact that human cloning will be a reality, some groups might create clones to be soldiers or slaves.

   Revise: _____

   _____

10. In 2050 of the future, we could face hard and difficult questions about what it means to be human in a world of machines.

    Revise: _____

    _____

EXPLORING ONLINE

www.youtube.com/watch?v=95Fxe3KnLz4

Watch "Microsoft's Vision for the World of Technology, 2020."

www.futuretimeline.net

Visit Future Timeline to learn more about what the experts see in our future.

PRACTICE 9   **CRITICAL THINKING AND WRITING**

Following are statements from real accident reports collected by an insurance company. As you will see, these writers need help with more than their fenders!

Read each statement and try to understand what each writer meant to say. Then revise each statement so that it says exactly and concisely what the writer intended.

1. "The guy was all over the place. I had to swerve a number of times before I hit him."
2. "The telephone pole was approaching fast. I was attempting to swerve out of its path when it struck my front end."
3. "Coming home, I drove into the wrong house and collided with a tree I don't have."
4. "I was on my way to the doctor's with rear-end trouble when my universal joint gave way, causing me to have an accident."
5. "I was driving my car out of the driveway in the usual manner when it was struck by the other car in the same place it had been struck several times before."

PRACTICE 10   **REVIEW**

Choose a paragraph or paper you wrote recently. Read it with a fresh eye, checking for exact and concise language. Then rewrite it, eliminating all vague or wordy language.

C. Turning Assignments into Paragraphs

In Chapter 3, Part B, you learned how to narrow a broad topic and write a specific topic sentence. Sometimes, however, your assignment may take the form of a specific question, and your job may be to answer the question in one paragraph.

For example, this question asks you to take a stand for or against a particular issue.

> Are professional athletes overpaid?

You can often turn this kind of question into a topic sentence:

> (1) Professional athletes are overpaid.
> (2) Professional athletes are not overpaid.
> (3) Professional athletes are sometimes overpaid.

- These three topic sentences take different points of view.
- The words *are*, *are not*, and *sometimes* make each writer's opinion clear.

Sometimes you will be asked to agree or disagree with a statement:

> **(4)** Salary is the most important factor in job satisfaction. Agree or disagree.

- This is really a question in disguise: *Is salary the most important factor in job satisfaction?*

In the topic sentence, make your opinion clear and repeat key words.

> **(5)** Salary is the most important factor in job satisfaction.
>
> **(6)** Salary is not the most important factor in job satisfaction.
>
> **(7)** Salary is only one among several important factors in job satisfaction.

- The words *is, is not,* and *is only one among several* make each writer's opinion clear.
- Note how the topic sentences repeat the key words from the statement—*salary, important factor, job satisfaction.*

Once you have written the topic sentence, follow the steps described in Chapters 2 and 3—freewriting, brainstorming, or clustering; selecting; grouping—and then write your paragraph. Be sure that all ideas in the paragraph support the opinion you have stated in the topic sentence.

PRACTICE 11   Here are four exam questions. Write one topic sentence to answer each of them.
REMEMBER: Make your opinion clear in the topic sentence and repeat key words from the question.

1. Should computer education be required in every public high school?

   Topic sentence: _____

   _____

2. Would you advise your best friend to buy a new car or a used car?

   Topic sentence: _____

   _____

3. Is there too much bad news on television news programs?

   Topic sentence: _____

   _____

4. How have your interests changed in the past five years?

   Topic sentence: _____

   _____

PRACTICE 12   Imagine that your instructor has just written the exam questions from Practice 11 on the board. Choose the question that most interests you and write a paragraph answering that question. Prewrite, select, and arrange ideas before you compose your paragraph. Then reread your work, making any needed corrections.

PRACTICE 13   Here are four statements. Agree or disagree, and write a topic sentence for each.

1. All higher education should be free. Agree or disagree.

   Topic sentence: _____

   _____

2. Expecting one's spouse to be perfect is the most important reason for the high divorce rate in the United States. Agree or disagree.

   Topic sentence: _____

   _____

3. Parents should give children money when they need it rather than give them an allowance. Agree or disagree.

   Topic sentence: _____

   _____

4. Silence is golden. Agree or disagree.

   Topic sentence: _____

   _____

PRACTICE 14   Choose the statement in Practice 13 that most interests you. Then write a paragraph in which you agree or disagree.

Chapter Highlights

To improve your writing, try these techniques:

- Organize your ideas by time order.
- Organize your ideas by space order.
- Organize your ideas by order of importance, either from the most important to the least or from the least important to the most.
- Use language that is exact and concise.
- Turn assignment questions into topic sentences.

EXPLORING ONLINE

lrs.ed.uiuc.edu/students/fwalters/cohere.html
Review ways to add coherence to your writing.

grammar.ccc.commnet.edu/grammar/quizzes/wordy_quiz.htm
Practice making wordy sentences lean and mean.

Visit **MindTap** for *Grassroots* to access this chapter's ebook, flashcards, additional practice and quizzes, and more!

CHAPTER 5

Illustration, Description, and Narration

A: Illustration

B: Description

C: Narration

Chapters 5, 6, and 7 present nine patterns of paragraph and essay organization that will help you become a more critical thinker and a better writer.

A common problem for many writers is not adequately developing their main idea. "This topic sentence needs more support," their instructor might write. To help with this problem, it is useful to know certain patterns that often are used in college or workplace writing. These **patterns of organization** also reflect **ways of thinking** about the world, ways in which the human brain naturally tries to make sense of experience. For instance, we might think of good *examples* to make our meaning clear or *compare* two things or search for the *reasons why* something happened. This chapter will teach you three useful patterns.

A. Illustration

One effective way to make your writing more specific is by thinking of one, two, or three **examples**. Someone might write, "Divers in Monterey Bay can observe many beautiful fish. For instance, tiger-striped treefish are common." The first sentence makes a general statement about the beautiful fish in Monterey Bay. The second sentence gives a specific example of such fish: *tiger-striped treefish*. This is called **illustration**.

Illustration is especially useful in fields requiring careful observation, like science, psychology, sociology, medicine, and design.

Topic Sentence

Here is the topic sentence of an illustration paragraph:

> Many of the computer industry's best innovators were young friends working in pairs when they first achieved success.

- The writer begins this paragraph with a topic sentence that makes a general statement.

- What generalization about many computer innovators does this sentence make?

_____

Paragraph and Plan

Here is the entire paragraph:

> Many of the computer industry's best innovators were friends working in pairs when they first achieved success. For example, buddies Larry Page and Sergey Brin were students in their twenties when they got the idea for Google, one of the Internet's most popular search engines. In 2004, just six years after launching their new company, Page and Brin became billionaires by selling Google shares to the public. Two more youthful examples are Chad Hurley and Steve Chen, who created the video-sharing website YouTube. The pair worked in Hurley's garage to solve a personal problem: they wanted to figure out an easier way to share video clips with each other via the Internet. The popularity of their site exploded, and one year later, Hurley and Chen sold YouTube to Google for $1.65 billion. A third pair of young computer geniuses are Brian Acton and Jan Koum, creators of the mobile, instant-messaging platform WhatsApp. After leaving their jobs at Google and being rejected by Facebook, the pair came up with their idea when they realized how important apps would become to smartphone users. In 2014, they sold their company to Facebook for $19.3 billion. Youth and collaboration, it seems, are common factors in digital breakthroughs.

- What three examples does this writer provide as support?

Example 1: _____

Example 2: _____

Example 3: _____

- Note that the topic sentence, examples, and concluding sentence make a rough **outline** for the paragraph. In fact, before drafting, the writer probably made just such an outline.

The simplest way to tell a reader that an example will follow is to say so, using **transitional expressions**: _For example, Larry Page . . . ._

Transitional Expressions for Illustration	
for instance	another instance of
for example	another example of
one illustration is	another illustration of

PRACTICE 1   Read this student's paragraph and answer the questions.

As a proud Californian, I separate glass, plastic, and paper and do what I can for the environment. Even if, like me, you rent and don't own a home, you can take simple actions that will help the earth and save money. For example, replace all your incandescent lightbulbs with compact fluorescents (CFLs). CFLs use 75 percent less electricity, last 10 times longer, and save money. Another way to make a difference is water use. Homeowners might install low-flow toilets, but renters can save water with a simple trick. Fill a one-liter plastic bottle with water and put it in the toilet tank. The bottle will displace enough water to save almost a gallon a flush—around ten gallons a day. Next, if you're handy, install a water filter on the kitchen faucet. By refilling stainless-steel bottles instead of buying plastic, a family of four can save $1,000 a year and keep 600 plastic bottles out of landfills. Finally, even if your landlord won't weather-strip those old windows, it is worth $50 or so to do it yourself. You will save a fortune in winter heating bills. Actions like these take a couple hours on a weekend, but the benefits last much longer.

James Lam, Student

1. Underline the topic sentence of this paragraph. Hint: It is not the first sentence.

2. How many examples of renters' actions are discussed?

   _____

3. What transitional expressions does Mr. Lam use?

   _____

PRACTICE 2   Each example in a paragraph must clearly relate to and explain the topic sentence. Each of the following topic sentences is followed by several examples. Circle the letter of any example that does *not* clearly illustrate the topic sentence. Be prepared to explain your choices.

EXAMPLE:

Some animals and insects camouflage themselves in interesting ways.
a. Snowshoe rabbits turn from brown to white in winter, thus blending into the snow.
b. The cheetah's spotted coat makes it hard to see in the dry African bush.
c. The bull alligator smashes its tail against the water and roars during mating season.
d. The walking stick is brown and irregular, much like the twigs among which this insect hides.

1. Many people are unaware that comic book superheroes include a number of Native American characters with special powers.
   a. Navajo Jason Strongbow became American Eagle, a comics hero with superhuman strength, through exposure to sonic energy and radiation.
   b. Female superhero Danielle Moonstar of the X-Men series is a Cheyenne who can create illusions with her thoughts.
   c. Writer Louise Erdrich, the author of 13 novels, identifies as Chippewa.
   d. The GI Joe series produced Spirit Iron-Knife, a Native American superhero highly attuned to nature.

2. Mrs. Makarem is well loved in this community for her generous heart.
   a. Her door is always open to neighborhood children, who stop by for lemonade or advice.

b. When the Padilla family had a fire, Mrs. Makarem collected clothes and blankets for them.

c. "Hello, dear," she says with a smile to everyone she passes on the street.

d. Born in Caracas, Venezuela, she has lived on Bay Road for 32 years.

3. Evidence now shows what many people instinctively understand—that time spent in nature improves physical and mental health.

a. Studies prove that hospital patients who can see trees, flowers, or outdoor vistas from their windows recover more quickly.

b. Strolling in a forest is especially healing, research shows, and the Japanese actually prescribe "forest bathing" to heal body and mind.

c. After the 9/11 terrorist attacks, record numbers of people visited parks, gardens, and other green spaces throughout the New York City area.

d. The National Park Service was created in 1916 by President Woodrow Wilson.

4. A number of unusual, specialized scholarships are available to college students across the United States.

a. The Icy Frost Bridge Scholarship at Indiana's DePauw University is awarded to female music students who sing or play the national anthem "with sincerity."

b. Brighton College, a secondary school for boys and girls in England, pays the full tuition of a student with the last name of *Peyton*.

c. Left-handed, financially needy students can get special scholarships at Juniata College in Pennsylvania.

d. The Collegiate Inventors Competition awards $25,000 to the undergraduate with the most original, socially useful invention.

5. Throughout history, artists, scientists, and inventors have gotten new ideas or solved problems in dreams.

a. In 1816, after a nightmare about a scientist bringing a hideous corpse back to life, Mary Shelley wrote *Frankenstein*, her famous horror story.

b. Biologist James Watson dreamed about spiral staircases, leading him to discover the structure of DNA and win the Nobel Prize.

c. Two weeks before he was shot and killed, President Abraham Lincoln dreamed he saw the body of a president lying in the White House.

d. The entire melody for the Beatles' hit song "Yesterday" came to Paul McCartney in a dream.

PRACTICE 3   The secret of good illustration lies in well-chosen and well-written examples. Think of one example that illustrates each of the following general statements. Write out the example in sentence form—one to three sentences—as clearly and exactly as possible.

1. Some professional athletes inspire young people with talent as well as good character.

    Example: _____

    _____

2. Certain unique foods are served in my culture (or family).

    Example: _____

    _____

3. Many films today have amazing special effects.

Example: _____

_____

PRACTICE 4 · CRITICAL VIEWING AND WRITING

Sometimes a writer notices specific examples first, sees a pattern, and then comes up with a generalization. Consider the three examples pictured and then craft your generalization into a topic sentence that includes all three.

PRACTICE 5 · WRITING AN ILLUSTRATION PARAGRAPH

Pick a topic from the list below or one that your instructor assigns. Draft a topic sentence that you can support well with examples. Now prewrite to get as many examples as possible and think critically as you pick the best three or four. Many students find it helpful to use a graphic organizer as they plan their paragraph. In your notebook or on the computer, create an outline for your illustration paragraph using an organizer like the one that follows.

- benefits of social media
- best places to study on campus
- people you most admire
- traditions typical of one culture or area
- people whose attitude is their worst enemy

- what not to wear for a job interview
- mistakes first-year college students make
- ads that use humor effectively
- ways to handle difficult customers
- best apps for a student (or sports or fashion lover)

ILLUSTRATION PARAGRAPH ORGANIZER

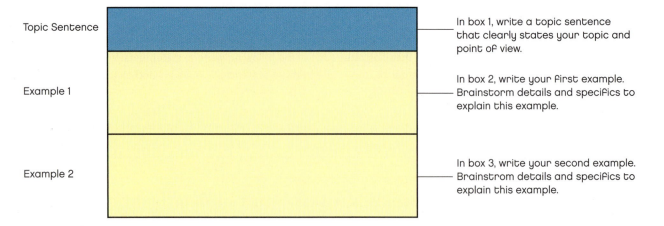

Example 3	In box 4, present your third example. Brainstorm details and specifics to explain this example.
Conclusion	Jot ideas for a lively concluding sentence or two, a final thought about your illustration.

Now write the best draft you can. Use transitional expressions of illustration to guide your reader from point to point. Let your draft cool for an hour or a day; then read it like a thoughtful stranger. Think critically as you read. Is the topic sentence clear and interesting? Does it "set up" the paragraph for the reader? Does each example develop the main idea? Proofread for grammar and spelling.

B. Description

Good **description** creates such a vivid word picture of a person, place, or object that a reader can experience it too. While detailed, exact language adds spark to any writing, it is the lifeblood of great description. Descriptive language appeals to our *senses*—sight, sound, smell, taste, and touch.

Imagine, for example, that you want your friends to try the creative new ice cream shop in town. You could say, "The ice cream is to die for," or you could describe one flavor that is startlingly purple, tastes a bit like sweet potatoes, and is called "Yam I Am." As you practice describing, you'll discover an amazing thing: The more you look, the more you see!

Descriptive ability is important in journalism, architecture, science, engineering, medicine, design, and many other fields.

Topic Sentence

Here is the first sentence of a descriptive paragraph:

> The windows at either end of the laundry room were open, but no breeze washed through to carry off the stale odors of fabric softener, detergent, and bleach.

- The topic sentence of a descriptive paragraph indicates what will be described. What will be the subject of this description?

  _____

- The topic sentence often also gives the reader an *overall impression* of the person, place, or thing to be described. Does this topic sentence give an overall impression of the laundry room?

  _____

Paragraph and Plan

Here is the entire paragraph:

> The windows at either end of the laundry room were open, but no breeze washed through to carry off the stale odors of fabric softener, detergent, and bleach. In the small ponds of soapy water that stained the concrete floor were stray balls of multicolored lint and fuzz. Along the left wall of the room stood ten rasping dryers, their round windows offering glimpses of jumping socks, underwear, and fatigues. Down the center of the room were a dozen washing machines, set back to back in two rows. Some were chugging like steamboats; others were whining and whistling and dribbling suds. Two stood forlorn and empty, their lids flung open, with crudely drawn signs that said "Broke!" A long shelf partially covered in blue paper ran the length of the wall, interrupted only by a locked door. Alone, at the far end of the shelf, sat one empty laundry basket and an open box of Tide. Above the shelf at the other end was a small bulletin board decorated with yellowed business cards and torn slips of paper: scrawled requests for rides, reward offers for lost dogs, and phone numbers without names or explanations. On and on the machines hummed and wheezed, gurgled and gushed, washed, rinsed, and spun.
>
> *Richard Nordquist*

- Do the details in this description help you see and feel this laundry room? The overall impression seems be that this is a stale and shabby place.

- List at least three details or sections that support this overall impression:

  _____

  _____

- How many senses does the writer appeal to in this paragraph? Underline your favorite descriptive words or parts.

  _____

- Like many descriptive paragraphs, this one is arranged according to space order.* Underline at least four transitional expressions that the writer uses to show where things are.

- Before composing this paragraph, the writer probably brainstormed or freewrote to gather the best details and then organized them into a rough **outline**.

------

*For more work on space order, see Chapter 4, "Improving Your Paragraphs," Part A.

Transitional expressions for descriptive paragraphs usually help readers "see" where things are.

Transitional Expressions Indicating Place or Position	
above, below	on top, underneath
near, far	to the left, right, in the center
next, to, near	behind, beside
up, down, between	front, back, middle

PRACTICE 6

Read this student's descriptive paragraph and answer the questions.

It is about two inches wide and two inches in height. It has three peaks on the top and one peak at the bottom center. Words are written across the top half, and in the middle are engravings of two men standing with a shield and an eagle between them. The lower half of this metal object displays numbers. On the back is a pin. This object carries a powerful meaning that calls up mixed feelings in some people. It is a symbol of authority and identifies a group of people who represent respect and discipline. You must attend an academy in order to enter this group, and then you can wear this object proudly on your chest or carry it in a wallet. It is a symbol of law enforcement, and sometimes good people die because of it.

Steven Rodriguez, Student

1. Rather than start with a general impression, this student describes an object in detail and puts his topic sentence at the end. Underline the topic sentence. Did you guess the object being described?

   _____

2. Does keeping the object a mystery add to or take away from the effectiveness of the paragraph?

   _____

3. The first five sentences give physical details. What kinds of details are given in the second half?

   _____

PRACTICE 7

The details in a descriptive paragraph should support the *overall impression* stated or implied in the topic sentence. In each of the following plans, one detail has nothing to do with the topic sentence and should be dropped. Find the irrelevant detail and circle its letter.

1. The patient presents with a painful rash down the left side of her head.
   a. patient well-dressed, designer handbag
   b. no fever, temperature 97.8 degrees
   c. vertical line of raised red blisters behind left ear to neck
   d. complains that left head and neck have hurt increasingly for three days

2. For two months every summer, Abuelita's house in the Dominican Republic was my tropical paradise.

   a. outdoor and courtyard walls painted pink

   b. giant banyan tree near the kitchen, my castle to play in

   c. huge vines and tiny lizards climbing the walls

   d. Haiti on one end of the island, DR on the other

   e. delicious smells of flowers and Abuelita's cooking

3. The pelican was oil-drenched and greatly distressed.

   a. weak from weight loss and dehydration

   b. feathers matted, separated, and glossy black with oil

   c. beak open, panting

   d. 105 oil spills just since 2000

PRACTICE 8   CRITICAL VIEWING AND WRITING

Study these photos of a tropical hotel that your marketing firm has been hired to promote, if possible, with several classmates. Your audience is adult couples who want a weekend away from it all without the children. Your goal is to describe this hotel—location, pool, views, guest rooms—in such enticing detail that guests will rush to make reservations and you will retire on your bonus checks. Take notes as you brainstorm. Then organize and craft your masterpiece of verbal salesmanship. Be prepared to share your work.

© Pakhnyushcha/Shutterstock.com

© Vitaly Titov & Maria Sidelnikova/Shutterstock.com

PRACTICE 9   WRITING A DESCRIPTIVE PARAGRAPH

Pick a topic from this list or one your instructor assigns. Think of one overall impression you wish to convey, and draft a topic sentence stating this impression. Prewrite to get rich descriptive details to support your topic sentence. Many students find it useful to use a graphic organizer as they plan their paragraph. In your notebook or on the computer, create an outline for your descriptive paragraph using an organizer like the one that follows.

- a workplace
- an object that says to you: *I have arrived*
- someone you know well
- a device or piece of equipment you use
- a sad (intense, dirty, quiet, historic, inspiring) place
- a photograph from the news
- your favorite meal (or worst meal)
- an animal at the zoo
- an object that deserves attention
- a "worthless" object that you treasure

DESCRIPTIVE PARAGRAPH ORGANIZER

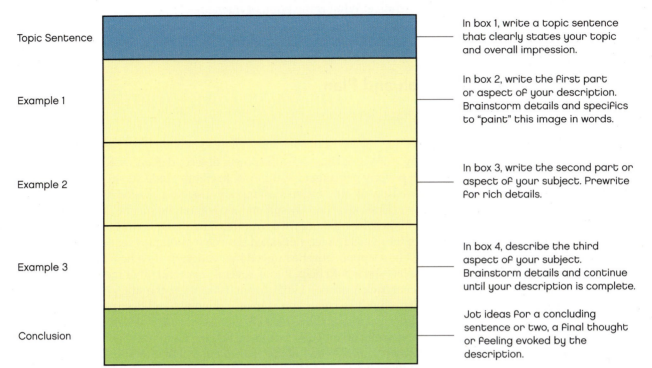

Topic Sentence	In box 1, write a topic sentence that clearly states your topic and overall impression.
Example 1	In box 2, write the first part or aspect of your description. Brainstorm details and specifics to "paint" this image in words.
Example 2	In box 3, write the second part or aspect of your subject. Prewrite for rich details.
Example 3	In box 4, describe the third aspect of your subject. Brainstorm details and continue until your description is complete.
Conclusion	Jot ideas for a concluding sentence or two, a final thought or feeling evoked by the description.

Now write the best draft you can. Use transitional expressions of description to guide your reader from detail to detail. Let your draft cool for an hour or a day. Then read it like a thoughtful stranger. Think critically as you read. Is the topic sentence clear and interesting? Does it "set up" the paragraph for the reader? Does each detail develop the main idea? Proofread for grammar and spelling.

C. Narration

From childhood on, most people love a good story. To **narrate** is to tell a story—to explain what happened, when it happened, and who was involved. When you tell a friend or relative about a funny, frightening, or annoying incident, you are sharing a narrative. Many writers and public speakers use stories to connect with their audiences and bring ideas to life. The key to a good narrative is that it has a clear **point**. The critical-thinking task of narrative is to ask "What is the point of this story? Why do I want to tell it?"

Narrative is a useful skill in any field that requires reports, such as sociology, psychology, business, nursing, and police work.

Topic Sentence

Here is the topic sentence of a narrative paragraph:

> The two lives of Victor Rios show the power of second chances.

- The topic sentence should indicate the subject or main idea of the narrative. Before you write, you should think about the *point* of your story. What do you want your readers to learn from reading your story? Do you hope to teach a lesson, to make them laugh, or perhaps inspire them to take action?

- The writer begins this paragraph with a topic sentence that reveals the point of the narrative. What is the point or main idea?

_____

Paragraph and Plan

Here is the entire paragraph:

> The two lives of Victor Rios show the power of second chances. Rios grew up in squalid poverty in Oakland, California. In eighth grade, he dropped out of school, joined a gang, and began stealing cars. The gang shaped his thinking: school was worthless, and the only sure money was on the streets. Then when Rios was 15, his best friend Smiley was murdered in a gang war. Rios saw clearly what his own future held. A teacher asked how he was doing after Smiley's death. "Fine," he snapped, but she hugged him and said when he was ready to change his life, she would help. It took several years and other mentors, but at last Rios went back to school. He discovered sociology, the study of human behavior—like why some smart young men and women self-destruct. Rios went on to earn a PhD and a college teaching job at the University of California. Today he mentors and writes about gang members, helping them transform. In 2012, Rios told TV interviewer Gwen Ifill that if an angel had said to him as an angry teen, "hang in there because at 34, you'll have an amazing life," he would have laughed. His message to kids in trouble: it's not a joke; your second chance exists.

- The body of a narrative is made up of small events or actions told in the order they occurred. Arranging these details in time, or chronological, order helps readers follow more easily.*

- List the smaller events in this paragraph in chronological order:

_____

_____

_____

- Underline at least three transitional expressions of time in this paragraph.

- Note that the topic sentence, events, and concluding sentences make a rough *outline* for the paragraph. Before drafting, the writer probably made just such an outline.

Using transitional expressions of time can help your readers follow the narrative.

Transitional Expressions of Time for Narratives		
afterward	first	next
currently	later	soon
finally	meanwhile	then

———

*For more work on time order, see Chapter 4, "Improving Your Paragraphs," Part A.

PRACTICE 10

Here are three plans for narrative paragraphs. The events in the plans are not in chronological order, and they each contain an event or detail that does not relate to the story. Number the events in time order and cross out the irrelevant one.

1. The invention of cornflakes was a happy accident.

   ____ Will decided to bake the boiled wheat flakes, liked the taste, and found that the patients loved them.

   ____ In the late 1800s, Dr. John Kellogg ran a health retreat, helped in the kitchen by his "slow" brother Will, a sixth-grade dropout.

   ____ Will had the brilliant idea of baking cornflakes as he had baked the wheat, and orders poured in.

   ____ Eating oatmeal might be good for the heart.

   ____ One day in 1894, after Will accidentally boiled some wheat too long, it fell into flaky pieces.

   ____ After John resigned, Will ran the W. W. Kellogg Company, proving himself to be a business and advertising genius.

2. I learned the hard way that a friend's envy is a serious warning sign.

   ____ After that conversation, we became best friends in high school.

   ____ Many students share apartments to keep costs down.

   ____ We shared an apartment in college, and after I decorated my bedroom, I was hurt when she just said, "I'd kill for this room" and walked out.

   ____ The first thing Lara said to me in high school was, "I want your hair," which I took as a compliment.

   ____ When Lara secretly interviewed for a job she knew I desperately wanted, I was shocked to realize that this woman was not my friend.

3. The largest unsolved art heist in history occurred quietly in Boston in 1990.

   ____ Working fast, the thieves removed 13 masterpieces from the walls, including paintings by Vermeer and Rembrandt, and then slipped into the night.

   ____ Art detectives, the FBI, and a five million dollar reward never turned up the missing works, which are valued at 500 million dollars.

   ____ Around midnight on March 18, two men posing as Boston police entered the security door of the small Isabella Stewart Gardner Museum.

   ____ They ordered the security guard to come away from his desk and then handcuffed him and the one other guard on duty.

   ____ Almost 400 years after his death, Vermeer is admired for the way he painted light.

PRACTICE 11

CRITICAL THINKING AND WRITING

Like many fairy tales, fables were told to convey a life lesson. In a small group, if possible, have someone read this fable, "The Frog and the Scorpion," aloud. What do you think the story is about? Finally, write the missing topic sentence.

The Frog and the Scorpion by Heidi Taillefer

Once you have read the fable below, can you explain why you think this artist painted partial armor on the frog? (There are no wrong answers in art.)

The ancient fable of the frog and the scorpion teaches a lesson about _____

_____

A poisonous scorpion wanted to cross a rushing river, but he could not swim. Spotting a frog sitting on the riverbank, the scorpion called to him, politely asking for a ride on the frog's back. "I'm sorry," said the frog, "but you will sting me, and then we will both die." The scorpion replied, "That makes no sense because I want to cross the river." This sounded reasonable, but the frog had a nagging worry. "Well, you might wait until we are almost across and then sting me." But the scorpion protested, "Never! Because I would be so grateful for your help." So the frog agreed, the scorpion hopped on his back, and off they went. About halfway across the river, the scorpion suddenly stung the frog hard. The frog's body started going numb, and he knew he was dying. "Why did you do that?" he gasped. The scorpion said, "Because it's my nature," and they both sank.

Does this story relate to your experience? Have you ever been a "frog" and let yourself get stung despite your common sense? Have you ever stung somebody else and then regretted it? Do we all have a bit of self-defeating frog or scorpion hiding in us? What do you think is the lesson or point of this fable? Then complete the topic sentence so that it clearly states this point.

PRACTICE 12   WRITING A NARRATIVE PARAGRAPH

Pick a topic from this list or one your instructor assigns. Draft a topic sentence that will get the reader's attention and/or states the point of your story. Prewrite to get as many narrative details as possible. Many students find it helpful to use a graphic organizer as they plan their paragraph. In your notebook or on the computer, create an outline for your narrative paragraph using an organizer like the one that follows.

- something I am (not) proud of
- a family story
- a parenting lesson
- a key event in history or science
- a lesson in dignity

- a career insight
- becoming a volunteer
- a cautionary college tale
- a decision to change jobs
- a turning point

Now write the best draft you can. Use transitional expressions of narration to guide your reader from event to event. Let your draft cool for an hour or a day. Then read it like a thoughtful stranger. Think critically as you read. Is the topic sentence clear and interesting? Does it "set up" the paragraph for the reader? Does each event or detail develop the main idea? Proofread for grammar and spelling.

NARRATIVE PARAGRAPH ORGANIZER

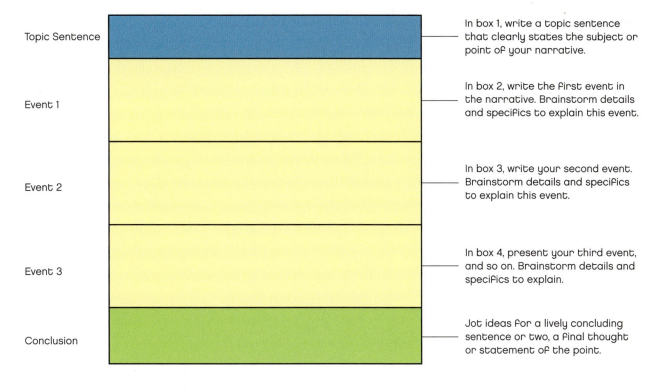

Topic Sentence — In box 1, write a topic sentence that clearly states the subject or point of your narrative.

Event 1 — In box 2, write the first event in the narrative. Brainstorm details and specifics to explain this event.

Event 2 — In box 3, write your second event. Brainstorm details and specifics to explain this event.

Event 3 — In box 4, present your third event, and so on. Brainstorm details and specifics to explain.

Conclusion — Jot ideas for a lively concluding sentence or two, a final thought or statement of the point.

Chapter Highlights

These paragraph patterns are often used in college and the workplace. They reflect different ways of thinking about a subject.

- The illustration paragraph develops the topic sentence with one, two, three, or more specific examples.

- The descriptive paragraph paints a vivid word picture of a person, place, or object.

- The narrative paragraph tells a story that makes a clear point.

EXPLORING ONLINE

writesite.cuny.edu/projects/keywords/example/hand2.html

Fill in the boxes to help you develop your idea with examples.

www.roanestate.edu/owl/describe.html

Good tips on writing effective narrative and descriptive essays from the Roane State OWL.

Visit **MindTap** for *Grassroots* to access this chapter's ebook, flashcards, additional practice and quizzes, and more!

CHAPTER 6

Process, Comparison-Contrast, and Classification

A: Process

B: Comparison-Contrast

C: Classification

This chapter will teach you three more paragraph patterns frequently used in college and business writing. Knowing these patterns of organization will help you become a more critical thinker and a better writer.

A. Process

A **process** paragraph explains *how to do something* or *how something gets done*. A recipe for cherry pie, the directions for your new scanner, or the stages in becoming a U.S. citizen are all processes. The goal of such directions is a delicious pie, a scanner that scans, and an understanding of the citizenship process. After reading a process paragraph, the reader should be able to do something or understand how something works. The process writer must think like the reader and not leave out a step.

Process writing is useful in technology, psychology, history, the sciences, business, and many other fields.

Topic Sentence

Here is the topic sentence of one student's process paragraph:

In just five easy steps, you can flunk almost any job interview.

- The topic sentence should clearly state the goal of the process. What should the reader be able to do once he or she finishes reading this paragraph?

- Based on the topic sentence, do you think this writer is being serious? What audience, or group of readers, is she addressing?

_____

Paragraph and Plan

Here is the entire paragraph:

> In just five easy steps, you can flunk almost any job interview. First, during the important pre-interview stage, keep these "don'ts" in mind. Don't take down the wild party pics from your Facebook page. Don't do any research about the company. Above all, don't practice interviewing with a friend, answering possible questions out loud. Second, on the big day, dress to express. Your team jersey is a solid choice, but a hilarious T-shirt is better, like "TXT Queen" or "It's all about ME." Third, make an unforgettable first impression. Arrive late without your résumé. Leave your tongue ring in; chewing gum will keep it flashing. Fourth, during the interview, it's important to act as detached as possible. Avoid the interviewer's eyes, say "Um" a lot, and check your phone every three minutes. Finally, the way you leave can seal the deal. Forget the interviewer's name as you say goodbye, and afterwards, skip the old-school thank you note. You will be the talk of the office for weeks to come.
>
> _Yesenia Ramos, Student_

- The body of a process paragraph consists of the steps to be completed in the order they should be done. Arranging these steps in time, or chronological,* order helps your readers understand the directions more easily.

- How many steps are there in this how-to paragraph and what are they?

_____

_____

- Note that the topic sentence, five main steps, and concluding sentence make an outline of the paragraph. In fact, after brainstorming or freewriting for ideas, the writer made just such an outline before she wrote.

To help readers follow the steps in a process, transitional expressions of time are useful.

Transitional Expressions of Time for Process		
Beginning a Process	**Continuing a Process**	**Ending a Process**
first	next, then	finally
initially	after that	last
the first step (or stage)	the second step (or stage)	the final step

*For more work on time order, see Chapter 4, "Improving Your Paragraphs," Part A.

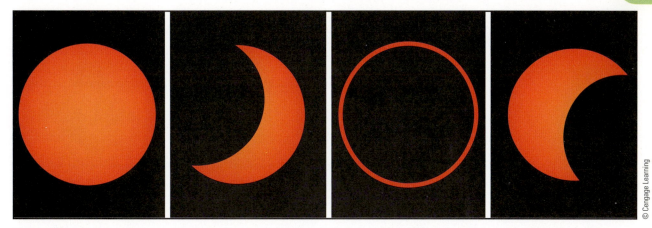

Just as these images show each stage of a solar eclipse—as the moon passes between the sun and Earth—your process paragraph should clearly describe each step or stage for the reader. Before writing, try to visualize the process as if it were a series of photographs.

PRACTICE 1

Read this student's process paragraph carefully and answer the questions.

> Properly shooting a basketball is a four-step process. First, position your body by squaring your shoulders in the direction of the hoop, holding the ball above your eyes, and aiming your shooting elbow at the basket. Next, bend your knees and explode upward to transfer power from your legs through your back to your shooting shoulder and arm, pushing the ball upward and forward toward the rim. Third, using only the fingertips of the shooting hand, apply a consistent and straight backspin as you release the basketball from your hands; your non-shooting hand should grip the ball as lightly as possible to stabilize it. Finally, snap your wrist as you release the ball. This fourth step not only ensures a tight rotation but also helps control the path of the shot. Mastering these four steps will help your shots float to the hoop with a nice arc and a tight, consistent backspin. Swish.
>
> *Jared Cohen, Student*

1. What process is described in this paragraph?

   _____

2. How many steps does the writer present?

   _____

3. What transitional expressions does this writer use to signal each new step in the process?

   _____

PRACTICE 2

Here are three plans for process paragraphs. The steps for the plans are not in the correct chronological order, and they contain irrelevant details that are not part of the process. Number the steps in the proper time sequence and cross out any irrelevant details.

1. Opening a Twitter account is as easy as one, two, three.

   ____ Create your Twitter username and complete the account setup.

   ____ Once on the site, click the box that says "Sign up."

_____ Facebook allows users to write longer posts than Twitter does.

_____ Go to **twitter.com**.

_____ Enter your full name, e-mail address or phone number, and a personal password.

_____ Start tweeting!

2. Stress, so common in modern life, is actually a process, with symptoms that will keep progressing if they are not addressed.

_____ Not getting enough sleep causes stress.

_____ After a time, a person enters the final phase, exhaustion, characterized by poor performance, lowered immunity, and a loss of zest for life.

_____ In the first, or alarm, stage, a threatening situation triggers strong "fight or flight" reactions—a racing heart, high blood pressure, and muscle tension.

_____ The second stage, resistance, occurs as the person anxiously attempts to keep coping with the stress, perhaps turning to overeating or drinking too much caffeine.

3. The creation of a woodblock print has four stages.

_____ Paper is laid over the inked block and is rubbed all over the raised design with a spoon.

_____ The artist sketches a design on a block of wood and then carves away all the wood around the design.

_____ Next the artist rolls ink across the raised surface of the design.

_____ Other prints are lithograph prints and silkscreens.

_____ When the paper is lifted away, the inked design is printed on it.

PRACTICE 3   CRITICAL THINKING AND WRITING

If you have ever tried to diet or quit smoking, you know how hard change can be. Behavioral change is actually a _process_, not an event. Look closely at this graphic (used by psychologists and addiction treatment experts) on the _five stages of change_, if possible, in a small group. Consider each stage and what a person might think or do at this stage. Which stages are most likely to cause trouble for a person hoping to change a behavior? Why do some people try to change but fail? Share examples if you wish.

Private journal assignment: Think of an important change you made or tried to make. Did you want to exercise more, quit drinking, or study more regularly? Describe your change process. Which stages were the hardest for you? What, if anything, did you learn?

THE STAGES OF BEHAVIORAL CHANGE

Precontemplation: Person is unaware or unwilling to change.

Contemplation: Person thinks about changing but has mixed feelings.

Preparation: Person takes small steps to prepare (e.g., buys a diet book).

Action: Person actually changes his or her behavior.

Maintenance: Person works to maintain the new behavior.

If relapse occurs, begin again.

PRACTICE 4   WRITING A PROCESS PARAGRAPH

Pick a topic from this list that interests you or one your instructor assigns. Draft a topic sentence to introduce your paragraph and catch the readers' interest. Visualize or go through the process, jotting facts and details. Don't leave out any steps. Many students find it helpful to use a graphic organizer as they plan the paragraph. In your notebook or on the computer, create an outline for your process paragraph using an organizer like the one that follows.

- how to turn a failure into success
- how to find (or get rid of) a roommate
- how to evaluate a website
- how to groom a dog
- how to become more _____
- how to use Instagram
- how to study for a test
- how to motivate yourself
- how to choose a major
- how to find a job

PROCESS PARAGRAPH ORGANIZER

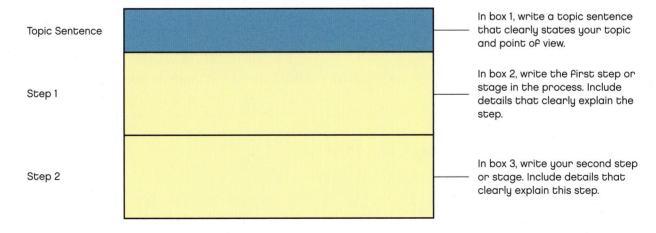

Topic Sentence — In box 1, write a topic sentence that clearly states your topic and point of view.

Step 1 — In box 2, write the first step or stage in the process. Include details that clearly explain the step.

Step 2 — In box 3, write your second step or stage. Include details that clearly explain this step.

Step 3

> In box 4, present your step, and so on until the process is complete.

Conclusion

> Jot ideas for a lively concluding sentence or two, a final thought about the importance of the process.

Now write the best draft you can. Use transitional expressions of process to guide your reader from step to step. Let your draft cool for an hour or a day. Then read it like a thoughtful stranger. Think critically as you read. Is the topic sentence clear and interesting? Does it "set up" the paragraph for the reader? Does each detail develop the main idea? Proofread for grammar and spelling.

B. Comparison-Contrast

To **contrast** two people, places, or things is to examine the ways in which they are different. To **compare** them is to examine the ways in which they are similar.

Contrast and comparison are extremely useful thinking skills in daily life, college, and work. When you shop, you might contrast two brands of running shoes or two flat-screen TVs to get the better value or style. In courses like English, history, psychology, and art, you will often be required to write comparison/contrast essays. Your employer might ask you to compare two overnight delivery services, two office chairs, or two child-care programs.

Topic Sentence

Here is the topic sentence of a contrast paragraph:

> Extroverts and introverts are two personality types that differ in important ways.

- The writer begins a contrast paragraph with a topic sentence that clearly states what two people, things, or ideas will be contrasted.

- What two things will be contrasted in this paragraph?

  _____

- What word or words tell you that the writer will contrast, not compare?

  _____

Paragraph and Plan

Here is the entire paragraph:

> Extroverts and introverts are two personality types that differ in important ways. Extroverts are outgoing "people persons" who draw energy from social situations, noise, and action. They usually have

many friends and love parties. Working on teams appeals to them, so the emphasis on teamwork in many businesses favors extroverts. In fact, American culture is geared to extroverts, whose ranks include Sofia Vergara and Michael Strahan. Introverts, on the other hand, tend to be more inward people who need private time to recharge. They often prefer a few close friendships and dislike parties, though they can be charming and fun in social gatherings if they choose. Introverts enjoy working alone, taking time to think deeply about a task. Recent books have highlighted the career strengths of introverts, whose traits make them good scientists, writers, doctors, and quiet leaders. Microsoft founder Bill Gates, actress Emma Watson, and author Toni Morrison are introverts. Understanding which type we are can help us make more satisfying career and life choices.

- To develop the topic sentence, the writer first provides information about (A) *extroverts* and then gives contrasting parallel information about (B) *introverts*.

- In column (A) list the main points given about extroverts, and in column (B) list the parallel points about introverts.

(A)   (B)

_____   _____

_____   _____

_____   _____

_____   _____

_____   _____

- When the writer makes a point about (A), he or she makes a similar point about (B). For example, "many friends" is balanced by "a few close friendships."

- Can you see why the contrast writer needs to make an *outline* before writing? Otherwise, keeping track of all the points would be too confusing, and important information might be left out. In fact, this writer's outline probably looked a lot like the chart you just filled in: two columns of balanced points presented in the same order.

- What *transitional expression* indicates that the writer has completed (A) and now is moving on to (B)?

_____

- The concluding sentence suggests how this information might help the reader. Could knowing about extroverts and introverts help you in life or work? Which personality type are you?

There are two ways to organize the details in comparison or contrast writing. You can visualize the first way like this:

First all A: Point 1
Point 2
Point 3

Then all B: Point 1
Point 2
Point 3

The other way to organize your points of contrast or comparison is to move back and forth between A and B. Present one point about A and then the parallel point about B. Move to the next point and do the same:

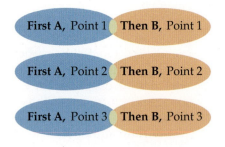

Transitional expressions in contrast paragraphs stress *differences*:

Transitional Expressions for Contrast	
however	on the contrary
in contrast	on the one hand
nevertheless	on the other hand

Transitional expressions in comparison paragraphs stress *similarities*:

Transitional Expressions for Comparison	
also	in a similar way
as well	in the same way
likewise	similarly

PRACTICE 5   Read this student's paragraph carefully and answer the questions.

"Two birds of a feather," so the family describes my mother and me, and it's true that we have much in common. First, we share the same honey-colored skin, hazel eyes, and pouting mouth. In addition, I like to think I've inherited her creative flair. Though we were poor, she taught me that beauty requires style, not money, and I see her influence in my small apartment, which I have decorated with colorful batiks and my paintings. A third similarity, I'm sorry to say, is procrastination. When I was growing up, we teased mom about waiting until the last minute to do the taxes, send out Christmas cards, or prepare for a family party. Once, the relatives were actually arriving at our house as she raced in, out of breath, with a grocery bag holding the chickens she had to cook. Now I'm the one who starts too many assignments the night before and decides to get gas when the tank is almost empty. Mostly, I thank my mother for the gift of who I am.

Cheri Baldwin, Student

1. What words in the topic sentence does this writer use to indicate that a comparison will follow?

_____

2. In what ways are the writer and her mother similar?

_____

3. Does the writer use the all A, then all B pattern or the AB, AB, AB pattern?

_____

4. Why do you think the writer saves procrastination for last?

_____

PRACTICE 6   Below are three plans for contrast paragraphs. The points of contrast in the second column do not follow the same order as the points in the first column. In addition, one detail is missing. First, number the points in the second column to match those in the first. Then fill in the missing detail.

1. Standard camera

1. takes great close-ups, clear shots
2. heavy to carry around
3. can be very expensive
4. some expertise required

Smartphone camera

___ no special expertise needed
___ price built into cost of phone
___ can't take close-up shots
___ _____

2. Beyoncé

1. 36, music veteran
2. stays true to R&B roots
3. focuses more on albums
4. started in group, Destiny's Child
5. _____

Rihanna

___ dominates radio with hit singles
___ started as solo artist
___ unmarried
___ more trendy pop, less R&B
___ 29, still on the way up

3. CT Scan

1. costs $1,200–$3,200
2. takes about 5 minutes
3. radiation of 1,000 X-rays
4. some risk of harm from radiation

MRI

___ no radiation, works magnetically
___ _____
___ costs $1,200–$4,000
___ takes about 30 minutes

PRACTICE 7   ## CRITICAL VIEWING AND WRITING

Nutrition expert Dr. Marion Nestle, a professor at New York University, writes about ways that "Big Soda" manufacturers take advantage of legal loopholes to avoid giving consumers the facts. Study these two soda labels in a group with several classmates, if possible. The label on the left is from a 20-ounce bottle of a popular cola. The new label on the right is proposed by consumer groups like the Center for Science in the Public Interest and by Dr. Nestle. List the six differences between the two labels. Do any facts on the proposed label surprise you? In what ways is the proposed label more honest? When you buy a can or bottle of soda, do you think of it as one serving—to drink all at once—or as 2 ½ servings? Be prepared to write about your findings.

CURRENT LABEL

Nutrition Facts

Serving Size 8 fl oz (240 mL)
Servings Per Container about 2.5

Amount Per Serving

Calories 110

	% Daily Value*
Total Fat 0g	0%
Sodium 70mg	3%
Total Carbohydrate 32g	10%
Sugars 30g	
Protein 0g	

*Percent Daily Values are based on a 2,000 calorie diet.

PROPOSED LABEL

Nutrition Facts

Serving Size 1 bottle (600 mL)
Servings Per Container 1

Amount Per Serving	% Daily Value*
Calories 275	14%
Total Fat 0g	0%
Sodium 175mg	7%
Total Carbohydrate 78g	26%
Sugars 75g	
Protein 0g	

*Percent Daily Values are based on a 2,000 calorie diet.

© Cengage Learning

PRACTICE 8

Here are ten topics for either contrast or comparison paragraphs. Choose your three favorites, and compose one topic sentence of either comparison or contrast for each of the three.

- two members of your family
- two cars you'd consider buying
- paper textbook vs. e-textbook
- two TV shows of the same type
- soccer and American football

- two places you have lived
- a phone call and FaceTime
- weeknight dinners and holiday dinners
- two teachers who have inspired you
- two careers you have considered

PRACTICE 9   WRITING A COMPARISON OR CONTRAST PARAGRAPH

Choose either the best topic sentence you wrote in Practice 8 or a topic your instructor assigns. Think and jot about the differences or similarities between A and B. Don't be satisfied with the first points you write; keep jotting to get as many ideas as possible. Now decide whether you will use the all A, all B pattern or AB, AB, AB. Many students find it helpful to use a graphic organizer as they plan their paragraph. In your notebook or on the computer, create an outline for your comparison or contrast paragraph using an organizer like the one that follows.

COMPARISON-CONTRAST PARAGRAPH ORGANIZER

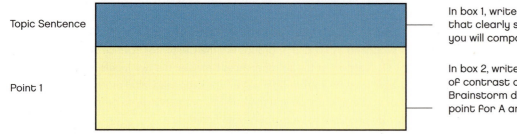

Topic Sentence

Point 1

In box 1, write a topic sentence that clearly states the two things you will compare or contrast.

In box 2, write your first point of contrast or comparison. Brainstorm details to support this point for A and B.

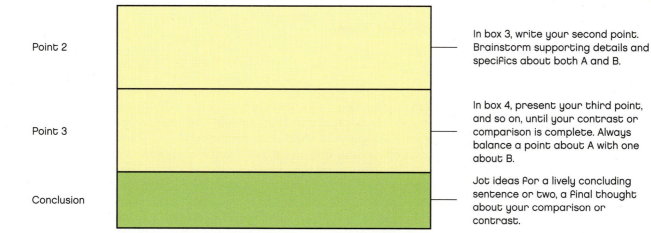

Point 2 — In box 3, write your second point. Brainstorm supporting details and specifics about both A and B.

Point 3 — In box 4, present your third point, and so on, until your contrast or comparison is complete. Always balance a point about A with one about B.

Conclusion — Jot ideas for a lively concluding sentence or two, a final thought about your comparison or contrast.

Now write the best draft you can. Use transitional expressions of comparison or contrast to guide your reader from point to point. Let your draft cool for an hour or a day. Then read it like a thoughtful stranger. Think critically as you read. Is the topic sentence clear and interesting? Does it "set up" the paragraph for the reader? Does each point develop the main idea? Proofread for grammar and spelling.

C. Classification

To **classify** is to sort things into types or categories, according to one basis of division. For example, you might classify your music by purpose (music for relaxing, music for working out, and so on). Animal species are classified by level of threat to their existence as vulnerable, threatened, endangered, or extinct. Experts rate hurricanes based on their wind speed and destructive force as category 1 through 5. In fact, classification is so common because it reflects one way our brains organize information.

For anyone in the sciences, medicine, retail, engineering, psychology, and many other fields, classification will be especially important.

Topic Sentence

Here is the topic sentence of a student's classification paragraph:

> Couples can be classified on the basis of their public displays of affection as get-a-room gropers, G-rated romantics, or cold customers.

- The writer begins a classification paragraph with a topic sentence that clearly states what group of people or things will be classified.

- What group of people will be classified in this paragraph? Into how many categories will they be divided?

_____

- Based on just the topic sentence, do you think the writer's tone is serious or humorous?

_____

Paragraph and Plan

Here is the entire paragraph:

> Couples can be classified on the basis of their public displays of affection as get-a-room gropers, G-rated romantics, or cold customers. Get-a-room gropers take public displays of affection to insane extremes. They can turn a kiss in a crowded elevator into an ear, nose, and throat exam. They grind and grab while disgusted parents cover their children's eyes. The next type, G-rated romantics, are affectionate but appropriate for general audiences. Strangers might feel that love is in the air as these two stroll down the street with their arms around each other, and G-rated romantics may kiss now and then, mouths closed, but they know when to quit. Walking with their hands in each other's back pockets is about as steamy as it gets. The last group is the cold customers. These pairs could pass for strangers except that they stay side by side for hours. In a restaurant, they can eat a whole meal in total silence. It's easy to wonder what put the chill in their relationship, but maybe they're just reacting to the gropers pawing each other at the next table.
>
> *Deirdre Chaudry, Student*

- What information does she provide about the first type, get-a-room gropers?

  _____

  _____

- What information does she provide about the second type, G-rated romantics?

  _____

  _____

- What information does she provide about the third type, cool customers?

  _____

  _____

- Note that the topic sentence, the three types, and the concluding sentence form an **outline** of this paragraph. In fact, the student brainstormed or freewrote to gather ideas and then made such an outline.

Transitional expressions in classification paragraphs stress *divisions* and *categories*:

Transitional Expressions for Classification	
can be divided	the first type (or class)
can be classified	the second kind (or group)
can be categorized	the last category

PRACTICE 10   Read the following classification paragraph carefully and answer the questions.

Everett Rogers' theory of consumer trends and how they spread is useful information for every business student. Rogers divided shoppers into five types, based on how quickly they respond to new products. The first type of shoppers, the innovators, are those techies, adventurers, or fashionistas who are first to stand in line for an iPad mini, a new snowboard, or edgy gladiator boots. While these cool leaders introduce a trend, the second group, the early adopters, establish the trend by joining it early on. Think of them as the popular crowd at school. Third comes the early majority, a large group of buyers who wait to buy their iPads until the trend is a sure thing. The late majority is even more cautious; they won't commit money to a snowboard until snowboarding has become an Olympic event. Finally come the laggards. These folks at last get the courage to buy gladiator boots when the trend is almost over, and innovators are already wearing the next hot thing. Marketers still rely on Rogers' categories to help them target buyers, create ad campaigns, and squeeze all the profit they can from a trend.

1. What group of people does Everett Rogers classify? Which sentence tells you this?

   _____

2. On what basis does he classify shoppers?

   _____

3. How many categories does he name and what are they?

   _____

4. Make an outline of this paragraph.

PRACTICE 11   Each group of things or people has been divided according to *one basis of classification*. However, one item in each group does not belong—it does not fit in that single basis of classification.

Read each group of items carefully; then circle the letter of each item that does not belong. Next, write the single basis of classification that includes the rest of the group.

EXAMPLE:

Jeans

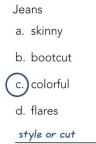

a. skinny

b. bootcut

c. colorful

d. flares

style or cut

1. Professors
   a. tough graders
   b. easy graders
   c. online graders
   d. moderate graders

   _____

2. Teenagers
   a. send fewer than 50 texts a day
   b. 50–150 daily texts
   c. daily send more than 150 texts
   d. 80% of teens text during class

   _____

3. Credit-card users
   a. pay in full monthly
   b. pay with another credit card
   c. never pay total amount due
   d. sometimes pay in full

   _____

4. Breakfast cereals
   a. 7–14 grams sugar per cup
   b. 1–6 grams sugar per cup
   c. 15 grams sugar or more in a cup
   d. 30 grams sugar or more in a soda

   _____

PRACTICE 12

Any group can be classified in different ways, depending on the basis of classification. For example, you might classify home-team football fans on the basis of how upset they are when their team loses (very upset, mildly upset, unfazed) or how many home games they attend (TV only, 1–3 games, 4 or more). Both are valid classifications.

For each group below, think of two ways in which each of the following groups could be classified.

Group	Basis of Classification
EXAMPLE: Home-team football fans	(A) *how upset they are when they lose* _____
	(B) *number of home games they attend* _____
1. Clothes in your closet	(A) _____
	(B) _____
2. Facebook users	(A) _____
	(B) _____
3. Fast-food burgers	(A) _____
	(B) _____
4. Ways to relax	(A) _____
	(B) _____
5. Vegetables at the market	(A) _____
	(B) _____

PRACTICE 13   ### CRITICAL VIEWING AND WRITING

You have been hired by Auto Galaxy, a large used-car dealer, to redesign its website. Customers have complained that they want more ways to search for cars than just the 12 clickable types shown. Study these types or categories—if possible, with several teammates. They show one important way to classify cars. What is that way? That is, from the 12 types shown in the chart below, what is the basis for this vehicle classification?

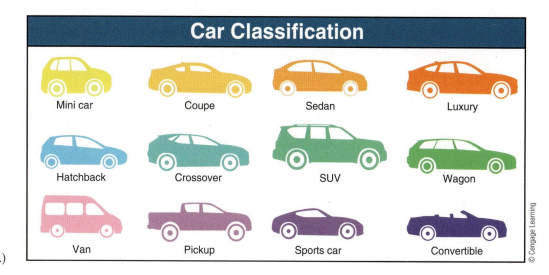

Car Classification

Mini car   Coupe   Sedan   Luxury

Hatchback   Crossover   SUV   Wagon

Van   Pickup   Sports car   Convertible

© Cengage Learning

This chart shows one way to classify cars: What is the *basis* of this classification? (See Practice 13.)

To improve the customers' search experience, your team has been tasked with adding to the website, this week, at least one more classification of cars on the lot. Your team has brainstormed four more possible bases for classification: (1) price, (2) year, (3) make (Ford, Toyota, etc.), and (4) mileage. Pick basis (2), (3), or (4) from this list, and then come up with types or categories that will include all the cars at Auto Galaxy.

EXAMPLE: Basis of car classification: *price*

Categories: *under $5000, $5000 to $15,000, $15,000 to $30,000, above $30,000*

PRACTICE 14   ### WRITING A CLASSIFICATION PARAGRAPH

Pick a topic from the list below or one your instructor assigns. Draft a topic sentence, using this form: "_____ *can be classified on the basis of* _____ *as A, B, C, and D.*" Think carefully as you plan your categories, which should cover the whole group. Then prewrite to get as many juicy details as possible. Many students find it helpful to use a graphic organizer as they plan their paragraph. In your notebook or on the computer, create an outline for your classification paragraph using an organizer like the one that follows.

- parenting styles
- detectives (or doctors) on TV
- attitudes toward saving money
- reactions to success (or failure)
- students in this class (or at this college)
- annoying co-workers
- jobs for college grads
- bosses
- YouTube videos
- dog (cat, or other pet) owners

CLASSIFICATION PARAGRAPH ORGANIZER

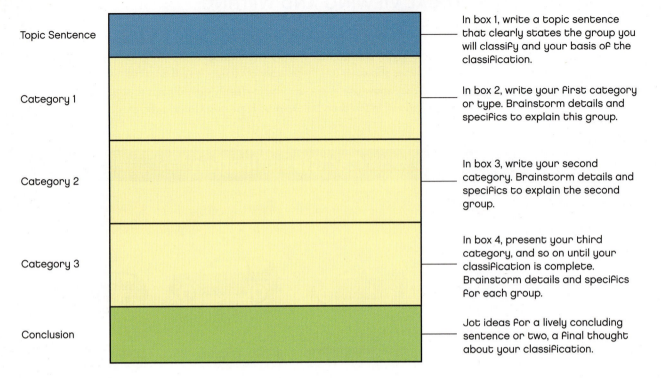

Topic Sentence

In box 1, write a topic sentence that clearly states the group you will classify and your basis of the classification.

Category 1

In box 2, write your first category or type. Brainstorm details and specifics to explain this group.

Category 2

In box 3, write your second category. Brainstorm details and specifics to explain the second group.

Category 3

In box 4, present your third category, and so on until your classification is complete. Brainstorm details and specifics for each group.

Conclusion

Jot ideas for a lively concluding sentence or two, a final thought about your classification.

Now write the best draft you can. Use transitional expressions of classification to guide your reader from category to category. Let your draft cool for an hour or a day. Then read it like a thoughtful stranger. Think critically as you read. Is the topic sentence clear and interesting? Does it "set up" the paragraph for the reader? Does each category develop the main idea? Proofread for grammar and spelling.

Chapter Highlights

These paragraph patterns are often used in college and the workplace. They reflect different ways of thinking about a subject.

- **A process paragraph explains step by step how to do something or how something gets done.**

- **The comparison or contrast paragraph examines the ways in which two people, places, or things are alike or different.**

- **The classification paragraph sorts things into types or categories, according to one basis of division.**

EXPLORING ONLINE

www.youtube.com/watch?v=32R30EYIW-U

This short video reviews the essentials of process writing.

lrs.ed.uiuc.edu/students/fwalters/compcontEx1a.html

Practice the transitional expressions for contrast writing, and get instant feedback.

www.youtube.com/watch?v=wm3ObvB0mLE

Excellent short video walks you through classification: how to divide your subject, create your topic sentence, and discuss your types.

Visit **MindTap** for *Grassroots* to access this chapter's ebook, flashcards, additional practice and quizzes, and more!

CHAPTER 7

Definition, Cause-Effect, and Persuasion

A: Definition

B: Cause-Effect

C: Persuasion

This chapter will teach you three more paragraph patterns that will help you become a more critical thinker and a better writer: definition, cause and effect, and perhaps the most important writing pattern of all, persuasion.

A. Definition

To **define** is to explain clearly what a word or term means. As you write for college and work, you will need to define words or terms your readers may not know. Often, a one-sentence definition will do. For example, "*diligent* means hardworking" or "*malware* is malicious software like viruses, worms, or spyware." Other terms, however—like *self-esteem*, *Custer's Last Stand*, and *climate change*—are harder to define. They challenge you to think and write with care so the reader understands exactly what you mean, and they usually require a paragraph or more.

Definition becomes more important as you advance in college or in fields like medicine, computer programming, science, psychology, sociology, and others because every field has its own vocabulary.

One-Sentence Definitions

To define a term, a one- or two-word definition is often sufficient. For instance, definitions by **synonym**, a word that means the same thing, are common in the dictionary:

> *Indolent* means lazy.
> A *fluke* is a chance event or coincidence.
> To *exult* means to rejoice greatly.

In college courses and work settings, however, **class definitions** may be necessary. A class definition has two parts: (1) the larger group or class in which the word belongs, and (2) the particular details that set it apart from others in that group. Here are some examples:

Word	Class	Distinguishing Details
A *cupcake* is	a small cake	that is baked in a cup-shaped container.
Cargo pants are	casual trousers	with many large pockets.
A *Yorkie* is	a very small terrier	with a long, glossy, tan and gray coat.

Notice that the definitions all have two parts: the class (small cake, casual trousers, and very small terrier) followed by details that make that one different or special in its class.

PRACTICE 1

CRITICAL THINKING AND WRITING

Review the class definition chart above (word, class, distinguishing details). Then write a *class definition* for each of the following words. You will see how much thinking is required just to define things we know well! Use this form:

A _____ is a _____

           (noun)   (class or group)

that _____.

        (distinguishing details)

1. turkey burger

   _____

2. laptop

   _____

3. lemonade

   _____

Tornado by Mario Carreno, MOMA, NY

Class definition of the event pictured: A tornado is a violent, whirling column of wind that is accompanied by a funnel cloud and cuts a narrow path of destruction across the land. How does the painting's "definition" differ from the verbal one?

4. goalie

_____

5. tricycle

_____

EXPLORING ONLINE

grammar.ccc.commnet.edu/grammar/definition_list.htm

Learning just a few "college words" a day will strengthen your vocabulary
and your writing. This excellent web page, "A Year's Worth of Words,"
is one of many vocabulary-building resources online.

quizlet.com/1070674/100-words-every-college-students-should-know-flash-cards

100 Words Every College Student Should Know

The Definition Paragraph: Topic Sentence

When a word is complex or important, a paragraph or essay may be needed to
define it well. Here is the topic sentence of a definition paragraph:

> The bystander* effect is the passive reaction of people in groups who see
> someone in trouble but do nothing to help him or her.

- The topic sentence of a definition paragraph should identify the word being
  defined and include its meaning.

- What word or term is defined in this paragraph?

_____

Paragraph and Plan

Here is the rest of the paragraph.

> The bystander effect is the passive reaction of people in groups who see
> someone in trouble but do nothing to help him or her. The first famous example
> was the 1964 murder of Kitty Genovese in Queens, NY—her neighbors
> supposedly heard her screams but did not call police. Although it now appears
> that some of Kitty's neighbors did call, psychologists say the bystander effect is
> real. In fact, the larger the crowd, the more likely it is that bystanders will assume
> someone else will take responsibility. For instance, hundreds of people might
> drive past a serious traffic accident, all assuming that someone else called 911.
> At schools across the country, many students witness verbal or physical bullying
> but fail to speak up. A current example of bystander effect is teenagers bullied on
> social media. Online witnesses who remain silent, like all bystanders, unknowingly
> encourage the bully. Successful new anti-bullying programs are focusing on the
> key role of the bystander. They teach people not to wait for someone else to act but
> to imagine the victim's feelings and find the courage to say something. Just one
> person taking action often stops a bully and might even save a life.

_____

* bystander: a person who watches an event but does not participate.

● One effective way to help your reader understand a definition is to provide *examples*. What four examples does the writer choose to explain *bystander effect*?

_____

_____

● After giving examples of "bystander effect," the writer discusses new anti-bullying programs. What do anti-bullying programs have to do with bystander effect?

_____

● Were you ever a silent bystander? What kept you from speaking up? Have you ever been the bystander who did speak up? Why did you take action?

Note that the topic sentence, examples, point about anti-bullying programs, and concluding sentence form an *outline* for the paragraph. In fact, before drafting, the writer probably prewrote and then made just such an outline.

There are no transitional expressions specifically for definition paragraphs, but phrases like "can be defined as . . ." and "means that . . ." alert the reader that a definition follows.

PRACTICE 2   Read this student's definition paragraph carefully and then answer the questions.

> Stress is an inner experience of pressure building up. Have you ever shaken up a bottle of soda pop and then opened it right afterwards? I have, and it explodes all over everything. When I think of stress, this picture is the first thing that comes to mind. For example, imagine it is Thursday and you have two important tests coming up on Monday, but you also have just realized your research paper is due on Friday. A bill just arrived that you thought was taken care of three months ago, and relatives from out of town decide to drop by at the last minute. Therefore, when you aren't working, your relatives expect you to spend time with them. Exhausted yet? Well, just when you think nothing else could come up, someone backs right into the driver's door of your car! By now your entire inside is so shaken up, it feels as though it is going to explode. This is what I call "stress."

> *Peggy Wheeler, Student*

1. Underline the topic sentence.

2. How does this student develop her definition?

_____

PRACTICE 3   ## CRITICAL THINKING AND WRITING

In a group with four or five classmates, if possible, consider and define the word *bully* or *bullying*. Write a one-sentence definition, and take notes for a composition about this important subject. What are typical behaviors of a bully? What motivates the bully? Who are the bully's ideal victims? What is the best way to stop a bully?

To learn more, check out PACER's National Bullying Prevention Center at **www.pacer .org/bullying** or watch the trailer for the powerful documentary *Bully* at **www.thebullyproject .com.** Take notes for further writing.

PRACTICE 4

Here are three topic sentences for definition paragraphs. Choose one that interests you, brainstorm or freewrite for ideas to develop the definition, and make a plan for a possible paragraph.

1. *Unemployed* means so much more than "out of work at the present time."

2. A *nurse* is the patient's guardian, cheerleader, and lifeline.

3. *Motivation* is the drive or incentive to act in ways that will advance one's goals.

PRACTICE 5 ## WRITING A DEFINITION PARAGRAPH

Pick a topic from this list that interests you, one from Practice 4, or one your instructor assigns. Draft a topic sentence that defines the word or term and introduces your paragraph. Think and freewrite about your term and what it really means. You might also discuss the term with a smart friend. Many students find it helpful to use a graphic organizer as they plan. In your notebook or on the computer, create an outline for your definition paragraph using an organizer like the one that follows.

- work ethic
- working mom (or dad)
- gossip

- veteran
- success
- AIDS or other illness

- wealth (or poverty)
- rap, country (or other music)
- honor

DEFINITION PARAGRAPH ORGANIZER

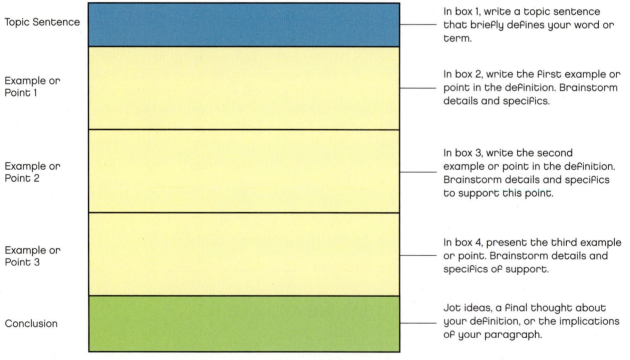

Topic Sentence — In box 1, write a topic sentence that briefly defines your word or term.

Example or Point 1 — In box 2, write the first example or point in the definition. Brainstorm details and specifics.

Example or Point 2 — In box 3, write the second example or point in the definition. Brainstorm details and specifics to support this point.

Example or Point 3 — In box 4, present the third example or point. Brainstorm details and specifics of support.

Conclusion — Jot ideas, a final thought about your definition, or the implications of your paragraph.

Now write the best draft you can. Use transitional expressions of definition to guide your reader from point to point. Let your draft cool for an hour or a day. Then read it like a thoughtful stranger. Think critically as you read. Is the topic sentence clear and interesting? Does it "set up" the paragraph for the reader? Does each example develop the main idea? Proofread for grammar and spelling.

B. Cause-Effect

Causes are the *reasons* for events. Humans naturally look for causes; we want to know *why*: Why am I afraid of public speaking? Why is my child diabetic? The mature human mind also tries to anticipate *effects*. **Effects** are the *results* or *consequences* of a cause or causes. If my nephew drops out of high school, what effects will it have on his life? If I take out this loan, how will it affect my finances going forward? You can see that ability to think critically about causes and effects is a vitally important skill in college, work, and daily life.

Cause and effect writing is particularly useful in medicine, pharmacy, psychology, science, electronics, business, history, and nearly every field.

Topic Sentence

Here is the topic sentence of a student's cause and effect paragraph:

> Although my parents don't believe it, online gaming has had positive effects on my life.

- The writer begins a cause and effect paragraph by clearly stating the subject and indicating whether causes or effects will be stressed.

- Will causes or effects be the focus? What words tell you this?

  _____

- Does this topic sentence make you want to read on? Why or why not?

  _____

Paragraph and Plan

Here is the entire paragraph:

> Although my parents don't believe it, online gaming has had positive effects on my life. For the last couple years, I have spent two hours every night playing *World of Warcraft*, an online role-playing game, with a team of 11 other people. I have always been a shy person, but having to communicate clearly with my team has developed my public-speaking skills and helped me become an effective team player. Our team bought special microphones so we can speak to each other directly during raids. Another important result might be hard to measure, but I believe I have become a better problem solver. As a guild leader, I have to make quick decisions that affect my entire team, and I'm learning to make critical choices with confidence. Finally, the most important effect is that gaming reduces my stress. As a new college student, I need that release each evening in order to face all the responsibilities waiting for me when I sign off with my team and join the real world again—studying, doing chores, and hearing my parents worry out loud that their "American" daughter must be addicted to the Internet.
>
> *Talia Bahari, Student*

● How many effects does the writer discuss? What are they?

_____

_____

● Do you play video games? Has this activity had positive or negative effects in your life?

_____

● Note that the topic sentence, three effects, and conclusion make a kind of *outline* for this paragraph. Indeed, this student jotted just such an outline before she started to write.

Transitional expressions in cause and effect paragraphs often imply order of importance or time order. Remember that the words *causes* and *reasons* refer to causes; the words *effects*, *results*, and *consequences* refer to effects.

Transitional Expressions for Cause and Effect	
To Show Causes	**To Show Effects**
the first cause (second, third)	one important effect
the first reason (second, third)	another result (or outcome)
yet another factor	consequently

PRACTICE 6   Read this student's cause-effect paragraph and answer the questions.

I never wanted to be a vegetarian. Pulled-pork sandwiches were my friends. But in this year of big personal changes, for three reasons, I decided to become a "veg head." The most important reason was saving money. Returning to college has me on a tight budget. Tuition, books, and rent are expenses I cannot control, but when I wrote down where my extra money was going, big items were meat, chicken, and fast food. I am saving at least $500 a year by cutting out meat and limiting fast food. Another motivation was weight. I gained 10 pounds in the first six months of college, all packed around my gut. It is so easy to eat pepperoni pizza while studying, Taco Bell with friends, and beef jerky when I'm stressed. A friend told me to research vegetarian diets online and see how people who eat vegetables, fruits, whole grains, and beans usually weigh less than meat eaters. Then, a final reason pushed me over the edge. My doctor made a big point this year about my family history of heart disease. Now that I am over 30, he said, this puts me at greater risk, but cutting saturated fat out of my diet now will help protect me from serious problems down the road. So good-bye, pulled pork. Good-bye, bacon cheeseburgers. Once I got the hang of eating green, I actually liked it and don't miss meat most of the time.

Ivan Akerstrom, Student

1. Underline the topic sentence. Hint: It is not the first sentence. Will this paragraph discuss causes or effects? How do you know?

_____

2. How many causes are discussed? What are they?

_____

3. Make an outline of this paragraph.

PRACTICE 7

To practice separating cause from effect, write the cause and the effect contained in each statement below.

EXAMPLE: Because it snowed during rush hour, there were several fender benders this morning.

Cause: _snow during rush hour_ _____

Effect: _several fender benders_ _____

1. With so many musicians in the family, I grew up with a love of music.

Cause: _____

Effect: _____

2. Three in ten young adults are moving back home with their parents, a trend experts blame on the weak economy.

Cause: _____

Effect: _____

3. People who do strenuous cardiovascular exercise three or four times a week score higher on intelligence tests.

Cause: _____

Effect: _____

4. Medical students who take art appreciation classes become better at observing and diagnosing their patients, according to Harvard University.

Cause: _____

Effect: _____

5. When white sunlight is split by rain or mist into colors, observers see a rainbow.

Cause: _____

Effect: _____

PRACTICE 8

List three causes or three effects that could support each topic sentence below. First, read the topic sentence to see whether causes or effects are called for. Then, think, jot, and list your three best ideas.

1. Public speaking courses would benefit nearly all college students.

2. Concerned citizens point to a number of factors to explain the empty storefronts downtown.

3. Dropping out of school often results in negative consequences.

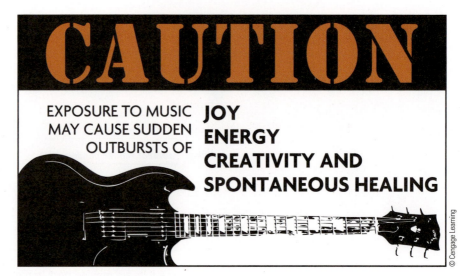

This upbeat sign is based on research studies showing the positive effects of playing a musical instrument. What are some of these effects?

PRACTICE 9

CRITICAL THINKING AND WRITING

Consider the fact that more and more companies are now declaring one day each week an e-mail–free or text-free day. On that day, employees cannot use e-mail or text but must walk to each other's desks or pick up the phone to make voice contact. In a group with several classmates, if possible, discuss why you think this is being done. What issues with e-mail or texting might have *caused* employers to take this step? What *effects* do you think executives are hoping to achieve with this policy? Take notes and list the most important three causes or effects of the no–e-mail policy. Be prepared to present your conclusions to the class.

PRACTICE 10

WRITING A CAUSE AND EFFECT PARAGRAPH

Pick a topic from this list that interests you or one your instructor assigns. Draft a topic sentence that states your subject and indicates whether causes or effects will be discussed. Prewrite to get as many points and details as possible. Many students find it helpful to use a graphic organizer as they plan their paragraph. In your notebook or on the computer, create an outline for your cause and effect paragraph using an organizer like the one that follows.

- causes for making a key decision
- why violent movies are popular
- reasons why some people don't vote
- what makes you (or another) happy
- why some people exercise regularly

- effects of teasing (or bullying) on the victim
- consequences of speaking two languages
- effects of traveling to another country
- effects of a relationship on someone
- consequences of passing a certain course

CAUSE AND EFFECT PARAGRAPH ORGANIZER

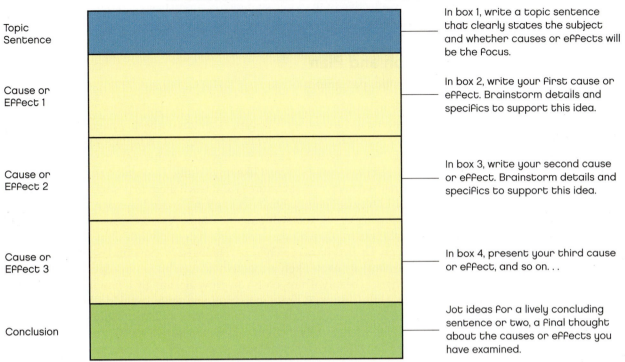

Topic Sentence	In box 1, write a topic sentence that clearly states the subject and whether causes or effects will be the focus.
Cause or Effect 1	In box 2, write your first cause or effect. Brainstorm details and specifics to support this idea.
Cause or Effect 2	In box 3, write your second cause or effect. Brainstorm details and specifics to support this idea.
Cause or Effect 3	In box 4, present your third cause or effect, and so on. . .
Conclusion	Jot ideas for a lively concluding sentence or two, a final thought about the causes or effects you have examined.

Now write the best draft you can. Use transitional expressions of cause and effect to guide your reader from point to point. Let your draft cool for an hour or a day. Then read it like a thoughtful stranger. Think critically as you read. Is the topic sentence clear and interesting? Does it "set up" the paragraph for the reader? Does each point develop the main idea? Proofread for grammar and spelling.

C. Persuasion

To **persuade** is to convince someone that a particular opinion or plan of action is the correct one. Persuasion is probably the most important thinking and writing pattern in college, work, and life. Any time you argue with a friend, champion a cause, write a college paper or a report at work, or broadcast a message on Twitter, you are trying to persuade people to agree with you, give you an A, or support your ideas.

Fair arguments are **logical and direct**, not emotional. This chapter will teach you basic techniques of logical persuasion that you will use again and again in college and in nearly every career. Understanding logical persuasion also will help you think critically about the ads, messages of bias, and even brainwashing that bombard us every day.

Topic Sentence

Here is the topic sentence of a persuasive paragraph:

> Parents should not enter their little girls in children's beauty pageants.

- The topic sentence of a persuasive paragraph clearly states what you are arguing for or against. It takes a **strong stand**.

- What will this persuasive paragraph argue against?

_____

- Words like *should* and *must* (or their negatives, *should not* and *must not*) are especially effective in the topic sentence of a persuasive paragraph because they show that the writing is taking a strong stand.

Paragraph and Plan

Here is the entire paragraph:

> Parents should not enter their little girls in children's beauty pageants. The first and most important reason to avoid these pageants is that they sexualize little girls. The "glitz pageants" in particular require contestants to wear heavy makeup and elaborate hairstyles, just like tiny adults. They encourage parents to dress their children in revealing costumes and teach them to gesture and dance suggestively. Little girls have no business prancing around on stage, winking at the judges, blowing kisses, and swinging their hips. A second reason to avoid these pageants is that girls who participate often develop unhealthy body images later on. Dr. Syd Brown, a child psychologist in Maryland, says that child beauty contestants are more likely either to hate their bodies in adolescence or to overvalue physical beauty. Third, costs can grow alarmingly if families commit to the pageant life. Costumes, props, coaching, and travel quickly add up to thousands of dollars per pageant. For example, Rick and Misty Simon of Atlanta, Georgia, told reporters that their credit card debt rose to $30,000 after two years of entering their daughter in a series of local pageants. Finally, most pageant moms claim that their daughters "just love dressing up" and want to enter pageants. They are fooling themselves. No four-year-old or seven-year-old is capable of wise life choices, whether it's choosing what food to eat, what time to go to bed, or whether to waste their childhoods in the ugly world of beauty contests.

- The first reason in this argument states some facts. What *facts* are given?

  _____

- The second reason supports the topic sentence by *referring to an authority*. Who is this authority and what does he say?

  _____

- The third reason in the argument *predicts a consequence*. If parents commit to the pageant life, what will the consequence be?

  _____

- The last reason *answers the opposition*. That is, this writer has tried to imagine what opponents in this argument might say. What point does the writer answer?

  _____

- Persuasive paragraphs either begin or end with the most important reason. Does this writer start with the most or least important reason? How do you know?

  _____

Before writing this paragraph, the writer made a plan that included the topic sentence and all the reasons in an order that seemed most persuasive.

Transitional expressions for persuasion signal each supporting point or reason. Sometimes, they also indicate the relative importance of a reason.

Transitional Expressions for Persuasion	
first, another, next	first (second, third)
another reason	last, finally, most important

When you argue or persuade, always keep your audience in mind. Who are your readers? What approach might convince them that you are right? Because people on both sides of an argument can have strong feelings, it is especially important to use logic, not emotional attack, to win over your opposition. Emotional attacks only make the other person angry, encouraging him or her to reject your views. As you compose an argument, a good memory prompt is **FAPO** (reminding you to include facts, authorities, prediction, and an answer to your opposition).

FAPO: Strategies of Persuasion

Facts Facts are statements of what is. Be sure to include the source of your facts (magazine article and date, for example), unless you are describing something widely known.

Authority Make sure any authority you quote is an expert in the subject you are discussing. Usain Bolt is an authority on sprinting, but you would not quote him in support of your argument that cooking classes should be required in high schools.

Predicting the Consequence Think critically about what really might happen if your opponent's ideas become reality: *If scholarship money is cut at this college, we will lose many bright students.* Do not exaggerate, which will undercut your credibility: *If women receive combat pay, the U.S. military will collapse.*

Answering the Opposition This might be the hardest and most important persuasive strategy. It is difficult to sympathize with opponents, but to reach them with logic, you must put yourself in their shoes, get inside their minds, and try to understand why they passionately hold the beliefs they do. Let's say you are arguing for certain gun restrictions. If your opposition believes that any gun control means all their firearms will be taken away, how can you answer them respectfully and convincingly?

PRACTICE 11   Read this student's persuasive paragraph and answer the questions.

Unpaid internships are not worth the effort. First, advisors tell students like me that an unpaid internship will give them work experience and a chance to show off their skills. I have had two unpaid internships in two years, one at a retail store and one at a newspaper, but my jobs had nothing to do with my associate degree in business. Instead, I made copies, got coffee, and broke down boxes to put in the trash. The second reason unpaid internships are a bad idea is the obvious: They are unpaid. With no money coming in, the bills add up, and there is less time to look for a paying job. Finally, the most important reason not to become an unpaid intern is that it won't help you get a full-time job. I interviewed Tara Cano, a career coach in Charlotte. She showed me the results of a 2012 survey by NACE, the National Association of Colleges and Employers. This survey found that 37 percent of unpaid interns get job offers, but 36 percent of students who were never unpaid interns also get job offers, so there is no advantage for an unpaid intern. On the other hand, 60 percent of paid interns get job offers. You do the math.

Domingo Reyes, Student

1. What is this paragraph arguing for or against?

    _____

2. What audience does the writer seem to be addressing?

    _____

3. How many reasons does the author provide? List them.

    _____

4. Which reason is an answer to the opposition?

    _____

5. Which reason combines quoting an authority with facts? How did the student find these facts?

    _____

6. Do you have any revision advice for this writer? What do you like best about his argument? Would you recommend any changes?

    _____

PRACTICE 12   CRITICAL THINKING AND WRITING

Choose one of the seven topics below. Working as a group, if possible, take a stand in answer to the question and express your stand in a strong topic sentence. Write four supporting sentences to build your argument—each sentence using one of the four FAPO methods: *facts, referring to an authority, predicting the consequences,* and *answering the opposition*. If you don't know the facts or an authority, just for this practice—never in real life—you can invent facts or an authority in support of your argument.

1. Should sugary drinks and snacks be taxed heavily, like cigarettes?
2. Should cell phones be banned in all classrooms?
3. Should all parents-in-waiting in this state be required to take parenting classes?
4. Do teachers treat males and females differently in the classroom?
5. Should contact sports be banned for children under 15?
6. Should students who test into developmental English or math be required to take those courses?
7. Should any athlete who takes performance-enhancing drugs be banned from the sport for life?

PRACTICE 13   CRITICAL VIEWING AND WRITING

In a group with four or five classmates, if possible, look closely at the following public service advertisement, sponsored by the World Wildlife Fund. Because the picture is detailed, examine it until you understand what is going on. Like many advertisements, this one is trying to *persuade* the viewer to adopt a certain point of view or to take action. What is the subject of the ad? Who is the intended audience? What is the persuasive message? Write down the ad's "topic sentence" and argument. How persuasive is this ad? Be prepared to support your opinion with evidence.

YOU CAN'T AFFORD TO BE SLOW IN AN EMERGENCY
ACT NOW FOR THE PLANET

PRACTICE 14   WRITING A PERSUASIVE PARAGRAPH

Pick a topic from Practice 12, from this list of questions, or from a topic your instructor assigns. Then take a stand by answering the question in a topic sentence that you can support with reasons. Prewrite to get as many ideas and reasons as possible, referring to the FAPO chart. Many students find that using a graphic organizer as they plan helps them build a strong paragraph. Fill your ideas and details in an organizer. In your notebook or on the computer, create an outline for your persuasive paragraph using an organizer like the one that follows.

- Is LeBron James the greatest athlete who ever lived?

- Should little boys play with dolls?

- Should two years of college be mandatory?

- Should colleges allow drinking on campus?

- Should public schools require uniforms?

- Should citizens be required by law to vote?

PERSUASIVE PARAGRAPH ORGANIZER

Topic Sentence

Reason 1

In box 1, write a topic sentence that clearly states your topic and point of view.

In box 2, write your first reason. Include details that clearly explain this reason.

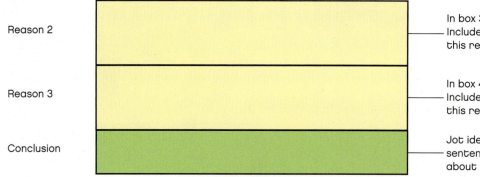

Reason 2 — In box 3, write your second reason. Include details that clearly explain this reason.

Reason 3 — In box 4, present your third reason. Include details that clearly explain this reason.

Conclusion — Jot ideas for a lively concluding sentence or two, a final thought about the issue and its importance.

Now write the best draft you can. Use transitional expressions of persuasion to guide your reader from reason to reason. Let your draft cool for an hour or a day. Then read it like a thoughtful stranger. Think critically as you read. Is the topic sentence clear and interesting? Does it "set up" the paragraph for the reader? Is each reason suited to the audience? Proofread for grammar and spelling.

Chapter Highlights

These paragraph patterns are often used in college and the workplace. They reflect different ways of thinking about a subject.

- The definition paragraph explains the meaning of a word or term.

- The cause and effect paragraph develops the topic sentence by explaining the causes (reasons for) or effects (results of) events.

- The persuasive paragraph takes a stand, providing reasons to convince the reader that a particular opinion or plan of action is correct.

EXPLORING ONLINE

www.youtube.com/watch?v=YXiT3x_VdW0

Excellent short video walks you through definition writing: how to develop an extended definition of a word or term.

lrs.ed.uiuc.edu/students/fwalters/cause.html

See a sample of cause-effect writing and the kinds of transitional expressions you will be expected to use in college and on the job.

www.une.edu.au/__data/assets/pdf_file/0010/10540/paragraph-argument.pdf

Tips on persuasive writing and two examples of persuasive paragraphs required in science courses and careers.

Visit **MindTap** for *Grassroots* to access this chapter's ebook, flashcards, additional practice and quizzes, and more!

CHAPTER 8

Moving from Paragraph to Essay

A: Defining the Essay and the Thesis Statement
B: The Process of Writing an Essay

So far, you have written single paragraphs, but to succeed in college and at work, you will need to handle longer writing assignments as well. This chapter will help you apply your paragraph-writing skills to planning and writing short essays.

A. Defining the Essay and the Thesis Statement

An **essay** is a group of paragraphs about one subject. In many ways, an essay is like a paragraph in longer, fuller form. Both have an introduction, a body, and a conclusion. Both explain one main idea with details, facts, and examples.

An essay is not just a padded paragraph, however. An essay is longer because it contains more ideas.

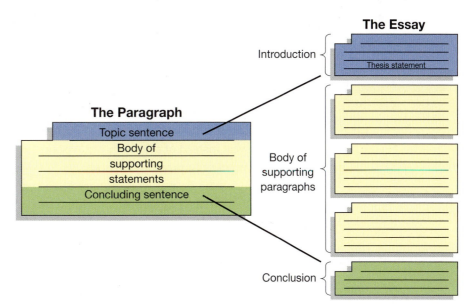

The paragraphs in an essay are part of a larger whole, so each one has a special purpose.

101

- The **introductory paragraph** opens the essay and tries to catch the reader's interest. It usually contains a **thesis statement**, one sentence that states the main idea of the entire essay.

- The **body** of an essay contains one, two, three, or more paragraphs, each one making a different point about the main idea.

- The **conclusion** brings the essay to a close. It might be a sentence or a paragraph long.

Here is a student essay:

Tae Kwon Do

Wineth Williams

(1) Tae kwon do is a Korean martial art. It is a way of fighting and self-defense based on an understanding of both body and mind. As a college student, I discovered tae kwon do. Even though I was physically fit and planned to become a police officer, I thought that women needed special skills to protect themselves. Tae kwon do teaches these skills and much more. The person who practices tae kwon do gains discipline, maturity, and a changed self-concept.

(2) First, the discipline of tae kwon do helps the student outfight and outsmart her opponent. For a while, I didn't appreciate the discipline. We had to move in certain ways, and we had to yell. Yelling made me laugh. Our teacher told us to shout with great force, "Keeah!" Yelling keeps the mind from focusing on being tired and helps the fighter call out the life force, or "chi," from inside her. Once we started sparring, I also had to get past not wanting to hurt anyone. Later I understood that if I punched or kicked my opponent, it meant that he or she should have been blocking and was not using good skills.

(3) Second, with practice, tae kwon do increases maturity. I have a hot temper. Before tae kwon do, I would walk dark streets and take chances, almost daring trouble. I reacted to every look or challenge. Practicing this martial art, I started to see the world more realistically. I developed more respect for the true danger in the streets. I spoke and behaved in ways to avoid trouble. My reactions became less emotional and more rational.

(4) Finally, after a year or so, tae kwon do can change the student's self-concept. This happened to me. On one hand, I became confident that I had the skills to take care of business if necessary. On the other hand, the better I got, the more I acted like a pussycat instead of a lion. That may sound strange, but inside myself, I knew that I had nothing to prove to anybody.

(5) Friends who do not work out are often surprised when I describe the way that tae kwon do changed me, but a serious exercise routine can do this for anyone. By committing to a routine or "practice," a person is setting a self-loving goal and working toward it. As I discovered firsthand, the rewards are discipline, the maturity to keep going despite discomfort, and finally, new confidence and self-respect.

- The last sentence in the introduction (underlined) is the *thesis statement*. The thesis statement must be general enough to include the topic sentence of every paragraph in the body of the essay.

- Underline the topic sentences of paragraphs (2), (3), and (4). Note that the thesis statement and the topic sentences make a rough plan of the entire essay.

- **Transitional expressions** are words and phrases that guide the reader from point to point and from paragraph to paragraph. What transition does this student use between paragraphs (1) and (2)? Between (2) and (3)? Between (3) and (4)?

  _____

- The last paragraph provides a brief _conclusion_.*

PRACTICE 1

To help you understand the structure of an essay, complete this plan for "Tae Kwon Do." Under each topic sentence, jot down the writer's two or three main supporting points as if you were making a plan for the essay. (In fact, the writer probably made such a plan before she wrote her first draft.)

Paragraph 1. INTRODUCTION

Thesis statement: The person who practices tae kwon do gains discipline, maturity, and a changed self-concept.

Paragraph 2. Topic sentence: First, the discipline of tae kwon do helps the student outfight and outsmart her opponent.

Point 1:_____

Point 2:_____

Point 3:_____

Paragraph 3. Topic sentence: Second, with practice, tae kwon do increases maturity.

Point 1:_____

Point 2:_____

Paragraph 4. Topic sentence: Finally, after a year or so, tae kwon do can change the student's self-concept.

Point 1:_____

Point 2:_____

Point 3:_____

Paragraph 5. CONCLUSION

PRACTICE 2

Discuss with several classmates or write your answers to these questions.

1. Did Wineth Williams's introduction (paragraph 1) catch and hold your interest? Would this essay be just as good or better if it had no introduction but started right in with the thesis statement? Why or why not?

2. In paragraph (4), the writer says she now can "take care of business." Is this language appropriate for a college essay? Will readers know what this means?

3. Is the conclusion effective, or is it too short?

_____

* To read essays by other students, see the Writers' Workshops in Units 3, 6, 7, and 8.

4. Williams's audience was her English class. Her purpose (though not directly stated in the essay) was to let people know some of the benefits that come from practicing tae kwon do. Did she achieve her purpose?

5. What did you like best about the essay? What, if anything, would you change?

© 2019 Cengage Learning, Inc. May not be scanned, copied or duplicated, or posted to a publicly accessible website, in whole or in part.

PRACTICE 3

Read this student's essay and answer the questions.

Confronting My Fear
ANGEL LINARES

(1) What brought me to this college was my dream of becoming a physician assistant. Having childhood asthma meant that I grew up spending a lot of time in doctors' offices. It was the kindness, caring, and helpful advice of my pulmonologist's PA that inspired me to pursue this career. In high school, I researched the requirements for a PA degree. I arrived on this campus with my goal and with good study habits, but I almost defeated myself with negative thoughts.

(2) The first thoughts of failure sneaked into my brain when I heard other students talking about Bio 23. I had always known that my curriculum would require hard work and that some of the subject matter would be tedious or difficult to learn. I also knew that biology was one of the hardest subjects. But the students I overheard said the course was so hard that very few students last term even passed it. On campus, I heard more testimonials from students who either failed Bio 23 or withdrew because they were failing. I began to doubt my own abilities. What if I failed Bio? I needed the course to achieve my dream.

(3) These negative ideas grew like mold. The more I let them stay in my head, the stronger and more toxic they got. I was scaring myself with my own thoughts. I started changing the mental channel, over and over again. Instead, I focused on my goal of becoming a physician assistant. I pushed all my fears to the back of my mind and registered for Bio 23. Once I entered the class, I studied all the material day and night. I took every pop quiz and test and poured my best effort into every assignment. In the end, I passed with a B.

(4) This experience increased my self-confidence. It taught me an important lesson that I will teach my children someday. I turned my self-destructive fear into victory because I tried.

1. Underline this writer's thesis statement. Based on this sentence, what do you expect this essay to be about?

_____

2. What is the main idea of paragraph 2? What is the main idea of paragraph 3?

_____

3. How effective is the conclusion? Is it too short, or does brevity give it power?

_____

4. Have you ever had the experience of defeating (or almost defeating) yourself with negative thinking? What happened?

_____

B. The Process of Writing an Essay

Whether you are writing a paragraph or an essay, the writing process is the same. Of course, writing an essay will probably take longer. In this section, you will practice these steps of the essay-writing process:

- Narrowing the subject and writing the thesis statement
- Generating ideas for the body of the essay
- Selecting and arranging ideas in a plan
- Writing and revising your essay

Narrowing the Subject and Writing the Thesis Statement

While an essay subject should be broader than a paragraph topic, a good essay subject also must be narrow enough to write about in detail. For example, the topic *jobs* is broad enough to fill a book. But the far narrower topic *driving a bulldozer at the town dump* could make a good essay. Remember to select or narrow your subject in light of your intended audience and purpose. Who are your readers, and what do you want your essay to achieve?

Writing the *thesis statement* forces you to narrow the topic further: *Driving a bulldozer for the Department of Highways was the best job I ever had.* That could be an intriguing thesis statement, but the writer could focus it even more: *For three reasons, driving a bulldozer for the Department of Highways was the best job I ever had.* The writer might discuss one reason in each of three paragraphs.

Here are two more examples of the narrowing process:

(1) Subject:	music
Narrowed subject:	Cuban singer Lucrecia
Thesis statement:	In talent and style, Cuban singer Lucrecia might be the next Celia Cruz.
(2) Subject:	pets
Narrowed subject:	pains and pleasures of owning a parrot
Thesis statement:	Owning a parrot will enrich your life with noise, occasional chaos, and lots of laughs.

- On the basis of each thesis statement, what do you expect the essays to discuss?

_____

_____

Although the thesis statement must include all the ideas in the body of the essay, it should also be **clear** and **specific**. Which of these thesis statements is specific enough for a good essay?

(1) Three foolproof techniques will help you avoid disastrous first dates.

(2) NBA basketball is the most exciting sport in the world.

(3) Dr. Villarosa is a competent and caring physician.

- Thesis statements (1) and (3) are both specific. From (1), a reader might expect to learn about the "three foolproof techniques," each one perhaps explained in a paragraph.

- On the basis of thesis statement (3), what supporting points might the essay discuss?

  _____

  _____

- Thesis statement (2), however, is too broad for an essay—or even a book. It gives the reader (and writer) no direction.

PRACTICE 4 Choose one of these topics for your own essay. Then narrow the topic and write a clear and specific thesis statement.

> The benefits of a sport or practice
>
> The most fascinating (or boring or important) job I ever had
>
> How to overcome fear (or laziness or negative family and friends)

Narrowed subject: _____

_____

Thesis statement: _____

_____

Generating Ideas for the Body of the Essay

Writers generate support for an essay just as they do for a paragraph—by prewriting to get as many interesting ideas as possible. Once you know your main point and have written a thesis statement, use your favorite prewriting method—freewriting, for example. If you feel stuck, change to brainstorming or clustering. Just keep writing.

PRACTICE 5 Generate as many good ideas as possible to support your thesis statement. Fill at least one or two pages with ideas. As you work, try to imagine how many paragraphs your essay will contain and what each will include.

Selecting and Arranging Ideas in a Plan

Next, underline or mark the most interesting ideas that support your thesis statement. Cross out the rest.

Make a rough **plan** or **outline** that includes an introductory paragraph, two or three paragraphs for the body of the essay, and a brief conclusion. Choose a logical order for presenting your ideas. Which idea will come first, second, third?

For example, the bulldozer operator might explain why that job was "the best" with three reasons, arranged in this order: (1) *On the job, I learned to operate heavy equipment.* (2) *Working alone at the controls gave me time to think.* (3) *One bonus was occasionally finding interesting items beside the road.* This arrangement moves logically from physical skills to mental benefits to a surprising bonus.

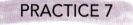

PRACTICE 6 Read over your prewriting pages, selecting your best ideas and a logical order in which to present them. Make an outline or a plan that includes an introduction and a thesis statement; two or three supporting paragraphs, each with a clear topic sentence; and a brief conclusion.

Writing and Revising Your Essay

Draft.   Now write your first draft. Try to express your ideas clearly and fully. If a section seems weak or badly written, put a check in the margin and go on; you can come back to that section later, prewriting again if necessary for fresh ideas. Set aside your draft for an hour or a day.

Revise.   Revising may be the most important step in the writing process. Reread your essay as if you were reading someone else's work, marking it up as you answer questions like these:

- Are my main idea and my thesis statement clear?

- Have I supported my thesis in a rich and convincing way?

- Does each paragraph in the body clearly explain the main idea?

- Does my essay have a logical order and good transitions?

- Are there any parts that don't belong or don't make sense?

- What one change would most improve my essay?*

You also might wish to ask a respected friend to read or listen to your essay, giving peer feedback before you revise.**

Proofread.   Now, carefully proofread your essay for errors in grammar, punctuation, and spelling. It is all-important not to skip or rush through this step. Read slowly, word by word, line by line.

The next chapter is devoted entirely to proofreading, teaching you some proven proofreading techniques that you will practice in Units 2 through 8. The units to come are your *proofreading handbook,* showing you how to spot and correct a wide range of serious errors.

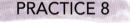

PRACTICE 7 Now read your first draft to see how you can improve it. Trust your instincts about what is alive and interesting and what is dull. Take your time. As you revise, try to make this the best paper you have ever written.

Finally, write a new draft of your essay, using the format preferred by your instructor. Proofread carefully, correcting any grammar or spelling errors.

PRACTICE 8 Exchange essays with a classmate. Write a one-paragraph evaluation of each other's work, saying as specifically as possible what you like about the essay and what might be improved. If you wish, use the Peer Feedback Sheet in Chapter 3, Part F.

Possible Topics for Essays

1. Three surefire ways to relax

2. A major decision

3. Should football be banned because it endangers players?

---

* See Chapter 3, Part F, for more revising ideas.

** See Chapter 3, Part F, for a sample Peer Feedback Sheet.

4. Should couples live together before marriage?

5. Tips for the new parent (college student, driver, and so forth)

6. A valuable (or worthless) television show

7. A good friend

8. Can anger be used constructively?

9. How I fell in love with reading (German shepherds, nursing, rock climbing, programming, and so forth)

10. What childhood taught me about _____.

Chapter Highlights

Checklist for Writing an Effective Essay

- Narrow the topic in light of your audience and purpose. Be sure you can discuss the topic fully in a short essay.

- Write a clear thesis statement. If you have trouble, freewrite or brainstorm first; then narrow the topic and write the thesis statement.

- Freewrite, brainstorm, or cluster to generate facts, details, and examples to support your thesis statement.

- Plan or outline your essay, choosing two or three main ideas to support the thesis statement.

- Write a topic sentence that expresses each main idea.

- Decide on a logical order in which to present the paragraphs.

- Plan the body of each paragraph, using all you have learned about support and paragraph development.

- Write the first draft of your essay.

- Revise as necessary, checking your essay for support, unity, and coherence.

- Proofread carefully for grammar, punctuation, and spelling.

EXPLORING ONLINE

www.powa.org/index.php/explain/subject-to-thesis

For help turning your subject into a good thesis statement, read "Subject to Thesis."

owl.english.purdue.edu/owl/resource/685/01

Purdue University's composition site reviews essay writing. At the bottom, click "Expository Essays" and "Argumentative Essays," the two essay types most assigned in college.

Visit **MindTap** for *Grassroots* to access this chapter's ebook, flashcards, additional practice and quizzes, and more!

CHAPTER 9

Proofreading to Correct Your Personal Error Patterns

A: Identifying and Tracking Your Personal Error Patterns

B: Proofreading Strategies

The important last step in the writing process is **proofreading**: slowly reading your revised paragraph or essay in order to find and correct any errors in grammar, punctuation, and spelling.

It is essential that you proofread work before turning it in because grammatical and other mistakes distract readers and give a negative impression of your skills and even intelligence. Often, employers won't interview a candidate whose letter or résumé contains errors. Yet many new writers avoid proofreading or rush through it so quickly that they set themselves up for failure.

In fact, the more mistakes you tend to make, the more important proofreading is for you. This chapter will give you tools to enhance your skills as an error detective and writer. Then Units 2 through 8 will further develop your proofreading skills, teaching you how to understand, spot, and correct many specific errors. In every coming chapter, you will practice a proofreading strategy that targets a particular mistake.

A. Identifying and Tracking Your Personal Error Patterns

Knowing what errors you tend to make and then proofreading for these errors will boost your success in college and at work.

Learn Your Error Patterns

An **error pattern** is any error you make two, three, or more times. For example, if a teacher has noted that one of your papers has several comma splices or numerous verb errors, those are *error patterns* that you need to work on. The first step in getting rid of these errors is becoming aware of them.

Here are four ways to discover your error patterns:

Papers. Study recently returned papers, making sure you understand the errors that have been marked. Check the inside back cover of this book for proofreading symbols your instructor might use, like *frag* for sentence fragment. Count the number of times each mistake appears.

Instructor. Ask your instructor to identify your error patterns. List them. Ask which three are the most serious.

Textbook. As you work through this book, notice chapters or practices where you keep making mistakes or writing incorrect answers. These are your error patterns.

Writing lab. Go to the writing lab with a paper you recently wrote. Ask a tutor to help identify the kinds of errors you make. Ask which three are the most serious.

PRACTICE 1 Consult your instructor, or bring a recent paper to the college writing lab. Seek help in identifying your error patterns and start a written list. Ask which three error patterns most harm your written communication and your grade.

Create a Personal Error Patterns Chart

Let's say your instructor marks 12 errors on your English paper, and 8 of them are verb agreement errors. This means that eight of your errors are really one error repeated eight times! Mastering this one error pattern would certainly improve your grade.

An excellent tool for tracking and beginning to master your errors is an **error chart** or **log**. This tool will show you what to study and what mistakes to watch for in your writing. Here is an example of one student's chart:

Personal Error Patterns Chart				
Error Type & Symbol	**Specific Error**	**Correction**	**Rule or Reminder**	**Assignment & Number of Errors**
Apostrophe error *apos*	My brothers fundraiser was a success.	My brother's fundraiser was a success.	's shows ownership by ONE brother.	Paper 1: 4 apos
Run-on *ro*	Jada is always late she can't decide what to wear.	Jada is always late because she can't decide what to wear.	Check for the end of each complete sentence. Join two sentences with a period or conjunction. See Ch. 18!	Paper 1: 5 ro #2: 3 ro #3: no run-ons!
Adverb *adv*	The patient did good.	The patient did well.	Good is an adjective; well is the adverb form.	#1: 4 adv #2: 3 adv

- Each time you receive a marked paper, write every *error name* or *type* in column 1 (like *apostrophe error* or *run-on*). Check the inside back cover to understand your instructor's proofreading symbols; for instance, *apos* for apostrophe error.

- In column 2, copy the error as you wrote it.

- In column 3, correct the error. If you have trouble understanding what you did wrong, ask the instructor, or search the index of this book for the pages you need.

- In column 4, jot the rule or ideas for fixing this type of mistake.

- In column 5, write the assignment number or date, plus the number of times you made this error. Add the error count for every later paper. Any error that appears in paper after paper will need a special plan of attack.

   Continue to add errors from future papers, instructor conferences, and tests. As you work in this textbook, add to your chart any grammatical concepts that still confuse you. Whenever you master the correction of an error, cross it off the chart and celebrate your achievement.

PRACTICE 2   Using a recent paper of yours that was graded by an instructor, begin your Personal Error Patterns Chart. You can use the blank chart in this book or create your chart as a Word file, adding rows as you need them. Some students design and draw their own charts. Follow this format:

Personal Error Patterns Chart				
Error Type & Symbol	Specific Error	Correction	Rule or Reminder	Assignment & Number of Errors

B. Proofreading Strategies

Whenever you write, honor your own writing process by setting aside enough time to perform each step, including proofreading. Just as it helps to take a break of hours or days between writing your first draft and revising, taking a break *before you proofread* is beneficial. Go for a walk. Call a friend. You cannot do a good job proofreading when you are tired. You will catch more errors with a rested mind and fresh outlook.

If possible, proofread in a quiet place where you won't be distracted—not at a dance club, not standing in the kitchen fixing dinner with the kids.

Many writers have found that the **proofreading strategies** described below help them see their own writing with a fresh eye. You will learn more strategies in subsequent chapters of this book. Try a number of methods and see which ones work best for you.

Proofreading Strategy: Allow enough time to proofread.

Many students don't proofread at all, or they skim their paper for grammatical errors two minutes before class. This just doesn't work. Set aside enough time to proofread slowly and carefully, searching for errors and hunting especially for your personal error patterns.

Proofreading Strategy: Work from a paper copy.

People who proofread on computers tend to miss more errors. If you write on a computer, do not proofread on the monitor. Instead, print a copy of your paper, perhaps enlarging the type to 14 point. Switching to a paper copy seems to help the brain see more clearly.

Proofreading Strategy: Read your words aloud.

Reading silently makes it easier to skip over small errors or mentally fill in missing details, whereas listening closely is a great way to hear mistakes. Listen and follow along on your printed copy, marking errors as you hear them.

   a. Read your paper aloud to *yourself*. Be sure to read *exactly* what's on the page, and read with enthusiasm.

   b. Ask a *friend* or *writing tutor* to read your paper out loud to you. Tell the reader you just want to hear your words and that you don't want any other suggestions right now.

Proofreading Strategy: Read "bottom up," from the end to the beginning.

One way to fool the brain into taking a fresh look at something you've written is to proofread the last sentence first. Read slowly, word by word. Then read the second-to-last sentence, and so on, all the way back to the first sentence.

Proofreading Strategy: Isolate your sentences.

If you write on a computer, spotting errors is often easier if you reformat so that each sentence appears isolated, on its own line. Double-space between sentences. This visual change can help the brain focus clearly on one sentence at a time.

Proofreading Strategy: Check for one error at a time.

If you make many mistakes, proofread separately all the way through your paper for each error pattern. Although this process takes time, you will catch many more errors this way and make real progress. You will begin to eliminate some errors altogether as you get better at spotting and fixing them. You will learn more recommended proofreading strategies in upcoming chapters.

PRACTICE 3

Win your Academy Award! In a group with several classmates, role-play discussions between W and several friends. The friends are committed to getting A's in their writing class, but W is getting Ds and Fs. He *says* he wants to earn a nursing degree, but his actions say otherwise. Last night the friends saw him "proofreading" his paper in a Mexican restaurant over margaritas with a buddy.

Pick someone to play W. Then, one at a time, each member of the group in turn should try to persuade him to take his writing seriously, and especially to work on his proofreading skills. At the end, ask W if anyone's argument got through to him. Be prepared to report to the class.

PRACTICE 4

Print out or make a photocopy of something you wrote recently for college or work. Ask someone to read the original out loud as you listen. On your copy, underline or highlight sentences or places that sound wrong. Also mark any places where the reader stumbles verbally. Rewrite the marked sentences.

PRACTICE 5

Choose a paper you wrote recently. Select one of the proofreading strategies and try it out on this paper. Read with full attention, keenly watching for your personal error patterns. Put a check in the margin beside each error. Then correct them neatly above the lines.

Chapter Highlights

- Proofreading for errors in grammar, punctuation, and spelling is a crucial step in the writing process. Proofreading skills can be learned.

- Keeping a Personal Error Patterns Chart and referring to it as they write helps writers spot and correct the errors that they habitually make.

- Using proofreading strategies can help writers recognize the errors in their own work. These strategies can help you too:

  - Allow enough time to proofread.
  - Work from a paper copy, not the monitor.
  - Read your words aloud.
  - Read "bottom up," from the last sentence to the first.
  - Isolate your sentences.
  - Read for one error at a time.

EXPLORING ONLINE

writing.wisc.edu/Handbook/Proofreading.html

Excellent proofreading advice from the University of Wisconsin OWL.

owl.english.purdue.edu/owl/resource/561/01

Proofreading tips from the Purdue University OWL, plus advice on correcting common errors made by college students.

Visit **MindTap** for *Grassroots* to access this chapter's ebook, flashcards, additional practice and quizzes, and more!

Writing Assignments

As you complete each writing assignment, remember to perform these steps:

- Write a clear, complete topic (or thesis) sentence.

- Use freewriting, brainstorming, or clustering to generate ideas for the body of your paragraph or essay.

- Arrange your best ideas in a plan.

- Revise for support, unity, coherence, and exact language.

- Proofread for grammar, punctuation, and spelling errors.

WRITING ASSIGNMENT 1 *Discuss your top two to three priorities in a job.* Complete this topic sentence: "My top two (or three) priorities in a job are _____." What matters the most to you when you think about your ideal job? Do you value salary over flexibility? Why? Do you care where you live, or would you go anywhere for a certain career? Do you want to pursue a passion or have a job with a prestigious title, or both? Begin by jotting down all of the priorities that you think are important in selecting your career path. Then choose the two or three that are the most essential and arrange them in order of importance—either from the least to the most essential or the reverse. Explain each priority, making clear to the reader why you feel as strongly as you do.

WRITING ASSIGNMENT 2 *Interview a classmate about an achievement.* Write about a time your classmate achieved something important, like winning a sales prize at work, losing 30 pounds, or helping a friend through a bad time. To gather interesting facts and details, ask your classmate questions like these and take notes: *Is there one accomplishment of which you are very proud? Why was this achievement so important? Did it change the way you feel about yourself?* Keep asking questions until you feel you have enough information to give your reader a vivid sense of your classmate's triumph.

In your first sentence, state the person's achievement—for instance, *Getting her first A in English was a turning point in Jessica's life.* Then explain specifically why the achievement was so meaningful.

WRITING ASSIGNMENT 3 *Develop a paragraph with examples.* Below are topic sentences for possible paragraphs. Pick the topic sentence that most interests you and write a paragraph, using one to three examples to explain the topic sentence.

a. A sense of humor can make difficult times easier to bear.

b. Mistakes can be great teachers.

c. Television commercials often insult my intelligence.

WRITING ASSIGNMENT 4 *Counsel a young person.* A young friend who is considering dropping out of high school urgently needs your advice. You have read the depressing statistics: more than 30 percent of dropouts end up trapped in poverty, as opposed to 13 percent of college graduates. As you plan your paragraph or essay, put yourself in this teenager's shoes. What pressures is he or she facing that brought on this crisis? What approach is most likely to be helpful to this particular teenager? You might wish to employ one of the paragraph types you learned in this unit, like persuasion, illustration, cause-effect, or contrast. REMEMBER: Keep your young reader firmly in mind as you write.

Review

Choosing a Topic Sentence

Each group of sentences could be unscrambled and written as a paragraph. Circle the letter of the sentence that would be the best topic sentence.

1. a. Rooftops and towers made eye-catching shapes against the winter sky.

   b. Far below, the faint sounds of slush and traffic were soothing.

   c. From the apartment-house roof, the urban scene was oddly relaxing.

   d. Stoplights changing color up and down the avenues created a rhythmic pattern invisible from the street.

2. a. Service members are eligible for insurance and retirement benefits.

   b. Financial support for a college education is a major advantage of military service.

   c. Being trained by the military can instill discipline and self-esteem.

   d. Many servicemen and women get to travel to new places and experience new cultures.

   e. Military service, despite its risks, offers many advantages.

Selecting Ideas

Here is a topic sentence and a brainstormed list of ideas for a paragraph. Check "Keep" for ideas that best support the topic sentence and "Drop" for ideas that do not.

Topic sentence: Simone Biles is a world-champion gymnast and role model.

Keep	Drop	
_____	_____	1. world's most decorated gymnast, 19 Olympic and world champion medals
_____	_____	2. grandparents got her into gymnastics classes by age six
_____	_____	3. the 795th most popular girl's name in 2017—Simone
_____	_____	4. inspired new generations of girls to try out for gymnastics
_____	_____	5. tiny Simone invited to take classes after her day-care visited a gymnastics center and she copied the gymnasts' moves
_____	_____	6. Shannon Miller, previously the most decorated U.S. gymnast
_____	_____	7. works obsessively hard but "never forgets to have fun"
_____	_____	8. most winning female gymnasts within 3 inches of 5 feet tall
_____	_____	9. she likes to wear glitter shadow and cat-eye makeup
_____	_____	10. known for generosity and leadership on her gymnastic teams

Examining a Paragraph

Read this paragraph and answer the questions.

(1) Students at some American colleges are learning a lot from trash by studying "garbology." (2) Wearing rubber gloves, they might sift through the local dump, counting and collecting treasures that they examine back at the laboratory. (3) First, they learn to look closely and to interpret what they see, thus reading the stories that trash tells. (4) More important, they learn the truth about what Americans buy, what they eat, and how they live. (5) Students at the University of Arizona, for instance, were surprised to find that low-income families in certain areas buy more educational toys for their children than nearby middle-income families do. (6) Most important, students say that garbology courses can motivate them to be better citizens of planet Earth. (7) One young woman, for example, after seeing from hard evidence in her town's landfill how many people really recycled their glass, cans, and newspapers and how many cheated, organized an annual recycling awareness day.

1. Write the number of the topic sentence in the paragraph. _____

2. What kind of order does this writer use? _____

3. Students learn three things in garbology courses. (a) Write the numbers of the sentences stating these. (b) Which two ideas are supported by examples?

   (a) _____   (b) _____

On Earth Day, garbology students at Western Kentucky University examine the contents of campus dumpsters to raise awareness about the impact of waste.

Writers' Workshop

Discuss Your Name

Good writers are masters of exact language and thoughtful observation. Read this student's paragraph about her name. Underline any words or details that strike you as well written, interesting, or powerful.

In this paragraph I will write about my name. My name YuMing is made up of two Chinese characters that mean "the universe" and "the crow of a bird." This may seem like a strange name to an American, but in fact it has a special meaning for me. In ancient Chinese literature, there is a story about a bird that was owned by God. This bird was rumored to have the most beautiful voice in the universe. A greedy king wanted this bird, so he had it captured and placed in a big cage. He sat next to this cage day after day waiting for the bird to sing, but the bird stayed silent. After three years, the impatient king threw open the cage door and set the bird free. As the bird flew up toward the heavens, it made its first crow in three years. The sound shocked everyone in the kingdom because they realized the legend was true—they had never heard such a beautiful voice before! My parents told me that they gave me this name because they want me to be like the bird in the story. Though I may stay silent for a while as I establish myself in society, they hope that I will "crow" one day when it is the right time for me, and crow loudly so everyone in the universe can hear.

YuMing Lai, Student

1. How effective is YuMing Lai's paragraph about the meaning of her name?

   _____ Good topic sentence?   _____ Rich supporting details?

   _____ Logical organization?   _____ Effective conclusion?

2. Underline the words, details, or sentences you like best. Put a check beside anything that needs improvement.

3. Now discuss your underlinings with your group or class. Try to explain as exactly as you can why you like something. For example, in the last sentence, the way that the writer ties her parents' wish for her to the meaning of the story is moving and surprising.

4. Is YuMing's topic sentence as good as the rest of her paragraph? If not, how might she change it?

5. Did YuMing's thoughts about her name make you think about your own name? Do you like your name? Why or why not? Do you know why your parents chose it?

6. What order does this paragraph employ?

Writing and Revising Ideas

1. Write about the meaning of your name or the name of someone close to you.

2. Visit the government's website below, which lists the most popular baby names in the United States, year by year. Do you see any patterns? How popular is your name? Your parents' names?
   www.ssa.gov/OACT/babynames

For help with writing your paragraph, see Chapter 3 and Chapter 4, Parts A and B. As you revise, pay special attention to writing a clear, catchy topic sentence supported by interesting details.

Writing Complete Sentences

The sentence is the basic unit of all writing, so good writers must know how to write clear and correct sentences. In this unit, you will

- Follow the MAP to better reading and writing

- Learn to spot subjects and verbs

- Practice writing complete sentences

- Learn to avoid or correct any sentence fragments

- Learn proofreading strategies to correct your own errors

Brian Jannsen/Alamy Stock Photo

Follow the MAP to Better Reading and Writing

MODEL

Read this paragraph carefully. Notice the way this writer, a media expert, uses strong, correct sentences to make a thought-provoking, even frightening, point about advertising. If possible, read the paragraph aloud.

Most people feel that advertising is not something to take seriously. Other aspects of the media are serious—the violent films, the trashy talk shows, the bowdlerization[1] of the news. But not advertising! Although much more attention has been paid to the cultural impact of advertising in recent years than ever before, just about everyone still feels personally exempt from its influence. What I hear more than anything else at my lectures is: "I don't pay attention to ads . . . I just tune them out . . . they have no effect on me." I hear this most from people wearing clothes emblazoned with logos. In truth, we are all influenced. There is no way to tune out this much information, especially when it is designed to break through the "tuning out" process. As advertising critic Sut Jhally put it, "To *not* be influenced by advertising would be to live outside of culture. No human being lives outside of culture."

Jean Kilbourne, "Jesus Is a Brand of Jeans," *New Internationalist*

ANALYSIS

- What is Kilbourne's main idea about advertising in this paragraph? Which sentences tell you this?

- Did any details or examples especially convince you that advertising affects people's behavior whether they know it or not?

PRACTICE

- Write about someone who loves clothes and accessories with logos.

- Write about a logo, product, or brand and what it says about the buyer.

---

1. bowdlerization: process of editing out offensive material

CHAPTER 10

Subjects and Verbs

A: Defining and Spotting Subjects

B: Spotting Singular and Plural Subjects

C: Spotting Prepositional Phrases

D: Defining and Spotting Action Verbs

E: Defining and Spotting Linking Verbs

F: Spotting Verbs of More Than One Word

A. Defining and Spotting Subjects

The sentence is the basic unit of all writing. To write well, you need to know how to write correct and effective sentences. This chapter will show you how. A **sentence** is a group of words that expresses a complete thought about something or someone. It contains a **subject** and a **verb**.

(1) _____ jumped over the black Buick, scaled the building, and finally reached the roof.

(2) _____ needs a new coat of paint.

These sentences might be interesting, but they are incomplete.

- In sentence (1), *who* jumped, scaled, and reached? Spider-Man, Ariana Grande, the English teacher?

- Depending on *who* performed the action—jumping, scaling, or reaching—the sentence can be exciting, surprising, or strange.

- What is missing is the *who* word—the *subject*.

- In sentence (2), *what* needs a new coat of paint? The house, the car, the old rocking chair?

- What is missing is the *what* word—the *subject*.

   For a sentence to be complete, it must contain a *who* **or** *what* **word—a** *subject*. **The subject tells you** *who* **or** *what* **does something or exists in a certain way**.

   The subject is often a *noun*, a word that names a person, place, or thing (such as *Ariana Grande, English teacher,* or *house*).* However, a *pronoun* (I, you, he, she, it, we, or *they*) also can be the subject.**

_____
* For more work on nouns, see Chapter 23.
** For more work on pronoun subjects, see Chapter 24, Part F.

PRACTICE 1

In each of these sentences, the subject (the *who* or *what* word) is missing. Fill in your own subject to make the sentence complete.

EXAMPLE: A(n) _____*fox*_____ dashed across the road.

1. The _____ skidded across the ice.

2. The _____ was eager to begin the semester.

3. Because of the crowd, the _____ slipped out unnoticed.

4. For years, _____ piled up in the back of the closet.

5. The cheerful yellow _____ brightened Sheila's mood.

6. _____ and _____ were scattered all over the doctor's desk.

7. The _____ believed that his _____ would return someday.

8. The _____ was in bad shape. The _____ was falling

   in, and the _____ were all broken.

As you may have noticed, the subject can be just one noun or pronoun. This single noun or pronoun is called **the simple subject**. The subject also can include *words that describe the noun or pronoun* (such as *the*, *cheerful*, or *yellow*). The noun and pronoun plus the words that describe it are called **the complete subject**.

> (3) Three scarlet roses grew near the path.
>
> (4) A large box was delivered this morning.

- The complete subject of sentence (3) is *three scarlet roses*.

- The simple subject is the noun *roses*.

- What is the complete subject of (4)? _____

- What is the simple subject of (4)? _____

Try This To find the subject, try turning the sentence into a question: *Who or what* grew near the path? *Three scarlet roses. Who or what* was delivered this morning? *A large box*.

PRACTICE 2

Circle the *simple* subject in each sentence. (A person's complete name—though more than one word—is considered a simple subject.)

EXAMPLE: (Stacie Ponder) blogs about horror movies.

(1) Many people love scary films. (2) Psychologists want to know why. (3) Dr. Leon Rappoport studies this fear factor among moviegoers. (4) Humans have always liked to explore their feelings of fear and anxiety, according to Rappoport. (5) Frightening movies allow them to master those emotions and work through them. (6) People do not wish to meet Hannibal Lecter in daily life. (7) They like to watch him onscreen, however,

Movie poster, 1958

Horror movies allow people to face their fears in a safe way, claim psychologists.

in the absence of any real danger. (8) Horror films and stories provide opportunities for such experiences. (9) Also, some moviegoers like to explore their uncivilized, antisocial nature in safe settings. (10) Many teenagers, in particular, need to test their tolerance for threatening situations. (11) In addition, parents often declare horror movies inappropriate. (12) Therefore, adolescents want to see this forbidden entertainment more than ever.

PRACTICE 3

In these sentences, the complete subject has been omitted. You must decide where it belongs and fill in a complete subject (a *who* or *what* word along with any words that describe it to make a complete sentence). Write in any complete subject that makes sense.

EXAMPLE: raced down the street

My worried friend raced down the street.

1. trained day and night for the big event

_____

2. has a dynamic singing voice

_____

3. landed in the cornfield

_____

4. after the show, applauded and screamed for fifteen minutes

_____

5. got out of the large gray van

_____

B. Spotting Singular and Plural Subjects

Besides being able to spot subjects in sentences, you need to know whether a subject is singular or plural.

> (1) The man jogged around the park.

- The subject of this sentence is *the man*.
- Because *the man* is one person, the subject is *singular*.

Singular means only one of something.

> (2) The man and his friend jogged around the park.

- The subject of sentence (2) is *the man and his friend*.
- Because *the man and his friend* refers to more than one person, the subject is *plural*.

Plural means more than one of something.*

PRACTICE 4

Here is a list of possible subjects of sentences. If the subject is singular, write *S* next to it; if the subject is plural, write *P* next to it.

EXAMPLES: an elephant   <u>S</u>

   children   <u>P</u>

1. our cousins _____
2. a song and a dance _____
3. Kansas _____
4. their website _____
5. women _____
6. a rock star and her band _____
7. his three pickup trucks _____
8. salad dressing _____

PRACTICE 5

Circle the complete subjects in these sentences. Then, in the space at the right, write *S* if the subject is singular or *P* if the subject is plural.

EXAMPLE: (This young comedian and writer) is getting national attention.   <u>S</u>

1. High school classmates voted him "most likely to write for *The Simpsons*." _____
2. Comedy and television had always intrigued him. _____
3. Now Donald Glover was a student in dramatic writing at New York University. _____
4. This *Simpsons* fanatic sent a script to the comedy show *30 Rock*. _____
5. Incredibly, *30 Rock* executives gave Glover a writing job. _____
6. Tina Fey mentored the talented 23-year-old. _____
7. His talents soon led to even more success. _____
8. African-American culture was underrepresented on TV, in Glover's view. _____

_____

* For much more on singulars and plurals, see Chapter 23, Nouns.

9. The show *Atlanta* was the result, written by and starring Glover.   _____

10. A music manager and his rapper cousin are its main characters.   _____

C. Spotting Prepositional Phrases

A **preposition** is a word like *on*, *through*, and *before*. Prepositions usually indicate location, direction, or time. For example, the plane sat *on the runway*, flew *through a thunderstorm*, and landed *before dark*. These humble words can be confusing, so it's important to be able to recognize them.

Common Prepositions			
about	beneath	inside	through
above	beside	into	throughout
across	between	like	to
after	beyond	near	toward
against	by	of	under
along	despite	off	underneath
among	down	on	until
around	during	onto	up
at	except	out	upon
before	for	outside	with
behind	from	over	within
below	in	past	without

One group of words that may confuse you as you look for the subjects of sentences is the prepositional phrase. A **prepositional phrase** contains a *preposition* and its *object* (the noun or pronoun that follows the preposition). Here are some prepositional phrases:*

Prepositional Phrase	=	Preposition	+	Object
at work		at		work
behind her		behind		her
of the students		of		the students
on the blue table		on		the blue table

The object of a preposition *cannot* be the subject of a sentence. Therefore, crossing out prepositional phrases can help you find the real subject.

(1) On summer evenings, girls in white dresses stroll under the trees.

(2) ~~On summer evenings~~, girls ~~in white dresses~~ stroll ~~under the trees~~.

(3) From dawn to dusk, we hiked.

(4) The president of the college will speak tonight.

● In sentence (1), you may have trouble spotting the subject. Is it *evening*, *girls*, or *dresses*?

_____

* For more work on prepositions and a list of many English expressions containing prepositions, see Chapter 26, Prepositions.

- However, once the prepositional phrases are crossed out in (2), the subject, *girls*, is easy to see.
- Cross out the prepositional phrase in sentence (3). What is the subject of the sentence? _____
- Cross out the prepositional phrase in sentence (4). What is the subject of the sentence? _____

Try This   If you have trouble finding prepositional phrases, circle all the prepositions, referring to the prepositions list. Then locate the rest of the words in each prepositional phrase.

PRACTICE 6   Underline all the prepositional phrases in the following sentences. Some sentences include more than one prepositional phrase.

1. In college or the workplace, a knowledge of your learning style can help you master any subject.
2. A learning style is a person's preferred way of learning new information.
3. The four types of learning styles are visual, auditory, reading/writing, and hands-on.
4. Most people learn in all four ways, with one favored style.
5. People with a visual learning style understand best from diagrams, images, or videos.
6. Auditory learners, on the other hand, learn by reading aloud, talking, and listening.
7. Learners with a reading/writing style absorb information easily through written words.
8. After a class, they should write notes and summaries of the material.
9. Hands-on learners show a strong preference for movement and action.
10. For example, they handle objects, perform, or conduct experiments.

PRACTICE 7   Now cross out the prepositional phrase or phrases in each sentence. Then circle the *simple* subject of the sentence.

EXAMPLE: (Millions) of people walk on the Appalachian Trail each year.

1. The famous trail stretches 2,158 miles from Springer Mountain in Georgia to Mount Katahdin in Maine.
2. The majority of walkers hike for just one day.
3. Trail names are used by nearly all hikers instead of their real names.
4. Examples include Bobcat, All In, Wild Child, and Hard Time.
5. Of the millions of trail users, 200 people trek the entire length every year.
6. These lovers of the wilderness start in spring to reach Mount Katahdin before winter.
7. On average, the trip through 14 states consumes five months and four or five pairs of shoes.
8. Men and women battle heat, humidity, bugs, blisters, muscle strains, and food and water shortages.
9. After beautiful green scenery in the South, the trail becomes rocky and mountainous.
10. Hikers in the White Mountains of New Hampshire struggle against fierce winds.

11. A pebble from Georgia is sometimes added to the pile of stones at the top of Mount Katahdin.

12. At the base of the mountain, conquerors of the Appalachian Trail add their names to the list of successful hikers.

D. Defining and Spotting Action Verbs

> (1) The pears _____ on the trees.
>
> (2) Robert _____ his customer's hand and _____ her dog on the head.

These sentences tell you what or who the subject is—*the pears* and *Robert*—but not what each subject does.

- In sentence (1), what do the pears do? Do they *grow, ripen, rot, stink,* or *glow*?

- All these *action verbs* fit into the blank space in sentence (1), but the meaning of the sentence changes depending on which action verb you use.

- In sentence (2), what actions did Robert perform? Perhaps he *shook, ignored, kissed, patted,* or *scratched*.

- Depending on which verb you use, the meaning of the sentence changes.

- Some sentences, like sentence (2), contain two or more action verbs.

For a sentence to be complete, it must have a *verb*. **An** *action verb* **tells what action the subject is performing**.

PRACTICE 8   Fill in each blank with an action verb.

1. Blake Griffin _____ through the air for a slam dunk.

2. An artist _____ the scene at the waterfront.

3. When the rooster _____, the dogs _____.

4. A fierce wind _____ and _____.

5. The audience _____ while the conductor _____.

6. This new kitchen gadget _____ and _____ any vegetable you can imagine.

7. When the dentist _____ his drill, Charlene _____.

8. Usher _____ and _____ across the stage.

PRACTICE 9   Circle the action verbs in these sentences. Some sentences contain more than one action verb.

(1) Sometimes the combination of talent and persistence explodes into well-deserved fame and fortune. (2) For almost a year, J. K. Rowling survived on public assistance in Edinburgh, Scotland. (3) Almost every day that year, she brought her baby to a coffee

shop near their damp, unheated apartment. (4) In the warmth of the café, the divorced, unemployed mother sat and wrote. (5) Almost at the end of her endurance, she finally finished her first book. (6) Today, Rowling's *Harry Potter* books sell hundreds of millions of copies in sixty languages. (7) Each book tells about Harry's adventures, both in the everyday world (the Muggles' world) and at a new grade level at Hogwarts School of Witchcraft and Wizardry. (8) The imaginative and very funny series about the courageous young wizard-in-training attracts and enthralls adults as well as children. (9) In fact, the *New York Times* began a children's bestseller list for the first time—after months of *Harry Potter* books in slots 1, 2, and 3 on the adult bestseller list.

E. Defining and Spotting Linking Verbs

The verbs you have been examining so far show action, but a second kind of verb simply links the subject to words that describe or rename it.

> (1) Aunt Claudia sometimes seems a little strange.

- The subject in this sentence is *Aunt Claudia*, but there is no action verb.
- Instead, *seems* links the subject, *Aunt Claudia*, with the descriptive words *a little strange*.

Aunt Claudia	seems	a little strange.
↓	↓	↓
subject	linking verb	descriptive words

> (2) They are reporters for the newspaper.

- The subject is *they*. The word *reporters* renames the subject.
- What verb links the subject, *they*, with the word *reporters*? _____

For a sentence to be complete, it must contain a *verb*. A *linking verb* links the subject with words that describe or rename that subject.

Here are some linking verbs you should know:

Common Linking Verbs	
be (am, is, are, was, were)	look
act	remain
appear	seem
become	smell
feel	sound
get	taste

● The most common linking verbs are the forms of *to be—am, is, are, was, were*—but verbs of the senses, such as *feel, look,* and *smell,* also may be used as linking verbs.

PRACTICE 10   The complete subjects and descriptive words in these sentences are underlined. Circle the linking verbs.

1. Jerry sounds sleepy today.

2. Sunetra always was the best debater on the team.

3. His brother often appeared relaxed and happy.

4. By evening, Harvey felt confident about the exam.

5. Mara and Maude became talent scouts.

PRACTICE 11   Circle the linking verbs in these sentences. Then underline the complete subject and the descriptive word or words in each sentence.

1. The sweet potato pie tastes delicious.

2. You usually seem energetic.

3. During the summer, she looks calm.

4. Under heavy snow, the new dome roof appeared sturdy.

5. Raphael is a gifted animal trainer.

6. Lately, I feel very competent at work.

7. Luz became a medical technician.

8. Yvonne acted surprised at her baby shower.

F.   Spotting Verbs of More Than One Word

All the verbs you have dealt with so far have been single words—*look, walked, saw, are, were,* and so on. However, many verbs consist of more than one word.

> (1) Sarah is walking to work.

● The subject is *Sarah.* What is *Sarah* doing?

● Sarah is walking.

● *Walking* is the *main verb. Is* is the *helping verb;* without *is, walking* is not a complete verb.

> (2) Should I have written sooner?

● The subject is *I.*

● *Should have written* is the *complete verb.*

● *Written* is the *main verb. Should* and *have* are the *helping verbs;* without *should have, written* is not a complete verb.

(3) Do you eat fish?

- What is the subject? _____
- What is the main verb? _____
- What is the helping verb? _____

The *complete verb* **in a sentence consists of all the helping verbs and the main verb.**

PRACTICE 12

The blanks following each sentence tell you how many words make up the complete verb. Fill in the blanks with the complete verb; then circle the main verb.

EXAMPLE: Language researchers at the University of Arizona have been studying parrots.

     _____*have*_____   _____*been*_____   _____(*studying*)_____

1. Dr. Irene Pepperberg has worked with Alex, an African Gray parrot, for 10 years.

     _____   _____

2. Nearly 100 words can be used by this intelligent bird.

     _____   _____   _____

3. Alex is believed to understand the words, not just "parrot" sounds.

     _____   _____

Alex, the talking parrot, with his trainer, Dr. Irene Pepperberg

Rick Friedman/Corbis Historical/Getty Images

4. For example, from a tray of objects, Alex can select all the keys, all the wooden items, or all the blue items.

   _____   _____

5. Dr. Pepperberg might show Alex a fuzzy cloth ball.

   _____   _____

6. The bird will shout, "Wool!"

   _____   _____

7. Alex has been counting to six.

   _____   _____   _____

8. Currently, he and the other parrots are learning letters and their sounds.

   _____   _____

9. Can these birds really be taught to read?

   _____   _____   _____

10. Scientists in animal communication are excited by the possibility.

    _____   _____

PRACTICE 13   Box the simple subject, circle the main verb, and underline any helping verbs in each of the following sentences.

EXAMPLE: Most people have wondered about the beginning of the universe.

1. Scientists have developed one theory.

2. According to this theory, the universe began with a huge explosion.

3. The explosion has been named the Big Bang.

4. First, all matter must have been packed into a tiny speck under enormous pressure.

5. Then, about 15 billion years ago, that speck burst with amazing force.

6. Everything in the universe has come from the original explosion.

7. In fact, the universe still is expanding from the Big Bang.

8. All of the planets and stars are moving away from each other at an even speed.

9. Will it expand forever?

10. Experts may be debating that question for a long time.

Chapter Highlights

■ **A sentence contains a subject and a verb, and expresses a complete thought:**

      S   *V*

Jennifer swims every day.

         S   *V*

The two students have tutored in the writing lab.

■ **An action verb tells what the subject is doing:**

Toni Morrison writes novels.

■ **A linking verb links the subject with words that describe or rename it:**

Her novels are bestsellers.

■ **Don't mistake the object of a prepositional phrase for a subject:**

      S   *PP*

The red car [in the showroom] *is a Corvette.*

  PP   *S*

[In my dream,] *a sailor and his parrot were singing.*

PROOFREADING STRATEGY

Being able to recognize subjects and verbs will help you know whether or not your sentences are complete. To test for completeness, **cross out** and **color code**:

1. Read each sentence slowly, crossing out any prepositional phrases.

2. Then either circle the subject and underline the verb or *color code your subjects and verbs,* using two different highlighters, like this:

   My hometown has been hit very hard ~~by the recession~~.

   Many ~~of my neighbors~~ have lost their jobs, including both ~~of my brothers~~.

3. Finally, read each sentence slowly to make sure it expresses a complete thought and ends with a period.

WRITING AND PROOFREADING ASSIGNMENT

Whether you have just graduated from high school or have worked for several years, the first year of college can be difficult. Imagine that you are writing to an incoming student who needs advice and encouragement. Pick one serious problem you had as a first-year student and explain how you coped with it. State the problem clearly. Use examples from your own experience or the experience of others to make your advice more vivid. After you write and revise your composition, take a break before you proofread. Then, cross out your prepositional phrases and mark or highlight every subject and verb. Check each sentence for completeness.

CHAPTER REVIEW

Circle the simple subjects, crossing out any confusing prepositional phrases. Then underline the complete verbs. If you prefer, color code the subjects and verbs. If you have difficulty with this review, consider rereading the lesson.

Target Practice: Setting Attainable Goals

(1) Successful people know an important secret about setting and reaching goals. (2) These high achievers break their big goals into smaller, more manageable steps or targets. (3) Then they hit the targets, one by one. (4) Otherwise, a huge goal might seem impossible.

(5) To turn a major goal into smaller steps, many achievers think backward. (6) Dillon, for example, wanted to lose 20 pounds by graduation. (7) That much weight must be lost gradually. (8) So Dillon decided to set smaller targets for himself. (9) First, Dillon eliminated between-meal snacks. (10) On the new plan, he might eat an occasional apple, but only in emergencies. (11) Second, Dillon gave up second helpings at any meal—no matter what. (12) His third target was a walk after dinner. (13) Every night, this purposeful dieter would check off the day's successes.

(14) Even high achievers do not complete a major goal, like losing a lot of weight, every day. (15) Yet they can feel satisfaction about moving forward one step at a time. (16) The photographer at Dillon's graduation captured his beaming smile. (17) Under that cap and gown, Dillon's weight had dropped by 22 pounds.

EXPLORING ONLINE

grammar.ccc.commnet.edu/grammar/quizzes/subjector.htm
Interactive quiz: Identify the subjects.

grammar.ccc.commnet.edu/grammar/quizzes/verbmaster.htm
Interactive quiz: Identify verbs of one or more words.

Visit **MindTap** for *Grassroots* to access this chapter's ebook, flashcards, additional practice and quizzes, and more!

CHAPTER 11

Avoiding Sentence Fragments

A: Writing Sentences with Subjects and Verbs

B: Writing Sentences with Complete Verbs

C: Completing the Thought

A. Writing Sentences with Subjects and Verbs

Which of these groups of words is a sentence? Be prepared to explain your answers.

(1) People will bet on almost anything.

(2) For example, every winter the Nenana River in Alaska.

(3) Often make bets on the date of the breakup of the ice.

(4) Must guess the exact day and time of day.

(5) Recently, the lucky guess won $300,000.

- In (2), you probably wanted to know what the Nenana River *does*. The idea is not complete because there is no *verb*.

- In (3) and (4), you probably wanted to know *who* often makes bets on the date of the breakup of the ice and *who* must guess the exact day and time of day.

  The ideas are not complete. What is missing? _____

- But in sentences (1) and (5), you knew *who did what*. These ideas are complete. Why? _____

Below are the same groups of words written as complete sentences:

(1) People will bet on almost anything.

(2) For example, every winter the Nenana River in Alaska freezes.

(3) The townspeople often make bets on the date of the breakup of the ice.

(4) Someone must guess the exact day and time of day.

(5) Recently, the lucky guess won $300,000.

Every *sentence* **must have both a subject and a verb—and must express a complete thought.**

A *fragment* **is not a complete sentence because it lacks either a subject or a complete verb—or does not express a complete thought.**

PRACTICE 1

All of the following are *fragments* because they lack a subject, a verb, or both. Add a subject, a verb, or both to make the fragments into sentences.

EXAMPLE: Raising onions in the backyard.

Rewrite: *Charles is raising onions in the backyard.*

1. Melts easily.

    Rewrite: _____

2. That couple on the street corner.

    Rewrite: _____

3. One of the fans.

    Rewrite: _____

4. Manages a GameStop store.

    Rewrite: _____

5. The tip of her nose.

    Rewrite: _____

6. DVR players.

    Rewrite: _____

7. Makes me nervous.

    Rewrite: _____

8. A person who likes to take risks.

    Rewrite: _____

Sentence fragments are considered a serious and distracting error in college and at work, so it is important that you learn to eliminate them from your writing.

B. Writing Sentences with Complete Verbs

Do not be fooled by incomplete verbs.

(1) She leaving for the city.

(2) We done that chapter already.

- *Leaving* seems to be the verb in (1).
- *Done* seems to be the verb in (2).

But . . .

- An *-ing* word like *leaving* is not by itself a verb.

- A word like *done* is not by itself a verb.

(1) She $\left.\begin{array}{l} \textit{is} \\ \textit{was} \end{array}\right\}$ leaving for the city.

(2) We $\left.\begin{array}{l} \textit{have} \\ \textit{had} \end{array}\right\}$ done that chapter already.

- To be a verb, an *-ing* word (called a *present participle*) must be combined with some form of the verb *to be*.*

Helping Verb		Main Verb
am	were	
is	has been	
are	have been	jogging
was	had been	

- To be a verb, a word like *done* (called a *past participle*) must be combined with some form of *to have* or *to be*.**

Helping Verb		Main Verb
am	have	
is	had	
are	has been	
was	have been	forgotten
were	had been	
has		

PRACTICE 2

All of the following are fragments; they have only a partial or an incomplete verb. Complete each verb in order to make these fragments into sentences.

EXAMPLE: Both children grown tall this year.

Rewrite: *Both children have grown tall this year.*

1. The Australian winning the tennis match.

   Rewrite: _____

2. Her friends seen her at the mall every Saturday.

   Rewrite: _____

---

* For a detailed explanation of present participles, see Chapter 15.

** For a detailed explanation of past participles, see Chapter 14.

3. Steve's letter published in the *Miami Herald*.

    Rewrite: _____

4. My physics professor always forgetting the assignment.

    Rewrite: _____

5. You ever been to Hawaii?

    Rewrite: _____

PRACTICE 3   Fragments are most likely to occur in paragraphs or longer pieces of writing. Proofread the paragraph below for fragments; check for missing subjects, missing verbs, or incomplete verbs. Circle the number of every fragment; then write your corrections above the lines.

(1) On a routine day in 1946, a scientist at the Raytheon Company his hand into his pants pocket for a candy bar. (2) The chocolate, however, a messy, sticky mass of gunk. (3) Dr. Percy Spencer had been testing a magnetron tube. (4) Could the chocolate have melted from radiation leaking from the tube? (5) Spencer sent out for a bag of popcorn kernels. (6) Put the kernels near the tube. (7) Within minutes, corn popping wildly onto the lab floor. (8) Within a short time, Raytheon working on the development of the microwave oven. (9) Microwave cooking the first new method of preparing food since the discovery of fire more than a million years ago. (10) Was the first cooking technique that did not directly or indirectly apply fire to food.

PRACTICE 4   Proofread the paragraph below for fragments; check for missing subjects, missing verbs, or incomplete verbs. Try combining some sentences. Circle the number of every fragment; then write your corrections above the lines.

(1) The next time you about to toss an empty plastic bottle in a trash can, picture it floating in ocean waves. (2) Littered with plastic trash. (3) Plastic pollution in our oceans become a serious problem in recent years. (4) Every square mile of ocean now contains 46,000 pieces of floating plastic. (5) Like water bottles, margarine containers, six-pack rings, bottle caps, and plastic bags. (6) Some of this marine debris litters the world's beaches. (7) Even more drifts in the sea, where it will injure or kill millions of seabirds, sea turtles, fish, and marine mammals. (8) These creatures mistake it for food or get tangled up and slowly die. (9) Because plastic cannot biodegrade, it remains in the sea. (10) Breaking down

into smaller and smaller pieces full of dangerous chemicals. (11) These toxins may wind up in the fish dinner you order at your favorite seafood restaurant. (12) The next time you consider trashing some plastic, think for a moment and keep it for a recycling bin instead. (13) Even better, stop buying bottled water and other single-use plastic items. (14) One sturdy, refillable water bottle to significantly reduce plastic waste. (15) Take home your groceries in reusable cloth bags. (16) Instead of plastic bags. (17) Through reducing, reusing, and recycling plastics, our oceans cleaner and safer for all.

Eight billion new tons of trash litter Earth's oceans and beaches every year.

PRACTICE 5 **CRITICAL THINKING AND WRITING**

Plastic in our oceans has become a global threat to wildlife and, increasingly, human health. Over 30 billion plastic bags are used every year in the United States alone; less than 3 percent of them are recycled. Think about and answer the following question, in a group with several classmates if possible. If more people were educated about the horrible deaths of so many seabirds, fish, and mammals caused by plastic bags and objects, would they be motivated not to toss away plastic carelessly? If not, what can be done to reverse the damage to our oceans?

C. Completing the Thought

Can these ideas stand by themselves?

(1) Because oranges are rich in vitamin C.

(2) Although Sam is sleepy.

- These ideas have a subject and a verb (find them), but they cannot stand alone because you expect something else to follow.

- Because oranges are rich in vitamin C, *then what*? Should you *eat them*, *sell them*, or *make marmalade*?

- Although Sam is sleepy, what will he do? Will he *wash the dishes*, *walk the dog*, or *go to the gym*?

> (1) Because oranges are rich in vitamin C, *I eat one every day.*
>
> (2) Although Sam is sleepy, *he will work late tonight.*

- These sentences are now complete.

- Words like *because* and *although* make an idea incomplete unless another idea is added to complete the thought.

You will learn more about words like this, called *subordinating conjunctions*, in Chapter 18, but here is a list of the most common ones.*

Common Subordinating Conjunctions			
after	because	though	whenever
although	before	unless	where
as	if	until	whether
as if	since	when	while

Fragments often begin with these *subordinating conjunctions*. When you spot one of these words in your writing, check to make sure you have completed the thought.

PRACTICE 6   Make these fragments into sentences by adding some idea that completes the thought.

    EXAMPLE: Because I miss my family, _I am going home for the weekend._

1. As May stepped off the elevator, _____

2. If you are driving to Main Street, _____

3. While Kimi studied chemistry, _____

4. Because you believe in yourself, _____

5. Although spiders scare most people, _____

Can these ideas stand by themselves?

> (3) Graciela, who has a one-year-old daughter.
>
> (4) A course that I will always remember.
>
> (5) Vampire stories, which are popular now.

---

* For more work on this type of sentence, see Chapter 18, Subordination.

● In each of these examples, you expect something else to follow. Graciela, who has a one-year-old daughter, *is doing what*? Does she *attend town meetings, knit sweaters*, or *fly planes*?

● A course that I will always remember *is what*? The thought must be completed.

● Vampire stories, which are popular now, *do what*? The thought must be completed.

> (3) Graciela, who has a one-year-old daughter, *attends Gordon College.*
>
> (4) A course that I will always remember *is documentary filmmaking.*
>
> (5) Vampire stories, which are popular now, *exist in cultures all over the world.*

● These sentences are now complete.*

Try This   Try this "fragment test," which works for some people. Ask, "Is it true that . . ." followed by the test sentence:

Is it true that _The mango salad that you brought_____? **NO**

Is it true that _The mango salad that you brought is delicious_____? **YES**

If the answer is *no*, this is a fragment. If the answer is *yes*, the sentence is correct.

PRACTICE 7

Make these fragments into sentences by completing the thought.

EXAMPLE: Kent, who is a good friend of mine, _rarely writes to me._____

1. The horoscopes that appear on this app _____

2. Couples who never argue _____

3. Alonzo, who is a superb pole vaulter, _____

4. Satellite radio, which offers hundreds of channels, _____

5. A person who has coped with a great loss _____

6. My dog, which is the smartest animal alive, _____

PRACTICE 8

Proofread the paragraph below for fragments. Circle the number of every fragment, and then write your corrections above the lines.

(1) The word *meditate* might call to mind the image of a spiritual seeker. (2) Sitting for hours in a cross-legged pose. (3) According to psychologists, however, you practicing meditation any time you quiet your mind, focus on your breath, let thoughts and feelings occur without judging them, and ignore all distractions around you. (4) Engaging in this form of "mindfulness" for just five minutes a day can produce remarkable benefits. (5) Small

---

* For more work on this type of sentence, see Chapter 21, Part A.

daily doses of meditation can improve intellectual function. (6) Including concentration and memory. (7) In one study, a group that practiced mindfulness 20 minutes a day for four days performed significantly better on brain tests. (8) Than a group of people who did not meditate. (9) Meditation also shifts brain activity toward more positive emotional states. (10) Many people who meditate regularly. (11) Report a decrease in feelings of depression, anxiety, anger, and stress. (12) Finally, meditation appears to have beneficial physical effects. (13) Such as pain management, lower blood pressure, improved cardiovascular fitness, and a stronger immune system. (14) Try mindfulness meditation the next time you are sitting quietly—on the bus, in a waiting room, in the bathtub, or anywhere. (15) Sink into the present moment and come alive. (16) Body, mind, and spirit.

PRACTICE 9   Proofread the paragraph for fragments. Circle the number of every fragment, and then write your corrections above the lines.

(1) Ralph Gilles won fame as the designer of the Chrysler 300C. (2) Which earned many design awards. (3) Raised in Canada by Haitian parents, Gilles was in awe of his mother. (4) Because she gave her all to various thankless jobs and still told her children success stories. (5) When he was a boy. (6) Gilles loved to draw futuristic cars in his notebooks. (7) An aunt noticed his design gifts and urged him to write to Lee

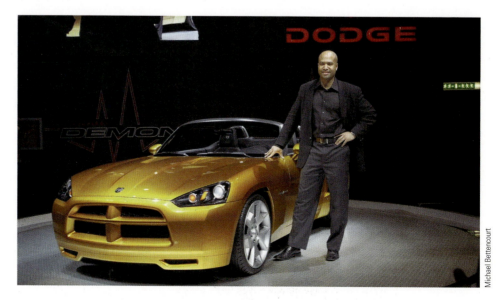

Ralph Gilles poses with the Dodge Demon concept car.

Iacocca.   (8) Who was then chairman of the Chrysler Corporation. (9) Amazingly, after the embarrassed fourteen-year-old sent a letter and some sketches. (10) An executive responded with encouragement. (11) And a list of colleges from which Chrysler hired designers. (12) Later Gilles took the advice, attended Detroit's College for Creative Studies, and landed his first job at Chrysler. (13) Talent and hard work earned him many promotions, the current title of head of global design for Fiat Chrysler Automobiles, and star status in the industry. (14) While Gilles is designing the next generation of vehicles. (15) He is also inspiring the next generation of young people. (16) He tells the kids who write him or attend his talks, "Dream out loud."

Chapter Highlights

A sentence fragment is an incomplete sentence because it lacks

- **a subject:**   Was buying a gold ring. (*incorrect*)
  Diamond Jim was buying a gold ring. (*correct*)

- **a verb:**   The basketball game Friday at noon. (*incorrect*)
  The basketball game *was played* Friday at noon. (*correct*)

- **a complete thought:**   While Teresa was swimming. (*incorrect*)
  While Teresa was swimming, she lost a contact lens. (*correct*)

  The woman who bought your car. (*incorrect*)
  The woman who bought your car is walking down the highway. (*correct*)

PROOFREADING STRATEGY

Sentence fragments are a serious error. To spot and correct them more easily in your writing, try the **bottom-up proofreading technique**. Start by reading the last sentence of your paper, slowly, word by word. Then read the second-to-last sentence, and so on, all the way from the "bottom to the top." For each sentence, ask:

1. Does this sentence have a *subject*, a *complete verb*, and express a *complete thought*?

2. Is this an incomplete thought beginning with a word like *because*, *although*, or *when*? If so, such fragments often can be fixed by connecting them to the sentence before or after.

3. Is this an incomplete thought containing *who*, *which*, or *that*? If so, such fragments often can be fixed by connecting them to the sentence before or after.

If sentence fragments are one of your error patterns, log them in your Personal Error Chart and proofread every paper once through just for fragments.

WRITING AND PROOFREADING ASSIGNMENT

Choose one of the sentences below that could begin a short story, working in a small group if possible.

1. Noah read the text message and ran to the wall safe.
2. A small black drone landed on the dock.
3. The boss's heels clicked down the hallway toward my pathetic cubicle.

Next, working individually, write a short story, starting with that sentence. First decide what type of story yours will be—science fiction, romance, action, comedy, murder mystery, and so on. As you write, be careful to avoid fragments, making sure each sentence has a subject and a complete verb—and expresses a complete thought. Now, re-read your paper carefully, using the bottom-up technique to check for fragments.

If you're working in a group, exchange papers and use the bottom-up technique to check each other's work for fragments. If time permits, read the papers aloud. Are you surprised by the different ways in which that first sentence was developed?

CHAPTER REVIEW

Circle the number of each fragment. Correct it in any way that makes sense, changing it into a separate idea or adding it to another sentence. You might try the bottom-up proofreading strategy.

A. (1) For years, the average American home just kept getting larger. (2) Doubling in size since 1950. (3) Recently, however, some people are buying or building "tiny houses." (4) A tiny house usually under 500 square feet. (5) With an emphasis on clever design instead of size. (6) It might feature folding furniture, storage stairs, a bathtub hidden under the sofa, hanging bookshelves, or a roof deck for parties. (7) Most tiny-house buyers are millennials or others under 50. (8) Who are willing to simplify quite radically. (9) They declare that their priority is experiences, not stuff. (10) They prefer to spend money on travel, education, or leisure. (11) Rather than a mortgage, high rent, and the debt of home ownership. (12) Tiny-house fans are often eco-friendly, wanting to reduce their pollution footprint. (13) Some tiny-house owners complain, however, that their homes feel just too cramped. (14) Causing physical and emotional stress.

B. (1) Many people seem to forget all about good manners. (2) When they use a cell phone. (3) They rudely allow the ringing phone to interrupt conversations, meetings, appointments, performances, and romantic dinner dates. (4) The ringtones, which range

"It keeps me from looking at my phone every two seconds."

from roaring motorcycles to mooing cows. (5) Blare out in classrooms and concert halls. (6) Many people even answer these calls in church or at funerals. (7) And then proceed to talk loudly. (8) Forcing others to listen or wait for them to finish talking. (9) Public relations consultant Carol Page, known as the "Miss Manners of Cell Phones." (10) Believes we can stop cell rudeness. (11) We should fix a "cell glare" on any cell phone user who is behaving badly. (12) If that doesn't work. (13) We can interrupt and gently ask if the phone conversation might be postponed. (14) Setting a good example when you use your own cell phone probably the best way to teach good cellular phone manners to others.

C.   (1) Ultrasound, or sonography, safely creates detailed pictures inside the human body. (2) With sound waves, not radiation. (3) These images help doctors visualize internal organs, blood vessels. (4) Or a baby developing in the womb. (5) The technician who performs sonograms is called a *diagnostic medical sonographer*. (6) This career is projected to grow by 24 percent through 2024. (7) Offering many job opportunities and salaries of $50,000 to $90,000 a year. (8) An excellent sonographer should possess good technical skills, a keen eye for detail, people skills, and writing ability to record test results clearly for the doctor. (9) An associate's or bachelor's degree is usually required. (10) Although some people earn their degree in a related field and then take a certificate program in diagnostic sonography.

(11) While this career can be physically demanding. (12) Job satisfaction is often high.

EXPLORING ONLINE

www.bls.gov/ooh

Visit this helpful career website, which describes the duties and future outlook for hundreds of professions. Choose one career that interests you, research it, take notes, and write a report on the pros and cons of the job for you.

D.   (1) These days, many people turn to multitasking. (2) Which is doing two or more things at once. (3) They think that this saves time. (4) Ironically, multitasking almost always takes longer. (5) Than completing each task separately. (6) Because each task requires attention, and switching attention back and forth takes extra time. (7) Even worse, multitasking is surprisingly dangerous. (8) Especially when one of the tasks is driving. (9) In laboratory studies with college students, students who simulated driving in a city and talking on a hands-free cell phone. (10) Crashed four times more often than other students. (11) An even more frightening study videotaped real truck drivers on the road. (12) Some of these truck drivers sent text messages as they drove. (13) Because they switched their attention back and forth from texting to driving. (14) Their reaction times were slow. (15) The texting drivers were an amazing 23 times more likely to crash. (16) Than other drivers.

E.   (1) Braille, which is a system of reading and writing now used by blind people all over the world. (2) Was invented by a 15-year-old French boy. (3) In 1824, when Louis Braille entered a school for the blind in Paris. (4) He found that the library had only 14 books for the blind. (5) These books used a system that he and the other blind students found hard to use. (6) Most of them just gave up. (7) Louis Braille devoted himself to finding a better way. (8) Working with the French army method called night writing. (9) He came up with a new system in 1829. (10) Although his classmates liked and used Braille. (11) It not widely accepted in England and the United States for another hundred years.

EXPLORING ONLINE

grammar.ccc.commnet.edu/grammar/quiz2/quizzes-to-fix/fragments_add2.html

Interactive quiz: Find the correct sentence in each group.

grammar.ccc.commnet.edu/grammar/quizzes/fragment_fixing.htm

Try your skills with this interactive fragment test.
Can you find and fix all the fragments?

Visit **MindTap** for *Grassroots* to access this chapter's ebook, flashcards, additional practice and quizzes, and more!

Writing Assignments

As you complete each writing assignment, remember to perform these steps:

- Write a clear, complete topic sentence.

- Use freewriting, brainstorming, or clustering to generate ideas for your paragraph, essay, or memo.

- Arrange your best ideas in a plan.

- Revise for support, unity, coherence, and exact language.

- Proofread for grammar, punctuation, and spelling errors.

WRITING ASSIGNMENT 1 *Plan to achieve a goal.* Did you know that nearly all successful people are good goal-planners? Choose a goal you would truly love to achieve, and write it down. Next, write down three to six smaller steps or targets that will lead you to your goal. Arrange these in time order. Have you left out any crucial steps? To inspire you and help you plan, reread "Target Practice: Setting Attainable Goals," Chapter 10 Review. You could also view the goal-planning tips from Oregon State University, scroll down, and click the printable Goal-Setting Worksheet at **success.oregonstate.edu/learning-corner/time-management/goal-setting**.

WRITING ASSIGNMENT 2 *Describe your place in the family.* Your psychology professor has asked you to write a brief description of your place in the family—as an only child, the youngest child, the middle child, or the oldest child. Did your place provide you with special privileges or lay special responsibilities on you? For instance, youngest children may be babied, whereas oldest children may be expected to act like parents. Does your place in the family have an effect on you as an adult? In your topic sentence, state what role your place in the family played in your development: *Being the _____ child in my family has made me _____.* Proofread for fragments.

WRITING ASSIGNMENT 3 *Write about someone who changed jobs.* Did you, someone you know, or someone you know about change jobs because of a new interest or love for something else? Describe the person's first job and feelings of job satisfaction (or lack of them). What happened to make the person want to make a job switch? How long did the switch take? Was it difficult or easy to accomplish? Describe the person's new job and feelings of job satisfaction (or lack of them). Proofread for fragments.

WRITING ASSIGNMENT 4 *Ask for a raise.* Compose a memo to a boss, real or imagined, attempting to persuade him or her to raise your pay. In your first sentence, state that you are asking for an increase. Be specific: note how the quality of your work, your extra hours, or any special projects you have been involved in have made the business run more smoothly or become more profitable. Do not sound vain, but do praise yourself honestly. Use the memo style shown here. Proofread for fragments.

MEMORANDUM

DATE:	Today's date
TO:	Your boss's name
FROM:	Your name
SUBJECT:	Salary Increase

Review

Proofreading and Revising

Proofread the following essay to eliminate all sentence fragments. Circle the number of every fragment. (You should find 10.) Then correct the fragments in any way you choose—by connecting them to a sentence before or after, by completing any incomplete verbs, and so on. Make your corrections above the lines.

Too Much Screen Time

(1) Children today are surrounded. (2) By screens. (3) Screens on laptops, computer tablets, smartphones, video games, and televisions all capture their attention. (4) Kids as young as two know how to access games, videos, and apps. (5) Some parents brag about their kids' educational gains. (6) While others just give in to temptation and use screens as babysitters. (7) Experts warn that too much screen time for kids under eight can be harmful.

(8) First, excessive time with electronic devices deprives kids of the kind of play that really does develop young brains and creativity. (9) According to child development experts, children learn best by interacting with people and things in the real world. (10) They need to move their bodies and manipulate objects. (11) Using all their senses and letting their imaginations run free. (12) They need to explore outdoors, ride bikes, build forts. (13) And dream up their own ways to play. (14) Even the most advanced educational apps and games cannot duplicate the brain-building effects of playing with real blocks, sticks, cardboard boxes, sand. (15) And other children.

(16) Second, too much screen time inhibits the development of relationships, social skills, and coping skills. (17) When children are absorbed in hours of solitary digital play. (18) They interact less with family, friends, and classmates. (19) This limits their opportunities to develop communication and conflict management skills. (20) Even worse, if parents give kids electronic gadgets to distract them from difficult emotions like boredom, grief, or frustration, children are robbed of chances to learn to cope with these feelings. (21) When a screen is always within reach. (22) A child may never learn to sit quietly and explore his or her own thoughts.

Jade and Bertrand Maitre/Flickr/Getty Images

Do you agree with experts that too much screen time can harm the development of children under eight?

(23) For all these reasons, the American Academy of Pediatrics recommends keeping children two and under away from any screens at all. (24) And limiting older children's screen time. (25) Experts urge parents to entice kids away from screens with time outdoors, trips to the playground, and toys that require imagination. (26) Such as dolls, Play-Doh, and musical instruments. (27) When it comes to raising happy, well-adjusted humans. (28) Screens are no substitute for old-fashioned play and personal interaction.

EXPLORING ONLINE

www.screenfree.org

Visit the website and read for ideas. Click "In Your Home" to plan a screen-free week in your home. Keep notes on any reactions or changes. Use these notes to write about the experience.

Writers' Workshop

Discuss an Event that Influenced You

Readers of a final draft can easily forget that they are reading the *end result* of someone else's writing process. The following paragraph is one student's response to the assignment *Write about an event in history that influenced you.*

In your class or group, read it aloud if possible. As you read, underline any words or lines that strike you as especially powerful.

Though the Vietnam War ended almost before I was born, it changed my life. My earliest memory is of my father. A grizzled Vietnam warrior who came back spat upon, with one less brother. He wore a big smile playing ball with my brother and me, but even then I felt the grin was a coverup. When the postwar reports were on, his face became despondent. What haunted his heart and mind, I could not know, but I tried in my childish way to reason with him. A simple "It'll be all right, Dad" would bring a bleak smirk to his face. When he was happy, I was happy. When he was down, I was down. Soon the fatherly horseplay stopped, and once-full bottles of liquor were empty. He was there in body. Yet not there. Finally, he was physically gone. Either working a sixty-hour week or out in the streets after a furious fight with my mother. Once they divorced, she moved us to another state. I never came to grips with the turmoil inside my father. I see him as an intricate puzzle, missing one piece. That piece is his humanity, tangled up in history and blown up by a C-19.

Brian Pereira, Student

1. How effective is Brian Pereira's paragraph?

   _____ Good topic sentence?　　　_____ Rich supporting details?

   _____ Logical organization?　　　_____ Effective conclusion?

2. Discuss your underlinings with the group or class. Did others underline the same parts? Explain why you feel particular words or details are effective. For instance, the strong words *bleak smirk* say so much about the father's hopeless mood and the distance between him and his young son.

3. The topic sentence says that the writer's life changed, yet the body of the paragraph speaks mostly about his troubled father. Does the body of the paragraph explain the topic sentence?

4. What order, if any, does this writer follow?

5. If you do not know what a "C-19" is in the last sentence, does that make the conclusion less effective for you?

6. Would you suggest any changes or revisions?

7. Proofread for grammar and spelling. Do you notice any error patterns (two or more errors of the same type) that this student should watch out for?

Brian Pereira's fine paragraph was the end result of a difficult writing process. Pereira describes his process this way:

> The floor in my room looked like a writer's battleground of crumpled papers. Before this topic was assigned, I had not the slightest idea that this influence even existed, much less knew what it was. I thought hard, started a sentence or two, and threw a smashed paper down in disgust, over and over again. After hours, I realized it—the event in history that influenced me was Vietnam, even though I was too young to remember it! That became my topic sentence.

Writing and Revising Ideas

1. Discuss an event that influenced you.

2. Choose your best recent paper and describe your own writing process—what you did well and not so well.

For help with writing your paragraph, see Chapter 3 and Chapter 4, Part A (see "Time Order"). Give yourself plenty of time to revise. Stick with it, trying to write the best possible paper. Pay special attention to fully supporting your topic with interesting facts and details.

Using Verbs Effectively

Every sentence contains at least one verb. Because verbs often are action words, they add interest and punch to any piece of writing. In this unit, you will

- Follow the MAP to better reading and writing

- Learn to use present, past, and other verb tenses correctly

- Learn when to add *-s* or *-ed*

- Recognize and use past participle forms

- Recognize *-ing* verbs, infinitives, and other special forms

- Learn proofreading strategies to find and correct your own errors

Follow the MAP to Better Reading and Writing

MODEL

Read this model paragraph, noticing how vividly the writer describes this solitary athlete and the court at dusk. His verbs are underlined.

Russell Thomas <u>places</u> the toe of his right sneaker one inch behind the three-point line. Inspecting the basket with a level gaze, he <u>bends</u> twice at the knees, <u>raises</u> the ball to shoot, then suddenly <u>looks</u> around. What <u>is</u> it? <u>Has</u> he <u>spotted</u> me, watching from the opposite end of the playground? No, something else <u>is</u> up. He <u>is</u> <u>lifting</u> his nose to the wind like a spaniel; he <u>appears</u> to be gauging air currents. Russell <u>waits</u> until the wind <u>settles</u>, bits of trash feathering lightly to the ground. Then he <u>sends</u> a twenty-five-foot jump shot arcing through the soft summer twilight. It <u>drops</u> without a sound through the dead center of the bare iron rim. So <u>does</u> the next one. So <u>does</u> the one after that. Alone in the gathering dusk, Russell <u>begins</u> to work the perimeter against imaginary defenders, unspooling jump shots from all points.

Darcy Frey, *The Last Shot*

ANALYSIS

- Simple but well-chosen *verbs* help bring this description to life. Which verbs most effectively help you see and experience the scene?

- Do you think that the writer realistically captures this young athlete at practice? What, if anything, do you learn about Russell Thomas—his abilities, personality, even his loves—from reading this short passage?

PRACTICE

- Write about a person practicing or performing some sport, art, or task.

- Write about a time when you watched or overheard someone in a public place.

CHAPTER 12

Present Tense (Agreement)

A: Defining Agreement

B: Troublesome Verbs in the Present Tense: TO BE, TO HAVE, TO DO (+ NOT)

C: Changing Subjects to Pronouns

D: Practice in Agreement

E: Special Problems in Agreement

A. Defining Agreement

A subject and a present tense verb **agree** if you use the correct form of the verb with each subject. The chart below shows which form of the verb to use for each kind of pronoun subject (we discuss other kinds of subjects later).

Verbs in the Present Tense
(example verb: to write)

Singular			Plural		
If the subject is	the verb is		If the subject is	the verb is	
1st person: I	write		1st person: we	write	
2nd person: you	write		2nd person: you	write	
3rd person: he she it	writes		3rd person: they	write	

PRACTICE 1   Fill in the correct present tense form of the verb.

1. You *ask* questions.
2. They *decide*.
3. I *remember*.

   1. He _____ questions.
   2. She _____.
   3. He _____.

4. They *wear* glasses.   4. She _____ glasses.

5. We *hope* so.   5. He _____ so.

6. I *laugh* often.   6. She _____ often.

7. We *study* daily.   7. He _____ daily.

8. He *amazes* me.   8. It _____ me.

Add -s or -es to a verb in the present tense only when the subject is *third person singular (he, she, it).*

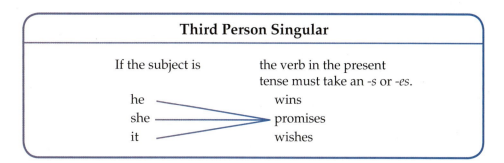

Third Person Singular

If the subject is   the verb in the present
                          tense must take an -s or -es.

he ——————————— wins
she ——————————— promises
it ——————————— wishes

PRACTICE 2

First, underline the subject (always a pronoun) in each sentence below. Then circle the correct verb form. REMEMBER: If the subject of the sentence is *he, she,* or *it* (third person singular), the verb must end in *-s* or *-es* to agree with the subject.

1. According to researcher Deborah Tannen, we sometimes (fail, fails) to understand how men and women communicate on the job.

2. When working together, they sometimes (differ, differs) in predictable ways.

3. In Tannen's book *Talking from 9 to 5: Women and Men at Work*, she (describe, describes) the following misunderstanding between Amy, a manager, and Donald, her employee.

4. She (read, reads) Donald's report and (find, finds) it unacceptable.

5. She (meet, meets) with him to discuss the necessary revisions.

6. To soften the blow, she (praise, praises) the report's strengths.

7. Then, she (go, goes) on to explain in detail the needed revisions.

8. The next day, he (submit, submits) a second draft with only tiny changes.

9. She (think, thinks) that Donald did not listen to her.

10. He (believe, believes) that Amy first liked his report, then changed her mind.

11. According to the author, they (represent, represents) different communication styles.

12. Like many women supervisors, she (criticize, criticizes) gently, adding positive comments to protect the other person's feelings.

13. Like many male employees, he (expect, expects) more direct—and to him, more honest—criticism.

14. Tannen says that both styles make sense, but they (cause, causes) confusion if not understood.

15. Stereotypes or truth? You (decide, decides) for yourself about the accuracy of Tannen's analysis.

B. Troublesome Verbs in the Present Tense: TO BE, TO HAVE, TO DO (+NOT)

A few present tense verbs are formed in special ways. The most common of these verbs are *to be*, *to have*, and *to do*.

Reference Chart: TO BE
(present tense)

	Singular			Plural	
	If the subject is	the verb is		If the subject is	the verb is
1st person:	I	am	1st person:	we	are
2nd person:	you	are	2nd person:	you	are
3rd person:	he / she / it	is	3rd person:	they	are

PRACTICE 3

Use the chart to fill in the present tense form of *to be* (*am*, *is*, *are*) that agrees with the subject.

1. She _____ a member of the Olympic softball team.

2. We _____ both carpenters, but he _____ more skilled than I am.

3. I _____ sorry about your accident; you _____ certainly unlucky with rollerblades.

4. They _____ salmon fishermen.

5. He _____ a gifted website designer.

6. I _____ too nervous to sleep because we _____ having an accounting exam tomorrow.

7. So you _____ the one we have heard so much about!

8. If it _____ sunny tomorrow, they _____ going hot-air ballooning.

Reference Chart: TO HAVE
(present tense)

	Singular			Plural	
	If the subject is	the verb is		If the subject is	the verb is
1st person:	I	have	1st person:	we	have
2nd person:	you	have	2nd person:	you	have
3rd person:	he / she / it	has	3rd person:	they	have

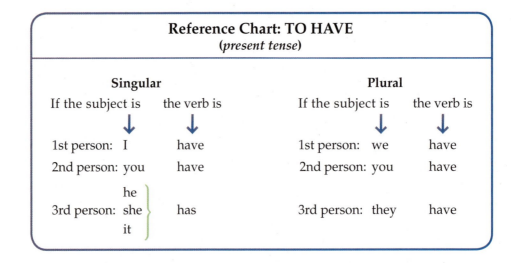

PRACTICE 4 Fill in the present tense form of *to have* (have, has) that agrees with the subject. Use the chart.

1. We _____ to taste these pickled mushrooms.
2. It _____ to be spring because the cherry trees _____ pink blossoms.
3. She _____ the questions, and he _____ the answers.
4. You _____ a suspicious look on your face, and I _____ to know why.
5. They _____ plans to build a fence, but we _____ plans to relax.
6. You _____ one ruby earring, and she _____ the other.
7. It _____ to be repaired, and I _____ just the person to do it for you.
8. If you _____ $50, they _____ an offer you can't refuse.

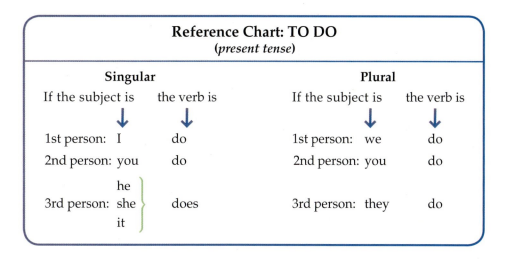

Reference Chart: TO DO
(*present tense*)

Singular		Plural	
If the subject is	the verb is	If the subject is	the verb is
1st person: I	do	1st person: we	do
2nd person: you	do	2nd person: you	do
3rd person: he she it	does	3rd person: they	do

PRACTICE 5 Use the chart to fill in the correct present tense form of *to do* (do, does).

1. She always _____ well in math courses.
2. I always _____ badly under pressure.
3. They most certainly _____ sell muscle shirts.
4. You _____ the nicest things for people!
5. If you _____ the dishes, I'll _____ the laundry.
6. He _____ seem sorry about forgetting your dog's birthday.
7. _____ they dance the tarantella?
8. _____ she want to be a welder?

To Do + Not

Once you know how to use *do* and *does*, you are ready for *don't* and *doesn't*.

$$do + not = don't$$
$$does + not = doesn't$$

PRACTICE 6 Fill in each blank with either *doesn't* or *don't*.

1. If they _____ turn down that music, I'm going to scream.
2. It just _____ make sense.
3. He _____ always lock his door at night.
4. We _____ mind the rain.
5. If she _____ stop calling so late, I _____ want to talk to her.
6. He _____ know the whole truth, and they _____ want to know.
7. Although you _____ like biking five miles a day to work, it _____ do your health any harm.
8. When I _____ try, I _____ succeed.

PRACTICE 7 **REVIEW**

As you read this paragraph, fill in the correct present tense form of *to be*, *to have*, or *to do* in each blank. Make sure all your verbs agree with their subjects.

(1) He _____ the expertise of an action hero, but he _____ a real-life member of the U.S. Navy SEALs. (2) After 35 weeks of brutal "adversity" training, he _____ whatever the mission requires. (3) Right now, he _____ calm although he _____ ready to leap from the open door of a Navy aircraft. (4) On his back, he _____ an oversized parachute capable of supporting both him and the extra hundred pounds of special equipment packed in his combat vest. (5) When he _____ hit the water, he _____ ready to face the real challenge: finding and defusing a bomb sixty feet under rough and frigid seas. (6) He _____ a mission and a tight time frame, and he _____ not want to let the enemy know he _____ there. (7) Swimming underwater in special scuba gear, he _____ not release any air bubbles to mark the water's surface. (8) Working in semidarkness, performing dangerous technical tasks, he quickly _____ the job. (9) However, unlike video-game heroes, he _____n't work alone. (10) It _____ precise teamwork for which the SEALs _____ famous. (11) Among the most respected special forces in the world, they _____ commando divers prepared for hazardous duty on sea, air, and land.

C. Changing Subjects to Pronouns

So far, you have worked on pronouns as subjects (*I, you, he, she, it, we, they*) and on how to make verbs agree with them. Often, however, the subject of a sentence is not a pronoun but a noun—like *dog, banjo, Ms. Callas, José and Robert, swimming* (as in *Swimming keeps me fit*).

To be sure that your verb agrees with your subject, *mentally* change the subject into a pronoun and then select the correct form of the verb. The chart below will show you how.

Reference Chart: Subject-Verb Agreement

If the subject is	it can be changed to the pronoun
1. the speaker himself or herself	I
2. masculine and singular (*Bill, one man*)	he
3. feminine and singular (*Sondra, a woman*)	she
4. neither masculine nor feminine and singular (a thing or an action) (*this pen, love, running*)	it
5. a group that includes the speaker (I) (*the family and I*)	we
6. a group of persons or things not including the speaker (*Jake and Wanda, several pens*)	they
7. the person or persons spoken to	you

PRACTICE 8 **REVIEW**

Change each subject into a pronoun. Then circle the present tense verb that agrees with that subject. (Use the Subject-Verb Agreement reference chart if you need to.)

EXAMPLES: Harry = __*he*__ Harry (whistle, (whistles)).

Sam and I = __*we*__ Sam and I ((walk), walks).

1. Camilla = _____ 1. Camilla (own, owns) a horse farm.

2. Their concert = _____ 2. Their concert (is, are) sold out.

3. You and Ron = _____ 3. You and Ron (seem, seems) exhausted.

4. The men and I = _____ 4. The men and I (repair, repairs) potholes.

5. This blender = _____

6. Folk dancing = _____

7. The museum and garden = _____

8. Aunt Lil and I = _____

5. This blender (grate, grates) cheese.

6. Folk dancing (is, are) our current passion.

7. The museum and garden (is, are) open.

8. Aunt Lil and I (like, likes) Swedish massages.

D. Practice in Agreement

PRACTICE 9   REVIEW

First identify the subject in each sentence. Then circle the correct verb, making sure it agrees with its subject.

Shark Tank: Entrepreneurs Get Their Shot

(1) *Shark Tank* (entertains, entertain) viewers, but this television show also (teaches, teach) valuable work and life lessons. (2) This combination (does, do) not occur often in reality TV. (3) On *Shark Tank*, hopeful entrepreneurs (presents, present) their products to "Sharks in the tank," five highly successful CEOs who (is, are) self-made millionaires or billionaires.

The Sharks seem amused by a contestant's new product.

Kelsey McNeal / Contributor/Getty Images

(4) They (includes, include) real-estate tycoon Barbara Corcoran, fashion guru Daymond John, and sports and Internet mogul Mark Cuban. (5) Contestants (tries, try) to convince one or more Sharks to invest in their companies and in them. (6) Each Shark (asks, ask) questions and (looks, look) for appealing presenters, good listeners, and money-making ideas. (7) If a contestant (has, have) a great product but (explains, explain) it poorly or (seems, seem) fuzzy on finances, he or she will not get a deal. (8) At home, viewers (guesses, guess) the outcome as contestants (reacts, react) to tough feedback.

(9) *Shark Tank* (differs, differ) from other reality shows because most contestants already (knows, know) their fields, whether smartphone apps, facial scrubs, or gym equipment. (10) Meeting top investors (tests, test) their ability to rise to the next level. (11) *Shark Tank* (exposes, expose) the complex realities of business ownership, and viewers (sees, see) how hard the owners (works, work). (12) To all career seekers, Shark Robert Herjavec (advises, advise), "A goal without a timeline is just a dream."

PRACTICE 10   REVIEW

In each blank, write the *present tense* form of one of the verbs from this list. Your sentences can be funny; just make sure that each verb agrees with each subject.

leap	spin	yip	woof	attend	win	compete
go	love	try	prance	wiggle	fly	encourage

(1) Dogs of every size and shape, their owners, and visitors all _____ the Great American Mutt Show. (2) Sponsored by Tails in Need, the Mutt Show _____ people to adopt mixed-breed dogs instead of buying pure breeds. (3) Pooches _____ in categories like Mostly Terrier, Most Misbehaved, Best Kisser, and Best Lap Dog Over 50 Pounds. (4) In one event, a shepherd mix named Top Gun _____ through the air to be crowned Best Jumper while a beagle named Jack _____ his stumpy tail, energetically claiming the coveted trophy for Best

Wag. (5) Four-legged hopefuls _____ and _____ trying to snag the

award for Best Bark. (6) The proud winner of Best in Show _____ home with a

trophy designed by Michael Graves—a red fire hydrant topped by a golden bone.

<table>
<tr><td>PRACTICE 11</td><td>**REVIEW**</td></tr>
</table>

The sentences that follow have singular subjects and verbs. To gain skill in verb agreement, rewrite each sentence, changing the subject from *singular* to *plural*. Then make sure the verb agrees with the new subject. Keep all verbs in the present tense.

> **EXAMPLE:** The train stops at Cold Spring.
>
> Rewrite: _The trains stop at Cold Spring._

1. The movie ticket costs too much.

   Rewrite: _____

2. The pipeline carries oil from Alaska.

   Rewrite: _____

3. A white horse grazes by the fence.

   Rewrite: _____

4. My brother knows American Sign Language.

   Rewrite: _____

5. The family needs good health insurance.

   Rewrite: _____

The sentences that follow have plural subjects and verbs. Rewrite each sentence, changing the subject from *plural* to *singular*. Then make sure the verb agrees with the new subject. Keep all verbs in the present tense.

6. The inmates watch *America's Most Wanted*.

   Rewrite: _____

7. Overhead, seagulls ride on the wind.

   Rewrite: _____

8. Good card players know when to bluff.

   Rewrite: _____

9. On Saturday, the pharmacists stay late.

   Rewrite: _____

10. The jewels from Bangkok are on display.

    Rewrite: _____

PRACTICE 12   REVIEW

This paragraph is written in the past tense. Rewrite it in the present tense by changing all the verbs. Write the present tense form of each verb above the lines. (Hint: You should change fourteen verbs.)

(1) At a rink in inner-city Chicago, two-year-old Shani Davis put on his first pair of roller skates. (2) Before long, he skated so fast that the rink guards chased him and warned him to slow down. (3) Then, at age six, Davis found ice skating, and the future star took off. (4) His mother recognized her son's gifts, moving the family to be near a speed-skating rink. (5) With his huge talent and a grueling work ethic, Davis became the first African American to join the U.S. Olympic speed-skating team. (6) Taller than other U.S. skaters, he bent low and held his upper body very still. (7) At the 2006 Winter Olympics in Turin, Italy, Davis scored a gold medal in the 1000-meter event and a silver in the 1500-meter. (8) In Vancouver in 2010, he did it again. (9) In 2016, the National Museum of African American History and Culture honored this ten-time Overall World Cup winner as a "game changer," alongside Muhammad Ali and Jackie Robinson. (10) Outside the rink, Shani Davis was a founder of ICE (Inner City Excellence), a skating program for urban children.

Speed skater Shani Davis flashes through the 1500-meter race, Nagano, Japan, 2016.

Atsushi Tomura - ISU/Getty Images

E. Special Problems in Agreement

So far, you have learned that if the subject of a sentence is third person singular (*he, she, it*) or a word like *Sasha, sister,* or *car* that mentally can be changed into *he, she,* or *it,* the verb takes *-s* or *-es* in the present tense.

In special cases, however, you will need to know more before you can make your verb agree with your subject.

Focusing on the Subject

> (1) A box of chocolates sits on the table.

- *What* sits on the table?

- Don't be confused by the prepositional phrase before the verb—*of chocolates.**

- Just one *box* sits on the table.

- *A box* is the subject. *A box* takes the third person singular verb—*sits.*

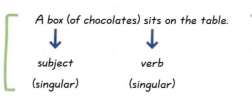

A box (of chocolates) sits on the table.

subject   verb

(singular)   (singular)

> (2) The children in the park play for hours.

- *Who* play for hours?

- Don't be confused by the prepositional phrase before the verb—*in the park.*

- *The children* play for hours.

- *The children* is the subject. *The children* takes the third person plural verb—*play.*

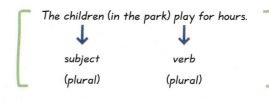

The children (in the park) play for hours.

subject   verb

(plural)   (plural)

> (3) The purpose of the exercises is to improve your spelling.

- *What* is to improve your spelling?

- Don't be confused by the prepositional phrase before the verb—*of the exercises.*

* For a detailed explanation of prepositional phrases, see Chapter 10, Part C, and Chapter 26.

- *The purpose is to improve your spelling.*

- *The purpose is the subject. The purpose takes the third person singular verb—is.*

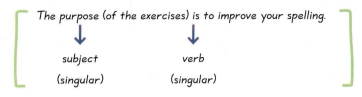

The purpose (of the exercises) is to improve your spelling.

subject   verb
(singular)   (singular)

As you can see from these examples, sometimes what seems to be the subject is really not the subject. Prepositional phrases (groups of words beginning with *of, in, at,* and so on) *cannot* contain the subject of a sentence. One way to find the subject of a sentence that contains a prepositional phrase is to ask yourself *what makes sense as the subject.*

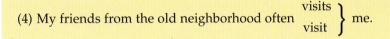

(4) My friends from the old neighborhood often { visits / visit } me.

- Which makes sense as the subject of the sentence: *my friends* or *the old neighborhood?*

(a) My friends . . . visit me.

(b) The old neighborhood . . . visits me.

- Obviously, sentence (a) makes sense; it clearly expresses the intention of the writer.

PRACTICE 13

In each of these sentences, cross out any confusing prepositional phrases, locate the subject, and then circle the correct verb.

1. Greetings around the world (differs, differ) from culture to culture.
2. A resident of the United States (shakes, shake) hands firmly to say hello.
3. Kisses on each cheek (is, are) customary greetings in Latin America and southern Europe.
4. Natives of Hawaii (hugs, hug) and (exchanges, exchange) breaths in a custom called *alo ha* (sharing of life breath).
5. The Maori people of New Zealand (presses, press) noses to greet each other.
6. A person in traditional Japanese circles (bows, bow) upon meeting someone.
7. A custom among Pakistanis (is, are) the *salaam*, bowing with the right hand on the forehead.
8. Hindus in India (folds, fold) the hands and (tilts, tilt) the head forward.
9. The Hindi word for the greeting (is, are) *namaste.*
10. This word (means, mean) "The divine in me (salutes, salute) the divine in you."

Spotting Special Singular Subjects

Either of the students
Neither of the students
Each of the students   } seems happy.
One of the students
Every one of the students

- *Either, neither, each, one,* and *every one* are the real subjects of these sentences.

- *Either, neither, each, one,* and *every one* are special singular subjects. They always take a singular verb.

- REMEMBER: The subject is never part of a prepositional phrase, so *of the students* cannot be the subject.

PRACTICE 14   Mentally cross out the prepositional phrases and then circle the correct verb.

1. One of the forks (is, are) missing.
2. Each of my brothers (wear, wears) cinnamon aftershave lotion.
3. Each of us (carry, carries) a snakebite kit.
4. Neither of those excuses (sound, sounds) believable.
5. One of the taxi drivers (see, sees) us.
6. Either of the watches (cost, costs) about $30.
7. Neither of those cities (is, are) the capital of Brazil.
8. One of the butlers (commit, commits) the crime, but which one?

PRACTICE 15   On a separate sheet of paper, write five sentences using the special singular subjects. Make sure your sentences are in the present tense.

Using THERE to Begin a Sentence

(1) *There* is a squirrel in the yard.
(2) *There* are two squirrels in the yard.

- Although sentences sometimes begin with *there*, *there* cannot be the subject of a sentence.

- Usually, the subject *follows* the verb in sentences that begin with *there*.

To find the real subject (so you will know how to make the verb agree), mentally drop the word *there* and rearrange the sentence to put the subject at the beginning.

(1) There is a squirrel in the yard.

becomes

A squirrel   *is in the yard.*
↓   ↓
subject   verb
(singular)   (singular)

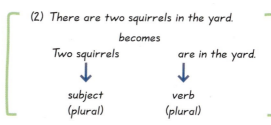

(2) *There are two squirrels in the yard.*

becomes

Two squirrels   *are in the yard.*

↓   ↓

subject   verb
(plural)   (plural)

BE CAREFUL: Good writers avoid using *there* to begin a sentence. Whenever possible, they write more directly: *Two squirrels are in the yard.*

PRACTICE 16   In each sentence, mentally drop the word *there* and rearrange the sentence to put the subject at the beginning. Then circle the verb that agrees with the subject of the sentence.

1. There (is, are) a daycare center on campus.

2. There (is, are) a scarecrow near the barn.

3. There (is, are) two scarecrows near the barn.

4. There (is, are) one good reason to quit this job—my supervisor.

5. There (is, are) six customers ahead of you.

6. There (is, are) a water fountain in the lounge.

7. There (is, are) a house and a barn in the wheat field.

8. There (is, are) only two shopping days left before my birthday.

PRACTICE 17   On paper or on a computer, rewrite each sentence in Practice 16 so that it does not begin with *there is* or *there are*. (You may add or change a word or two if you like.) Sentences (1) and (2) are done for you.

EXAMPLES: 1. *A daycare center is on campus.*

2. *A scarecrow hangs near the barn.*

Choosing the Correct Verb in Questions

(1) Where is Lucas?

(2) Where are Lucas and Jay?

(3) Why are they singing?

(4) Have you painted the hall yet?

- In questions, the subject usually *follows* the verb.
- In sentence (1), the subject is *Lucas*. *Lucas* takes the third person singular verb *is*.
- In sentence (2), the subject is *Lucas and Jay*. *Lucas and Jay* takes the third person plural verb *are*.
- What is the subject in sentence (3)? _____ What verb does it take?

  _____

- What is the subject in sentence (4)? _____ What verb does it take?

  _____

If you can't find the subject, mentally turn the question around:

(1) Lucas is . . .
(2) Lucas and Jay are . . .

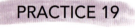

PRACTICE 18   Circle the correct verb.

1. Where (is, are) my leather bomber jacket?
2. (Have, Has) our waiter gone to lunch?
3. How (is, are) your children enjoying computer camp?
4. Who (is, are) those people on the fire escape?
5. Which (is, are) your day off?
6. Why (do, does) she want to buy another motorcycle?
7. (Have, Has) you considered taking a cruise next year?
8. Where (is, are) Don's income tax forms?

PRACTICE 19   On paper or on a computer, write five questions of your own. Make sure that your questions are in the present tense and that the verbs agree with the subjects.

Using WHO, WHICH, and THAT as Relative Pronouns

When you use a **relative pronoun**—*who, which,* or *that*—to introduce a dependent idea, make sure you choose the correct verb.*

(1) I know a woman *who* plays expert chess.

- Sentence (1) uses the singular verb *plays* because *who* relates or refers to *a woman* (singular).

(2) Suede coats, *which* stain easily, should not be worn in the rain.

- Sentence (2) uses the plural verb *stain* because *which* relates to the subject *suede coats* (plural).

_____

* For work on relative pronouns, see Chapter 21.

(3) Dishwashers *that* talk make me nervous.

- Sentence (3) uses the plural verb *talk* because *that* relates to what word?

_____

PRACTICE 20

Write the word that *who*, *which*, or *that* relates or refers to in the blank at the right; then circle the correct form of the verb.

EXAMPLE: I like people who (is, (are)) creative.   _____*people*_____

1. My office has a robot that (fetch, fetches) the mail.   _____
2. Never buy food in cans that (have, has) dents in them.   _____
3. My husband, who (take, takes) marvelous photographs, won the Nikon Prize.   _____
4. He likes women who (is, are) very ambitious.   _____
5. The old house, which (sit, sits) on a cliff above the sea, is called Balston Heights.   _____
6. Students who (love, loves) to read usually write well.   _____
7. I like a person who (think, thinks) for himself or herself.   _____
8. The only airline that (fly, flies) to Charlottesville is booked solid.   _____

PRACTICE 21

REVIEW

Proofread the following paragraph for a variety of verb agreement errors. First, locate the subject in each sentence. Then underline all present tense verbs and correct any errors above the lines.

(1) Many television viewers do not know Nina Tassler's name, but millions of them watches her hit shows every week. (2) President of CBS Entertainment from 2005 to 2015, she is the most powerful Latina in television. (3) Thanks to her ability to pick shows that audiences loves, CBS have the rank of most-watched TV network in America. (4) Tassler's successes include *The Big Bang Theory*, *NCIS*, and her first hit, *CSI*, which has three spinoffs and hold the record as one of the most successful TV franchises ever. (5) Tassler try to reflect social trends and concerns in her shows. (6) Appealing to frustrated employees everywhere, *Undercover Boss* show workers telling the truth to their bosses. (7) In *Mike and Molly* (with comedian Melissa McCarthy), the characters first meet at an Overeaters Anonymous meeting. (8) *The Good Wife* explores powerful women dealing with men who behaves badly. (9) Tassler believes in giving more women great roles, both as TV characters and as real-life executives.

Chapter Highlights

- **A subject and a present tense verb must agree.**

  The light flickers. (*singular subject, singular verb*)

  The lights flicker. (*plural subject, plural verb*)

- **Only third person singular subjects (*he, she, it*) take verbs ending in** *-s* **or** *-es.*

- **Three troublesome present tense verbs are** *to be, to have,* **and** *to do.*

- **When a prepositional phrase comes between a subject and a verb, the verb must agree with the subject.**

  The *chairs* on the porch *are* painted white.

- **The subjects** *either, neither, each, one,* **and** *every one* **are always singular.**

  Neither of the mechanics *repairs* transmissions.

- **In a sentence beginning with** *there is* **or** *there are,* **the subject follows the verb.**

  There are three *oysters* on your plate.

- **In questions, the subject usually follows the verb.**

  Where are *Kimi and Fred*?

- **Relative pronouns (*who, which,* and *that*) refer to the word with which the verb must agree.**

  A *woman who* has children must manage time skillfully.

PROOFREADING STRATEGY

If present tense verb agreement is one of your error patterns, you might **isolate and color code**. First, if you are writing on a computer, *isolate each sentence* on its own line. This will help your brain and eye focus on one sentence at a time. Next, find the subject and verb in each sentence; use highlighters to *color code* subjects yellow and verbs green. Cross out any confusing prepositional phrases.

Now check each color-coded pair for subject-verb agreement. (1) If you aren't sure, *change the subject to a pronoun*, and see if it agrees with the verb. (2) Do a final "audio check" and read the sentence aloud. Here are two examples:

it

The cafeteria ~~at my son's school~~ *serves* serve sweet-potato fries.

they want

Most parents wants the cafeteria to offer more fresh vegetables and fruits.

WRITING AND PROOFREADING ASSIGNMENT

In a group of three or four classmates, if possible, choose an area of the building or campus that contains some interesting action—the hallway, the cafeteria, or a playing field. Go there now and observe what you see, recording details and using verbs in the present tense. Choose as many dynamic action verbs as you can. Keep observing and writing for ten minutes. Then, write a first draft of a paragraph. Proofread for subject-verb agreement, using the strategy described above.

Next, exchange papers within your group. The reader should check for verb agreement and tell the writer what he or she liked about the writing and what could be improved.

CHAPTER REVIEW

Proofread this essay carefully for verb agreement. First, underline all present tense verbs. Then correct each verb agreement error.

Roadtrip to a Satisfying Career

(1) *Roadtrip Nation* is a documentary series on public television that aim to help people think about their career choices. (2) The program feature small teams of roadtrippers, ages eighteen to forty, that travels across the country in a van and interview career leaders they admires. (3) These leaders and role models, some famous and some not, represents a range of fascinating jobs. (4) Both the episodes and the *Roadtrip Nation* website is valuable resources for any job seeker or job changer.

(5) Each of the *Roadtrip* travel teams choose its role models, interviews them, and film the whole process. (6) The show emphasizes "meaningful conversations" between the career leaders and their interviewers, whose questions and comments inevitably raise key issues: "How do you handle your fear?" "How does you define success?" "My parents doesn't approve of my goals, but I want to please them." "Does hard work create passion?"

(7) The *Roadtrip Nation* website offer thousands of interview videos featuring information and career advice. (8) The "Explore" tab take you to videos classified by leader, interest, theme, and foundation. (9) It also connects to a personalized roadmap. (10) Clicking "All Leaders" bring up a long list of successful career men and women, including drummer Questlove, human rights attorney Brittan Heller, and Starbucks founder Howard Schultz. (11) Clicking "Interests" help you search by fields such as technology, entrepreneurship, sports, medicine, journalism, and more. (12) Clicking "Themes" let you search for words that feels right, like *determination, risk,* or *regrets,* while "Foundations" allow you to sort by type of organization. (13) Finally, "The Roadmap" customize your search by helping you to define your own career path.

EXPLORING ONLINE

roadtripnation.com

See whether the *Roadtrip Nation* website might be useful to your job search or interest. Click "Watch," "Explore," or "Participate" to see *Roadtrip Nation* TV shows (some free, some not), explore hundreds of interviews about real people's career journeys, or learn how to participate.

EXPLORING ONLINE

a4esl.org/q/j/kf/mc-svae.html

Interactive quiz: Test your verb agreement skills.

grammar.ccc.commnet.edu/grammar/quiz2/quizzes-to-fix/agreement_add3.html

This interactive quiz is a tricky one. Take the test and then view your score. Mark any mistakes on your Personal Error Pattern Chart.

Visit **MindTap** for *Grassroots* to access this chapter's ebook, flashcards, additional practice and quizzes, and more!

CHAPTER 13

Past Tense

A: Regular Verbs in the Past Tense

B: Irregular Verbs in the Past Tense

C: Troublesome Verb in the Past Tense: TO BE

D: Review

A. Regular Verbs in the Past Tense

Verbs in the past tense express actions that occurred in the past. The italicized words in the following sentences are verbs in the past tense.

> (1) They *noticed* a dent in the fender.
> (2) She *played* the guitar very well.
> (3) For years I *studied* yoga.

- What ending do all these verbs take? _____
- In general, what ending do you add to put a verb in the past tense? _____
- Verbs that add *-d* or *-ed* to form the past tense are called regular verbs.

PRACTICE 1

Some of the verbs in these sentences are in the present tense; others are in the past tense. Circle the verb in each sentence. Write *present* in the column at the right if the verb is in the present tense; write *past* if the verb is in the past tense.

1. Ricardo stroked his beard. _____
2. Light travels 186,000 miles in a second. _____
3. They donate blood every six months. _____
4. Magellan sailed around the world. _____
5. The lake looks as calm as glass. _____
6. Yesterday, Rover buried many bones. _____
7. Mount St. Helens erupted in 1980. _____
8. That chemical plant pollutes our water. _____
9. A robin nested in the mailbox. _____
10. He owns two exercise bikes. _____

PRACTICE 2 Change the verbs in this paragraph to past tense by writing the past tense form above each italicized verb.

(1) Again this year, Carnival *transforms* Rio de Janeiro, Brazil, into one of the most fantastic four-day parties on the planet. (2) On the Friday before Ash Wednesday, thousands of visitors *pour* into the city. (3) They *watch* all-night parades and *admire* the glittering costumes. (4) They *cheer, sweat,* and *dance* the samba. (5) Of course, preparation *starts* long before. (6) For months, members of the samba schools (neighborhood dance clubs) *plan* their floats, *practice* samba steps, and *stay* up for nights making their costumes. (7) Using bright fabrics, sequins, feathers, and chains, both men and women *create* spectacular outfits. (8) Each samba school *constructs* a float that *features* a smoke-breathing dragon or a spouting waterfall. (9) During Carnival, judges *rate* the schools on costumes, dancing, and floats, and then they *award* prizes. (10) Together, Brazilians and their visitors *share* great music, drink, food, fun, and the chance to go a little bit crazy.

As you can see from this exercise, many verbs form the past tense by adding either -d or -ed.

Furthermore, in the past tense, agreement is not a problem, except for the verb to be (see Part C of this chapter). This is because verbs in the past tense have only one form, no matter what the subject is.

PRACTICE 3 The verbs have been omitted from this paragraph. Choose verbs from the list below and write a past tense form in each blank space. Do not use any of the verbs twice.

arrive	cry	walk	help
install	climb	pound	learn
grab	hug	smile	work
paint	thank	shout	hurry

(1) Last month, Raoul and I _____ build a Habitat for Humanity house as part of our college's service learning program. (2) On the first day, we _____ at the construction site at dawn. (3) With three other volunteers, we _____ our hammers and _____ onto the roof. (4) We _____ nails for hours while other volunteers _____ the Sheetrock walls. (5) For three weeks, we _____ hard and _____ a lot about plumbing, wiring, and

interior finishes. (6) On our last day, the new homeowners _____ with joy and

_____ the whole crew.

PRACTICE 4   Fill in the past tense of each verb.

1. Erik Weihenmayer, blinded at age thirteen, _____ (dream) for years of climbing Mount Everest.

2. Mountaineers _____ (laugh) at the idea of a blind man scaling the world's tallest peak—a death trap of rock, wind, and cold.

3. But in 2001, Erik _____ (gather) a climbing team and _____ (start) the trek up Everest.

4. Before the climbers _____ (reach) the first of several camps on the way to the top, Erik _____ (slip) into a crevasse, but he _____ (survive).

5. When he finally _____ (stumble) into the first camp, weak and dehydrated, Erik _____ (wonder) whether he had made a serious mistake.

6. Nevertheless, he and his teammates _____ (vow) to continue the climb.

7. The group _____ (battle) upward through driving snow and icy winds.

8. Erik _____ (manage) to keep up and even _____ (edge) across the long, knife-blade ridge just below the peak, taking tiny steps and using his ice ax as an anchor.

9. Months after he began his journey, the blind mountaineer _____ (step) onto Everest's summit and _____ (stay) for ten minutes to savor his victory.

10. For many people around the world, this achievement _____ (symbolize) the nearly unstoppable human power to reach a goal.

Blind mountaineer Erik Weihenmayer successfully scaled Mount Everest.

Photo by Didrik Johnck

B. Irregular Verbs in the Past Tense

Instead of adding *-d* or *-ed*, some verbs form the past tense in other ways.

> (1) He *threw* a knuckleball.
> (2) She *gave* him a dollar.
> (3) He *rode* from his farm into the town.

- The italicized words in these sentences are also verbs in the past tense.

- Do these verbs form the past tense by adding *-d* or *-ed*? _____

- *Threw*, *gave*, and *rode* are the past tense of verbs that do not add *-d* or *-ed* to form the past tense.

- Verbs that do not add *-d* or *-ed* to form the past tense are called *irregular verbs*.

A chart listing common irregular verbs follows.

Reference Chart: Irregular Verbs

Simple Form	Past	Simple Form	Past
be	was, were	have	had
become	became	hear	heard
begin	began	hide	hid
blow	blew	hold	held
break	broke	hurt	hurt
bring	brought	keep	kept
build	built	know	knew
burst	burst	lay	laid
buy	bought	lead	led
catch	caught	leave	left
choose	chose	let	let
come	came	lie	lay
cut	cut	lose	lost
dive	dove (dived)	make	made
do	did	mean	meant
draw	drew	meet	met
drink	drank	pay	paid
drive	drove	put	put
eat	ate	quit	quit
fall	fell	read	read
feed	fed	ride	rode
feel	felt	ring	rang
fight	fought	rise	rose
find	found	run	ran
fly	flew	say	said
forget	forgot	see	saw
forgive	forgave	seek	sought
freeze	froze	sell	sold
get	got	send	sent
give	gave	set	set
go	went	shake	shook
grow	grew	shine	shone (shined)

Reference Chart: Irregular Verbs (*continued*)

Simple Form	Past	Simple Form	Past
shrink	shrank (shrunk)	take	took
sing	sang	teach	taught
sit	sat	tear	tore
sleep	slept	tell	told
speak	spoke	think	thought
spend	spent	throw	threw
spring	sprang	understand	understood
stand	stood	wake	woke
steal	stole	wear	wore
strike	struck	win	won
swim	swam	wind	wound
swing	swung	write	wrote

Learn the unfamiliar past tense forms by grouping together verbs that change from present tense to past tense in the same way. For example, some irregular verbs change *ow* in the present to *ew* in the past:

bl<u>ow</u>	bl<u>ew</u>	kn<u>ow</u>	kn<u>ew</u>
gr<u>ow</u>	gr<u>ew</u>	thr<u>ow</u>	thr<u>ew</u>

Another group changes from *i* in the present to *a* in the past:

beg<u>i</u>n	beg<u>a</u>n	s<u>i</u>ng	s<u>a</u>ng
dr<u>i</u>nk	dr<u>a</u>nk	spr<u>i</u>ng	spr<u>a</u>ng
r<u>i</u>ng	r<u>a</u>ng	sw<u>i</u>m	sw<u>a</u>m

As you write, refer to the chart. If you are unsure of the past tense form of a verb that is not in the chart, check a dictionary. For example, if you look up the verb *go* in the dictionary, you will find an entry like this:

go \ went \ gone \ going

The first word listed is used to form the *present* tense of the verb (I *go*, he *goes*, and so on). The second word is the *past* tense (I *went*, he *went*, and so on). The third word is the *past participle* (*gone*), and the last word is the *present participle* (*going*).

Some dictionaries list different forms only for irregular verbs. If no past tense is listed, you know that the verb is regular and that its past tense ends in *-d* or *-ed*.

PRACTICE 5

Circle the correct past tense form of each verb. If you aren't sure, check the chart.

(1) Emma (began, begun) her job search in an organized way. (2) She (thought, thinked) carefully about her interests and abilities. (3) She (spended, spent) time in the library and (readed, read) books like the latest edition of *What Color Is Your Parachute?* and *The Pathfinder: How to Choose or Change Your Career*. (4) On the library's computers, she (did, done) online research at sites like *Occupational Outlook Handbook* from the Bureau of Labor Statistics (**www.bls.gov/ooh/**). (5) To network, she (had, have) information-gathering interviews and (spoke, speaked) to people with jobs that appealed to her. (6) After Emma

(understanded, understood) her own goals, she (writed, wrote) a straightforward, one-page,
error-free résumé. (7) Her clear objective statement (telled, told) prospective employers
about her job preferences. (8) After listing her educational experience, she (gave, gived)
her past employment, with the most recent job first. (9) She (choosed, chose) lively action
verbs like *organized*, *filed*, *oversaw*, and *inspected* to describe her responsibilities at each
job. (10) Her references (was, were) four people who (knowed, knew) her work well. (11) At
last, Emma (felt, feeled) ready to create a *LinkedIn* profile and search for jobs online. (12)
She (put, putted) her résumé on *Monster.com* so that hundreds of companies would see
it. (13) Then, she (took, taked) a friend's good suggestion that they interview each other to
practice their skills. (14) A few days later, the phone (rang, ringed) and Emma (made, maked)
preparations for her first job interview.

PRACTICE 6   Look over the list of irregular verbs at the beginning of Part B. Pick out the ten verbs that
give you the most trouble and list them here.

Simple	**Past**	**Simple**	**Past**
_____	_____	_____	_____
_____	_____	_____	_____
_____	_____	_____	_____
_____	_____	_____	_____
_____	_____	_____	_____

Now, write one paragraph using *all ten* verbs. Your paragraph may be humorous;
just make sure your verbs are correct.

C. Troublesome Verb in the Past Tense: TO BE

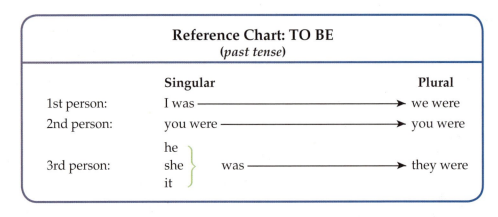

Reference Chart: TO BE
(past tense)

	Singular	**Plural**
1st person:	I was ──────────────────────→	we were
2nd person:	you were ────────────────────→	you were
3rd person:	he she } was ──────────────→ it	they were

- Note that the first and third person singular forms are the same—*was*.

PRACTICE 7   In each sentence, circle the correct past tense of the verb to be—either *was* or *were*.

1. Our instructor (was, were) a pilot and skydiver.
2. You always (was, were) a good friend.
3. Jorge Luis Borges (was, were) a great twentieth-century writer.
4. Why (was, were) they an hour early for the party?
5. I (was, were) seven when my sister (was, were) born.
6. Carmen (was, were) a Republican, but her cousins (was, were) Democrats.
7. The bride and groom (was, were) present, but where (was, were) the ring?
8. (Was, Were) you seasick on your new houseboat?
9. Either they (was, were) late, or she (was, were) early.
10. At this time last year, Sarni and I (was, were) in Egypt.

To Be + Not

Be careful of verb agreement if you use the past tense of *to be* with *not* as a contraction.

$$
\begin{array}{l}
was + not = wasn't \\
were + not = weren't
\end{array}
$$

PRACTICE 8   In each sentence, fill in the blank with either *wasn't* or *weren't*.

1. The wireless headphones _____ on sale.
2. That papaya _____ cheap.
3. He _____ happy about the opening of the nuclear power plant.
4. This fireplace _____ built properly.
5. The parents _____ willing to tolerate drug dealers near the school.
6. That _____ the point!
7. My pet lobster _____ in the aquarium.
8. That history quiz _____ so bad.
9. He and I liked each other, but we _____ able to agree about music.
10. Many young couples _____ able to afford homes.

D. Review

PRACTICE 9   **REVIEW**

All main verbs in this paragraph are underlined to help you spot them. Proofread the paragraph, checking every verb in this paragraph and correcting any past tense errors or incorrect verbs above the lines.

(1) Mohawk Indians <u>played</u> a major role in constructing American cities. (2) They <u>builded</u>

skyscrapers all over the United States and Canada, earning fame as skillful ironworkers.

(3) Almost 150 years ago, Mohawks first <u>began</u> to "walk high steel" when they <u>work</u> on a

Mohawk Indians and other ironworkers eat lunch on a beam during construction of Rockefeller Center. New York City, 1932.

bridge over the St. Lawrence River in Canada. (4) They <u>done</u> well at this dangerous job.

(5) Some people <u>sayed</u> that Mohawks <u>haved</u> no fear, but in fact they just <u>handled</u> their fear better than others. (6) Mohawk ironworking families <u>move</u> where the jobs <u>was</u>.

(7) They <u>putted</u> up the Sears Tower in Chicago (now the Willis Tower) and the San Francisco Bay Bridge. (8) In New York City, they proudly <u>taked</u> their place in history, working on the Chrysler Building, the Empire State Building, and the George Washington Bridge. (9) In the 1960s, the call <u>wented</u> out for ironworkers willing to climb the tallest buildings in the world.

(10) Five hundred Mohawks <u>signed</u> up to build the World Trade Center. (11) In 2001, after the Twin Towers <u>falled</u>, a new generation of Mohawk steelworkers <u>come</u> back to dismantle the twisted beams.

PRACTICE 10   REVIEW

This paragraph is written in the present tense. Underline every main verb. Then change the paragraph to the past tense by changing all the verbs, writing the past tense form of every verb above the lines.*

   (1) Above the office where I work is a karate studio. (2) Every day as I go through my email, make out invoices, and write letters, I hear loud shrieks and crashes from

———

* See also Chapter 27, "Consistent Tense," for more practice.

the studio above me. (3) All day long, the walls tremble, the ceiling shakes, and little pieces of plaster fall like snow onto my desk. (4) Sometimes, the noise does not bother me; at other times, I wear earplugs. (5) If I am in a very bad mood, I stand on my desk and pound out reggae rhythms on the ceiling with my shoe. (6) However, I appreciate one thing. (7) The job teaches me to concentrate no matter what.

Chapter Highlights

- **Regular verbs add** *-d* **or** *-ed* **to form the past tense.**

    We *decided*.

    The frog *jumped*.

    He *outfoxed* the fox.

- **Irregular verbs in the past tense change in irregular ways.**

    We *took* a marketing course.

    Owen *ran* fast.

    Jan *brought* pineapples.

- *To be* **is the only verb that takes more than one form in the past tense.**

    I *was*   we *were*

    you *were*   you *were*

    he

    she   } *was*   they *were*

    it

PROOFREADING STRATEGY

To proofread for past tense verb errors, especially if these are one of your error patterns, **highlight** and **read aloud**. First, read slowly through the text, underlining or highlighting the *main verb* in every sentence.

- Make sure that every *regular past tense verb* ends in *-d* or *-ed*.

- Carefully consider every *irregular past tense verb* to make sure it is in the correct form. If you aren't sure, check the past tense chart. Here are two examples:

    became

    The Civil War, which lasted from 1861 to 1865, become the deadliest war in

    died

    American history. Over 600,000 die in the conflict, a greater death toll than World War I and World War II together.

WRITING AND PROOFREADING ASSIGNMENT

With three or four classmates, invent a group fairy tale. Take five minutes to decide on a subject for your story. On a clean sheet of paper, the first student should write the first sentence—in the past tense, of course. Use vivid action verbs. Each student should write a sentence in turn until the fairy tale is finished.

Now proofread. Underline or highlight every main verb. Then have a group member read your story aloud. As you listen, make sure the verbs are correct. Should any verbs be replaced with livelier ones?

CHAPTER REVIEW

Proofread carefully for past tense verbs. Check every verb in this essay, correcting any past tense errors or incorrect verbs above the lines.

Homegrown Warrior

(1) Majora Carter growed up in a rough neighborhood of New York's South Bronx, and after college, she vowed never to return. (2) Like many inner-city areas, it was an industrial wasteland, with decaying buildings and gray air. (3) Soon, the expense of earning her master's degree bringed her back to live at her parents' house. (4) This twist of fate inspired an amazing career.

(5) Carter soon heard about plans to build yet another solid waste treatment plant in the South Bronx. (6) She and her neighbors discuss this pattern of dumping unwanted

Green roofs like this one in New York City reduce urban heat and pollution.

Reprinted with permission of Alyson Hurt and www.morethanthis.com

waste in poor communities and researched the toxic effects on health, especially asthma. (7) Angry and determined, Carter rallied the residents to fight. (8) Incredibly, they defeated the city's plan.

(9) Inspired by success, Carter seen how much more need to be done. (10) So in 2001, she founded Sustainable South Bronx (SSBx), an organization dedicated to community restoration and economic development. (11) The group assembled a workforce, built a park on the site of an old cement plant, and create green spaces like the "green roof." (12) Carter demonstrate how growing plants on city roofs cleans the air, cools buildings, provides healthy food, and reduces water pollution. (13) This idea catched on nationwide. (14) The changes winned new respect for SSBx, and artists and activists moved to the area.

(15) In 2005, at age 38, Majora Carter receive a MacArthur "Genius" Grant for vastly improving her community's quality of life. (16) Then her TED Talk help launch the inspiring *TED.com* website, which features videos of thought leaders. (17) In 2011, Carter's public radio series about people making a difference, The *Promised Land*, earned a prestigious Peabody Award. (18) In addition, Carter begun efforts to bring tech training and jobs into the South Bronx. (19) A career she never plan just kept growing.

EXPLORING ONLINE

grammar.ccc.commnet.edu/grammar/quizzes/chute.htm
Change present tense verbs to past tense in this passage from
a famous book.

www.manythings.org/wbg/verbs_past1-sw.html
Play the game! Try SpeedWord: see how many past
tense forms you can type before you time out.

Visit **MindTap** for *Grassroots* to access this chapter's ebook, flashcards, additional practice and
quizzes, and more!

CHAPTER 14

The Past Participle in Action

A: Past Participles of Regular Verbs

B: Past Participles of Irregular Verbs

C: Using the Present Perfect Tense

D: Using the Past Perfect Tense

E: Using the Passive Voice

F: Using Past Participles as Adjectives

A. Past Participles of Regular Verbs

Every verb has one form that can be combined with helping verbs like *has* and *have* to make verbs of more than one word. This form is called the **past participle**.

> (1) She has solved the problem.
>
> (2) I have solved the problem.
>
> (3) He had solved the problem already.

- Each of these sentences contains a two-part verb. Circle the first part, or *helping verb*, in each sentence, and write each helping verb in the blanks that follow:

    (1) _____

    (2) _____

    (3) _____

- Underline the second part, or *main verb*, in each sentence. This word, a form of the verb *to solve*, is the same in all three. Write it here: _____

- *Solved* is the past participle of *to solve*.

The past participle never changes, no matter what the subject is and no matter what the helping verb is.

Fill in the past participle in each series below:

Present Tense	Past Tense	Helping Verb + Past Participle
(1) Beth dances.	(1) Beth danced.	(1) Beth has _____.
(2) They decide.	(2) They decided.	(2) They have _____.
(3) He jumps.	(3) He jumped.	(3) He has _____.

● Are the verbs *to dance*, *to decide*, and *to jump* regular or irregular? _____ How do you know? _____

● What ending does each verb take in the past tense? _____

● Remember that any verb that forms its past tense by adding *-d* or *-ed* is a *regular* verb. What past participle ending does each verb take? _____

The past participle forms of regular verbs look exactly like the past tense forms. Both end in *-d* or *-ed*.

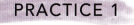

PRACTICE 1

The first sentence in each of these pairs contains a one-word verb in the past tense. Fill in the past participle of the same verb in the blank in the second sentence.

   EXAMPLE: She designed jewelry all her life.

   She has ____*designed*____ jewelry all her life.

1. Several students worked in the maternity ward.

   Several students have _____ in the maternity ward.

2. The pot of soup boiled over.

   The pot of soup has _____ over.

3. The chick hatched.

   The chick has _____.

4. We congratulated Jorge.

   We have _____ Jorge.

5. Nelson always studied in the bathtub.

   Nelson has always _____ in the bathtub.

PRACTICE 2 Write the missing two-part verb in each of the following sentences. Use the helping verb *has* or *have* and the past participle of the verb written in parentheses.

EXAMPLE: _____*Have*_____ you ever _____*wished*_____ (to wish) for a new name?

1. Some of us _____ _____ (to want) new names at one time or another.

2. Many famous people _____ _____ (to fulfill) that desire.

3. Some _____ _____ (to use) only one of their names.

4. Aubrey Drake Graham _____ _____ (to drop) everything but Drake.

5. Zendaya Maree Stoermer Coleman _____ _____ (to rename) herself Zendaya.

6. J Lo _____ _____ (to shorten) her name to a famous abbreviation.

7. Other celebrities _____ _____ (to abandon) all their birth names.

8. Changing three names, Peter Gene Hernandez _____ _____ (to turn) himself into Bruno Mars.

9. Replacing all her names, Stefani Joanne Angelina Germanotta _____ _____ (to transform) herself into Lady Gaga.

10. What new name would you _____ _____ (to pick) for yourself?

B. Past Participles of Irregular Verbs

Present Tense	Past Tense	Helping Verb + Past Participle
(1) He sees.	(1) He saw.	(1) He has seen.
(2) I take vitamins.	(2) I took vitamins.	(2) I have taken vitamins.
(3) We sing.	(3) We sang.	(3) We have sung.

- Are the verbs *to see*, *to take*, and *to sing* regular or irregular? _____

- Like all irregular verbs, *to see*, *to take*, and *to sing* do not add *-d* or *-ed* to show past tense.

- Most irregular verbs in the past tense are also irregular in the past participle—like *seen*, *taken*, and *sung*.

BE CAREFUL: Past participles must be used with helping verbs.*

Because irregular verbs change their spelling in irregular ways, there are no easy rules to explain these changes. Here is a list of some common irregular verbs.

_____
* For work on incomplete verbs, see Chapter 11, Part B.

Reference Chart: Irregular Verbs

Simple Form	Past	Past Participle
be	was, were	been
become	became	become
begin	began	begun
blow	blew	blown
break	broke	broken
bring	brought	brought
build	built	built
burst	burst	burst
buy	bought	bought
catch	caught	caught
choose	chose	chosen
come	came	come
cut	cut	cut
dive	dove (dived)	dived
do	did	done
draw	drew	drawn
drink	drank	drunk
drive	drove	driven
eat	ate	eaten
fall	fell	fallen
feed	fed	fed
feel	felt	felt
fight	fought	fought
find	found	found
fly	flew	flown
forget	forgot	forgotten
forgive	forgave	forgiven
freeze	froze	frozen
get	got	gotten (got)
give	gave	given
go	went	gone
grow	grew	grown
have	had	had
hear	heard	heard
hide	hid	hidden
hold	held	held
hurt	hurt	hurt
keep	kept	kept
know	knew	known
lay	laid	laid
lead	led	led
leave	left	left
let	let	let
lie	lay	lain

(continued)

Reference Chart: Irregular Verbs (*continued*)

Simple Form	Past	Past Participle
lose	lost	lost
make	made	made
mean	meant	meant
meet	met	met
pay	paid	paid
put	put	put
quit	quit	quit
read	read	read
ride	rode	ridden
ring	rang	rung
rise	rose	risen
run	ran	run
say	said	said
see	saw	seen
seek	sought	sought
sell	sold	sold
send	sent	sent
set	set	set
shake	shook	shaken
shine	shone (shined)	shone (shined)
shrink	shrank (shrunk)	shrunk
sing	sang	sung
sit	sat	sat
sleep	slept	slept
speak	spoke	spoken
spend	spent	spent
spring	sprang	sprung
stand	stood	stood
steal	stole	stolen
strike	struck	struck
swim	swam	swum
swing	swung	swung
take	took	taken
teach	taught	taught
tear	tore	torn
tell	told	told
think	thought	thought
throw	threw	thrown
understand	understood	understood
wake	woke (waked)	woken (waked)
wear	wore	worn
win	won	won
wind	wound	wound
write	wrote	written

You already know many of these past participle forms. One way to learn the unfamiliar ones is to group together verbs that change from the present tense to the past tense to the past participle in the same way. For example, some irregular verbs change from *ow* in the present to *ew* in the past to *own* in the past participle.

bl<u>ow</u>	bl<u>ew</u>	bl<u>own</u>
gr<u>ow</u>	gr<u>ew</u>	gr<u>own</u>
kn<u>ow</u>	kn<u>ew</u>	kn<u>own</u>
thr<u>ow</u>	thr<u>ew</u>	thr<u>own</u>

Another group changes from *i* in the present to *a* in the past to *u* in the past participle:

beg<u>i</u>n	beg<u>a</u>n	beg<u>u</u>n
dr<u>i</u>nk	dr<u>a</u>nk	dr<u>u</u>nk
r<u>i</u>ng	r<u>a</u>ng	r<u>u</u>ng
s<u>i</u>ng	s<u>a</u>ng	s<u>u</u>ng
spr<u>i</u>ng	spr<u>a</u>ng	spr<u>u</u>ng
sw<u>i</u>m	sw<u>a</u>m	sw<u>u</u>m

As you write, refer to the chart. If you are unsure of the past participle form of a verb that is not on the chart, check a dictionary. For example, if you look up the verb *see* in the dictionary, you will find an entry like this:

see \ saw \ seen \ seeing

The first word listed is the present tense form of the verb (I *see*, she *sees*, and so on). The second word listed is the past tense form (I *saw*, she *saw*, and so on). The third word is the past participle form (I *have seen*, she *has seen*, and so on), and the last word is the present participle form.

Some dictionaries list different forms only for irregular verbs. If no past tense or past participle form is listed, you know that the verb is regular and that its past participle ends in *-d* or *-ed*.

PRACTICE 3

Write the missing two-part verb in each of the following sentences. Use the helping verb *has* or *have* and the past participle of the verb in parentheses.

EXAMPLE: These drugs _have changed_ the world.

1. Since their discovery in 1927, antibiotics _____ (fight) serious bacterial infections like tuberculosis and pneumonia and _____ (make) humans healthier.

2. Overuse of these "miracle drugs" _____ (lead) to a medical crisis, however.

3. At the first sign of a child's runny nose, some parents _____ (run) to the clinic for antibiotics.

4. Doctors _____ (give) antibiotics to patients with colds or flu, conditions that antibiotics cannot help.

5. Worse, farmers _____ (feed) large doses of these drugs to poultry and animals, so the public _____ (take) antibiotics hidden in eggs, milk, and meat.

6. As a result, our bodies _____ (become) tolerant of these drugs, which then may not help us when we need them.

7. Now, some bacteria _____ (grow) into dangerous "superbugs" resistant to all known antibiotics.

8. The number of deaths from incurable infections _____ (rise) to 60,000 a year in the United States alone.

9. Fearing a deadly plague of superbugs, many doctors _____ (begin) to limit their antibiotic prescriptions.

10. Doctors like Sanjay Gupta _____ (tell) consumers, especially parents, to buy antibiotic-free eggs, milk, and meat if at all possible.

PRACTICE 4   REVIEW

For each verb in the chart that follows, fill in the present tense (third person singular form), the past tense, and the past participle. BE CAREFUL: Some of the verbs are regular, and some are irregular.

Simple	Present Tense (he, she, it)	Past Tense	Past Participle
know	knows	knew	known
catch			
stop			
break			
reach			
bring			
fly			
fall			
feel			
take			
go			

PRACTICE 5   REVIEW

Carefully proofread for verb errors in this essay, which contains both *regular* and *irregular* verbs. In every sentence, find and check any verbs containing a *helping verb* (*has* or *have*) and a *past participle*. Cross out the errors and make your corrections above the lines. Hint: sixteen verbs are incorrect.

EXAMPLES: Latin women have ~~achieve~~ *achieved* success in many fields.

The stereotyped Latina of TV and film ~~have~~ *has* begun to disappear.

Latinas Shatter the Glass Ceiling

(1) Many Latinas has broken through old stereotypes to forge successful careers. (2) They have enroll in college in record numbers and have rose in business, science, and the arts.

Latin American art expert Mari Carmen Ramirez discusses work by kinetic artist Carlos Cruz-Diez.

(3) Linda Alvarado, for instance, jokes that she have been mistaken for a cleaning lady and a secretary but never a powerful construction company CEO. (4) Born in New Mexico as one of six children, she grew up without indoor plumbing. (5) Alvarado has overcame prejudice and harassment in the male-dominated construction industry, and today Alvarado Construction has won national and international clients. (6) She has praise her parents for teaching her to keep working hard in the face of opposition.

(7) Another achiever, Ellen Ochoa, has flown to the stars as the first Latina astronaut. (8) She have always been good at science, earning a BS at San Diego State and then a MS and PhD at Stanford University. (9) Years of musical training has shown her that practice leads to excellence. (10) Ochoa has spend nine days in space aboard the shuttle *Discovery* and even played her flute in zero gravity. (11) Her fine work has earn her the title of director of the Johnson Space Center, and for inspiring younger people to explore science, she has have four schools named after her.

(12) Finally, one of *TIME* magazine's "25 Most Influential Hispanics in America," Mari Carmen Ramirez has help bring the world's attention to Latin American art. (13) Born in Puerto Rico and tired of Latin culture seeming invisible, she has brung to the United States a love of Latin American art and a refusal to be ignored. (14) With her keen eye, she has built a powerhouse collection of Latin American art at the Museum of Fine Arts,

Houston (MFAH). (15) Her bold shows have often ignore famous painters like Mexicans Frida Kahlo and Diego Rivera and instead have introduced unknown geniuses of painting, sculpture, and kinetic (moving) art, teaching art experts and the public to see with new eyes. (16) These Latina leaders have enrich Anglo culture and opened new doors for women to come.

PRACTICE 6   REVIEW

Check your work in the preceding exercises or have it checked. Do you see any *patterns* in your errors? Do you tend to miss regular or irregular verbs? To help yourself learn, copy all four forms of each verb that you missed into your notebook in a chart like the one that follows. Add specific mistakes to your Personal Error Patterns chart.

Personal Review Chart

Simple	Present Tense (he, she, it)	Past Tense	Past Participle
go	*goes*	*went*	*gone*

C. Using the Present Perfect Tense

The **present perfect tense** is composed of the present tense of *to have* (*has* or *have*) plus the past participle.

Present Perfect Tense

Singular	Plural
I *have* spoken	we *have* spoken
you *have* spoken	you *have* spoken
he	
she } *has* spoken	they *have* spoken
it	

Let us see how this tense is used.

(1) They *sang* together last Saturday.
(2) They *have sung* together for three years now.

● In sentence (1), the past tense verb *sang* tells us that they sang together on one occasion, Saturday, but are no longer singing together. The action began and ended in the past.

- In sentence (2), the present perfect verb *have sung* tells us something entirely different: that they have sung together in the past and *are still singing together now*.

> (3) Janet *sat* on the beach for three hours.
>
> (4) Valerie *has* just *sat* on the beach for three hours.

- Which woman is probably still sunburned? _____

- In sentence (3), Janet's action began and ended at some time in the past. Perhaps it was ten years ago that she sat on the beach.

- In (4), the present perfect verb *has sat* implies that although the action occurred in the past, it *has just happened*, and Valerie had better put some lotion on her sunburn *now*.

- Notice how the word *just* emphasizes that the action occurred very recently.

Use the *present perfect tense* to show either (1) that an action began in the past and has continued until now or (2) that an action has just happened.

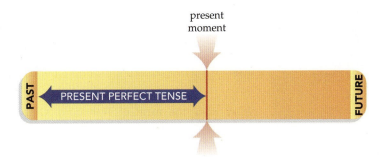

In writing about an action that began in the past and is still continuing, you will often use time words like *for* and *since*.

> (5) We have watched the fireworks *for* three hours.
>
> (6) John has sung in the choir *since* 2002.

In writing about an action that has just happened, you will often use words like *just*, *recently*, *already*, and *yet*.

> (7) I have *just* finished the novel.
>
> (8) They have *already* gone to the party.

PRACTICE 7   Paying close attention to meaning, circle the verb that best completes each sentence.

   EXAMPLES: Years ago, he (wanted, has wanted) to know how things worked. Since then, not much (changed, has changed).

   1. Even as a young boy in New York City, Dean Kamen (loved, has loved) science and invention.

2. While just a teenager, he (got, has gotten) the job of automating the Times Square ball drop for New Year's Eve.

3. Since that time, Kamen (invented, has invented) many amazing machines, including a stair-climbing wheelchair, a robotic scooter, and a small dialysis machine.

4. For several years now, he (lived and worked, has lived and worked) in a huge, six-sided house in New Hampshire.

5. Inside and out, the house (began, has begun) to look like a fabulous science museum.

6. The collection (expanded, has expanded) to include helicopters, a steam engine, a special Humvee, and a wind turbine.

7. Some years ago, Kamen (decided, has decided) to encourage children to enter science careers through FIRST (For Inspiration and Recognition of Science and Technology).

8. FIRST (helped, has helped) thousands of students and their mentors in hundreds of countries to build robots, compete, and grow as scientists.

9. In a speech, Kamen (said, has said), "Teenagers think they will become NBA stars and make millions, but their odds [of doing so] are less than 1 percent."

10. "However, many, many scientists and inventors (made, have made) big money and big contributions as well," he added. "Think about it."

PRACTICE 8   Fill in either the *past* tense or the *present perfect* tense form of each verb in parentheses.

(1) In 1976, the town of Twinsburg, Ohio, _____ (to begin) hosting a gathering of twins from around the world. (2) Every year since then, more and more twins _____ (to attend), wearing matching outfits, crazy hats, and posing for photographers. (3) Last year, 2,064 sets of twins from the United States, Africa, Europe, and South America _____ (to register) for Twins Days. (4) Over the years, fascinated tourists _____ (to double) the fun. (5) More important, the annual event _____ (to offer) scientists a rare research opportunity. (6) For example, researchers _____ (to study) identical twins (with identical genes) to see how DNA and environment affect diseases, hair loss, and even personality traits like shyness. (7) By the way, in the 1990s, researchers _____ (to find) that shyness is inherited. (8) Many twins _____ (to assist) scientists by standing in line for hours to answer questions, take tests, and donate their DNA. (9) The twins festival _____ (to afford) them the chance not only to meet other twins but also to contribute to human knowledge.

D. Using the Past Perfect Tense

The **past perfect tense** is composed of the past tense of *to have* (had) plus the past participle.

Past Perfect Tense	
Singular	**Plural**
I *had* spoken	we *had* spoken
you *had* spoken	you *had* spoken
he	
she } *had* spoken	they *had* spoken
it	

Let us see how this tense is used.

(1) Because Bob *had broken* his leg, he *wore* a cast for six months.

- The actions in both parts of this sentence occurred entirely in the past, but one occurred before the other.

- At some time in the past, Bob *wore* (past tense) a cast on the leg that he *had broken* (past perfect tense) at some time before that.

When you are writing in the past tense, use the *past perfect tense* to show that something happened at an even earlier time.

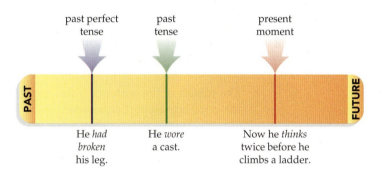

As a general rule, the present perfect tense is used in relation to the present tense, and the past perfect tense is used in relation to the past tense. Read the following pairs of sentences and note the time relation.

(2) Sid *says* (present) he *has found* (present perfect) a good job.

(3) Sid *said* (past) he *had found* (past perfect) a good job.

(4) Grace *tells* (present) us she *has won* (present perfect) first prize.

(5) Grace *told* (past) us she *had won* (past perfect) first prize.

PRACTICE 9 Choose either the present perfect or the past perfect tense of the verb in parentheses to complete each sentence. Match the present perfect tense with the present tense and the past perfect tense with the past tense.

1. The newspaper reports that the dictator _____ _____ (to leave) the country.

2. The newspaper reported that the dictator _____ _____ (to leave) the country.

3. I plan to buy a red convertible; I _____ _____ (to want) a convertible for three years now.

4. Last year, I bought a red convertible; I _____ _____ (to want) a convertible for three years before that.

5. Mel _____ _____ (to choose) the steepest trail up the mountain; he was thoroughly worn out.

6. Mel _____ _____ (to choose) the steepest trail up the mountain; he is thoroughly worn out.

7. I am worried about my cat; she _____ _____ (to drink) bubble bath.

8. I was worried about my cat; she _____ _____ (to drink) bubble bath.

E. Using the Passive Voice

So far in this chapter, you have combined the past participle with forms of *to have*. But the past participle can also be used with forms of *to be* (*am, is, are, was, were*).

> (1) That jam was made by Aunt Clara.

- The subject of the sentence is *that jam*. The verb has two parts: the helping verb *was* and the past participle *made*.

- Note that the subject, *that jam*, does not act but is acted on by the verb. *By Aunt Clara* tells us who performed the action.

> That jam *was made* by Aunt Clara.

When the subject is acted on or receives the action, it is passive, and the verb (*to be + past participle*) **is in the** *passive voice.*

Now compare the passive voice with the active voice in these pairs of sentences:

> (2) **Passive voice:** Free gifts are given by the bank.
> (3) **Active voice:** The bank gives free gifts.
>
> (4) **Passive voice:** We were photographed by a tourist.
> (5) **Active voice:** _____

- In sentence (2), the subject, *free gifts*, is passive; it receives the action. In sentence (3), *the bank* is active; it performs the action.

- Note the difference between the passive verb *are given* and the active verb *gives*.

- However, the tense of both sentences is the same. The passive verb *are given* is in the present tense, and so is the active verb *gives*.

- Rewrite sentence (4) in the active voice. Be sure to keep the same verb tense in the new sentence.

Write in the *passive voice* only when you want to emphasize the receiver of the action rather than the doer. Usually, however, write in the *active voice* because sentences in the active voice are livelier and more direct.

PRACTICE 10

Underline the verb in each sentence. In the blank to the right, write *A* if the verb is written in the active voice and *P* if the verb is in the passive voice.

> **EXAMPLE:**   The late Nelson Mandela is still <u>respected</u> worldwide as a leader.   ___*P*___

1. Nelson Mandela was born in South Africa on July 18, 1918, a member of the Xhosa tribe.   _____

2. Under the apartheid government, only whites, not the black majority, enjoyed basic rights.   _____

3. As a young lawyer, Mandela defended many black clients.   _____

4. They were charged with such crimes as "not owning land" or "living in the wrong area."   _____

5. Several times, Mandela was arrested for working with the African National Congress, a civil rights group.   _____

6. In 1961, he gave up his lifelong belief in nonviolence.   _____

7. Training guerrilla fighters, he was imprisoned again, this time with a life sentence.   _____

8. Twenty-seven years in jail did not break Mandela.   _____

9. Offered freedom to give up his beliefs, he said no.   _____

10. Finally released in 1990, this man became a symbol of hope for a new South Africa.   _____

11. In 1994, black and white South Africans lined up to vote in the first free elections.   _____

12. Gray-haired, iron-willed Nelson Mandela was elected president of his beloved country.   _____

PRACTICE 11

Whenever possible, write in the active, not the passive, voice. Rewrite each sentence, changing the verb from the passive to the active voice. Make all necessary verb and subject changes. Be sure to keep each sentence in the original tense.

> **EXAMPLE:**   Good medical care is deserved by all human beings.
>
> *All human beings deserve good medical care.*

1. Doctors Without Borders was created by a small group of French doctors in 1971.

_____

Doctors Without Borders provides urgently needed HIV-AIDS care at clinics like this one in Myanmar.

2. Excellent health care was provided by them to people in poor or isolated regions.

    _____

3. Soon they were joined by volunteer doctors and nurses from all over the world.

    _____

4. Today drugs and medical supplies are brought by the organization to people in need.

    _____

5. Vaccinations are received by children in eighty countries.

    _____

6. Crumbling hospitals and clinics are restored by volunteers.

    _____

7. Victims of wars also are treated by the DWB staff.

    _____

8. Information about humanitarian crises is gotten by the world.

    _____

9. Each year, thousands are given the gifts of health and life by these traveling experts.

    _____

F.   Using Past Participles as Adjectives

Sometimes a past participle is not a verb at all but an *adjective*, a word that describes a noun or pronoun.*

> (1) Jay is *married*.
>
> (2) The *broken* window looks terrible.
>
> (3) Two *tired* students slept in the hall.

———
*For more work on adjectives, see Chapter 25.

- In sentence (1), *married* is the past participle of the verb *to marry*, but here it is not a verb. Instead, it describes the subject, *Jay*.

- *Is* links the subject, *Jay*, with the descriptive word, *married*.

- In sentence (2), *broken* is the past participle form of *to break*, but it is used as an adjective to describe the noun *window*.

- In sentence (3), what past participle is an adjective? _____

- Which word does it describe? _____

Past participles like *married*, *broken*, and *tired* are often used as adjectives.

Some form of the verb *to be* usually links descriptive past participles with the subjects they describe, but here are a few other common linking verbs that you learned in Chapter 10, Part E.

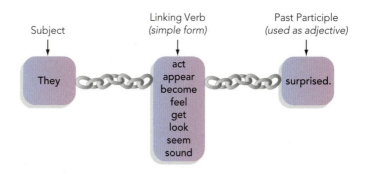

Subject	Linking Verb (simple form)	Past Participle (used as adjective)
They	act appear become feel get look seem sound	surprised.

PRACTICE 12   Underline the linking verb in each sentence. Then circle the descriptive past participle or participles that complete the sentences.

EXAMPLES: The window <u>was</u> (polish, (polished)).

Paolo <u>seems</u> very (worry, (worried)) these days.

1. This product is (guarantee, guaranteed) not to explode.

2. Nellie seems (qualify, qualified) for the job.

3. Your aunt appears (delight, delighted) to see you again.

4. After we read the chapter, we were still (confuse, confused).

5. The science laboratory is (air-condition, air-conditioned).

6. Dwayne feels (appreciate, appreciated) in his new job.

7. Did you know that one out of two American couples gets (divorce, divorced)?

8. We were (thrill, thrilled) to meet Venus and Serena Williams.

9. During the holidays, Paul feels (depress, depressed).

10. Are the potatoes (fry, fried), (bake, baked), or (boil, boiled)?

PRACTICE 13   Proofread the following website copy for past participle errors. First, underline all the past participles. Then make any corrections above the lines.

(1) Comic-Con International San Diego has grown into a thrilling annual event, attend

by nearly 150,000 fans and professionals in comics, film, and science fiction. (2) Visitors can explore floor booths on virtual reality or computer graphics, attend panel discussions with admire filmmakers, designers, and cartoonists, or just mingle with others who are interest in the same things. (3) Valued for its fun and creativity, Comic-Con can also be use as a job fair. (4) Job seekers are attracted by the chance to network in their fields, exchange business cards, or check out workplaces. (5) A game designer, for instance, might seek out companies and contacts with shared interests. (6) Cosplay, or costume play, has became a belove aspect of Comic-Con. (7) Motivated by their favorite heroes and villains, hundreds arrive dress as characters like Spider-Man, the Joker, Chewbacca from *Star Wars*, or Lady Sinestra from *World of Warcraft*. (8) Each character is outfitted, paint, and accessorize in detail. (9) Comic-Con San Diego is sometimes call the world's greatest geek gathering, but it has inspire even larger conventions, like Comiket in Tokyo, Japan; Gamescom in Cologne, Germany; Lucca Comics and Games in Lucca, Italy; and New York Comic Con.

PRACTICE 14

Combine each pair of short sentences. First, find and underline the past participle. Then rewrite the two short sentences as one smooth sentence, using the past participle as an adjective.

> **EXAMPLE:**   The book is lost. It is worth $1,000.
> *The lost book is worth $1,000.*

1. This rug has been dry-cleaned. It looks new.

   _____

2. His grades have fallen. He can bring them up.

   _____

3. The envelope was sealed. Harriet opened it.

   _____

4. The weather forecast was revised. It calls for sunshine.

   _____

5. These gold chains are overpriced. Do not buy them.

   _____

PRACTICE 15   The sentences in the left column are in the present tense; those in the right column are in the past tense. If the sentence is shown in the present tense on the left, write the sentence in the past tense on the right, and vice versa. REMEMBER: Only the *linking verb*, never the past participle, changes to show tense.

EXAMPLES: Smoking is forbidden.   *Smoking was forbidden.*

Lunches are served.   Lunches were served.

Present Tense	Past Tense
1. Your car is repaired.	1. _____
2. _____	2. The store looked closed.
3. _____	3. My feelings were hurt.
4. The seats are filled.	4. _____
5. She is relaxed.	5. _____
6. _____	6. You seemed qualified for the job.
7. He is supposed to meet us.*	7. _____
8. They are used to hard work.*	8. _____
9. _____	9. It was written in longhand.
10. You are expected at noon.	10. _____

Chapter Highlights

- **Past participles of regular verbs add** *-d* **or** *-ed,* **just like their past tense forms:**

Present	Past	Past Participle
decide	decided	decided
jump	jumped	jumped

- **Past participles of irregular verbs change in irregular ways:**

Present	Past	Past Participle
bring	brought	brought
see	saw	seen
take	took	taken

- **Past participles can combine with** *to have:*

    He *has edited* many articles for us. (*present perfect tense*)

    He *had edited* many articles for us. (*past perfect tense*)

---

* For more work on *supposed* and *used,* see Chapter 36, "Look-Alikes/Sound-Alikes."

> ■ **Past participles can combine with** *to be*:
>
>   The report *was edited* by Mary. (*passive voice*)
>
> ■ **Past participles can be used as adjectives:**
>
>   The *edited* report arrived today. (*adjective*)

PROOFREADING STRATEGY

If past participle problems are among your error patterns, read your draft one word at a time and **search for the helping verbs** *has, have, had, is, am, are, was,* **and** *were*. Every time you find a helping verb, highlight or underline it. If you are using a computer, use the *Find* feature to locate these words in your draft. Whenever these helping verbs are part of a past participle verb, **check the past participle form**. If it's a regular verb, it should end in *-d* or *-ed*. If it's an irregular verb and you aren't sure, check the verb chart. How should the writer correct the two incorrect past participles in these examples?

CORRECT   INCORRECT
I have registered for classes next semester, but I haven't yet buy my textbooks.
INCORRECT   CORRECT
The floor was stain a rich brown and polished to a high gloss.

WRITING AND PROOFREADING ASSIGNMENT

In a group of four or five classmates, write a wacky restaurant menu, using all the past participles that you can think of as adjectives: steamed fern roots, fried cherries, caramel-coated hamburgers, and so forth. Brainstorm. Get creative. Then arrange your menu in an order that makes sense (if that is the correct term for such a menu!). Don't forget to proofread.

CHAPTER REVIEW

Proofread this student's essay for past participle errors. Correct each error above the line.

Three Ways to Be a Smarter Learner

(1) Once in a great while, a person is born with a photographic memory, allowing him or her

to memorize a lot of information with almost no effort. (2) However, most of us have struggle

on our own to find the best ways to learn. (3) We have stayed up all night studying. (4) We

have mark up our textbooks, highlighting and underlining like skill tattoo artists. (5) Maybe, in

frustration, we have even questioned our own intelligence. (6) Although everyone has his or

her own learning style, three action steps have make me a better learner.

(7) The first step is simple—sit at the front of the class! (8) A student who has choose to sit up front is more likely to stay alert and involve and less likely to play with a smartphone. (9) By avoiding windows, talkative friends, and other distractions, many students discover that they take a greater interest in the classroom subject and take better notes. (10) An extra benefit of sitting up front is that teachers are often impress by students with whom they make eye contact, students whose behavior says, "I care about this class."

(11) Second, make a smart friend. (12) During the first week of class, exchange phone numbers with another front-row student. (13) You are looking for an intelligent, responsible classmate who seems committed to learning—not for a pizza buddy or a date. (14) Students who have agree in advance to help each other can call if they miss a class. (15) What was discuss that day? (16) Was homework assign or a test announced? (17) Two students who "click" might want to become study partners, meeting regularly to review material and prepare for tests.

(18) Third, ask questions. (19) The student who has sit up front, made a study friend, and pay close attention in class should not be worried about asking the professor questions. (20) Learning a subject is like building a tower. (21) Each new level of understanding must be build solidly on the level below. (22) If an important point or term is unclear, ask for help, in or after class.

(23) Students who take these steps will be rewarded with increase understanding and better grades—even before they have pull out their pastel highlighters.

Maurice Jabbar, Student

EXPLORING ONLINE

a4esl.org/q/j/ck/fb2-irregularverbs.html
Fill in the verb forms to test your past tense and past participle skills.

grammar.ccc.commnet.edu/grammar/quizzes/passive_quiz.htm
Ready, action! Revise the passive sentences in this interactive quiz, and make them active.

Visit **MindTap** for *Grassroots* to access this chapter's ebook, flashcards, additional practice and quizzes, and more!

CHAPTER 15

Progressive Tenses
(TO BE **+** -*ING* Verb Form)

A: Defining and Writing the Present Progressive Tense

B: Defining and Writing the Past Progressive Tense

C: Using the Progressive Tenses

D: Avoiding Incomplete Progressives

A. Defining and Writing the Present Progressive Tense

Verbs in the *present progressive tense* have two parts: the present tense form of *to be* (*am, is, are*) plus the *-ing* (or present participle) form of the main verb.

Present Progressive Tense *(example verb: to play)*	
Singular	**Plural**
I *am playing*	we *are playing*
you *are playing*	you *are playing*
he	
she ⎬ *is playing*	they *are playing*
it	

Compare the present tense with the present progressive tense below.

(1) Luria works at the bookstore.

(2) Luria is working at the bookstore.

- Sentence (1) is in the present tense. Which word tells you this? _____
- Sentence (2) is also in the present tense. Which word tells you this? _____
- Note that the main verb in sentence (2), *working*, has no tense. Only the helping verb *is* shows tense.

PRACTICE 1

Change each one-word present tense verb in the left-hand column to a two-part present progressive verb in the right-hand column. Do this by filling in the missing helping verb (*am, is,* or *are*).

EXAMPLES: I fly.   I _____*am*_____ flying.

He wears my sweater.   He _____*is*_____ wearing my sweater.

Present Tense	**Present Progressive Tense**
1. Elsa and I set goals together.	1. Elsa and I _____ setting goals together.
2. They eat quickly.	2. They _____ eating quickly.
3. He plans the wedding.	3. He _____ planning the wedding.
4. Our work begins to pay off.	4. Our work _____ beginning to pay off.
5. We pose for the photographer.	5. We _____ posing for the photographer.
6. Maryann smiles.	6. Maryann _____ smiling.
7. Sal does his Elvis impression.	7. Sal _____ doing his Elvis impression.
8. I speak Portuguese to Manuel.	8. I _____ speaking Portuguese to Manuel.
9. My grandson gets silly.	9. My grandson _____ getting silly.
10. You probably wonder why.	10. You _____ probably wondering why.

REMEMBER: **Every verb in the present progressive tense must have two parts: a helping verb (*am, is,* or *are*) and a main verb ending in *-ing*. The helping verb must agree with the subject.**

PRACTICE 2

Below are sentences in the regular present tense. Rewrite each one in the present progressive tense by changing the verb to *am* or *is*, and changing the form of the main verb to the *-ing* form.

EXAMPLE: We play cards.

We are playing cards.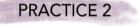

1. The cell phone rings.

_____

2. Dexter wrestles with his math homework.

_____

3. James and Sylvia work in the emergency room.

_____

4. I keep a journal of thoughts and observations.

_____

5. We polish all our old tools.

_____

B. Defining and Writing the Past Progressive Tense

Verbs in the *past progressive tense* have two parts: the past tense form of *to be* (*was* or *were*) plus the *-ing* form of the main verb.

Past Progressive Tense (*example verb: to play*)	
Singular	**Plural**
I *was playing*	we *were playing*
you *were playing*	you *were playing*
he	
she } *was playing*	they *were playing*
it	

Compare the past tense with the past progressive tense below.

(1) Larry worked at the bookstore.

(2) Larry was working at the bookstore.

- Sentence (1) is in the past tense. Which word tells you this? _____
- Sentence (2) is also in the past tense. Which word tells you this? _____
- Notice that the main verb in sentence (2), *working*, has no tense. Only the helping verb *was* shows tense.

PRACTICE 3

Change each one-word past tense verb in the left-hand column to a two-part past progressive verb in the right-hand column. Do this by filling in the missing helping verb (*was* or *were*).

EXAMPLES: I flew.   I ___*was*___ flying.

He wore my sweater.   He ___*was*___ wearing my sweater.

Past Tense	Past Progressive Tense
1. Elsa and I set goals together.	1. Elsa and I _____ setting goals together.
2. They ate quickly.	2. They _____ eating quickly.
3. He planned the wedding.	3. He _____ planning the wedding.
4. Our work began to pay off.	4. Our work _____ beginning to pay off.
5. We posed for the photographer.	5. We _____ posing for the photographer.
6. Maryann smiled.	6. Maryann _____ smiling.
7. Sal did his Elvis impression.	7. Sal _____ doing his Elvis impression.
8. I spoke Portuguese to Manuel.	8. I _____ speaking Portuguese to Manuel.

9. My grandson got silly.

9. My grandson _____ getting silly.

10. You probably wondered why.

10. You _____ probably wondering why.

PRACTICE 4

Below are sentences in the past tense. Rewrite each sentence in the past progressive tense by adding the helping verb *was* or *were* and changing the form of the main verb to the *-ing* form.

EXAMPLE: You cooked dinner.

You were cooking dinner.

1. The two linebackers growled at each other.

_____

2. Leroy examined his bank receipt.

_____

3. We watched the news.

_____

4. Mila read the *Wall Street Journal* online.

_____

5. He painted like a professional artist.

_____

C. Using the Progressive Tenses

As you read these sentences, do you hear the differences in meaning?

(1) Lenore *plays* the piano.

(2) Dave *is playing* the piano.

- Which person is definitely at the keyboard right now?
- If you said Dave, you are right. He is *now in the process of playing* the piano. Lenore, on the other hand, *does* play the piano; she may also paint, write novels, and play center field, but we do not know from the sentence what she *is doing right now*.
- The present progressive verb *is playing* tells us that the action is *in progress*.

  Here is another use of the present progressive tense:

(3) Tony *is coming* here later.

- The present progressive verb *is coming* shows *future* time: Tony is going to come here.

(4) Linda *washed* her hair last night.

(5) Linda *was washing* her hair when we arrived for the party.

- In sentence (4), *washed* implies a completed action.

- The past progressive verb in sentence (5) has a special meaning: that Linda was *in the process* of washing her hair when something else happened (we arrived).

- To say, "Linda *washed* her hair *when* we arrived for the party" means that first we arrived, and then Linda started washing her hair.

Writers in English use the progressive tenses *much less often* than the present tense and past tense. Use the progressive tense only when you want to emphasize that something is or was in the process of happening.

Use the *present progressive tense* (*am, is, are* + *-ing*) **to show that an action is in progress now or that it is going to occur in the future.**

Use the *past progressive tense* (*was, were* + *-ing*) **to show that an action was in progress at a certain time in the past.**

PRACTICE 5   Read each sentence carefully. Then circle the verb or verbs that best express the meaning of the sentence.

> **EXAMPLE:**   Right now, we (write, are writing) letters.

1. Thomas Edison (held, was holding) 1,093 patents.

2. Where is Ellen? She (drives, is driving) to Omaha.

3. Most mornings we (get, are getting) up at seven.

4. Believe it or not, I (thought, was thinking) about you when you phoned.

5. My dog Gourmand (eats, is eating) anything.

6. At this very moment, Gourmand (eats, is eating) the sports page.

7. Max (fried, was frying) onions when the smoke alarm (went, was going) off.

8. Please don't bother me now; I (study, am studying).

9. Newton (sat, was sitting) under a tree when he (discovered, was discovering) gravity.

10. The *Andrea Doria*, a huge pleasure ship, (sank, was sinking) on July 25, 1956.

D. Avoiding Incomplete Progressives

Now that you can write both present and past progressive verbs, avoid mistakes like this one:

> We having fun. (*incomplete*)

- Can you see what is missing?

- All by itself, the *-ing* form *having* is not a verb. It has to have a helping verb.

- Because the helping verb is missing, *we having fun* has no time. It could mean *we are having fun* or *we were having fun*.
- *We having fun* is not complete. It is a fragment of a sentence.*

PRACTICE 6   Each group of words below is an incomplete sentence. Put an *X* over the exact spot where a word is missing. Then, in the Present Progressive column, write the word that would complete the sentence in the *present progressive tense*. In the Past Progressive column, write the word that would complete the sentence in the *past progressive tense*.

	Present Progressive	**Past Progressive**
EXAMPLE: Ẋ He having fun.	*is*	*was*
	(He is having fun.)	(He was having fun.)
1. Fran and I watching the sunrise.	_____	_____
2. You taking a computer course.	_____	_____
3. A big log floating down the river.	_____	_____
4. Her study skills improving.	_____	_____
5. I trying to give up caffeine.	_____	_____
6. Fights about money getting me down.	_____	_____
7. Thick fog blanketing the city.	_____	_____
8. That child reading already.	_____	_____
9. Your pizza getting cold.	_____	_____
10. They discussing the terms of the new contract.	_____	_____

Chapter Highlights

- **The progressive tenses combine *to be* with the *-ing* verb form:**

    present progressive tense: I *am reading.* He *is reading.*

    past progressive tense: I *was reading.* He *was reading.*

- **The *-ing* verb form must have a helping verb to be complete:**

    She playing the tuba. (*incorrect*)

    She *is playing* the tuba. (*correct*)

- **The present progressive tense shows that an action is in progress now:**

    Aunt Belle *is waxing* her van.

- **The present progressive tense can also show that an action will take place in the future:**

    Later today, Aunt Belle *is driving* us to the movies.

- **The past progressive tense shows that an action was in progress at a certain time in the past:**

    Aunt Belle *was waxing* her van when she heard thunder.

---

* For more on this type of fragment, see Chapter 11, Part B.

PROOFREADING STRATEGY

If you make progressive tense errors, you are probably leaving out one of the verb's two parts: either the helping verb (*am, is, are, was,* or *were*) or the main verb ending in *-ing*.

First, check for sentences in which the verb needs to express ongoing, continuous action. **Underline or highlight** those verbs and make sure that the **main verb ends in** *-ing*.

CORRECT   INCORRECT

The clock was striking midnight, but they still moving furniture into the house.

Then, check the helping verb. If the **helping verb** is missing, add one, making sure that it **agrees** with the subject of the sentence.

were

The clock was striking midnight, but they still moving furniture into the house.

WRITING AND PROOFREADING ASSIGNMENT

Write a brief account that begins, "We are watching an amazing scene on TV. A man/woman/child/couple/group/animal is trying to _____." Fill in the blank, and then write four or five more sentences describing the unfolding action in the *present progressive* tense—as if the action is taking place right now. Now carefully proofread what you have written, checking the verbs.

Now rewrite the whole account in the *past progressive* tense. The new version will begin, "We were watching an amazing scene on TV. A man/woman/child/couple/group/animal was trying to _____."

CHAPTER REVIEW

Proofread this paragraph for incomplete progressive verbs. Write the missing verbs above the lines.

(1) The sluggish economy prompting many people to seek new career directions.

(2) They hoping to find jobs with bright futures. (3) By checking trusted sources like the U.S.

Bureau of Labor Statistics at **www.bls.gov/ooh,** job-seekers learning about opportunities

in growth fields like health care. (4) People always need doctors, nurses, and other medical

professionals to help them stay healthy, but now, as baby boomers are aging, many jobs

in the health sciences experiencing higher than average growth. (5) Some of these require

only a two-year degree. (6) One example is the position of dental hygienist. (7) After they

pass biology, science, and other courses, dental hygienists earn an associate's degree and

must pass a certification exam. (8) Then they work in dentists' offices, cleaning patients'

teeth and teaching them how to maintain oral health. (9) A typical full-time dental hygienist now earning an annual income of about $60,000 or less in some areas. (10) The number of positions will likely increase by 36 percent before 2018, so economists predicting excellent employment opportunities for these technicians.

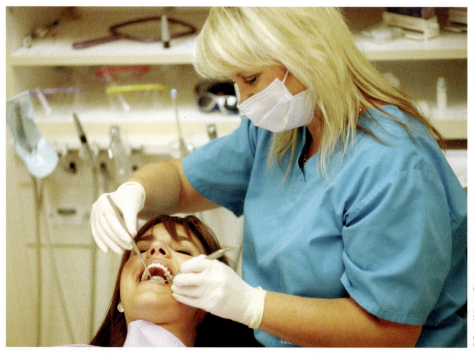

Excellent employment opportunities exist for dental hygienists and other medical professionals.

© Tracy Whiteside/Shutterstock.com

EXPLORING ONLINE

a4esl.org/q/h/vm/sp_or_pc.html

Read each sentence, aloud, if possible. Say the correct verb form. Then click to check your answer.

www.grammar.cl/Games/Present_vs_Progressive.htm

Present tense or present progressive? Choose the one that works best in each sentence as the game clock totals your points.

Visit **MindTap** for *Grassroots* to access this chapter's ebook, flashcards, additional practice and quizzes, and more!

CHAPTER 16

Fixed-Form Helping Verbs and Verb Problems

A: Defining and Spotting the Fixed-Form Helping Verbs

B: Using the Fixed-Form Helping Verbs

C: Using CAN and COULD

D: Using WILL and WOULD

E: Writing Infinitives

F: Revising Double Negatives

A. Defining and Spotting the Fixed-Form Helping Verbs

You already know the common—and changeable—helping verbs: *to have, to do,* and *to be.* Here are some helping verbs that do not change:

Fixed-Form Helping Verbs	
can	could
will	would
may	might
shall	should
must	

The fixed-form helping verbs do not change, no matter what the subject is. They always keep the same form.

PRACTICE 1   Fill in each blank with a fixed-form helping verb.

1. You _____ do it!

2. This _____ be the most exciting presidential debate ever held.

3. I _____ row while you watch for crocodiles.

4. Rico _____ go to medical school.

5. In South America, the elephant beetle _____ grow to twelve inches in length.

6. If the committee _____ meet today, we _____ have a new budget on time.

7. We _____ rotate the crops this season.

8. Violent films _____ cause children to act out violently.

9. You _____ have no difficulty finding a sales position.

10. Janice _____ teach users to do research on the Internet.

B.   Using the Fixed-Form Helping Verbs

> (1) Al will stay with us this summer.
>
> (2) Harper can shoot a rifle well.

- *Will* is the fixed-form helping verb in sentence (1). What main verb does it help? _____

- *Can* is the fixed-form helping verb in sentence (2). What main verb does it help? _____

- Notice that *stay* and *shoot* are the simple forms of the verbs. They do not show tense by themselves.

When a verb has two parts—a fixed-form helping verb and a main verb—the main verb keeps its simple form.

PRACTICE 2   In the left column, each sentence contains a verb made up of some form of *to have* (the changeable helping verb) and a past participle (the main verb).

Each sentence in the right column contains a fixed-form helping verb and a blank. Write the form of the main verb from the left column that correctly completes each sentence.

Have + Past Participle	Fixed-Form Helping Verb + Simple Form
EXAMPLES:	
I have talked to him.	I may ___*talk*___ to him.
She has flown to Ireland.	She will ___*fly*___ to Ireland.
1. Irena has written a song.	1. Irena must _____ a song.
2. We have begun.	2. We can _____.
3. Joy has visited Graceland.	3. Joy will _____ Graceland.
4. He has slept all day.	4. He could _____ all day.
5. I have run three miles.	5. I will _____ three miles.

6. We have seen an eclipse.

7. It has drizzled.

8. Avery has gone on vacation.

9. Has he studied?

10. Della has been promoted.

6. We might _____ an eclipse.

7. It may _____.

8. Avery could _____ on vacation.

9. Should he _____?

10. Della might _____ promoted.

C. Using CAN and COULD

(1) He says that I *can* use any tools in his garage.

(2) He said that I *could* use any tools in his garage.

- What is the tense of sentence (1)? _____
- What is the tense of sentence (2)? _____
- What is the helping verb in sentence (1)? _____
- What is the helping verb in sentence (2)? _____
- As you can see, *could* may be used as the past tense of *can*.

Present tense: Today, I *can* touch my toes.

Past tense: Yesterday, I *could* touch my toes.

Can means *am/is/are able*. **It may be used to show present tense.**

Could means *was/were able* **when it is used to show the past tense of** *can*.

(3) If I went on a diet, I *could* touch my toes.

(4) Rod wishes he *could* touch his toes.

- In sentence (3), the speaker *could* touch his toes *if* . . . . Touching his toes is a possibility, not a certainty.
- In sentence (4), Rod *wishes* he *could* touch his toes, but probably he cannot. Touching his toes is a wish, not a certainty.

Could **also means** *might be able*, **a possibility, a wish, or a request.**

PRACTICE 3

Fill in the helper *can* or the helper *could*, whichever is needed. To determine whether the sentence indicates the present or the past, look at the other verbs in the sentence or look for words like *now* and *yesterday*.

1. When I am rested, I _____ study for hours.

2. When I was rested, I _____ study for hours.

3. Jorge insists that he _____ play the trumpet.

4. Jorge insisted that he _____ play the trumpet.

5. A year ago, Zora _____ jog for only five minutes at a time.

6. Now Zora _____ jog for nearly an hour at a time.

7. If you're so smart, how come you _____ never find your own socks?

8. If you were so smart, how come you _____ never find your own socks?

9. When the air was clear, you _____ see the next town.

10. When the air is clear, you _____ see the next town.

PRACTICE 4

Circle either *can* or *could*.

1. Hilaria thinks that she (can, could) carry a tune.

2. Yesterday, we (can, could) not go to the town meeting.

3. I wish I (can, could) pitch like Johan Santana.

4. You should meet Naveed: he (can, could) lift a two-hundred-pound weight.

5. Everyone I meet (can, could) do a cartwheel.

6. Until the party, everyone thought that Harry (can, could) cook.

7. She (can, could) ice skate better now than she (can, could) last year.

8. On the night that Smithers disappeared, the butler (can, could) not be found.

9. When my brother was younger, he (can, could) name every car on the road.

10. I hope that the snow leopards (can, could) survive in captivity.

PRACTICE 5

On a separate paper, write five sentences using *can* to show present tense and five sentences using *could* to show past tense.

D. Using WILL and WOULD

> (1) You know you *will* do well in that class.
>
> (2) You knew you *would* do well in that class.

- Sentence (1) says that *you know* now (present tense) that you *will* do well in the future. *Will* points to the future from the present.
- Sentence (2) says that *you knew* then (past tense) that you *would* do well after that. *Would* points to the future from the past.

Would **may be used as the past tense of** *will*, **just as** *could* **may be used as the past tense of** *can*.

> (3) *If* you studied, you *would* pass physics.
>
> (4) Juanita wishes she *would* get an A in French.

- In sentence (3), the speaker *would* pass physics *if* . . . . Passing physics is a possibility, not a certainty.

• In sentence (4), Juanita *wishes* she *would* get an A, but this is a wish, not a certainty.

Would **can also express a possibility, a wish, or a request.**

PRACTICE 6   Fill in the *will* or the *would*. To determine whether the sentence is in the present or the past, look at the other verbs in the sentence.

1. The meteorologist predicts that it _____ snow on Friday.

2. The meteorologist predicted that it _____ snow on Friday.

3. Hernan said that he _____ move to Colorado.

4. Hernan says that he _____ move to Colorado.

5. Roberta thinks that she _____ receive financial aid.

6. Roberta thought that she _____ receive financial aid.

7. I _____ marry you if you propose to me.

8. Unless you stop adding salt, no one _____ want to eat that chili.

9. Hugo thinks that he _____ be a country and western star someday.

10. Because she wanted to tell her story, she said that she _____ write an autobiography.

PRACTICE 7   Circle either *will* or *would*.

1. You (will, would) find the right major once you start taking courses.

2. When the house is painted, you (will, would) see how lovely the old place looks.

3. Yolanda wishes that her neighbor (will, would) stop raising ostriches.

4. The instructor assumed that everyone (will, would) improve.

5. They insisted that they (will, would) pick up the check.

6. The whole town assumed that they (will, would) live happily ever after.

7. When we climb the tower, we (will, would) see for miles around.

8. If I had a million dollars, I (will, would) buy a big house on the ocean.

9. Your flight to Mars (will, would) board in fifteen minutes.

10. Because we hated waiting in long lines, we decided that we (will, would) shop somewhere else.

E. Writing Infinitives

Every verb can be written as an **infinitive**. An infinitive has two parts: *to* + the simple form of the verb—*to kiss, to gaze, to sing, to wonder, to help*. Never add endings to the infinitive form of a verb: no *-ed*, no *-s*, no *-ing*.

(1) Quinn has *to take* a course in environmental law.

(2) Neither dictionary seems *to contain* the words I need.

• In sentences (1) and (2), the infinitives are *to take* and *to contain*.

• *To* is followed by the simple form of the verb: *take, contain*.

Don't confuse an infinitive with the preposition *to* followed by a noun or a pronoun.

(3) Tamara spoke *to Sam*.

(4) I gave the award *to her*.

- In sentences (3) and (4), the preposition *to* is followed by the noun *Sam* and the pronoun *her*.

- *To Sam* and *to her* are prepositional phrases, not infinitives.*

PRACTICE 8   Find the infinitives in the following sentences and write them in the blanks at the right.

Infinitive

EXAMPLE: Many people don't realize how hard   it is to write a funny essay.   *to write*   _____

1. Our guests started to leave at midnight.   _____

2. Marlena has decided to run for mayor.   _____

3. Han has to get a B on his final exam or he   will not transfer to Wayne State.   _____

4. It is hard to think with that radio blaring!   _____

5. The man wanted to buy a silver watch to   give to his son.   _____

PRACTICE 9   Write an infinitive in each blank in the following sentences. Use any verb that makes sense. Remember that the infinitive is made up of *to* plus the simple form of the verb.

1. They began _____ in the cafeteria.

2. Few people know how _____ well.

3. Would it be possible for us _____ again later?

4. He hopes _____ an operating-room nurse.

5. It will be easy_____ _____.

F.   Revising Double Negatives

The most common **negatives** are *no, none, not, nowhere, no one, nobody, never,* and *nothing*.

The negative *not* is often joined to a verb to form a contraction: *can't, didn't, don't, hasn't, haven't,* and *won't,* for example.

However, a few negatives are difficult to spot. Read these sentences:

(1) There are hardly any beans left.

(2) By noon, we could scarcely see the mountains on the horizon.

- The negatives in these sentences are *hardly* and *scarcely*.

_____

* For more work on prepositions, see Chapter 10, Part C, and Chapter 26.

- They are negatives because they imply that there are *almost* no beans left and that we *almost couldn't* see the mountains.

Use only one negative in each idea. The double negative is an error you should avoid.

> (3) **Double negative:** I *can't* eat *nothing*.

- There are two negatives in this sentence—*can't* and *nothing*—instead of one.
- Double negatives cancel each other out.

  To revise a double negative, simply drop one of the negatives.

> (4) **Revised:** I *can't* eat anything.
>
> (5) **Revised:** I can eat *nothing*.

- In sentence (4), the negative *nothing* has been changed to the positive *anything*.
- In sentence (5), the negative *can't* has been changed to the positive *can*.

  When you revise double negatives that include the words *hardly* and *scarcely*, keep those words and change the other negatives to positives.

> (6) **Double negative:** They couldn't hardly finish their papers on time.

- The two negatives are *couldn't* and *hardly*.

> (7) **Revised:** They could hardly finish their papers on time.

- Change *couldn't* to *could*.

PRACTICE 10   Revise the double negatives in the following sentences.

EXAMPLE: I don't have no more homework to do.

Revised: _I don't have any more homework to do._ _____

1. I can't hardly wait for Christmas vacation.

   Revised: _____

2. Ms. Chandro hasn't never been to Los Angeles.

   Revised: _____

3. Fido was so excited that he couldn't scarcely sit still.

   Revised: _____

4. Nat won't talk to nobody until he's finished studying.

   Revised: _____

5. Yesterday's newspaper didn't contain no ads for large-screen television sets.

   Revised: _____

6. Alice doesn't have no bathing suit with her.

   Revised: _____

7. If Vasily were smart, he wouldn't answer no one in that tone of voice.

   Revised: _____

8. Kylie claimed that she hadn't never been to a rodeo before.

   Revised: _____

9. Some days, I can't seem to do nothing right.

   Revised: _____

10. Umberto searched, but he couldn't find his gold bow tie nowhere.

    Revised: _____

Chapter Highlights

- **Fixed-form verbs do not change, no matter what the subject is:**

  I *can*.

  He *can*.

  They *can*.

- **The main verb after a fixed-form helping verb keeps the simple form:**

  I will *sleep*.

  She might *sleep*.

  Sarita should *sleep*.

- **An infinitive has two parts, *to* + the simple form of a verb:**

  to drive

  to exclaim

  to read

- **Do not write double negatives:**

  I didn't order no soup. (*incorrect*)

  I didn't order any soup. (*correct*)

  They couldn't hardly see. (*incorrect*)

  They could hardly see. (*correct*)

PROOFREADING STRATEGY

To proofread for the errors discussed in this chapter, **isolate your sentences** and **find key words.** If you write on a computer, reformat your draft to isolate your sentences, one sentence on each line. This can trick your eye and brain into seeing your words anew.

Now use your eyes or the *"Find"* feature to focus on terms related to your problem areas. For instance, if you have trouble with **fixed-form helping verbs** like *can, could, will,* and *would,* search for and highlight these words; then check the main verb following each one. If you write **double negatives,** find all the "negatives" in your paper (words like *no, none, not, nowhere, no one, nobody, never, nothing*) and check for correctness. Here is an example:

Make sure your paper doesn't have no fixed-form errors or double negatives.

(above "no" is written "any")

WRITING AND PROOFREADING ASSIGNMENT

Review this chapter briefly. What part was most difficult for you? Write a paragraph explaining the difficult material to someone who is having the same trouble you had. Your purpose is to make the lesson crystal clear to him or her. As you proofread, search for key words that help you see your trouble spots.

CHAPTER REVIEW

Proofread the following essay for errors in fixed-form verbs, infinitives, and double negatives. Cross out each incorrect word and correct the error above the line.

Urban Farming Pioneer

(1) Will Allen couldn't never be happy just taking it easy. (2) He grew up working hard on the family farm, learning good habits that led him to graduated from college, play professional basketball, and succeed in a corporate career. (3) Because he still weren't fulfilled, Allen quit his job in 1993 and returned to farming and the soil. (4) Soon he would became a hero in his Wisconsin community and one of the most influential urban farmers in the world.

(5) Allen bought a vacant plant nursery in Milwaukee, just a few blocks from a big public housing project. (6) Fresh food wasn't hardly ever sold in the area, so he decided to grew and sell nourishing food on his new urban farm. (7) Soon, young people from the neighborhood bombarded him with questions. (8) Inspired, Allen created a program for teens to work with him while they learned about good food and sustainable farming.

Darren Hauck/The New York Times/Redux Pictures

Urban farmer Will Allen surveys one of Growing Power's greenhouses.

(9) Growing Power, Inc., has become a thriving nonprofit urban farming center with gardens, greenhouses, crops, animals, poultry, and fish. (10) It can fed thousands and empower people who once didn't eat nothing but junk food to making healthy decisions about what they eat and where their food comes from. (11) Michelle Obama asked Allen to been the first national spokesman for her campaign to end childhood obesity. (12) Allen's work now might took him around the world, but he stays rooted in Milwaukee, coming home to teach and to farming the worm-rich soil.

EXPLORING ONLINE

www.bbc.co.uk/skillswise/game/en31vari-game-double-negatives
Click the picture of the woman being interviewed and then
"start" to play the double negatives game!

leo.stcloudstate.edu/grammar/doubneg.html
Good review of double negatives from St. Cloud State University.

Visit **MindTap** for *Grassroots* to access this chapter's ebook, flashcards, additional practice and quizzes, and more!

Writing Assignments

As you complete each writing assignment, remember to perform these steps:

- Write a clear, complete topic sentence.

- Use freewriting, brainstorming, or clustering to generate ideas for the body of your paragraph, essay, or letter.

- Arrange your best ideas in a plan.

- Revise for support, unity, coherence, and exact language.

- Proofread for grammar, punctuation, and spelling errors.

WRITING ASSIGNMENT 1 *Tell a family story.* Many of us heard family stories as we were growing up—how our great-grandmother escaped from Poland, how Uncle Chester took his sister for a joyride in the Ford when he was six. Assume that you have been asked to write such a story for a scrapbook that will be given to your grandmother on her eightieth birthday. Choose a story that reveals something important about a member of your family. As you revise, make sure that all your verbs are correct. Consider sharing your story online at a website that invites viewers to share their personal experiences. Try **madeintoamerica.org** or **www.pbs.org/weta/finding-your-roots**.

WRITING ASSIGNMENT 2 *Describe a person who takes a risk to help others.* In this unit, you might have read about Majora Carter, who vastly improved the quality of life for her South Bronx neighbors. She stood up and fought for the common good. Do you know someone who is a community crusader, a champion of children, or a person who otherwise helps others? Write a verbal portrait of this person, describing his or her activities and contributions. Select vivid verbs that capture his or her actions for the greater good.

WRITING ASSIGNMENT 3 *Describe a lively scene.* To practice choosing and using verbs, go where the action is—to a sports event, a busy store, a club, a public park, even the woods or a field. Observe carefully as you take notes and freewrite. Capture specific sounds, sights, colors, actions, and smells. Then write a description of what takes place, using lively verbs. Choose either present or past tense and make sure to use that tense consistently throughout.

WRITING ASSIGNMENT 4 *Describe a few intense moments.* Read paragraph A in the following section, Unit 3: Review, which uses lively verbs to describe the saving of someone's life at a health club. This writer uses the present tense, as if the action is happening now. Describe some brief but dramatic event—the birth of a child, the opening of an important letter, the arrival of a blind date, or the reaction of the person to whom you just proposed. Decide whether present or past tense would be better, and choose varied, interesting verbs. As you revise, make sure the verbs are correct.

Review

Transforming

A. Rewrite this paragraph, changing every *I* to *she*, every *me* to *her*, and every *us* to *them*. Do not change any verb tenses. Be sure all verbs agree with their new subjects, and make any other necessary changes.

(1) I am at the gym, training a client. (2) A man near us gets off the treadmill and suddenly collapses onto the floor. (3) I know that I must act quickly. (4) I shout, "Call 911!" (5) I dash to the portable defibrillator on the wall, open the box, and remove the device. (6) I press the green start button and quickly tear off the unconscious man's T-shirt. (7) I place the two electrode pads on his chest and plug them into the machine. (8) The defibrillator analyzes the man's heartbeat to determine whether his heart needs to be shocked. (9) It does. (10) The machine charges itself and warns me not to touch the patient. (11) When I press the orange button, the machine delivers a jolt and then checks to see if the patient needs another. (12) One is enough. (13) The man's skin almost instantly turns from gray to pink, and he has a pulse. (14) When the paramedics arrive, they tell me that the defibrillator and I probably saved his life.

Marcel Alfonso, Student

B. Rewrite this paragraph, changing the verbs from present tense to past tense.

(1) It is the morning of August 29, 2005. (2) Hurricane Katrina churns over the warm waters of the Gulf of Mexico and bears down on the coasts of Louisiana and Mississippi. (3) When it makes landfall at 6:10 A.M., it is a monster storm, packing 125-mile-an-hour winds and dumping 10 to 15 inches of rain. (4) Hurricane-force winds rage 120 miles outward from its center. (5) In the city of New Orleans, the storm whips up huge waves in Lake Pontchartrain. (6) These waves slam into the levees around the city, causing the levees to break. (7) Lake water pours into the city and floods low-lying areas. (8) Winds and torrents rip down telephone and power lines, wash away streets and bridges, and level whole neighborhoods. (9) Many of the people still in their homes swim for their lives. (10) Others scramble to their rooftops, where they wait, sometimes in vain,

for rescue. (11) The most destructive storm in U.S. history, Hurricane Katrina costs over $100 billion in damages. (12) Far worse, it leaves over 1,800 people dead, shatters millions of lives, and raises deeply disturbing questions.

Proofreading

The following essay contains both past tense errors and past participle errors. First, proofread for verb errors, underlining all the incorrect verbs. Then correct the errors above the lines. (You should find a total of thirteen errors.)

Protector of the Chimps

(1) Dr. Jane Goodall, DBE*, has did more than anyone else to understand the lives of chimpanzees. (2) Always an animal lover, she was too poor to go to college to study animals. (3) She worked as a waitress until the age of twenty-five. (4) Then she fulfilled a lifelong dream and gone to East Africa. (5) There she was thrilled by the beauty of the land and the wild animals.

(6) In Africa, she meet Louis Leakey, a famous naturalist. (7) Leakey recognize Goodall's curiosity, energy, and passion for the natural world. (8) He hired her for a six-month study of the wild chimpanzees in a national park in Tanzania. (9) Despite malaria, primitive living conditions, and hostile wildlife, this determined woman followed

Dr. Jane Goodall, DBE, Founder of the Jane Goodall Institute, communicates with a chimpanzee.

_____
* DBE: Dame of the British Empire, an honorary title in England, like "Knight."

the activities of a group of chimps in the Gombe Forest. (10) For months, she watch the chimps through binoculars. (11) She moved closer and closer until she eventually become part of their lives. (12) Dr. Goodall named the chimps and recorded their daily activities. (13) She learned that chimps was capable of feeling happiness, anger, and pain. (14) They formed complex societies with leaders, politics, and tribal wars. (15) One of her most important discoveries were that chimps made and used tools. (16) Dr. Goodall expected to stay in Gombe for six months; instead she studied the chimps there for almost forty years. (17) Her studies lead to a totally new understanding of chimps, and she became world famous.

(18) However, her life changed completely in 1986. (19) She attend a conference in Chicago, where she heard horrible stories about the fate of chimps outside Gombe. (20) She learned about the destruction of the forests and the wildlife of Africa. (21) From that day on, Dr. Goodall committed herself to education and conservation. (22) Since then, she has traveled, lectured, gave interviews, and met with people. (23) She established both the Jane Goodall Institute and a young people's group, Roots & Shoots, and is a UN Messenger of Peace. (24) These worldwide organizations have already carry out many important conservation and educational projects. (25) The author of remarkable books and the subject of inspiring television specials, Dr. Goodall is knowed for her total commitment to chimps and to a healthy natural world.

EXPLORING ONLINE

www.janegoodall.org
www.worldwildlife.org

Visit the Jane Goodall Institute or the World Wildlife Fund
to learn more about endangered species.

Writers' Workshop

Tell a Family Story

A **narrative** tells a story. It presents the most important events in the story, usually in time order. Here, a student tells of her mother-in-law's inspiring journey to self-realization.

In your group or class, read this narrative essay aloud, if possible. As you read, underline any words or details that strike you as vivid or powerful.

Somebody Named Seeta

(1) Someone I deeply admire is my mother-in-law, Seeta, who struggled for years to become her best self. She was born in poverty on the sunny island of Trinidad. Seeta's father drank and beat his wife, and sadly, her mother accepted this lifestyle. Her parents did not believe in sending girls to school, so Seeta's daily chores began at 4:00 A.M. when she milked the cows. Then she fed the hens, scrubbed the house, cooked, and tended babies (as the third child in a family of ten children). During stolen moments, she taught herself to read. At age sixteen, this skinny girl with long black hair ran away from home.

(2) Seeta had nowhere to go, so her friend's family took her in. They believed in education, yet Seeta struggled for years to catch up and finish school. Even so, she calls this time her "foot in the door." She married my father-in-law and had four children, longing inside to become "somebody" someday. When their oldest was nine and the youngest two months, Seeta's husband died. She had to get a job fast. She cut sugar cane in the fields, wrapping her baby in a sheet on the ground. In the evenings, she hiked home to care for the other children. Word got around on the sugar estate that she was bringing a baby to work, so she was given a job indoors. All the while, Seeta stayed patient and hopeful that God would help her someday.

(3) In fact, after seven years, she moved with her children to America. She was so poor that she owned only one pot and one spoon. After she finished

cooking, the children would all gather around the pot, and sitting on the floor, they passed the spoon from one to another. My mother-in-law got a job at a department store, selling by day and cleaning offices at night. All the time, in the back of her head, she wanted to be somebody. A plan was taking shape. Eight years ago, my mother-in-law enrolled at this college, first for her GED and then for a college degree. She graduated and became a registered nurse.

(4) When I first met Seeta, I thought she did not like me. Was I wrong! She was just checking me out to see what I was made of. Did I too have goals to be conquered? She taught me that patience is a virtue but that one should never give up. She told me that even in modern America where women have their independence, she had to fight to hold on to hers. Today my mother-in-law is attending Lehman College at night for her master's degree in surgical nursing.

Rosalie Ramnanan, Student

1. How effective is Rosalie Ramnanan's essay?

   _____ Clear thesis statement?   _____ Rich supporting details?
   _____ Logical organization?   _____ Effective conclusion?

2. Underline the thesis statement (main idea sentence) for the whole essay. The rest of the paper—a narrative—develops this idea.

3. Ramnanan uses different action verbs to help the reader see and hear the story, especially in paragraphs (1), (2), and (3). Can you identify them?

4. Why do you think the writer chose the title she did? How effective is it?

5. Proofread for grammar and spelling. Do you notice any error patterns (two or more errors of the same type) that this student should watch out for?

Writing and Revising Ideas

1. Tell an inspiring story about one or more of your family members.

2. Use narrative to develop this topic or thesis sentence: Poverty or difficult circumstances can make some people stronger and more ambitious.

For help writing your paragraph or essay, see Chapters 3 to 8. As you revise, make sure that your main idea is clear and that your paper explains it. To add punch to your writing as you revise, replace *is*, *was*, *has*, and *had* with action verbs whenever possible.

Joining Ideas Together

Too many short, simple sentences can make your writing sound monotonous. This unit will show you five ways to create interesting sentences. In this unit, you will

- Follow the MAP to better reading and writing
- Join ideas through coordination and subordination
- Use semicolons and conjunctive adverbs correctly
- Spot and correct run-ons or comma splices
- Join ideas with *who*, *which*, and *that*
- Join ideas by using *-ing* modifiers
- Learn proofreading strategies to find and correct your own errors

Image Source/Alamy Stock Photo

Follow the MAP to Better Reading and Writing

MODEL

Here, writer Brent Staples uses several methods of joining ideas as he describes his first passionate kiss (at least, *he* was passionate). If possible, read the paragraph aloud.

I stepped outside and pulled the door closed behind me, and in one motion encircled her waist, pulled her to me, and whispered breathlessly that I loved her. There'd been no rehearsing this; the thought, deed, and word were one. "You do? You love me?" This amused her, but that didn't matter. I had passion enough for the two of us. When I closed in for the kiss, she turned away her lips and offered me her cheek. I kissed it feverishly and with great force. We stood locked this way until I came up for air. Then she peeled me from her and went inside for the flour.

Brent Staples, *Parallel Time*

ANALYSIS

- Brent Staples mixes simple sentences with sentences that join ideas in different ways. Sentences 2, 4, 6, and 8, for example, combine ideas in ways you will learn in this unit.

- Can you recognize what any of these methods are?

- How do you think the writer now feels about this incident from his youth? Does his tone seem angry, frustrated, or amused? Which sentences tell you?

PRACTICE

- Write about your first crush or romantic encounter.
- Write about a time you discovered that a loved one's view of the relationship was very different from your view of it.

CHAPTER 17

Coordination

As a writer, you will sometimes want to join short, choppy sentences to form longer sentences. One way to join two ideas is to use a comma and a **coordinating conjunction**.

> (1) This car has many special features, and it costs less than $20,000.
>
> (2) The television picture is blurred, but we will watch the football game anyway.
>
> (3) She wants to practice her Italian, so she is going to Italy.

- Can you break sentence (1) into two complete and independent ideas or thoughts? What are they? Underline the subject and verb in each.

- Can you do the same with sentences (2) and (3)? Underline the subjects and verbs.

- In each sentence, circle the word that joins the two parts of the sentence together. What punctuation mark comes before that word?

- *And*, *but*, and *so* are called *coordinating conjunctions* because they coordinate, or join together, ideas. Other coordinating conjunctions are *for*, *nor*, *or*, and *yet*.

To join two complete and independent ideas, use a coordinating conjunction preceded by a comma. To help you remember these words, just think FANBOYS (the first letter of *for*, *and*, *nor*, *but*, *or*, *yet*, **and** *so*).

Now let's see just how coordinating conjunctions connect ideas:

Coordinating Conjunctions		
and	*means*	in addition
but, yet	*mean*	in contrast
for	*means*	because
nor	*means*	not either
or	*means*	either, a choice
so	*means*	as a result

BE CAREFUL: *Then*, *also*, and *plus* are not coordinating conjunctions. By themselves, they cannot join two ideas.

Incorrect: He studied, then he went to work.

Correct: He studied, and then he went to work.

Read this paragraph, aloud if possible.

Lucky found me over the Thanksgiving holiday. She was a gray and white tabby. She looked like a skeleton cat wearing a fur blanket. It was clear that she was starving. Her ribs and rump bone were sticking out. I got to work. I cut up some leftover turkey from the fridge. I popped it into the microwave for thirty seconds. My scrawny visitor ate every bit. I made a second plate and a third. Finally, she curled up on the kitchen mat. That day, Lucky joined our family.

This might have been a good paragraph, but all the short sentences sound monotonous, even childish. Here is the same paragraph, rewritten:

Lucky found me over the Thanksgiving holiday. She was a gray and white tabby, *but* she looked like a skeleton cat wearing a fur blanket. It was clear that she was starving, *for* her ribs and rump bone were sticking out. I got to work. I cut up some leftover turkey from the fridge, *and* I popped it into the microwave for thirty seconds. My scrawny visitor ate every bit, *so* I made a second plate and a third. Finally, she curled up on the kitchen mat. That day, Lucky joined our family.

- Can you hear the difference? This paragraph sounds smoother and more sophisticated because it uses coordinating conjunctions to connect ideas.
- This writer has joined some of the short sentences into longer ones, using *but*, *for*, *and*, and *so*.
- Because these conjunctions join two complete ideas, a comma precedes the conjunction.
- Three times in this paragraph, *and* is used to join words that are *not* complete ideas. No comma is needed because they are not complete ideas. Find these three *ands*.

_____

_____

REMEMBER: Coordinating conjunctions can join not just two independent ideas but also two words, two phrases, and two dependent clauses. **A comma goes before the conjunction *only* if it links two independent ideas.**

PRACTICE 1

Read these sentences for meaning. Then fill in the coordinating conjunction (FANBOYS) that best expresses the relationship between the two complete thoughts. REMEMBER: Do you want to *add*, *contrast*, *give a reason*, *show a result*, or *indicate a choice*?

EXAMPLE: War is no game, _____*yet*_____ games are transforming modern warfare.

1. Young men and women today grew up playing computer games, _____ the U.S. Army is using video games to recruit and train soldiers.

AP Photo/Sue Ogrocki

Soldiers train for combat on a new simulator that uses video game technology.

2. Since 2002, an online version of *America's Army* has attracted 6.5 million registered players, _____ the game has been used for real combat training.

3. Video games can teach many skills needed in battle, _____ they expose players to lifelike war zones such as deserts, jungles, and bombed-out villages.

4. Flashes, explosions, and deadly surprises are part of war, _____ similar computer effects help players adjust to stressful conditions.

5. Some games teach the soldier to load, aim, and fire realistic weapons, _____ he or she must engage in "deadly" combat with other players.

6. Virtual soldiers gain rewards for showing teamwork and bravery, _____ they are penalized for sloppy preparation or safety violations.

7. In one scenario, a Humvee driver and gunner must work together, _____ they both will "die."

8. The Army started its own $50 million video game division in 2010, _____ its programmers can create even better and more realistic training games.

9. Critics say that military-themed video games are morally dangerous, _____ they make killing a human enemy less real.

10. Some object to using games to sharpen the skills of shooters and snipers, _____ for now, these games—like war—are here to stay.

EXPLORING ONLINE

www.americasarmy.com

Explore the *America's Army* website and perhaps play a video game. Do you think this site would encourage young men and women to enlist in the military? Why or why not? Jot down three reasons for your opinion, and write specifically about why this website would or would not inspire volunteers to enlist.

PRACTICE 2   Punctuate these sentences correctly by adding any missing commas. Write a *C* for "correct" next to a sentence that does not need a comma. To determine if a comma is needed, first locate the coordinating conjunction(s) in each sentence. Any coordinating conjunction that joins two *independent ideas* must be preceded by a comma.

1. Residents of the Greek island of Ikaria live longer, healthier lives than most humans and scientists want to know why.

2. Many Ikarians thrive well into their 90s but the average American lives only to 78.

3. Americans lose years of life to heart disease and cancers yet these diseases are rare in Ikaria.

4. A key factor in Ikarians' longevity seems to be a diet packed with beans and vegetables but low in meat and sugar.

5. Ikarians consume wild local greens, herbal teas, and goat's milk so their risk of high blood pressure and heart disease is reduced.

6. This healthy diet is essential but regular exercise is another key factor.

7. Ikaria is a mountainous island so its steep terrain gives inhabitants a workout every time they leave home.

8. In addition, Ikarians refuse to rush through life and get lots of rest, including daily naps.

9. Ikarian natives are lucky to share a strong sense of community for close bonds with family and friends promote longevity.

10. Ikarians may be some of the healthiest people on earth but adopting the right habits can help anyone lead a longer, better life.

PRACTICE 3   Each of these thoughts is complete by itself, but you can join them together to make more interesting sentences. Combine pairs of these thoughts, using *and, but, for, nor, or, so,* or *yet*, and write six new sentences on the lines that follow. Punctuate correctly.

> babies need constant supervision
> Rico overcame his disappointment
> in the 1840s, American women began to fight for the right to vote
> I will write my essay at home tonight
> the ancient Chinese valued peaches
> he decided to try again
> they are the best Ping-Pong players on the block
> you should never leave them by themselves
> I will write it tomorrow in the computer lab
> they did not win that right until 1920
> they can't beat my cousin from Cleveland
> they believed that eating peaches made a person immortal

1. _____

   _____

2. _____

3. _____

4. _____

5. _____

6. _____

PRACTICE 4   Finish these sentences by adding a second complete idea after the coordinating conjunction.

1. She often interrupts me, but _____

2. Yuri has lived in the United States for ten years, so _____

3. Len has been married three times, and _____

4. I like owning a car, for _____

5. I like owning a car, but _____

PRACTICE 5   On the lines below or on a computer, write seven sentences of your own, using each of the coordinating conjunctions—*and, but, for, nor, or, so,* and *yet*—to join two independent ideas. Punctuate correctly.

1. _____

2. _____

3. _____

4. _____

5. _____

6. _____

7. _____

Chapter Highlights

■ **A comma and a coordinating conjunction join two independent ideas:**

The fans booed, _but_ the umpire paid no attention.

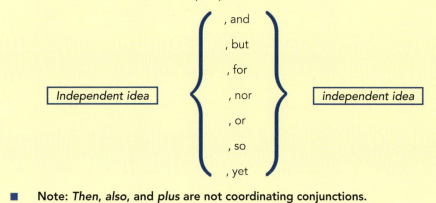

■ **Note:** _Then, also,_ and _plus_ are not coordinating conjunctions.

PROOFREADING STRATEGY

Using coordination will improve your writing. Just proofread to make sure that you punctuate correctly.

1. **Search** for the seven coordinating conjunctions, or FANBOYS, and **highlight or underline** each one. If you are using a computer, use the "_Find_" feature to locate these words in your draft.

2. Check to see if each coordinating conjunction joins two complete ideas. Can the words on either side of it stand alone as complete sentences? If so, put a _comma_ before the conjunction. Make sure you understand these examples.

CORRECT   CORRECT

The boss and his partner were very supportive but intolerant of those who arrived late for work.

INCORRECT   CORRECT

We paid, but later Blanca and I regretted sending that check.
        ^

WRITING AND PROOFREADING ASSIGNMENT

Whether you are a teenager, a young adult, middle-aged, elderly, single, or part of a couple, there are characters in TV sitcoms who are supposed to represent you. Do these characters correctly portray the kind of person you are, or are you seeing one or more irritating exaggerations?

Write a letter of praise or complaint to a network that broadcasts one of these sitcoms. Make clear why you think a certain character does or does not correctly portray someone like you. Use examples and specific details. As you revise and proofread, avoid choppy sentences by joining ideas with coordinating conjunctions.

CHAPTER REVIEW

Read this paragraph of short, choppy sentences. Then rewrite it, using different coordinating conjunctions to combine some pairs of sentences. Keep some short sentences for variety. Copy your revised paragraph on a fresh sheet of paper. Punctuate with care.

(1) Super Bowl parties everywhere owe a debt to Rebecca Webb Carranza. (2) Most people don't even know her name. (3) This Mexican-born entrepreneur invented the tortilla chip in 1948. (4) At the time, Carranza and her husband ran the El Zarape Tortilla Factory in Los Angeles. (5) Some tortillas always came off the conveyor belt in strange shapes. (6) Carranza threw them away. (7) She hated this waste of food. (8) One day before a family party, she cut some discarded tortillas into triangles and fried them. (9) The relatives loved the chips. (10) They could easily grab a handful or dip the crunchy morsels in sauce. (11) Carranza began selling her chips for 10 cents a bag in her Mexican delicatessen and factory. (12) By the 1960s, she had named them Tort Chips. (13) Her factory now manufactured nothing but this irresistible snack. (14) Demand for the chips took off. (15) Carranza is now recognized as a snack-food industry pioneer. (16) She received awards for her work, including, appropriately, two Golden Tortillas.

EXPLORING ONLINE

web2.uvcs.uvic.ca/elc/studyzone/330/grammar/coconj1.htm
Fill in the right coordinating conjunction; the computer checks your answers.

grammar.ccc.commnet.edu/grammar/quizzes/nova/nova1.htm
Interactive quiz: Place commas in sentences with coordinating conjunctions.

Visit **MindTap** for *Grassroots* to access this chapter's ebook, flashcards, additional practice and quizzes, and more!

CHAPTER 18

Subordination

A: Defining and Using Subordinating Conjunctions

B: Punctuating Subordinating Conjunctions

A. Defining and Using Subordinating Conjunctions

Another way to join ideas together is with a **subordinating conjunction**. Read this paragraph:

A great disaster happened in 1857. The SS *Central America* sank. This steamship was carrying six hundred wealthy passengers from California to New York. Many of them had recently struck gold. Battered by a storm, the ship began to flood. Many people on board bailed water. Others prayed and quieted the children. Thirty hours passed. A rescue boat arrived. Almost two hundred people were saved. The rest died. Later, many banks failed. Three tons of gold had gone down with the ship.

This could have been a good paragraph, but notice that all the sentences are short and choppy.

Here is the same paragraph, rewritten to make it more interesting:

A great disaster happened in 1857 *when* the SS *Central America* sank. This steamship was carrying six hundred wealthy passengers from California to New York. Many of them had recently struck gold. Battered by a storm, the ship began to flood. Many people on board bailed water *while* others prayed and quieted the children. *After* thirty hours passed, a rescue boat arrived. Almost two hundred people were saved *although* the rest died. Later, many banks failed *because* three tons of gold had gone down with the ship.

- Note that the paragraph now reads more smoothly and is more interesting because the following words were used to join some of the choppy sentences: *when*, *while*, *after*, *although*, and *because*.

- *When, while, after, although*, and *because* are part of a large group of words called *subordinating conjunctions*. As you can see from the paragraph, these conjunctions join ideas.

BE CAREFUL: Once you add a *subordinating conjunction* to an idea, that idea can no longer stand alone as a complete and independent sentence. It has become a subordinate or dependent idea; it must rely on an independent idea to complete its meaning.*

(1) He is tired.

(2) Because he is tired, _____

(3) I left the room.

(4) As I left the room, _____

(5) You speak Spanish.

(6) If you speak Spanish, _____

- (1), (3), and (5) are all complete sentences, but once a subordinating conjunction is added, they become dependent ideas. They must be followed by something else—a complete and independent thought.

- (2), for example, could be completed like this: Because he is tired, *he won't go out to eat with us.*

- Add an independent idea to complete each dependent idea on the lines above.

  Below is a partial list of subordinating conjunctions.

Common Subordinating Conjunctions		
after	even though	when
although	if	whenever
as	since	where
as if	so that	whereas
as though	though	wherever
because	unless	whether
before	until	while

Each subordinating conjunction expresses a specific *relationship* between two ideas in a sentence. Let's look at some of these relationships:

Subordinating Conjunctions	Meaning	One Example
after, as, before, since, until, when, whenever, while	To show different time relationships	*When* her son was diagnosed with autism, Monique started her research.

———

* For more work on sentence fragments of this type, see Chapter 11, Part C.

although, even though, though, whereas, while	To show a contrast or contradiction	I love classical music *even though* my parents did not.
as though, as if	To show something *seems* true but is not	He acts *as if* he owned the club.
because, since, so that	To show a reason, a cause, or an effect	He told the truth *because* he respects you.
even if, if, unless, whether	To show a condition for something to happen	*Even if* one has a college degree, good jobs can be hard to find.

PRACTICE 1 Read these sentences for meaning. Then fill in the subordinating conjunction that best expresses the relationship between the two ideas.

1. _____ you are like most people, you resist admitting mistakes or hurtful actions.

2. _____ it is commonly thought that apologizing shows weakness, an apology actually requires great strength.

3. A genuine apology is a powerful tool _____ it can repair damaged relationships, heal humiliation, and encourage forgiveness.

4. _____ we learn to apologize sincerely, psychologists say, we can prevent grudges, revenge, and a lot of pain.

5. _____ you apologize to someone, remember the key ingredients of a successful apology.

6. _____ you have hurt someone's feelings or betrayed that person, you must first admit your wrongdoing.

7. Specifically describe what you did _____ you reveal an understanding of your offense and its impact.

8. Say, for example, "I'm sorry for hurting you _____ I criticized you in front of your friends."

9. _____ you apologize, you must communicate remorse with both your words and your body language.

10. The other person will question your sincerity _____ you seem truly distressed and sorry.

11. _____ you end your apology, say that you will not repeat such actions again.

12. _____ it might be difficult, a sincere apology will be worth the effort.

PRACTICE 2   Now that you understand how subordinating conjunctions join thoughts together, try these sentences. Here you have to supply one idea. Make sure that the ideas you add have subjects and verbs.

1. The cafeteria food improved when _____

_____

2. Because Damon and Luis both love basketball, _____

_____

3. If _____

Peyton plans to get legal advice.

4. I was repairing the roof while _____

_____

5. Before _____

you should get all the facts.

B. Punctuating Subordinating Conjunctions

As you may have noticed in the preceding exercises, some sentences with subordinating conjunctions use a comma whereas others do not. Here is how it's done.

> (1) Because it rained very hard, we had to leave early.
>
> (2) We had to leave early because it rained very hard.

● Sentence (1) has a comma because the dependent idea comes before the independent idea.

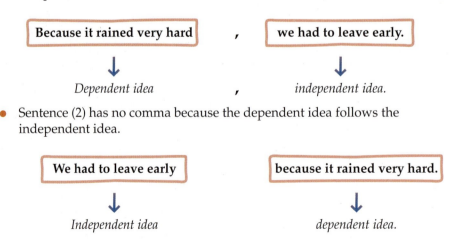

● Sentence (2) has no comma because the dependent idea follows the independent idea.

Use a comma after a dependent idea; do not use a comma before a dependent idea.

PRACTICE 3

If a sentence is punctuated correctly, write *C* in the blank. If it is not, punctuate it correctly by adding or deleting a comma.

1. Whenever Americans get hungry they want to eat quickly.   _____

2. When McDonald's opened in 1954 it started a trend that continues today.   _____

3. Whether you are talking about pizza or hamburgers fast food is big business—earning more than $215 billion a year.   _____

4. Fast food is appealing because it is cheap, tasty, and—of course—fast.   _____

5. While it has many advantages fast food also presents some health hazards.   _____

6. Although the industry is booming many people are worried about the amount of fat in fast foods.   _____

7. Whereas some nutritionists recommend eating only 35 grams of fat a day you often eat more than that in just one fast-food meal.   _____

8. If you order a Burger King Double Whopper with cheese you take in a whopping 68 grams of fat.   _____

9. That goes up to 74 fat grams whenever you devour a McDonald's Big Mac, large fries, and chocolate shake.   _____

10. Now some fast-food restaurants are claiming to serve low-fat items so that they can attract health-conscious customers.   _____

11. However, you still must pay attention to the ingredients, if you want to make sure that your meal is healthy.   _____

12. For example, most grilled or roasted chicken sandwiches are relatively
    low in fat before they are slathered with mayonnaise and special sauces. _____

13. Because just one tablespoon of mayonnaise or salad dressing contains
    eleven fat grams these tasty toppings add gobs of extra fat and calories. _____

14. Although they might taste delicious cheese and cheese sauces also
    add surprising quantities of fat to a meal. _____

15. When you next order your favorite fast food don't forget to say,
    "Hold the sauce!" _____

PRACTICE 4

Correctly combine each pair of ideas in two ways: with the subordinating conjunction at the beginning of the sentence and with the subordinating conjunction in the middle of the sentence. For each pair, write in the subordinating conjunction that expresses the relationship between these ideas. Then make sure you punctuate each sentence correctly.

EXAMPLE: ___*Although*___ marriage exists in all societies, every culture has unique wedding customs.

Every culture has unique wedding customs ___*although*___ marriage exists in all societies.

1. _____ young couples in India marry the ceremony may last for days.
   The ceremony may last for days _____ young couples in India marry.

2. _____ the wedding takes place at the bride's home everyone travels to the groom's home for more celebration.
   Everyone travels to the groom's home for more celebration _____ the wedding takes place at the bride's home.

3. Ducks are often included in Korean wedding processions _____ they mate for life.
   _____ they mate for life ducks are often included in Korean wedding processions.

4. Iroquois brides gave grain to their mothers-in-law _____ mothers-in-law gave meat to the brides.
   _____ Iroquois brides gave grain to their mothers-in-law mothers-in-law gave meat to the brides.

5. _____ the food was exchanged the bride and groom were considered married.
   The bride and groom were considered married _____ the food was exchanged.

6. _____ the tradition went out of style Finnish brides and grooms used to exchange wreaths.
   Finnish brides and grooms used to exchange wreaths _____ the tradition went out of style.

7. A Zulu wedding is not complete _____ the bride, groom, and bridal party dance special dances.
   _____ the bride, groom, and bridal party dance special dances a Zulu wedding is not complete.

8. The bride stabs at imaginary enemies with a knife _____ she dances wildly and gloriously.

   _____ the bride dances wildly and gloriously she stabs at imaginary enemies with a knife.

9. _____ the wedding ring is a very old symbol the elaborate wedding cake is even older.

   The wedding ring is a very old symbol _____ the elaborate wedding cake is even older.

10. _____ the ring symbolizes the oneness of the new couple the cake represents fertility.

    The cake represents fertility _____ the ring symbolizes the oneness of the new couple.

PRACTICE 5   Now try writing sentences of your own. Fill in the blanks, being careful to punctuate correctly. Do not use a comma before a dependent idea.

1. _____ because

   _____ .

2. Although _____

   _____ .

3. _____ whenever

   _____ .

4. Unless _____

   _____ .

Chapter Highlights

- **A subordinating conjunction joins a dependent idea and an independent idea:**

  When I registered, all the math courses were closed.

  All the math courses were closed *when* I registered.

- **Use a comma after a dependent idea.**

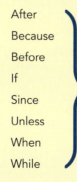

  After
  Because
  Before
  If
  Since
  Unless
  When
  While

  dependent idea, independent idea.

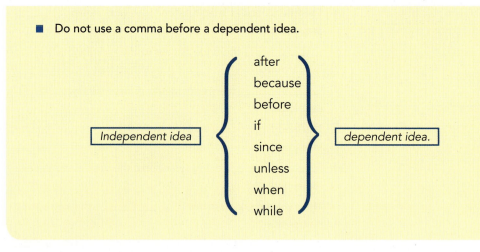

- Do not use a comma before a dependent idea.

Independent idea { after / because / before / if / since / unless / when / while } dependent idea.

PROOFREADING STRATEGY

Joining ideas with subordinating conjunctions will add sophistication to your writing, but be sure to proofread for correct punctuation.

1. **First, search the document for any subordinating conjunctions** (like *although, because, before, when,* etc.). **Highlight or underline** these words.

2. If a dependent idea comes first in the sentence, **use a comma to separate the dependent from the independent idea**. You know you have the comma in the right spot if there is a complete sentence *after* the comma. Here are two examples:

   Independent idea ———————— dependent idea
   Lia enrolled in classes every semester until she finished her associate degree.

   Dependent idea ———————— independent idea
   When Jorge gets home from work, he takes his dogs for a walk.

WRITING AND PROOFREADING ASSIGNMENT

Imagine that you are a teacher planning a lesson on courtesy for a class of young children. Use a personal experience, either positive or negative, to illustrate your point. Brainstorm, freewrite, or cluster to generate details for the lesson. Then write what—and how—you plan to teach. Keeping in mind that you are trying to reach young children, make sure that the significance of the experience you will describe is clear. When you finish drafting, read over your lesson and look for ideas you can join with subordinating conjunctions. Underline the subordinating conjunctions you use, and check your punctuation.

Form small groups to discuss one another's lessons. Which are most convincing? Why? Would children learn more from examples of good behavior or from examples of bad behavior?

CHAPTER REVIEW

Read this paragraph of short, choppy sentences. Then revise it by making changes above the lines, using different subordinating conjunctions to combine pairs of sentences. Keep some short sentences for variety. Punctuate with care.

(1) Jacob Lawrence was a great American painter, a powerful teller of stories on canvas. (2) Young Jacob joined his mother in Harlem in 1930. (3) He began to paint the people around him. (4) Luckily, he found excellent art classes in Harlem. (5) The big art academies often excluded blacks then. (6) He was only 23. (7) He gained fame for his 60-picture Migration Series. (8) A New York gallery displayed these paintings. (9) No major commercial gallery had showcased an African-American artist before. (10) The *Migration Series* depicts southern blacks journeying north to find work after World War I. (11) The paintings show people searching for a better life. (12) Lawrence's work portrays the poverty and prejudice the migrants endured. (13) He also wanted viewers of his work "to experience the beauty of life." (14) During his long career, Lawrence painted many more energetic canvases and series. (15) His work reminds us that we are all migrants. (16) We are always on the move. (17) We are seeking something more.

EXPLORING ONLINE

www.whitney.org/Collection/JacobLawrence
See Lawrence's paintings at the Whitney Museum of Art online.

www.phillipscollection.org/collection/migration-series
Learn about Lawrence's *Migration Series* at the Phillips Collection.
Describe your favorite painting for someone who has never seen it.

Migration Series, Panel 3,
by Jacob Lawrence

EXPLORING ONLINE

a4esl.org/q/h/vm/conj02.html

Quiz with answers: Combine sentences with a conjunction.

web2.uvcs.uvic.ca/elc/studyzone/330/grammar/subcon.htm

Explanation of subordination followed by interactive practice sets.

Visit **MindTap** for *Grassroots* to access this chapter's ebook, flashcards, additional practice and quizzes, and more!

CHAPTER 19

Avoiding Run-Ons and Comma Splices

Now that you have had practice in joining ideas together, here are two serious errors to watch out for: the **run-on** and the **comma splice**. If run-ons and comma splices are among your personal error patterns, pay close attention to this chapter.

> **Run-on:** Herb talks too much nobody seems to mind.

- There are two complete ideas here: *Herb talks too much* and *nobody seems to mind.*
- A *run-on* incorrectly runs together two complete ideas without using a conjunction or punctuation.

> **Comma splice:** Herb talks too much, nobody seems to mind.

- A *comma splice* incorrectly joins two complete ideas with a comma but no conjunction.

BE CAREFUL: Run-ons and comma splices are considered serious mistakes in college and the workplace because they force readers to stop, back up, and try to figure out where one idea ends and another begins.

Here are three ways to correct a run-on or a comma splice:

1. **Write two separate sentences, making sure each is complete.**	Herb talks too much. Nobody seems to mind.
2. **Use a comma and a coordinating conjunction or FANBOYS** (*for, and, nor, but, or, yet, so*).*	Herb talks too much, *but* nobody seems to mind.
3. **Use a subordinating conjunction** (for example, *although, because, if,* or *when*).**	*Although* Herb talks too much, nobody seems to mind.

* For more work on coordinating conjunctions, see Chapter 17.
** For more work on subordinating conjunctions, see Chapter 18.

Try This   Try this "run-on" test, which works for some people. Ask **"Is it true that . . ."** followed by the test sentence. If the answer is *yes*, the sentence is correct; if the answer is *no*, it is a run-on or comma splice.

Is it true that *Many drivers in my city don't use their blinkers to warn the driver behind*

them that they are going to turn this reckless behavior really frustrates me **?** **NO**

This confusing example gets a *no*, so try breaking it into possible sentences:

Is it true that *Many drivers in my city don't use their blinkers to warn the driver behind*

them that they are going to turn **?** **YES**

Is it true that *this reckless behavior really frustrates me* **?** **YES**

PRACTICE 1

Many of these sentences contain run-ons or comma splices. If a sentence is correct, write *C* in the right-hand column. If it contains a run-on or a comma splice, write either *RO* or *CS*. Then correct the error in any way you wish. Use each method at least once.

EXAMPLE: ~~Painkiller~~ *After painkiller* addiction became a national ~~crisis~~ *crisis,* people began
_____ *RO* _____ to wake up.

1. America is gripped by an opioid epidemic, since 2000, overdose deaths have risen by 400 percent. _____

2. Opioids are powerful painkillers that include prescription drugs like OxyContin and illegal drugs like heroin. _____

3. Opioids can help a burn victim or surgical patient deal with terrible pain someone with a minor injury should not receive these drugs. _____

4. Many doctors write too many opioid prescriptions they almost never warn patients about the great risk of addiction. _____

5. These strong painkillers sit in millions of medicine cabinets, they might seem harmless. _____

6. People tend to hide their substance abuse, a young person's overdose might be his or her parents' first awareness of a problem. _____

7. Prescription opioids and heroin have very similar effects, but heroin is deadlier. _____

8. Both drugs change the brain craving replaces the brain's ability to make good choices. _____

9. In 2010, a new type of OxyContin was approved as "abuse resistant" it could not be crushed and snorted. _____

10. The surprise result was that many OxyContin abusers turned to heroin, heroin-related deaths became tragic local news all over the country. _____

11. Recovery is difficult an addict needs willingness, serious rehab to retrain body and brain, and perhaps a drug like Suboxone to help him or her stay off opioids.   _____

12. Someone conquers substance abuse, his or her triumph encourages others to seek help.   _____

PRACTICE 2   Label each sentence *RO* or *CS*. Then correct each run-on (RO) or comma splice (CS) in two ways. Be sure to punctuate correctly.

> **EXAMPLE:**   "Awesome" is an overused word awe can change us. *RO*
>
>   a. *"Awesome" is an overused word, but awe can change us.*
>
>   b. *Although "awesome" is an overused word, awe can change us.*

1. A child might feel awe gazing at the Grand Canyon, wonder and reverence fill her.

    a. _____

    _____

    b. _____

    _____

2. Researchers tested 63 students, they wanted to study the effects of awe.

    a. _____

    _____

    b. _____

    _____

3. They showed different videos to two groups they recorded the reactions.

    a. _____

    _____

    b. _____

    _____

4. Some students watched waterfalls, whales, and astronauts in space this group felt awe.

    a. _____

    _____

    b. _____

    _____

5. Others watched scenes of people having fun this group felt happiness.

   a. _____

   _____

   b. _____

   _____

6. Later, the awe group felt that time slowed down stress lifted.

   a. _____

   _____

   b. _____

   _____

7. The other group did not feel this slowing of time their to-do lists still worried them.

   a. _____

   _____

   b. _____

   _____

8. People who often feel awe are more creative, they are better problem solvers.

   a. _____

   _____

   b. _____

   _____

9. Children who experience awe feel more connected to others, they are kinder people.

   a. _____

   _____

   b. _____

   _____

10. The ocean, a night sky, a thrilling concert, a wild animal all can evoke awe what experiences would bring you more awe?

   a. _____

   _____

   b. _____

   _____

Chapter Highlights

Avoid run-ons and comma splices:

Error: Her house faces the ocean the view is breathtaking. (*run-on*)

Error: Her house faces the ocean, the view is breathtaking. (*comma splice*)

Use these techniques to avoid run-ons and comma splices:

- Write two complete sentences.

  Her house faces the ocean. The view is breathtaking.

- Use a coordinating conjunction (*for, and, nor, but, or, yet, so*).

  Her house faces the ocean, *so* the view is breathtaking.

- Use a subordinating conjunction (*although, before, because, when,* etc.).

  Because her house faces the ocean, the view is breathtaking.

PROOFREADING STRATEGY

Proofread your work very carefully if comma splices are among your error patterns.

1. Go back through your draft and **circle every comma** in every sentence.

2. For each comma, ask yourself, *"Would substituting a period for this comma create a complete sentence that could stand alone?"*

   NO   YES
   Before he joined the Army, he completed his associate's degree, he also married his high-school sweetheart.

3. If the answer is yes, you have written a comma splice and will need to replace the comma with **a period or keep the comma and add a coordinating conjunction after it**.

   Before he joined the Army, he completed his associate's degree, and he married his high-school sweetheart.

WRITING AND PROOFREADING ASSIGNMENT

When you apply for a job, the cover letter (or email) that accompanies your résumé is a vital job-search tool. It introduces you to the employer and always includes a paragraph that summarizes your qualifications for a particular job. Write a summary of your work experience, beginning with your very first job and moving in chronological order from that job to your current job. Include both paid and volunteer positions. For each job, provide your dates of employment and a brief description of your major responsibilities. The cover letter (or email) must be error-free, so proofread it carefully. Exchange papers with a classmate and check each other's work, especially for comma splices and run-ons.

CHAPTER REVIEW

Run-ons and comma splices are most likely to occur in paragraphs or longer pieces of writing. Proofread each of the following paragraphs for run-ons and comma splices. Correct them in any way that makes sense: make two separate sentences, add a coordinating conjunction, or add a subordinating conjunction. Make your corrections above the lines. Punctuate with care.

A. (1) Sodas and other sugary drinks are hugely popular, earning the beverage companies a whopping $60 billion a year. (2) The average American male 12 to 19 years old drinks 898 cans of soda a year, that's 2 ½ cans a day. (3) The average young female drinks about 675 cans a year. (4) Every can of Coke, Dr Pepper, 7UP, or other soda contains at least 10 teaspoons of added sugar, these days, fast-food chains and manufacturers are pushing larger and larger sodas. (5) A 20-ounce bottle of soda has 20 teaspoons of sugar a 1-liter bottle has 31 teaspoons. (6) No wonder soda has been called "liquid candy." (7) Except for water, sugar is the main ingredient in every brand. (8) Soda companies don't want customers to know that their products are a major factor in America's obesity and diabetes epidemics. (9) Drinking a can of soda a day puts on 15 pounds a year, a daily 20-ounce soda packs on 25 pounds. (10) Sarah Bradley was a self-described soda addict, 40 pounds overweight, she and her two children decided enough was enough. (11) They cut out all soda and fruit juice and encouraged each other to get more active. (12) Sarah and the kids have lost 35 pounds among them. (13) "It's up to us to get healthy," Sarah says, "or the soda companies will just get rich by making us fat and sick."

B. (1) Tony Hawk not only has created a skateboarding revolution he has turned his mastery of the sport into a business empire. (2) In 1999, at 31 years of age, Hawk was the first skater ever to complete a "900," this is a 360-degree spin done two-and-a-half times in midair. (3) As a result, he was dubbed "the Michael Jordan of skateboarding." (4) Hawk flew, he defied the laws of physics, inventing amazing new feats of aerial acrobatics. (5) Millions of admiring kids took up skateboarding, skate parks sprang up across the country. (6) Applying his skating expertise to the growing video game industry, Hawk created his *Tony Hawk's Pro Skater* game series, it was hugely popular. (7) *Tony Hawk's Underground* series came next each game told a story, with new characters and new tricks. (8) Through 2015, Hawk released 19 skateboarding video games and sold 30 million copies. (9) Hawk's history-making moves and his video games that capture the thrill of skateboarding have changed America more young people now skateboard than play baseball.

C. (1) What do you do every night before you go to sleep and every morning when you wake up? (2) You probably brush your teeth, most people in the United States did not start brushing their teeth until after the 1850s. (3) People living in the nineteenth century did not have toothpaste, Dr. Washington Wentworth Sheffield developed a tooth-cleaning substance, which soon became widely available. (4) With the help of his son, this Connecticut dentist changed our daily habits by making the first toothpaste it was called Dr. Sheffield's Crème Dentifrice. (5) The product was not marketed cleverly enough, the idea of using toothpaste caught on slowly. (6) Then toothpaste was put into tin tubes everyone wanted to try this new product. (7) Think of life without tubes of mint-flavored toothpaste then thank Dr. Sheffield for his idea.

Last Words

D. (1) Every 14 days, a language somewhere in the world dies. (2) For example, the last fluent speaker of the Alaskan language of Eyak was Chief Marie Jones, when she passed away in 2008, Eyak died with her. (3) Languages are disappearing on every continent. (4) North America has 200 Native American languages, only about 50 now have more than a thousand speakers. (5) The endangered Gaelic language is undergoing a revival in Ireland, the other Celtic languages in northwestern Europe have been declining for generations. (6) The death of languages is most noticeable in isolated communities in Asia, South America, and Australia, however. (7) Each tiny community might have its own language only a few people speak it.

(8) In such small communities, a whole language can die if one village perishes. (9) When Westerners explored a rain forest in Venezuela in the 1960s they carried a flu virus into a tiny community. (10) The virus killed all the villagers, their language disappeared with them. (11) However, most languages fade out when a smaller community comes into close contact with a larger, more powerful one, people begin to use the "more important" language.

A teacher at the Nixyaawii Community School in Mission, Oregon, gives a lesson in an endangered Native American language.

(12) A language that gives better access to education, jobs, and new technology usually prevails over a native mother tongue.

(13) According to scholars who study languages, almost half of the world's 7,000 languages are in danger of extinction. (14) That statistic represents more than the loss of specific languages, every language represents a way of looking at the world. (15) Whenever a language disappears, we lose a unique point of view. (16) No other language can really take its place.

PRACTICE 3   CRITICAL THINKING AND WRITING

You have been asked to suggest ways to address the heroin epidemic in the United States. First, reread Practice 1 in this chapter about this epidemic. Now study the following chart, if possible in a group with several classmates. What is the *main idea* expressed in this poster? Do any facts or statistics here surprise you? Why? Note that some of the addictive substances listed are legal, others illegal. What steps should be taken to slow or stop the heroin epidemic and the suffering and death it brings? Draw on experiences of friends or acquaintances if you wish. Now organize your ideas and write a persuasive paragraph or essay setting forth two to three actions to help solve this devastating social problem.

Heroin use is part of a larger substance abuse problem.

Nearly all people who used heroin also used at least 1 other drug.

Most used at least 3 other drugs.

Heroin is a highly addictive opioid drug with a high risk of overdose and **death** for users.

People who are addicted to...

ALCOHOL	MARIJUANA	COCAINE	Rx OPIOID PAINKILLERS
are	are	are	are
2x	**3x**	**15x**	**40x**

...more likely to be addicted to heroin.

National Survey on Drug Use and Health (NSDUH), 2011-2013

EXPLORING ONLINE

depts.dyc.edu/learningcenter/owl/exercises/run-ons_ex1.htm

Interactive quiz: Correct the run-ons and click for your score.

grammar.ccc.commnet.edu/grammar/quizzes/nova/nova4.htm

Interactive quiz: Find and fix the comma splices in these sentences.

web2.uvcs.uvic.ca/elc/studyzone/490/grammar/sentence-problems1.htm

Moment of truth! Have you learned to slay the three grade-killers—run-ons, comma splices, and fragments?

Visit **MindTap** for *Grassroots* to access this chapter's ebook, flashcards, additional practice and quizzes, and more!

CHAPTER 20

Semicolons and Conjunctive Adverbs

A: Defining and Using Semicolons

B: Defining and Using Conjunctive Adverbs

C: Punctuating Conjunctive Adverbs

A. Defining and Using Semicolons

So far you have learned to join ideas together in two ways.

Coordinating conjunctions (*and, but, for, nor, or, so, yet*) can join ideas:

(1) This is the worst food we have ever tasted, *so* we will never eat in this restaurant again.

Subordinating conjunctions (for example, *although, as, because, if,* and *when*) also can join ideas:

(2) *Because* this is the worst food we have ever tasted, we will never eat in this restaurant again.

Another way to join ideas is with a **semicolon**:

(3) This is the worst food we have ever tasted; we will never eat in this restaurant again.

A *semicolon* joins two related independent ideas without a conjunction; do not capitalize the first word after a semicolon unless it is a word that is always capitalized, like someone's name.

Use the semicolon for variety. In general, use no more than one or two semicolons in a paragraph.

PRACTICE 1

Each independent idea that follows is the first half of a sentence. Add a semicolon and a second complete idea, one that can stand alone.

EXAMPLE: Domingo was a cashier at Food City : *now he manages the store.*

1. My cat spotted a mouse _____

_____

2. The garage became an art studio _____

_____

3. Beatrice has an unlisted phone number _____

_____

4. I felt sure someone had been in the room _____

_____

5. Roslyn's first car had a stick shift _____

_____

Semicolons should connect two *related independent ideas.* If two ideas do not have a close relationship—such as a cause and its effect, a comparison of two like things, or a time order relationship—the sentences probably should be separated with a period.

BE CAREFUL: Do not use a semicolon between a dependent idea and an independent idea.

> Although he is never at home, he is not difficult to reach at the office.

- You cannot use a semicolon in this sentence because the first idea (*although he is never at home*) cannot stand alone.

- The word *although* requires that another idea be added in order to make a complete sentence.*

PRACTICE 2   Which of these ideas can be followed by a semicolon and an independent thought? Check them (✔).

1. When Molly peered over the counter   _____

2. The library has installed new computers   _____

3. After he finishes cleaning the fish   _____

4. She suddenly started to laugh   _____

5. My answer is simple   _____

6. I cannot find my car keys   _____

7. The rain poured down in buckets   _____

8. Before the health fair is over   _____

9. Unless you arrive early   _____

10. Because you understand, I feel better   _____

_____

* For work on subordinating conjunctions, see Chapter 18.

Now copy the sentences you have checked, add a semicolon, and complete each sentence with a second independent idea. You should have checked sentences 2, 4, 5, 6, 7, and 10.

2. _____

_____

4. _____

_____

5. _____

_____

6. _____

_____

7. _____

_____

10. _____

_____

PRACTICE 3   Proofread for incorrect semicolons and capital letters. Make your corrections above the lines.

(1) The Swiss Army knife is carried in the pockets and purses of millions of travelers, campers, and just plain folks. (2) Numerous useful gadgets are folded into its famous red handle; These include knife blades, tweezers, scissors, toothpick, screwdriver, bottle opener, fish scaler, and magnifying glass. (3) Because the knife contains many tools; it is also carried by explorers, mountain climbers, and astronauts. (4) Lives have been saved by the Swiss Army knife. (5) It once opened the iced-up oxygen system of someone climbing Mount Everest; It saved the lives of scientists stranded on an island, who used the tiny saw on the knife to cut branches for a fire. (6) The handy Swiss Army knife was created for Swiss soldiers in 1891; and soon became popular all over the world. (7) It comes in many models and colors many people prefer the classic original. (8) The Swiss Army knife deserves its reputation for beautiful design and usefulness; a red one is on permanent display in New York's famous Museum of Modern Art.

B. Defining and Using Conjunctive Adverbs

Another excellent method of joining ideas is to use a semicolon and a special kind of adverb. This special adverb is called a **conjunctive adverb** because it is part *conjunction* and part *adverb*.

(1) (a) He received an A on his term paper; *furthermore,*

(b) the instructor exempted him from the final.

- *Furthermore* adds idea (b) to idea (a).
- The sentence might have been written, "He received an A on his term paper, *and* the instructor exempted him from the final."
- However, *furthermore* is stronger and more emphatic.
- Note the punctuation.

(2) (a) Luzette has never studied finance; *however,*

(b) she plays the stock market like a pro.

- *However* contrasts ideas (a) and (b).
- The sentence might have been written, "Luzette has never studied finance, *but* she plays the stock market like a pro."
- However, the word *however* is stronger and more emphatic.
- Note the punctuation.

(3) (a) The complete dictionary weighs 30 pounds; *therefore,*

(b) I have a dictionary app on my phone.

- *Therefore* shows that idea (a) is the cause of idea (b).
- The sentence might have been written, "*Because* the complete dictionary weighs 30 pounds, I have a dictionary app on my phone."
- However, *therefore* is stronger and more emphatic.
- Note the punctuation.

A *conjunctive adverb* **may be used with a semicolon only when both ideas are independent and can stand alone.**

Here are some common conjunctive adverbs and their meanings:

Common Conjunctive Adverbs		
consequently	*means*	as a result
for example	*means*	as one example
furthermore	*means*	in addition
however	*means*	in contrast
in fact	*means*	in truth, to emphasize
instead	*means*	in place of
meanwhile	*means*	at the same time
nevertheless	*means*	in contrast
otherwise	*means*	as an alternative
therefore	*means*	for that reason

Conjunctive adverbs are also called **transitional expressions**. They help the reader see the transitions, or changes in meaning, from one idea to the next.

PRACTICE 4   Add an idea after each conjunctive adverb. The idea you add must make sense in terms of the entire sentence, so keep in mind the meaning of each conjunctive adverb. If necessary, refer to the chart.

> **EXAMPLE:**   Several students had questions about the final; therefore, *they stayed*
> *after class to chat with the instructor.*

1. Aunt Bessie did a handstand; meanwhile, _____

   _____

2. Anna says whatever is on her mind; consequently, _____

   _____

3. I refuse to wear those red cowboy boots again; furthermore, _____

   _____

4. Travis is a good role model; otherwise, _____

   _____

5. Kim wanted to volunteer at the hospital; however, _____

   _____

6. My mother carried two bulky pieces of luggage off the plane; furthermore,

   _____

7. I have many chores to do today; nevertheless, _____

   _____

8. The gas gauge on my car does not work properly; therefore, _____

   _____

C. Punctuating Conjunctive Adverbs

Notice the punctuation pattern:

> Complete idea; conjunctive adverb, complete idea.

- The conjunctive adverb is preceded by a semicolon.
- It is followed by a comma.

PRACTICE 5   Highlight or underline the conjunctive adverb in each sentence. Then punctuate each sentence correctly.

1. For centuries, humans have tried to understand why we dream consequently many different theories have been proposed.

2. To the ancients, dreams had divine meaning for example the Greeks thought a god actually entered the sleeper and delivered a message.

3. The ancient Egyptians also looked for divine guidance in dreams furthermore, they built dream temples for this purpose.

4. In 1899, Sigmund Freud brought attention to dreams again in fact his book *The Interpretation of Dreams* helped create modern psychology.

5. According to Freud, dreams don't deal with conscious problems at all instead they reveal our *unconscious* thoughts, desires, and fears.

6. A dream about being fired might reveal a hidden wish for a new career therefore analyzing such a dream might expand one's self-knowledge.

7. In the last ten years, brain scientists have proposed many new theories about why we dream furthermore two of these have become widely accepted.

Fantastic images like this ship appear to us in dreams. Do dreams send messages, solve problems, or just discharge brain static?

8. The first idea is that we dream to exercise our brains, consequently our minds will be alert in the morning.

9. The second idea is that we dream to solve problems from the day before in fact college students given a logic problem right before bed often discovered the answers in their sleep.

10. We may not study or even remember our dreams, however; dreaming seems to play an important role in our lives.

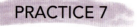 **PRACTICE 6**

WRITING ASSIGNMENT

Have you ever had a dream that sparked a new idea or new insights? Has a dream ever helped you find a solution to a problem you faced? Have you ever gained new awareness of your hidden thoughts and feelings because of a dream?

Write a description of an important dream you have had, and then explain the effects, if any, this dream had on your actions and decisions.

PRACTICE 7

Combine each set of sentences into one, using a conjunctive adverb. Choose a conjunctive adverb that expresses the relationship between the two ideas. Punctuate with care.

1. a. Belkys fell asleep on the train.
   b. She missed her stop.

   Combination: _____

   _____

2. a. Last night Channel 20 televised a special about gorillas.
   b. I did not get home in time to see it.

   Combination: _____

   _____

3. a. Roberta writes to her nephew every month.
   b. She sends a gift with every letter.

   Combination: _____

   _____

4. a. It takes me almost an hour to get to school each morning.
   b. The scenery makes the drive a pleasure.

   Combination: _____

   _____

5. a. Luke missed work on Monday.
   b. He did not proofread the quarterly report.

   Combination: _____

   _____

BE CAREFUL: Never use a semicolon and a conjunctive adverb when the conjunctive adverb does not join two independent ideas.

> (1) *However,* I don't climb mountains.
>
> (2) I don't, *however,* climb mountains.
>
> (3) I don't climb mountains, *however.*

- Why aren't semicolons used in sentences (1), (2), and (3)?
- These sentences contain only one independent idea; therefore, a semicolon cannot be used.

Never use a semicolon to join two ideas if one of the ideas is subordinate to the other.

> (4) If I climbed mountains, *however,* I would hike in the Rockies.

- Are the two ideas in sentence (4) independent?
- *If I climbed mountains* cannot stand alone as an independent idea; therefore, a semicolon cannot be used.

Chapter Highlights

- **A semicolon joins two related independent ideas:**

  I like hiking; she prefers fishing.

- **Do not capitalize the first word after a semicolon unless it is always capitalized:**

  | Independent idea | ; | independent idea. |

- **A semicolon and a conjunctive adverb join two independent ideas:**

  We can't go rowing now; *however,* we can go on Sunday.

  Lou earned an 83 on the exam; *therefore,* he passed physics.

- **Use a semicolon only when the conjunctive adverb joins two independent ideas:**

  I wasn't sorry; however, I apologized. (*two independent ideas*)

  I apologized, however. (*one independent idea*)

  If you wanted to go, however, you should have said so. (*one dependent idea + one independent idea*)

PROOFREADING STRATEGY

Use semicolons and conjunctive adverbs to add style and variety to your writing; just proofread with care, especially for punctuation errors. **Highlight or underline any conjunctive adverbs** (like *however*, *consequently*, and *for example*). Make sure the ideas on both sides of the conjunctive adverb are complete. Add any missing semicolons and commas.

Now **circle the semicolons.** Make sure the ideas on both sides are complete, closely related thoughts. No word after a semicolon should be capitalized unless it is always capitalized, like the pronoun "I" or someone's name. Here are two examples:

My dog Garbo badly needed a bath; ~~She~~ *she* was sprayed by a skunk.

Randy grabbed the dog shampoo and filled the wading pool with water *water; however,* however;

Garbo had other ideas.

WRITING AND PROOFREADING ASSIGNMENT

Many people find that certain situations make them nervous or anxious—for example, taking a test or meeting strangers at a social gathering. Have you ever conquered such an anxiety yourself or even learned to cope with it successfully?

Write to someone who has the same fear you have had; encourage him or her with your success story, explaining how you managed the anxiety. Describe the steps you took.

Use one or two semicolons and at least one conjunctive adverb in your paper. Make sure that you are joining two independent ideas. Finally, highlight your conjunctive adverbs and circle your semicolons. Check for correctness.

CHAPTER REVIEW

Proofread this paragraph for semicolon errors, conjunctive adverb errors, and punctuation or capitalization errors. You might use the proofreading strategy above.

(1) Shakira is more than a gifted Colombian singer and songwriter she is also a philanthropist, determined to give children a brighter future. (2) By the age of eight, Shakira had decided she would succeed as a professional musician; In addition she vowed to use her fame and money to help children. (3) In her hometown of Barranquilla, Colombia, she saw countless children struggle in poverty consequently; at 18 she released *Pies Descalzos* ("Bare Feet"), her breakthrough album in Latin America. (4) As her fame grew, Shakira started the Pies Descalzos Foundation to provide education for poor children. (5) Because violence and conflict have long plagued Colombia; many families have lost their stable communities. (6) Today, Pies Descalzos sponsors seven schools and 77,000

David Vaaknin/Getty Images

Shakira meets
with Israeli and
Palestinian children as
a UNICEF Goodwill
Ambassador.

children and adults, offering classes and family services. (7) Subjects include reading,
writing, and art, furthermore, the schools aim to help students grow emotionally and
socially. (8) Shakira's work with children extends beyond her foundation; she has served as
a UNICEF Goodwill Ambassador and honorary chairperson of the Global Campaign
for Education. (9) This exceptional woman wants education and a bright future for every
child, meanwhile; she is collaborating with other Latin superstars like Ricky Martin and
Carlos Vives and producing her long-awaited eleventh album. (10) Once asked what part
of her body she likes best, Shakira replied, "My brain."

EXPLORING ONLINE

owl.english.purdue.edu/owl/resource/607/04
Comma or semicolon? Review the rules.

depts.dyc.edu/learningcenter/owl/exercises/semicolons_ex1.htm
If you ace Exercise 1, congratulations. If you ace Exercise 2,
you are now Master of the Semicolon!

Visit **MindTap** for *Grassroots* to access this chapter's ebook, flashcards, additional practice and
quizzes, and more!

CHAPTER 21

Relative Pronouns

A: Defining and Using Relative Pronouns

B: Punctuating Ideas Introduced by WHO, WHICH, or THAT

A. Defining and Using Relative Pronouns

To add variety to your writing, you sometimes may wish to use **relative pronouns** to combine two sentences.

> (1) My grandfather is 80 years old.
>
> (2) He collects stamps.

- Sentences (1) and (2) are grammatically correct.
- They are so short, however, that you may wish to combine them.

> (3) My grandfather, *who* is 80 years old, collects stamps.

- Sentence (3) is a combination of (1) and (2).
- *Who* has replaced *he*, the subject of sentence (2). *Who* introduces the rest of the idea, *is 80 years old*.
- *Who* is called a *relative pronoun* because it *relates* "is 80 years old" to "my grandfather."*

BE CAREFUL: An idea introduced by a relative pronoun cannot stand alone as a complete and independent sentence. It is dependent; it needs an independent idea (like "My grandfather collects stamps") to complete its meaning.

Here are some more combinations:

> (4) He gives great singing lessons.
>
> (5) All his pupils love them.
>
> (6) He gives great singing lessons, *which* all his pupils love.

---

* For work on subject-verb agreement with relative pronouns, see Chapter 12, Part E.

(7) I have a large dining room.

(8) It can seat 20 people.

(9) I have a large dining room *that* can seat 20 people.

● As you can see, *which* and *that* can also be used as relative pronouns.

● In sentence (6), what does *which* relate or refer to? _____

● In sentence (9), what does *that* relate or refer to? _____

When *who, which,* and *that* are used as relative pronouns, they usually come directly after the words they relate to.

My grandfather, who . . .

. . . singing lessons, which . . .

. . . dining room that . . .

Relative Pronouns
BE CAREFUL: *Who, which,* and *that* cannot be used interchangeably.
Who **refers to people.**
Which **refers to things.**
That **refers to things.**

PRACTICE 1   Combine each set of sentences into one sentence. Make sure to use *who, which,* and *that* correctly.

EXAMPLE: a. The garden is beginning to sprout.

b. I planted it last week.

Combination: _The garden that I planted last week is beginning to sprout._

1. a. My uncle is giving me diving lessons.

   b. He was a state champion.

   Combination: _____

   _____

2. a. Our marriage ceremony was quick and sweet.

   b. It made our nervous parents happy.

   Combination: _____

   _____

3. a. The manatee is a sea mammal.

   b. It lives along the Florida coast.

   Combination: _____

   _____

4. a. Donna bought a new backpack.

   b. The backpack has thickly padded straps.

   Combination: _____

   _____

5. a. This walking tour has 32 stops.

   b. It is a challenge to complete.

   Combination: _____

   _____

6. a. Hockey is a fast-moving game.

   b. It often becomes violent.

   Combination: _____

   _____

7. a. Andrew Jackson was the seventh U.S. president.

   b. He was born in South Carolina.

   Combination: _____

   _____

8. a. At the beach, I always use sunscreen.

   b. It prevents burns and lessens the danger of skin cancer.

   Combination: _____

   _____

B. Punctuating Ideas Introduced by WHO, WHICH, or THAT

Ideas introduced by relative pronouns can be one of two types, **restrictive** or **nonrestrictive**. Punctuating them must be done carefully.

Restrictive

Never eat peaches *that are green*.

- A *relative clause* has (1) a subject that is a relative pronoun and (2) a verb.

- What is the relative clause in the sentence in the box? _____

- Can you leave out *that are green* and still keep the basic meaning of the sentence?

- No! You are not saying *don't eat peaches*; you are saying don't eat *certain kinds* of peaches—*green* ones.

- Therefore, *that are green* is *restrictive*; it restricts the meaning of the sentence.

A *restrictive clause* **is not set off by commas because it is necessary to the meaning of the sentence.**

Nonrestrictive

My guitar, *which is a Martin,* was given to me as a gift.

- In this sentence, the relative clause is _____.

- Can you leave out *which is a Martin* and still keep the basic meaning of the sentence?

- Yes! *Which is a Martin* merely adds a fact. It does not change the basic idea of the sentence, which is *my guitar was given to me as a gift.*

- Therefore, *which is a Martin* is *nonrestrictive;* it does not restrict or change the meaning of the sentence.

A *nonrestrictive clause* **is set off by commas because it is not necessary to the meaning of the sentence.**

Note: *Which* **is often used as a nonrestrictive relative pronoun.**

PRACTICE 2   Underline or highlight the relative pronoun in each sentence. Punctuate correctly. Write a C next to each correct sentence.

1. People who need help are often embarrassed to ask for it.   _____

2. Ovens that clean themselves are the best kind.   _____

3. Paint that contains lead can be dangerous to children.   _____

4. The anaconda which is the largest snake in the world can weigh 550 pounds.   _____

5. Edward's watch which tells the time and the date was a gift from his wife.   _____

6. Carol who is a flight attendant has just left for Pakistan.   _____

7. Joel Upton who is a dean of students usually sings in the yearly talent show.   _____

8. Exercise that causes severe dehydration is dangerous.   _____

PRACTICE 3   Complete each sentence by completing the relative clause.

EXAMPLE: Boxing is a sport that ____*upsets me*_____.

1. My aunt, who _____, rescued a cat last week.

2. A family that _____ can solve its problems.

3. I never vote for candidates _____.

4. This T-shirt, which _____, was a gift.

5. Paris, _____, is an exciting city to visit.

6. James, who _____, just enlisted in the Air Force.

7. I cannot resist stores that _____.

8. This company, which _____, provides health benefits and retirement plans for employees.

PRACTICE 4   On paper or on a computer, write four sentences using restrictive relative clauses and four using nonrestrictive relative clauses. Punctuate with care.

Chapter Highlights

- **Relative pronouns (*who*, *which*, and *that*) can join two independent ideas:**

    We met Krizia Stone. She runs an advertising agency.

    We met Krizia Stone, *who* runs an advertising agency.

    My favorite radio station is WQDF. It plays mostly jazz.

    My favorite radio station is WQDF, *which* plays mostly jazz.

    Last night, I had a hamburger. It was too rare.

    Last night, I had a hamburger *that* was too rare.

- **Restrictive relative clauses change the meaning of the sentence. They are not set off by commas:**

    The uncle *who is helping me through college* lives in Texas.

    The car *that we saw Ned driving* was not his.

- **Nonrestrictive relative clauses do not change the meaning of the sentence. They are set off by commas:**

    My uncle, *who lives in Texas*, owns a supermarket.

    Ned's car, *which is a 1992 Mazda*, was at the repair shop.

PROOFREADING STRATEGY

If *who*, *which*, *that* errors are one of your error patterns, **search your drafts for the words *who*, *which*, and *that* and highlight or underline** them. If you are using a computer, use the "*Find*" feature to locate these words. Whenever *who*, *which*, or *that* is being used as a relative pronoun, ask yourself, "***Have I selected the correct relative pronoun?***" *Who* is for people, *which* and *that* for things.

  Now check your punctuation. Would omitting the *who*, *which*, or *that* clause *change* the meaning of the sentence? If the answer is "No," then use commas to set off this *nonrestrictive* clause. Here is an example:

                    YES   NO
The man who caused the accident did not see the stop sign, which was hidden under thick vines.

WRITING AND PROOFREADING ASSIGNMENT

In a small group, discuss a change that would improve life in your neighborhood—a new traffic light or more police patrols, for instance. Your task is to write a flier that will convince neighbors that this change is important; your purpose is to win them over to your side. The flier might note, for instance, that a child was killed at a certain intersection or that several burglaries could have been prevented. Each group member should write his or her own flier, including two sentences with relative pronouns and correct punctuation. Then read the fliers aloud; decide which are effective and why. Finally, exchange papers and check for correct relative pronoun use.

CHAPTER REVIEW

Proofread the following paragraph for relative pronoun errors and punctuation errors. Correct each error above the line.

(1) Charles Anderson is best known as the trainer of the Tuskegee Airmen who were the first African-American combat pilots. (2) During a time when African Americans were prevented from becoming pilots, Anderson was fascinated by planes. (3) He learned about flying from books. (4) At age 22, he bought a used plane which, became his teacher. (5) Eventually he met someone, who helped him become an expert flyer. (6) Battling against discrimination, Anderson became the first African American to earn

Seven of the famous African-American pilots of World War II, the Tuskegee Airmen

Bettmann/Getty Images

an air transport pilot's license. (7) He and another pilot made the first round-trip flight across America by black Americans. (8) In 1939 Anderson started a civilian pilot training program at Tuskegee Institute in Alabama. (9) One day Eleanor Roosevelt, which was first lady at the time insisted on flying with him. (10) Soon afterward, Tuskegee Institute was chosen by the Army Air Corps for a special program. (11) Anderson who was chief flight instructor gave America's first African-American World War II pilots their initial training. (12) During the war, the Tuskegee Airmen showed great skill and heroism which were later recognized by an extraordinary number of honors and awards.

EXPLORING ONLINE

grammar.ccc.commnet.edu/grammar/quizzes/which_quiz.htm

Interactive quiz: Choose *who*, *which*, or *that*.

wwwedu.ge.ch/cptic/prospective/projets/anglais/exercises/whowhich.htm

Test your relatives (*who*, *which*, and *that*, that is).

Visit **MindTap** for *Grassroots* to access this chapter's ebook, flashcards, additional practice and quizzes, and more!

CHAPTER 22

-*ING* Modifiers

A: Using -*ING* Modifiers

B: Avoiding Confusing Modifiers

A. Using -*ING* Modifiers

Another way to join ideas together is with an **-*ing* modifier**, or **present participle**.

> (1) Beth was learning to ski. She broke her ankle.
>
> (2) Learning to ski, Beth broke her ankle.

- It seems that *while* Beth was learning to ski, she had an accident. Sentence (2) emphasizes this time relationship and also joins two short sentences in one longer one.

- In sentence (2), *learning* without its helping verb, *was*, is not a verb. Instead, *learning to ski* refers to or modifies *Beth*, the subject of the new sentence.

> Learning to ski, Beth broke her ankle.

- Note that a comma follows the introductory -*ing* modifier, setting it off from the independent idea.

PRACTICE 1 Combine the two sentences in each pair, using the -*ing* modifier to connect them. Drop unnecessary words. Draw an arrow from the -*ing* word to the word or words to which it refers.

EXAMPLE: Tom was standing on the deck. He waved good-bye to his family.

Standing on the deck, Tom waved good-bye to his family.

1. Kyla was searching for change. She found her lost earring.

   _____

2. The children worked all evening. They completed the jigsaw puzzle.

   _____

3. They were hiking cross-country. They made many new friends.

_____

4. She was visiting Santa Fe. She decided to move there.

_____

5. You are replacing the battery pack in your camera. You spot a grease mark on the lens.

_____

6. Seth was mumbling to himself. He named the 50 states.

_____

7. Judge Smithers was pounding his gavel. He called a recess.

_____

8. The masons built the wall carefully. They were lifting huge rocks and cementing them in place.

_____

B. Avoiding Confusing Modifiers

Be sure that your *-ing* modifiers say what you mean!

(1) Hanging by the toe from the dresser drawer, Joe found his sock.

- Probably the writer did not mean that Joe spent time hanging by his toe. What, then, was hanging by the toe from the dresser drawer?
- *Hanging* refers to the *sock*, of course, but the order of the sentence does not show this. We can clear up the confusion by turning the ideas around.

Joe found his sock hanging by the toe from the dresser drawer.

Read your sentences in Practice 1 to make sure the order of the ideas is clear, not confusing.

(2) Visiting my cousin, our house was robbed.

- Does the writer mean that *our house* was visiting my cousin? To whom or what, then, does *visiting my cousin* refer?
- *Visiting* seems to refer to *I*, but there is no *I* in the sentence. To clear up the confusion, we would have to add or change words.

Visiting my cousin, I learned that our house was robbed.

PRACTICE 2 Rewrite the following sentences to clarify any confusing *-ing* modifiers.

1. Biking and walking daily, Cheryl's commuting costs were cut.

   Rewrite: _____

2. Leaping from tree to tree, Professor Fernandez spotted a monkey.

   Rewrite: _____

3. Painting for three hours straight, the bathroom and the hallway were finished by Theresa.

   Rewrite: _____

4. My son spotted our dog playing soccer in the schoolyard.

   Rewrite: _____

5. Lying in the driveway, Tonya discovered her calculus textbook.

   Rewrite: _____

PRACTICE 3 Write three sentences of your own, using *-ing* modifiers to join ideas.

Chapter Highlights

- **An *-ing* modifier can join two ideas:**

  (1) Sol was cooking dinner.

  (2) He started a small fire.

  (1) + (2) *Cooking* dinner, Sol started a small fire.

- **Avoid confusing modifiers:**

  I finally found my cat riding my bike. (*incorrect*)

  Riding my bike, I finally found my cat. (*correct*)

PROOFREADING STRATEGY

If confusing *-ing* modifiers are one of your error patterns:

1. **Search your draft for *-ing* words or phrases**, and circle them. If you are using a computer, use the *"Find"* feature to locate these words.

2. If an *-ing* word or phrase is used as a modifier, ask yourself, *"**What word in the sentence is being modified?**"* Draw an arrow to that word.

3. Ask yourself, *"Does the -ing word or phrase come immediately before or after the word it modifies?"* If the answer is no, rewrite to move the modifier to its rightful place. Is the modifier in the sentence below positioned correctly?

INCORRECT

The seal delighted the children performing tricks for fish treats.

CORRECT

Performing tricks for fish treats, the seal delighted the children.

WRITING AND PROOFREADING ASSIGNMENT

Some people feel that much popular music degrades women and encourages violence. Others feel that popular songs expose many of the social ills we suffer from today. What do you think?

Prepare to take part in a debate to defend or criticize popular music. Your job is to convince the other side that your view is correct. Use specific song titles and artists as examples to support your argument. After you write, take a break. Then revise to use one or two -*ing* modifiers to join ideas. Proofread for correct punctuation.

PRACTICE 4

Highlight or underline all the -*ing* modifiers in this paragraph. Then proofread the following paragraph for comma errors and confusing modifiers. Correct each error above the line.

(1) Harming native plants, animals, and human health *invasive species* are plants and animals brought to the United States from other places. (2) Once here, they take over or attack native species. (3) The list includes Burmese pythons, killer bees, and saltwater crocodiles, but the most deadly invasive species of all is a fragrant flowering vine from Japan called kudzu. (4) Experts urged Americans to plant kudzu as a decorative plant, an erosion control, or a food for animals, admiring this vine at a 1865 garden show. (5) Climbing trees and strangling to death all greenery in its path, people soon saw that kudzu grew too well. (6) "Mile-a-minute-vine," as it was called, first thrived in the South. (7) Its roots, which must be destroyed to kill it, run wide and deep. (8) In 1970 the United States declared kudzu a weed and in 1997, a very dangerous weed. (9) Kudzu has become a nightmare for environmental scientists, now smothering whole forests as far North as New England. (10) Like a green tsunami, this monster vine has destroyed 7 million acres with no end in sight.

EXPLORING ONLINE

grammar.ccc.commnet.edu/grammar/quizzes/niu/niu9.htm

Are your modifiers misplaced? Take this quiz to improve your skills.

Visit **MindTap** for *Grassroots* to access this chapter's ebook, flashcards, additional practice and quizzes, and more!

Writing Assignments

As you complete each writing assignment, remember to perform these steps:

- Write a clear, complete topic sentence.

- Use freewriting, brainstorming, or clustering to generate ideas for the body of your paragraph, essay, or letter.

- Arrange your best ideas in a plan.

- Revise for support, unity, coherence, and exact language.

- Proofread for grammar, punctuation, and spelling errors.

WRITING ASSIGNMENT 1 *Explore an occupation.* Select one career that you are considering and gather information about it. As you explore, take lots of notes. You might search in the library—for job duties, qualifications needed, salary, and whether or not this is a career that is growing—or search online at sites like **www.careeronestop.org/ExploreCareers/explore-careers.aspx** and **www.bls.gov/ooh**. Now, think of ways to contact someone working in this field. Can you set up a phone call or a meeting in which you might interview him or her? Organize and write up your findings, discussing how well this career fits your interests and skills. Use a number of techniques for joining ideas, and proofread for run-ons and comma splices.

WRITING ASSIGNMENT 2 *Be a witness.* You have just witnessed a fender-bender involving a car and an ice cream truck. No one was hurt, but the insurance company has asked you to write an eyewitness report. First, visualize the accident and how it occurred. Then jot down as many details as possible to make your description of the accident as vivid as possible. Use subordinating conjunctions that indicate time (*when, as, before, while,* and so on) to show the order of events. Use as many techniques for joining ideas as you can, being careful about punctuation. Proofread for run-ons and comma splices.

WRITING ASSIGNMENT 3 *Post your thoughts online.* Many websites, blogs, and social media platforms invite readers to respond by posting their comments or opinions. Find a website forum or social media discussion on a topic you find interesting, such as music, sports, health/fitness, movies, or technology. Select a site you already know and like, or find a new one. First, compose your thoughts into a short paragraph that utilizes several ways of joining ideas. Proofread for run-ons and comma splices, and then post what you've written. Sample sites: Review a film not yet on the discussion board: **www.moviequotesandmore.com/movie-reviews**. Search by subject, explore, and comment: **medium.com/the-mission**. Learn and post about parenting: **www.parents.com**.

WRITING ASSIGNMENT 4 *Evaluate reality shows.* A local newspaper has asked readers to write a 100- to 300-word response to this question: "Has reality television gone too far?" In many popular reality programs—like *Survivor* and *The Bachelor*—contestants are often humiliated or forced to do bizarre things. State whether these reality competition shows have or have not "gone too far." Then explain specifically what you mean by going too far, using vivid details and examples from programs to support your main point. Use a variety of techniques for joining ideas; proofread for run-ons and comma splices. Your goal is to have your response chosen and published in the newspaper.

Review

Five Useful Ways to Join Ideas

In this unit, you have combined simple sentences by means of a **coordinating conjunction**, a **subordinating conjunction**, a **semicolon**, and a **semicolon** and **conjunctive adverb**. Here is a review chart of the sentence patterns discussed in this unit.

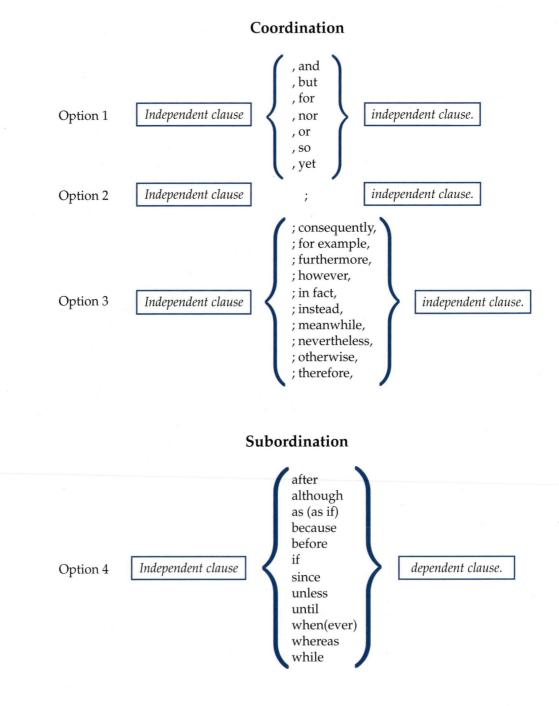

Coordination

Option 1   *Independent clause*   { , and / , but / , for / , nor / , or / , so / , yet }   *independent clause.*

Option 2   *Independent clause*   ;   *independent clause.*

Option 3   *Independent clause*   { ; consequently, / ; for example, / ; furthermore, / ; however, / ; in fact, / ; instead, / ; meanwhile, / ; nevertheless, / ; otherwise, / ; therefore, }   *independent clause.*

Subordination

Option 4   *Independent clause*   { after / although / as (as if) / because / before / if / since / unless / until / when(ever) / whereas / while }   *dependent clause.*

Option 5 {
After
Although
As (as if)
Because
Before
If
Since
Unless
Until
When(ever)
Whereas
While
} *dependent clause, independent clause.*

Proofreading

The student composition below has been changed to contain run-ons, comma splices, and misused semicolons. Proofread for these errors. Then correct them above the lines in any way you choose. (You should find eight errors.)

Managing Time in College

(1) When I started college, time was a problem. (2) I was always desperately reading an assignment just before class or racing to get to work on time. (3) The stress became too much. (4) It took a while now I know how to manage my time. (5) The secret of my success is flexible planning.

(6) At the beginning of each semester, I mark a calendar with all the due dates for the term these include deadlines for assignments, papers, and tests. (7) I also write in social events and obligations, therefore; I know at a glance when I need extra time during the next few months.

(8) Next, I make out a model weekly study schedule. (9) First, I block in the hours when I have to sleep, eat, work, go to class, and tend to my family then I decide what time I will devote to study and relaxation. (10) Finally, I fill in the times I will study each subject, making sure I plan at least one hour of study time for each hour of class time. (11) Generally, I plan some time just before or after a class that way I can prepare for a class or review my notes right after a lecture.

(12) In reality, I don't follow this schedule rigidly, I vary it according to the demands of the week and day. (13) In addition, I spend more time on my harder subjects and less time on the easy ones. (14) I also try to study my harder subjects in the morning; when I am most awake.

(15) I find that by setting up a model schedule but keeping it flexible, I can accomplish all I have to do with little worry. (16) This system may not help everyone, it has certainly worked for me.

Jesse Rose, Student

Combining

Read each pair of sentences below to determine the relationship between them. Then join each pair in two different ways, using the conjunctions shown. Punctuate correctly.

1. The tide had not yet come in.

    We went swimming.

    (although) _____

    _____

    (but) _____

    _____

2. Michael enjoys drinking coffee.

    He needs to limit his caffeine intake.

    (yet) _____

    _____

    (nevertheless) _____

    _____

3. Alexis plays the trumpet very well.

    She hopes to have her own band someday.

    (and) _____

    _____

    (furthermore) _____

    _____

4. The lecture starts in five minutes.

    We had better get to our seats.

    (because) _____

    _____

    (so) _____

    _____

5. He knows how to make money.

   He doesn't want to start another company.

   (although) _____

   _____

   (however) _____

   _____

Revising

Read through this essay of short, choppy sentences. Then revise it, combining some sentences. Use one coordinating conjunction, one subordinating conjunction, and any other ways you have learned to join ideas together. Keep some short sentences for variety. Make your corrections above the lines, and punctuate with care.

The Fastest Growing Job in America

(1) One job in the nation is growing faster than all others. (2) Applicants cannot be afraid of heights. (3) Wind turbine technicians climb 300 feet up to a tiny "room" full of equipment. (4) These intrepid mechanics repair the tall turbines that turn wind into electricity. (5) The demand for clean energy grows. (6) Wind turbine technicians are increasingly in demand.

(7) The government estimates that this career will grow 108 percent by 2024. (8) The pay is appealing. (9) Salaries average $53,000. (10) Wind turbine technicians often receive job offers. (11) They are still in college. (12) Andrew Swapp directs wind energy technology training at Mesalands Community College in New Mexico. (13) In 2016, five companies courted all 27 students in his program. (14) A wind industry leader is General Electric. (15) It is hiring technicians to avoid a shortage in the future.

(16) Jobs in renewable energy are helping many communities. (17) Unemployment is high. (18) Large wind projects are underway in Texas, Iowa, Oklahoma, Kansas, California, Ohio, Maine, and more. (19) Native Americans traditionally honor the earth. (20) It makes sense that many tribes are training people for both wind and solar careers. (21) Henry Red Cloud of Pine Ridge, South Dakota, trains Lakota Sioux solar workers at Lakota Solar Enterprises. (22) He also has helped other tribes create wind farms and train wind technicians.

(23) You don't fear heights or occasional fierce weather. (24) You might add wind turbine repair to your occupational short list.

Writers' Workshop

Describe a Detour off the Main Highway

When a writer really cares about a subject, often the reader will care too. In your group or class, read this student's paragraph, aloud if possible. As you read, underline any words or details that strike you as vivid or powerful.

Sometimes detours off the main highway can bring wonderful surprises, and last week this happened to my husband and me. On the Fourth of July weekend, we decided to drive home the long way, taking the old dirt farm road. Pulling over to admire the afternoon light gleaming on a field of wet corn we saw a tiny farm stand under a tree. No one was in sight, but a card table covered with a red checkered cloth held pints of tomatoes, jars of jam, and a handwritten price list. Next to these was a vase full of red poppies and tiny American flags. We bought tomatoes, leaving our money in the tin box stuffed with dollar bills. Driving home we both felt so happy—as if we had been given a great gift.

Kim Lee, student

1. How effective is Kim Lee's paragraph?

   _____ Clear topic sentence?   _____ Rich supporting details?
   _____ Logical organization?   _____ Effective conclusion?

2. Discuss your underlinings with one another, explaining as specifically as possible why a particular word or sentence is effective. For instance, the "red poppies and tiny American flags" are so exact that you can see them.

3. This student supports her topic sentence with a single *example,* one brief story told in detail. If you were to support the same topic sentence, what example from your own life might you use?

4. The concluding sentence tells the reader that she and her husband felt they had been given "a great gift." Do you think that the gift was being trusted to be honest?

5. Proofread for grammar and spelling. Do you notice any error patterns (two or more errors of the same type) that this student should watch out for?

About her writing process, Kim Lee says:

> I wrote this paper in my usual way—I sort of plan, and then I freewrite on the subject. I like freewriting—I pick through it for certain words or details, but of course it is also a mess. From my freewriting I got "light gleaming on a field of wet corn" and the last sentence, about the gift.

Writing and Revising Ideas

1. Develop the topic sentence "Sometimes detours off the main highway can bring wonderful [disturbing] surprises."
2. Write about a time when you were trusted or distrusted by a stranger. What effect did this have on you?

As you plan your paragraph, try to angle the subject toward something that interests *you*—chances are, it will interest your readers too. Consider using one good example to develop your paragraph. As you revise, make sure that the body of your paragraph perfectly fits the topic sentence.

Choosing the Right Noun, Pronoun, Adjective, Adverb, or Preposition

Choosing the right form of many words in English can be tricky. This unit will help you avoid some common errors. In this unit, you will

- Follow the MAP to better reading and writing
- Learn about singular and plural nouns
- Choose correct pronouns
- Use adjectives and adverbs correctly
- Choose the right prepositions
- Learn proofreading strategies to find and correct your own errors

Follow the MAP to Better Reading and Writing

Model

Here two researchers set forth new findings about happiness. If possible, read the paragraph aloud.

In study after study, four traits characterize happy people. First, especially in individualistic Western cultures, they like themselves. They have high self-esteem and usually believe themselves to be more ethical, more intelligent, less prejudiced, better able to get along with others, and healthier than the average person. Second, happy people typically feel personal control. Those with little or no control over their lives—such as prisoners, nursing home patients, severely impoverished groups or individuals, and citizens in totalitarian regimes—suffer lower morale and worse health. Third, happy people are usually optimistic. Fourth, most happy people are extroverted. Although one might expect that introverts would live more happily in the serenity of their less stressed lives, extroverts are happier—whether alone or with others.

David G. Myers and Ed Diener, "The Pursuit of Happiness," *Scientific American.*

Analysis

- This well-organized paragraph tells us the traits of happy people. They see themselves as "more *ethical,* more *intelligent,* less *prejudiced,* better *able* . . . , and *healthier.* . . ." Does this sound true to you?

- All five parts of speech discussed in this unit are used here: nouns, pronouns, adjectives, adverbs, and prepositions. Can you identify one of each?

- If you don't know the meaning of the words *extrovert* and *introvert,* look them up. Which refers to you?

Practice

- Analyze how happy you are, based on the four traits mentioned above.

- Describe an extrovert or an introvert you have observed.

CHAPTER 23

Nouns

A: Defining Singular and Plural

B: Signal Words: Singular and Plural

C: Signal Words with OF

A. Defining Singular and Plural

A **noun** names a person, a place, or a thing. Nouns may be **singular** or **plural**. *Singular* means one. *Plural* means more than one.

Singular	Plural
a reporter	the reporters (person nouns)
a forest	the forests (place nouns)
a couch	the couches (thing nouns)

● Most nouns in English form the plural by adding *-s* or *-es*.

Other nouns form their plurals in unusual ways. Learning them is easier if they are divided into groups.

Some nouns form their plurals by changing their spelling:

Singular	Plural
child	children
foot	feet
goose	geese
man	men
mouse	mice
person	people
tooth	teeth
woman	women

Many nouns ending in *-f* or *-fe* change their endings to *-ves* in the plural:

Singular	Plural
half	halves
knife	knives
leaf	leaves
life	lives

scarf	scarves
shelf	shelves
wife	wives
wolf	wolves

Most nouns that end in *-o* add *-es* in the plural:

echo + *es* = echoes	potato + *es* = potatoes
hero + *es* = heroes	veto + *es* = vetoes

● Here are some exceptions to memorize:

pianos	solos
radios	sopranos

Other nouns do not change at all to form the plural. Here is a partial list:

Singular	Plural
deer	deer
fish	fish
moose	moose
sheep	sheep

Hyphenated nouns usually form plurals by adding *-s* or *-es* to the first word:

Singular	Plural
brother-in-law	brothers-in-law
maid-of-honor	maids-of-honor
mother-to-be	mothers-to-be
runner-up	runners-up

If you are ever unsure about the plural of a noun, check a dictionary. For example, if you look up the noun *woman* in the dictionary, you will find an entry like this:

woman / women

The first word listed, *woman,* is the singular form of the noun; the second word, *women,* is the plural. Some dictionaries list the plural form of a noun only if the plural is unusual. If no plural is listed, the noun probably adds *-s* or *-es.*

PRACTICE 1   Make the following nouns plural.* If you are not sure of a particular plural, check the charts in the beginning of this section.

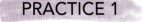

	Singular	Plural		Singular	Plural
1.	notebook	_____	4.	brother-in-law	_____
2.	hero	_____	5.	technician	_____
3.	man	_____	6.	shelf	_____

_____

* For help with spelling, see Chapter 35.

7. half _____

8. bridge _____

9. deer _____

10. runner-up _____

11. woman _____

12. radio _____

13. tooth _____

14. potato _____

15. mouse _____

16. child _____

17. flight _____

18. wife _____

19. place _____

20. maid-of-honor _____

REMEMBER: **Do not add an** -s **to words that form plurals by changing an internal letter or letters. For example, the plural of** man **is** men, **not** mens; **the plural of** woman **is** women, **not** womens; **the plural of** foot **is** feet, **not** feets.

PRACTICE 2

Proofread the following paragraph for incorrect plural nouns. Cross out the errors and correct them above the lines.

(1) Many peoples consider Glacier National Park the jewel of the National Park Service. (2) Its many mountains, glaciers, waterfalls, blue-green lake, and amazing wildlifes are in the remote Rocky Mountains in the northwest corner of Montana. (3) Several road take visitors into the park, especially Going-to-the-Sun Road, which clings to the mountainside and offers spectacular, stomach-churning views. (4) At Logan Pass—6,646 foot high—the road crosses the Continental Divide. (5) From this line along the spine of the Rocky, all river flow either west to the Pacific Ocean, south to the Gulf, or east. (6) Because Glacier is truly a wilderness park, it is best seen by hikers, not drivers. (7) Most men, woman, and childs who hike the park's 700 miles of trails come prepared—with hats, long-sleeved shirts, and on their feets, proper hiking shoes. (8) Their equipments includes bottled water and, just in case, bear spray. (9) Glacier has a large population of grizzly bears, which can weigh up to 1,400 pounds, have four-inch claws, and dislike surprises. (10) Besides grizzlies, one might glimpse mountain lions, wolfs, black bear, white mountain goats, moose, bighorn sheeps, elk, and many smaller mammals. (11) Salmon, trouts, and other fishs swim in the ice-cold rivers and lakes. (12) Scientist worry that the glaciers are melting too quickly, but Glacier Park remains a treasure.

EXPLORING ONLINE

www.nps.gov/findapark

Visit the National Park Service website. Use the find-a-park search tool to explore the many parks the public can visit and select one (Glacier National Park or some other) that you might like to learn about. Read, explore, and jot down any writing—or travel—ideas.

B. Signal Words: Singular and Plural

A *signal word* **tells you whether a singular or a plural noun usually follows.**
These **signal words** tell you that a *singular noun* usually follows:

Signal Words

a(n)
another
a single
each   } motorboat
every
one

These signal words tell you that a *plural noun* usually follows:

all
both
few
many   } motorboats
several
some
two (or more)

PRACTICE 3

In the blank following each signal word, write either a singular or a plural noun. Use as many different nouns as you can think of.

EXAMPLES: a single ___*stamp*___

most ___*fabrics*___

1. a(n)   _____
2. some   _____
3. few   _____
4. nine   _____
5. one   _____
6. all   _____

7. another _____
8. each   _____
9. a single _____
10. every   _____
11. both   _____
12. many   _____

PRACTICE 4

Read the following essay and underline or highlight the signal words. Then check for incorrect singular or plural nouns. Cross out the errors and correct them above the lines.

The Best Medicine

(1) Many researcher believe that laughter improves people's health. (2) In fact, laughing seems to lower stress, improve memory, and help most patient heal faster. (3) To put this theory into practice, many medical center have introduced humor routines into their treatment programs. (4) At one hospitals in Washington, D.C., a Laugh Café is open to patients and their families. (5) Folks meet for an hour just to have fun, and the price of admission is a single jokes.

(6) A sense of humor protects against heart disease. (7) Who knew? (8) Laughing also strengthens the immune system. (9) Dr. Mary Bennett, who has studied many health benefit of humor, performed one study in which she extracted immune cells from women who had just watched a comedy videos and from other woman who had viewed a boring informational video. (10) Dr. Bennett then mixed their cells with cancer cells. (11) The humor group had much stronger immune responses.

(12) So if you're getting a cold or feeling stressed, watch a funny movie or attend open mic night at a comedy club. (13) Take a breaks from studying, and hang out with several hilarious friend. (14) Your good health may depend on it.

PRACTICE 5

On paper or on a computer, write three sentences using signal words that require singular nouns. Then write three sentences using signal words that require plural nouns.

C. Signal Words with OF

Many signal words are followed by *of . . .* or *of the. . . .* Usually, these signal words are followed by a *plural* noun (or a collective noun) because you are really talking about one or more from a larger group.*

$$
\left.\begin{array}{l}
\text{many of the} \\
\text{a few of the} \\
\text{lots of the}
\end{array}\right\} \text{ houses are . . .}
$$

BE CAREFUL: The signal words *one of the* and *each of the* are followed by a *plural* noun, but the verb is *singular* because only the signal word (*one, each*) is the real subject.**

$$
\left.\begin{array}{l}
\text{one of the} \\
\text{each of the}
\end{array}\right\} \text{ houses is . . .}
$$

(1) *One* of the apples *is* spoiled.

(2) *Each* of the trees *grows* quickly.

- In sentence (1), *one* is the subject, not *apples*.
- In sentence (2), *each* is the subject, not *trees*.

———

* For more work on collective nouns, see Chapter 24, Part D.
** For more work on this type of construction, see Chapter 12, Part E.

PRACTICE 6   Fill in your own nouns in the following sentences. Use a different noun in each sentence.

1. Many of the _____ enrolled in Chemistry 202.

2. Sipho lost one of his _____ at the beach.

3. This is one of the _____ that everyone liked.

4. Each of the _____ carried a sign.

5. You are one of the few _____ who can do somersaults.

6. Few of the _____ produced calves.

PRACTICE 7   Write five sentences, using the signal words with *of* provided in parentheses. Use a different noun in each sentence.

EXAMPLE: (many of those . . .) ___*I planted many of those flowers myself.*___

1. (one of my . . .) _____

_____

2. (many of the . . .) _____

_____

3. (lots of the . . .) _____

_____

4. (each of these . . .) _____

_____

5. (a few of your . . .) _____

_____

PRACTICE 8   Proofread the following paragraph for correct plural nouns. Underline or highlight any signal words. Then cross out the errors and correct them above the lines.

(1) In 1782 the bald eagle became the national symbol of the United States. (2) Sadly, over the years, many of these magnificent bird suffered destruction of their habitat, poisoning of their food sources, and illegal extermination by farmers, ranchers, and hunters. (3) By the 1960s, these majestic raptors were declared an endangered species. (4) Today, however, eagles are back in American skies, thanks to some of the new recovery method used by wildlife specialists. (5) In one such method, scientists remove each of the egg from a wild eagle's nest and place it in an incubator. (6) Baby eagles must not attach

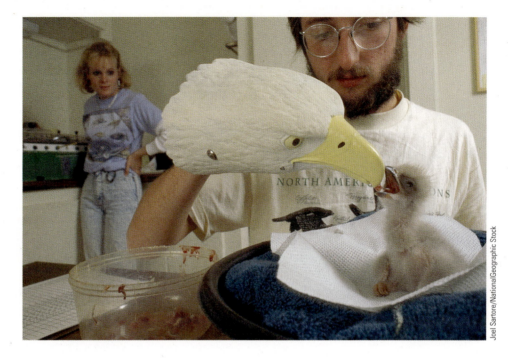

Eagle puppet feeding a three-day-old bald eaglet.

themselves to people, so all of the hatchling are fed first with tweezers and later with eagle puppets. (7) In this way, they learn to recognize Mom and Dad. (8) Protected and well fed, lots of the chick grow strong enough to be placed in the nests of adult eagles. (9) Instinct kicks in, and the adults adopt and raise the chicks as their own. (10) Today, many of our wild eagle got their start in eaglet nurseries.

Chapter Highlights

- **Most plural nouns are formed by adding -s or -es to the singular noun:**

   job/jobs   watch/watches

- **Some plurals are formed in other ways:**

   child/children   woman/women   wolf/wolves

- **Some nouns ending in -o add -es; others add -s:**

   echo/echoes   solo/solos

- **Some nouns have identical singular and plural forms:**

   fish/fish   equipment/equipment

- **Hyphenated nouns usually add -s or -es to the first word:**

   father-in-law/fathers-in-law

- **Signal words, with and without *of*, indicate whether a singular or a plural noun usually follows:**

   another musician   *many of the* musicians

PROOFREADING STRATEGY

Incorrect singular and plural nouns are considered serious errors, so proofread with care if these are among your error patterns.

First, **search each sentence for signal words and phrases** (such as *an, each, one, many, several, a few*) that "announce" the need for either a singular or a plural noun. Underline or color code these signal words. Code in a different color all phrases like *one of the . . .* and *a few of the . . .* that are *always* followed by a plural. **Locate the noun** following each signal word and check for correctness.

Notice how the color-coded signal words in this example make it easier to see if the nouns are correct.

> *ideas*   *suggestions*
> The teams generated several ~~idea,~~ but only a few of the ~~suggestion~~ seemed like workable solutions.

WRITING AND PROOFREADING ASSIGNMENT

For some families, shopping—whether for food, clothing, or electronics—is a delightful group outing, a time to be together and share. For other families, it is an ordeal, a time of great stress, with arguments about what to purchase and how much to spend.

Describe a particularly enjoyable or awful family shopping experience. Your first sentence might read, "Shopping for _____ was (is) a(n) _____ experience." Explain in detail what made it so good or so bad: What were you shopping for? Where? Exactly what went right (or wrong)? Proofread your work for the correct use of singular and plural nouns. Be especially careful of nouns that follow signal words.

CHAPTER REVIEW

Proofread the following essay for incorrect singular and plural nouns. First underline or highlight the signal words. Then cross out the errors and correct them above the lines.

Pros and Cons of Facebook

(1) Worldwide, about 2 billion peoples use Facebook, the giant social networking site started in 2004. (2) More woman are active on Facebook than man, but both genders log on regularly. (3) Many of America's 214 million user are 18 to 29 years old; they often jump onto Facebook as soon as they wake up. (4) All Facebook users should know both its powerful advantages and disadvantage.

(5) One of the major benefit of Facebook is the ease of connecting with friends, family, and interest groups. (6) Most members post photos, links, and informations about their lifes and activities. (7) Others rely on Facebook for updates in their career fields, while many business view the site as vital to sales. (8) Locating people is easier than it was in the past, so users can find like-minded groups, an old classmate, or even a birth parents. (9) The bright side of Facebook is staying easily connected worldwide.

(10) But Facebook has a dark side that includes loss of privacy, made worse because too many user post personal information that might lead to embarrassment or theft. (11) Teens and childrens, especially, may see nothing wrong with posting their home address or school. (12) Online bullying is increasing. (13) Recently, because so many Facebook user trust the site and repost sensational story without checking facts, fake news has become a real problem. (14) The company admits that far too many of its "news" article are false, invented as "click bait" to make money or promote extremist group. (15) So enjoy Facebook, but be alert; we can all be manipulated by hidden trolls who are definitely not our friends.

EXPLORING ONLINE

web2.uvcs.uvic.ca/elc/studyzone/330/grammar/irrplu1.htm
This quiz is short but tricky. Look up any plurals you don't know.

grammar.ccc.commnet.edu/grammar/quizzes/cross/plurals_gap.htm
Now try this longer plurals quiz.

grammar.ccc.commnet.edu/grammar/noun_exercise2.htm
Art Class! Study Bruegel's famous painting and hunt for nouns.

Visit **MindTap** for *Grassroots* to access this chapter's ebook, flashcards, additional practice and quizzes, and more!

Pronouns

A. Defining Pronouns and Antecedents

Pronouns take the place of or refer to nouns or other pronouns. The word or words that a pronoun refers to are called the **antecedent** of the pronoun.

> (1) *Tory* said that *he* was tired.
>
> (2) *Sonia* left early, but I did not see *her* until later.
>
> (3) *Robert and Tyrone* have been good friends ever since *their* college days.

- In sentence (1), *he* refers to *Tory*.
- *Tory* is the antecedent of *he*.

- In sentence (2), *her* refers to *Sonia*.
- *Sonia* is the antecedent of *her*.

- In sentence (3), *their* refers to *Robert and Tyrone*.
- *Robert and Tyrone* is the antecedent of *their*.

A pronoun must **agree** with its antecedent. In sentence (1), the antecedent *Tory* requires the singular, masculine pronoun *he*. In sentence (2), the antecedent *Sonia* requires the singular, feminine pronoun *her*. In sentence (3), the antecedent *Robert and Tyrone* requires the plural pronoun *their*.

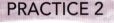

PRACTICE 1

In each of the following sentences, circle the pronoun. In the columns on the right, write the pronoun and its antecedent as shown in the example.

	Pronoun	Antecedent
EXAMPLE: Susan B. Anthony promoted women's rights before (they) were popular.	*they*	*rights*

1. Susan B. Anthony deserves praise for her accomplishments. _____ _____

2. Anthony became involved in the antislavery movement because of her principles. _____ _____

3. She helped President Lincoln develop his plans to free the slaves during the Civil War. _____ _____

4. Eventually, Anthony realized that women wouldn't be fully protected by law until they could vote. _____ _____

5. When Anthony voted in the presidential election of 1872, she was arrested. _____ _____

6. She was found guilty and given a $100 fine, but she refused to pay it. _____ _____

7. The judge did not sentence Anthony to jail because a sentence would have given her grounds for an appeal. _____ _____

8. If the Supreme Court had heard her appeal, it might have ruled that women had the right to vote. _____ _____

9. Audiences in England and Germany showed their appreciation of Anthony's work with standing ovations. _____ _____

10. Unfortunately, women in the United States had to wait until 1920 before they could legally vote. _____ _____

PRACTICE 2

Read this paragraph for meaning; then circle each pronoun you find and write its antecedent above the pronoun.

(1) Driverless cars are already making their way along the freeways of Los Angeles. (2) In 2012, the Google company secured a new bill in California that allowed its fleet of driverless cars to bring visitors from the airport to company headquarters. (3) Although much attention focused on amazing videos of a blind man doing his errands in a car with

no one at the wheel, the complex technology is still being developed. (4) Because human error accounts for 77 to 90 percent of traffic accidents, the goal is to take human drivers out of the equation, rather than try to improve their driving skills. (5) Twenty large companies including Google, Toyota, Uber, and BMW are racing to get their self-driving vehicles on the road by 2021. (6) Tesla claims its vehicles will be ready by 2018. (7) Not everyone wants his or her car making all the decisions; however, newer cars already offer self-driving features like lane-change alarms, automatic parking, and forward-collision braking, so consumers are getting used to them.

B. Referring to Indefinite Pronouns

Indefinite pronouns do not point to a specific person.

anybody
anyone
each
everybody
everyone   } Indefinite pronouns are usually *singular*.
no one   A pronoun that refers to an indefinite
nobody   pronoun should also be singular.
somebody
someone

(1) *Everyone* should do what *he* or *she* can to help.

(2) *Each* wanted to read *his* or *her* composition aloud.

(3) If *someone* smiles at you, give *him* or *her* a smile in return.

- In sentence (1), *everyone* is a singular antecedent and must be used with the singular pronoun *he* or *she*.

- In sentence (2), *each* is a singular antecedent and must be used with the singular pronoun *his* or *her*.

- In sentence (3), *someone* is a singular antecedent and must be used with the singular pronoun *him* or *her*.

   In the past, writers used *he, his,* or *him* to refer to both men and women. Now, however, many writers use *he or she, his or her,* or *him or her.* Of course, if *everyone* is a woman, use *she* or *her;* if *everyone* is a man, use *he, his,* or *him.**

Someone left *her* purse in the classroom.

Someone left *his* wallet on the bus.

Someone left *his* or *her* glasses on the back seat.

---

* For more work on pronoun reference, see Chapter 28, "Consistent Person."

It is often best to avoid the repetition of *his or her* and *he or she* by changing the indefinite pronoun to a plural.

> (4) *Everyone* in the club agreed to pay *his or her* dues on time.
>
> *or*
>
> (5) The club *members* agreed to pay *their* dues on time.

PRACTICE 3 Fill in the blanks with the correct pronouns. Then write the antecedent of each pronoun in the column on the right.

Antecedent

EXAMPLE: Everyone should do _____*his or her*_____ best.   _____*everyone*_____

1. The average citizen does not take _____ right to vote
    seriously enough.   _____

2. If a person chooses a career in accounting,
    _____ must enjoy working with numbers.   _____

3. Each player gave _____ best in the women's
    basketball finals.   _____

4. Anyone can learn to do research on the Internet if
    _____ will put the time into it.   _____

5. Amir and Fatima always do _____ housecleaning
    on Tuesday.   _____

6. Someone left _____ fingerprints on the
    windshield.   _____

7. Everyone should see _____ dentist at least
    once a year.   _____

8. Nobody wanted to waste _____ money on a
    singing stapler.   _____

PRACTICE 4 As you read this paragraph, determine which pronoun correctly refers to the antecedent and circle it. If you have trouble, locate the antecedent of the pronoun in question.

(1) Educational expert Dr. Ken Robinson says that to make the right career choice, everyone needs to understand how (his or her, their) passions and talents come together. (2) For example, someone who loves to draw will probably be happiest and most successful if (they pursue, he or she pursues) an artistic profession. (3) Anyone who enjoys interacting with people and has a knack for selling may enjoy a career in which (they, he or she) can express these gifts—entrepreneur or sales manager, for example. (4) Dr. Robinson says that

everyone should first ask (himself or herself, themselves), "What do I love to do?" (5) Then, (they, he or she) should ask, "What am I good at?" (6) This second question is difficult because many people tend to exclude answers that don't seem relevant to (his or her, their) career options (like dribble a soccer ball, play the banjo, or create new recipes). (7) No one should limit (themselves, himself or herself) only to standard academic majors or jobs with society's stamp of approval. (8) Because a career choice is one of the most important decisions a person ever makes, it should arise from who that person is and what (he or she enjoys, they enjoy).

PRACTICE 5   On paper or on a computer, write three sentences using indefinite pronouns as antecedents.

C. Referring to Special Singular Constructions

each of . . .
either of . . .
every one of . . .   } Each of these constructions is *singular*. Pronouns that refer to them must also be singular.
neither of . . .
one of . . .

(1) *Each* of the women did her work.
(2) *Neither* of the men finished his meal.
(3) *One* of the bottles is missing from its place.

- In sentence (1), *each* is a singular antecedent and is used with the singular pronoun *her*.
- Do not be confused by the prepositional phrase *of the women*.
- In sentence (2), *neither* is a singular antecedent and is used with the singular pronoun *his*.
- Do not be confused by the prepositional phrase *of the men*.
- In sentence (3), *one* is a singular antecedent and is used with the singular pronoun *its*.
- Do not be confused by the prepositional phrase *of the bottles*.*

PRACTICE 6   Fill in the blanks with the correct pronouns. Then write the antecedent of each pronoun in the column on the right.

Antecedent

EXAMPLE: Each of my nephews did ___*his*___ homework.   ___*each*___

* For more work on these special constructions, see Chapter 12, Part E.

1. One of the hikers filled _____ canteen.   _____

2. Every one of the women scored high on _____
   entrance examination.   _____

3. Each of the puzzles has _____ own solution.   _____

4. Either of them should be able to learn _____
   lines before opening night.   _____

5. One of my brothers does not have a radio in _____ car.   _____

6. Neither of the dental technicians has had _____
   lunch yet.   _____

7. Every one of the children sat still when _____
   photograph was taken.   _____

8. Lin Li and her mother opened _____ boutique
   in 1998.   _____

PRACTICE 7

As you read this paragraph, determine which pronoun correctly refers to the antecedent and circle it. If you have trouble, locate the antecedent of the pronoun in question.

(1) Cal Newport is the author of *So Good They Can't Ignore You: Why Skills Trump Passion in the Quest for Work You Love*. (2) On most college campuses, he says, each of the students has been told to follow (his or her, their) passion and this will lead to a great job. (3) This assumes, however, that a student knows what (their, his or her) passion is. (4) If the student doesn't know, Newport claims, (he or she is, they are) better off developing excellent skills and letting the passion follow. (5) Newport was one of those students who didn't know (their, his or her) passion, so he attended Massachusetts Institute of Technology (the famous MIT) and worked very hard to earn a degree in engineering. (6) There wasn't much to love in the exhausting workload and long hours. (7) But today Newport is a computer science professor—and one of the lucky people who loves (his or her, their) job. (8) He advises, "Put in the hard work, make yourself valuable to society, and your passion will follow."

PRACTICE 8

On paper or on a computer, write three sentences that use special singular constructions as antecedents.

D. Referring to Collective Nouns

Collective nouns imply more than one person but are generally considered *singular*. Here is a partial list:

Common Collective Nouns

board	family	panel
class	flock	school
college	government	society
committee	group	team
company	jury	tribe

---

(1) The *jury* meets early today because *it* must decide on a verdict.

(2) *Society* must protect *its* members from violence.

- In sentence (1), *jury* is a singular antecedent and is used with the singular pronoun *it*.

- In sentence (2), *society* is a singular antecedent and is always used with the singular pronoun *it*.

- Use *it* or *its* when referring to collective nouns.

- Use *they* or *their* only when referring to collective nouns in the plural (*schools*, *companies*, and so forth).

PRACTICE 9

Write the correct pronoun in the blank. Then write the antecedent of the pronoun in the column on the right.

Antecedent

EXAMPLE: The society sent _____*its*_____ latest recommendations for the butterfly exhibit.   ____*society*____

1. Wanda's company will have _____ annual picnic next week.   _____

2. The two teams picked up _____ gloves and bats and walked off the field.   _____

3. My high school class will soon have _____ tenth reunion.   _____

4. The city is doing _____ best to build a new stadium.   _____

5. Many soap operas thrive on _____ viewers' enjoyment of "a good cry."   _____

6. Each band has _____ guitar player and drummer.   _____

7. The panel made _____ report public.   _____

8. This college plans to train _____ student teachers in classroom management.   _____

PRACTICE 10   Proofread this paragraph carefully for errors in pronoun reference. Cross out any errors and write the correct pronouns above the lines.

(1) Last year, the board of directors at Blue Pines College decided they would invest much more money to create a superior learning experience for all students. (2) As a result, Blue Pines is undergoing major changes. (3) Many of their classroom buildings are being updated with the latest technology. (4) With a tap of the finger, an architecture instructor can take his or her students from a tour of an ancient Aztec pyramid to a wildly imaginative building by architect Zaha Hadid. (5) Classes will be able to hear a mathematician lecture in Buenos Aires and then interact live with them online. (6) In addition, the college encourages their instructors to bring leaders from local businesses into the classroom. (7) For example, the Premier Athletic Equipment Company, based in town, sent their personnel director to campus. (8) Students learned just what skills Premier is looking for in their entry-level employees. (9) Other companies have sent its representatives, too, giving students a realistic picture of what it takes to get hired and what it takes to move up. (10) This year, the state panel on higher education gave Blue Pines College their Medal of Excellence.

PRACTICE 11   On paper or on a computer, write three sentences using collective nouns as antecedents.

E. Avoiding Vague and Repetitive Pronouns

Vague Pronouns

Be sure that all pronouns *clearly* refer to their antecedents. Be especially careful of the pronouns *they* and *it*. If *they* or *it* does not refer to a *specific* antecedent, change *they* or *it* to the exact word you have in mind.

> (1) **Vague pronoun:** At registration, they said I should take Math 101.
>
> (2) **Revised:** At registration, an adviser said I should take Math 101.
>
> (3) **Vague pronoun:** On the beach, it says that no swimming is allowed.
>
> (4) **Revised:** On the beach, a sign says that no swimming is allowed.

- In sentence (1), who is *they*? The pronoun *they* does not clearly refer to an antecedent.
- In sentence (2), the vague *they* has been replaced by *an adviser*.
- In sentence (3), what is *it*? The pronoun *it* does not clearly refer to an antecedent.
- In sentence (4), the vague *it* has been replaced by *a sign*.

Repetitious Pronouns

Don't repeat a pronoun directly after its antecedent. Use *either* the pronoun *or* the antecedent—not both.

> (1) **Repetitious Pronoun:** The doctor, she said that my daughter is in perfect health.
>
> (2) **Revised:** *The doctor* said that my daughter is in perfect health.
>
> *or*
>
> *She* said that my daughter is in perfect health.

- In sentence (1), the pronoun *she* unnecessarily repeats the antecedent *doctor*, which is right before it.
- In sentence (2), use either *the doctor* or *she*, not both.

PRACTICE 12   Rewrite the sentences that contain vague or repetitious pronouns. If a sentence is correct, write *C*.

EXAMPLE: Dyslexia, it is a learning disorder that makes reading difficult.

Revised: _Dyslexia is a learning disorder that makes reading difficult._

1. Many dyslexic persons, they have achieved success in their chosen professions.

   Revised: _____

   _____

2. For example, Albert Einstein, he was dyslexic.

   Revised: _____

   _____

3. In his biography, it says that he couldn't interpret written words the way others could.

   Revised: _____

   _____

4. At his elementary school, they claimed that he was a slow learner.

   Revised: _____

   _____

5. However, this slow learner, he changed the way science looked at time and space.

   Revised: _____

   _____

6. Even politics has had its share of dyslexic leaders.

    Revised: _____

    _____

7. American history, it teaches us that President Woodrow Wilson and Vice President Nelson Rockefeller, they were both dyslexic.

    Revised: _____

    _____

8. Authors can have this problem too; the well-known mystery writer Agatha Christie, she had trouble reading.

    Revised: _____

    _____

9. Finally, in several magazines, they report that both Jay Leno and Cher are dyslexic.

    Revised: _____

    _____

10. Cher, she wasn't able to read until she was 18 years old.

    Revised: _____

    _____

F. Using Pronouns as Subjects, Objects, and Possessives

Pronouns have different forms, depending on how they are used in a sentence. Pronouns can be *subjects*, *objects*, or *possessives*. They can be in the *subjective case*, *objective case*, or *possessive case*.

Pronouns as Subjects

A pronoun can be the *subject* of a sentence:

(1) *He* loves the summer months.

(2) By noon, *they* had reached the top of the hill.

- In sentences (1) and (2), the pronouns *he* and *they* are subjects.

Pronouns as Objects

A pronoun can be the *object* of a verb:

(1) Graciela kissed *him*.

(2) Sheila moved *it* to the corner.

- In sentence (1), the pronoun *him* tells whom Graciela kissed.

- In sentence (2), the pronoun *it* tells what Sheila moved.

- These objects answer the questions *kissed whom?* and *moved what?*

A pronoun can also be the *object* of a preposition (a word like *to, for,* or *at*).*

(3) The umpire stood between *us.*

(4) Near *them,* the children played.

- In sentences (3) and (4), the pronouns *us* and *them* are the objects of the prepositions *between* and *near.*

Sometimes the prepositions *to* and *for* are understood, usually after words like *give, send, tell,* and *bring.*

(5) I gave *her* the latest sports magazine.

(6) Carver bought *him* a cowboy hat.

- In sentence (5), the preposition *to* is understood before the pronoun *her*: I gave *to* her . . .

- In sentence (6), the preposition *for* is understood before the pronoun *him*: Carver bought *for* him . . .

Pronouns That Show Possession

A pronoun can show *possession* or ownership.

(1) Manolo took *his* report and left.

(2) The climbers spotted *their* gear on the slope.

- In sentences (1) and (2), the pronouns *his* and *their* show that Manolo owns *his* report and that the climbers own *their* gear.

The chart below can help you review all the pronouns discussed in this part.

Pronoun Case Chart					
Singular Pronouns			**Plural Pronouns**		
Subjective	**Objective**	**Possessive**	**Subjective**	**Objective**	**Possessive**
1st person: I	me	my (mine)	we	us	our (ours)
2nd person: you	you	your (yours)	you	you	your (yours)
3rd person: he	him	his	they	them	their (theirs)
she	her	her (hers)			
it	it	its			

---

* See the list of prepositions in Chapter 26, Part A.

PRACTICE 13   Underline the pronouns in this paragraph. Then, over each pronoun, write an *S* if the pronoun is in the subjective case, an *O* if it is in the objective case, and a *P* if it is in the possessive case.

(1) The *iReport* page at *CNN.com* publishes stories submitted by you, me, or anyone in the world. (2) It features thumbnails of fascinating photos and videos posted by everyday people. (3) To view them, you just search "CNN iReport" and click on what interests you. (4) My friend Mahit and I have joined thousands of citizen reporters who capture important or strange events as they unfold near us, often before the professional media knows they are happening. (5) Using our smartphones, we snap pictures or videos, add our words, and send them off. (6) CNN posts but doesn't screen or edit our submissions. (7) Mahit became an iReporter when he posted his dramatic photographs of flooding in Mississippi. (8) Sending in my video of a Cleveland man offering free hugs after the election got me hooked. (9) I scan the iReports to see what real people notice and what matters to them. (10) Mahit and I think we look at the world more deeply now and spot more wonderful details, even though his parents say we are just playing a game. (11) Still, we wouldn't dream of leaving home without our smartphones, a pen, and a little paper tablet.

G. Choosing the Correct Pronoun Case

Correct Case After AND or OR

When nouns or pronouns are joined by *and* or *or*, be careful to use the correct pronoun case after the *and* or the *or*.

(1) **Incorrect:** *Carlos* and *her* have to leave soon.

(2) **Revised:** *Carlos* and *she* have to leave soon.

- In sentence (1), the pronoun *her* should be in the *subjective case* because it is part of the subject of the sentence.
- In sentence (2), change *her* to *she*.

(3) **Incorrect:** The dean congratulated *Charles* and *I*.

(4) **Revised:** The dean congratulated *Charles* and *me*.

- In sentence (3), the pronoun *I* should be in the *objective case* because it is the object of the verb *congratulated*.

- The dean congratulated *whom*? The dean congratulated *me*.

- In sentence (4), change *I* to *me*.

> (5) **Incorrect:** Is that letter for *them* or *he*?

- In sentence (5), both objects of the preposition *for* must be in the *objective case*.

  What should *he* be changed to? _____

Try This One simple way to make sure that you have the right pronoun case is to leave out the *and* or the *or* and the word before it. You probably would not write these sentences:

> (6) **Incorrect:** *Her* have to leave soon.
>
> (7) **Incorrect:** The dean congratulated *I*.
>
> (8) **Incorrect:** Is that letter for *he*?

These sentences look and sound strange, and you would know that they have to be corrected.

PRACTICE 14

In the sentences below, circle the correct pronoun in the parentheses. If the pronoun is a *subject*, use the *subjective case*. If the pronoun is the *object* of a verb or a preposition, use the *objective case*.

1. Frieda and (I, me) were born in Bogotá, Colombia.
2. (We, Us) girls are determined to make an A on the next exam.
3. For (we, us), a swim in the ocean on a hot day is one of life's greatest joys.
4. If it were up to Angelo and (he, him), they would spend all their time snow skiing.
5. Our lab instructor expects Dan and (I, me) to hand in our report today.
6. Between you and (I, me), I don't like spinach.
7. Robert and (they, them) have decided to go to Rocky Mountain National Park with Jacinto and (she, her).
8. Either (he, him) or (she, her) must work overtime.

Correct Case in Comparisons

Pronouns in comparisons usually follow *than* or *as*.

> (1) Ferdinand is taller *than* I.
>
> (2) These guidelines help you as much *as* me.

- In sentence (1), the comparison is completed with a pronoun in the subjective case, *I*.
- In sentence (2), the comparison is completed with a pronoun in the objective case, *me*.

> (3) Ferdinand is taller than I . . . (am tall).
>
> (4) These guidelines help you as much as . . . (they help) . . . me.

- A comparison is really a kind of shorthand that omits repetitious words.

By completing the comparison mentally, you can choose the correct case for the pronoun.

BE CAREFUL: The case of the pronoun you place after *than* or *as* can change the meaning of the sentence.

> (5) Diana likes Tom more than *I* . . . (more than *I* like him).
>
> *or*
>
> (6) Diana likes Tom more than *me* . . . (more than she likes *me*).

- Sentence (5) says that Diana likes Tom more than I like Tom.
- Sentence (6) says that Diana likes Tom more than she likes me.*

PRACTICE 15

Circle the correct pronoun in these comparisons.

1. You study more often than (I, me).
2. The movie scared us more than it did (he, him).
3. Diego eats dinner earlier than (I, me).
4. She ran a better campaign for the local school board than (he, him).
5. Stan cannot memorize vocabulary words faster than (he, him).
6. I hate doing laundry more than (they, them).
7. Sometimes our children are more mature than (we, us).
8. Remembering birthdays seems easier for me than for (he, him).

PRACTICE 16

Proofread this paragraph carefully for errors in pronoun case. Cross out any errors and write the correct pronouns above the lines.

(1) My sister Tina and me visited Miami for the first time this year. (2) Our cousin JJ met her and I at their airport and drove us to Wynwood, where he lives. (3) JJ is a graphic designer. (4) He has always been more artistic and trendy than us. (5) JJ loves living

---

* For more work on comparisons, see Chapter 25, Part C.

Shepard Fairey's Wall of Heroes, Wynwood Walls, Miami

in Wynwood, which is Miami's design district. (6) Of all the things we saw, my favorite was the Wynwood Walls, many city blocks of whitewashed warehouse walls painted with colorful cartoons and graphics by some of the world's best street artists. (7) We saw the Wall of Heroes by Shepard Fairey, who painted the famous poster portrait of Obama. (8) A mural about modern life by Liqen from Spain amazed Tina and I. (9) It shows creatures, part human, part insect or animal, trapped inside concrete chambers. (10) A Brazilian artist named Kobra painted huge colorful murals with images from the past, like roller coasters. (11) Liqen's vision of life was much darker than him. (12) My sister took pictures of a giant lobster between JJ and I. (13) I took one of JJ and she pretending to ride a painted motorcycle. (14) All this inspiring work is art, not graffiti, we decided. (15) On that day, no one could have been happier than me.

EXPLORING ONLINE

thewynwoodwalls.com

To explore the Wynwood Walls, visit this site. You might look for the work of Fairey and Liqen. Do you think this is graffiti or art? What is the difference?

PRACTICE 17 On paper or on a computer, write three sentences using comparisons that are completed with pronouns. Choose each pronoun case carefully.

H. Using Pronouns with -*SELF* and -SELVES

Pronouns with -*self* and -*selves* are used in two ways.

> (1) José admired *himself* in the mirror.
>
> (2) The teacher *herself* thought the test was too difficult.

- In sentence (1), José did something to *himself*; he admired *himself*. In this sentence, *himself* is called a **reflexive pronoun**.

- In sentence (2), *herself* emphasizes the fact that the teacher—much to her surprise—found the test too hard. In this sentence, *herself* is called an **intensive pronoun**.

This chart will help you choose the right reflexive or intensive pronoun.

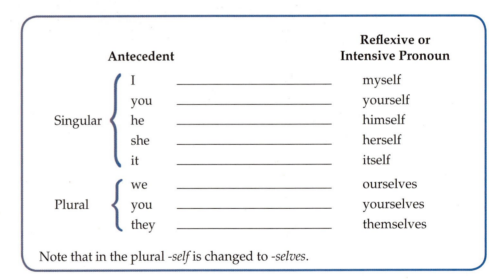

	Antecedent		Reflexive or Intensive Pronoun
Singular	I	_____	myself
	you	_____	yourself
	he	_____	himself
	she	_____	herself
	it	_____	itself
Plural	we	_____	ourselves
	you	_____	yourselves
	they	_____	themselves

Note that in the plural -*self* is changed to -*selves*.

PRACTICE 18 Write the correct reflexive or intensive pronoun in each sentence. Be careful to match the pronoun with the antecedent.

EXAMPLES: I should have stopped ____*myself*____.

Roberta ____*herself*____ made this bracelet.

1. We built all the cabinets _____.

2. He _____ was surprised to discover that he had a green thumb.

3. Did you give _____ a party after you graduated?

4. Rick, look at _____ in the mirror!

5. Don't bother; Don and André will hang the pictures _____.

6. These new lamps turn _____ on and off.

7. The oven cleans _____.

8. Because he snores loudly, he wakes _____ up several times each night.

PRACTICE 19   On paper or on a computer, write three sentences, using either a reflexive or an intensive pronoun in each.

Chapter Highlights

■ **A pronoun takes the place of or refers to a noun or another pronoun:**

Louise said that *she* would leave work early.

■ **The word that a pronoun refers to is its antecedent:**

I have chosen *my* seat for the concert.

(*I* is the antecedent of *my*.)

■ **A pronoun that refers to an indefinite pronoun or a collective noun should be singular:**

Everyone had cleared the papers off *his* or *her* desk.

The *committee* will give *its* report Friday.

■ **A pronoun after *and* or *or* is usually in the subjective or objective case:**

Dr. Smythe and *she* always work as a team. (*subjective*)

The bus driver wouldn't give the map to Ms. Tallon or *me*. (*objective*)

■ **Pronouns in comparisons usually follow *than* or *as*:**

Daisuke likes Sally more than *I*.
(*subjective*: . . . more than I like Sally)

Daisuke likes Sally more than *me*.
(*objective*: . . . more than he likes me)

■ **A pronoun ending in *-self* (singular) or *-selves* (plural) may be used as a reflexive or an intensive pronoun. A reflexive pronoun shows that someone did something to himself or to herself; an intensive pronoun is used for emphasis:**

On his trip, Martin bought nothing for *himself*.

The musicians *themselves* were almost late for the street fair.

PROOFREADING STRATEGY

One of the most common pronoun errors is using the plural pronouns *they*, *them*, or *their* incorrectly to refer to a singular antecedent. If this is one of your error patterns, **search your draft for *they*, *them*, and *their* and highlight or underline** them. If you are using a computer, use the *"Find"* feature to locate these words.

Take a moment to **identify the antecedent** for each of these highlighted words by drawing an arrow from the highlighted word to its antecedent, as in this example. Do the two words agree?

The **people** who work here usually clean up <mark>their</mark> messes, but

his or her

somebody let <mark>their</mark> lunch splatter in the microwave and didn't wipe it up.

(*Somebody* means *one*, so *their* must be changed to *his* or *her*.)

WRITING AND PROOFREADING ASSIGNMENT

In a small group if possible, discuss the factors that seem absolutely necessary for a successful marriage or long-term relationship. As a group, brainstorm to identify four or five key factors.

Now imagine that a friend with very little experience has asked you for written advice about relationships. Each member of the group should choose just one of the factors and write a letter to this person. Explain in detail why this factor—for example, honesty or mutual respect—is so important to a good relationship.

Read the finished letters to one another. Which letters give the best advice or are the most convincing? Why? Exchange letters with a partner, proofreading for the correct use of pronouns.

CHAPTER REVIEW

Proofread the following essay for pronoun errors. Cross out any incorrect, vague, or repetitious pronouns and make your corrections above the lines. Use nouns to replace vague pronouns. Hint: There are 14 errors.

The Devastating Cost of Concussions

(1) Professional football players are America's gladiators. (2) Each of them is a nearly superhuman young man who crashes into their opponents at high speeds. (3) Concussions—brain injuries caused by a blow—are common in football and other contact sports. (4) Until recently, a concussion was thought to be a minor injury. (5) One of the players who suffered a concussion might just say their "bell was rung" and be sent back into the game. (6) In the last 15 years, however, they have exposed the tragic, long-term effects of head hits on the human brain.

(7) Dr. Bennet Omalu, a forensic pathologist* and neurologist, first discovered a new disease in football players caused by repeated blows to his or her heads. (8) He called its CTE** and published his findings in 2005. (9) The National Football

---

*Forensic pathologist: doctor who examines bodies for cause of death.
**CTE: chronic traumatic encephalopathy or progressive brain disease caused by a blow to the head.

League mocked he and his research, claiming that not one of their players had brain damage. (10) Tragically, in 2011 and 2012, six retired NFL players killed themself and left notes asking that his or her brains be studied. (11) Autopsies showed that all of them had CTE, which causes memory loss, violent outbursts, depression, and suicidal thoughts. (12) By 2016, brain studies of 91 deceased NFL strongmen showed that 87 had CTE.

(13) Public pressure on the NFL finally forced them to take some steps, with a new policy for handling concussions, helmet improvements, and stiffer penalties for head hits. (14) Top doctors say this is not enough. (15) Is the NFL more worried about player safety or protecting their financial empire? (16) Violence sells, and football is America's favorite sport. (17) They bring in $13 billion a year. (18) In the 2015 movie *Concussion*, Will Smith made Dr. Omalu's research famous. (19) Later, Smith said he was surprised that Americans kept watching football once they knew the facts.

(20) For now, every parent can only keep a watchful eye on the concussion policy at their children's school because a child's or teenager's brain is at even greater risk if they get a concussion.

PRACTICE 20   CRITICAL THINKING AND WRITING

Think about the issue of concussions and brain damage in the NFL and, if possible, discuss in a group with several classmates. Should the rules and nature of football change even more in order to protect players' brains? Do you agree with some experts who say that professional football can never sufficiently protect players' brains, so the sport should be banned? Be prepared to defend your stand.

EXPLORING ONLINE

grammar.ccc.commnet.edu/grammar/quiz2/quizzes-to-fix/pronouns_add2.htm
Choose the correct pronouns. Submit to get your score.

web2.uvcs.uvic.ca/elc/studyzone/330/grammar/poss1.htm
Can you choose the right possessive pronouns?

Visit **MindTap** for *Grassroots* to access this chapter's ebook, flashcards, additional practice and quizzes, and more!

CHAPTER 25

Adjectives and Adverbs

A. Defining and Writing Adjectives and Adverbs

Adjectives and adverbs are two kinds of descriptive words. An **adjective** describes a noun or a pronoun. It tells *which one*, *what kind*, or *how many*.

(1) The *red* coat belongs to me.

(2) He looks *healthy*.

- In sentence (1), the adjective *red* describes the noun *coat*.

- In sentence (2), the adjective *healthy* describes the pronoun *he*.

   An **adverb** describes a verb, an adjective, or another adverb. Adverbs often end in *-ly*. They tell *how, to what extent, why, when,* or *where*.

(3) Laura sings *loudly*.

(4) My biology instructor is *extremely* short.

(5) Lift this box *very* carefully.

- In sentence (3), *loudly* describes the verb *sings*. How does Laura sing? She sings *loudly*.

- In sentence (4), *extremely* describes the adjective *short*. How short is the instructor? *Extremely* short.

- In sentence (5), *very* describes the adverb *carefully*. How carefully should you lift the box? *Very* carefully.

PRACTICE 1   Complete each sentence with an appropriate adjective from the list below.

funny	orange	sarcastic	energetic
old	tired	bitter	little

1. Bella is _____.
2. He often wears a(n) _____ baseball cap.
3. _____ remarks will be his downfall.
4. My daughter collects _____ movie posters.
5. This coffee tastes _____.

PRACTICE 2   Complete each sentence with an appropriate adverb from the list below.

quietly	loudly	wildly	convincingly
madly	quickly	constantly	happily

1. The waiter _____ cleaned the table.
2. Mr. Huff whistles _____.
3. The lawyer spoke _____.
4. They charged _____ down the long hallway.
5. _____, he entered the rear door of the church.

Many adjectives can be changed into adverbs by adding an *-ly* ending. For example, *glad* becomes *gladly, thoughtful* becomes *thoughtfully,* and *wise* becomes *wisely.*

Be especially careful of the adjectives and adverbs in this list; they are easily confused.

Adjective	Adverb	Adjective	Adverb
awful	awfully	quick	quickly
bad	badly	quiet	quietly
easy	easily	real	really
poor	poorly	sure	surely

(6) This chair is a *real* antique.

(7) She has a *really* bad sprain.

- In sentence (6), *real* is an adjective describing the noun *antique.*
- In sentence (7), *really* is an adverb describing the adjective *bad.* How bad is the sprain? The sprain is *really* bad.

PRACTICE 3   Change each adjective in the left-hand column into its adverb form.*

EXAMPLE: You are polite.   You answer _____*politely*_____.

Adjective	Adverb
1. She is honest.	1. She responds _____.

_____

* If you have questions about spelling, see Chapter 35, Part E.

2. They are loud.
3. It is easy.
4. We are careful.
5. He is creative.
6. She was quick.
7. It is perfect.
8. It is real.
9. He is eager.
10. We are joyful.

2. They sing _____.
3. It turns _____.
4. We decide _____.
5. He thinks _____.
6. She acted _____.
7. It fits _____.
8. It is _____ hot.
9. He waited _____.
10. We watch _____.

PRACTICE 4

Circle the adjective or adverb form of the word in parentheses.

EXAMPLE: Lovers of nature argue (passionate, (passionately)) that we must protect the Galápagos Islands.

1. These (remote, remotely) islands lie in the Pacific Ocean 600 miles off the coast of Ecuador.
2. They are (actual, actually) just piles of volcanic lava.
3. Nevertheless, they are home to (abundant, abundantly) wildlife.
4. For centuries, the Galápagos Islands remained (complete, completely) isolated and undisturbed by humans.
5. As a result, some (rare, rarely) animal species developed there.
6. For example, giant tortoises up to six feet long from head to tail lumber (slow, slowly) across the hills and beaches.
7. The world's only swimming iguanas (lazy, lazily) sun themselves on jet-black rocks.
8. The islands are also home to many (amazing, amazingly) birds.
9. Blue-footed boobies waddle (comic, comically) over the boulders.

Blue-footed boobies of the Galápagos Islands engage in a courtship dance.

greenglobaltravel.com

10. Flightless cormorants, which live only in the Galápagos, dive (graceful, gracefully) into the sea, searching for eel and octopus.

11. Tiny Galápagos penguins, the only ones north of the equator, hop (easy, easily) into and out of the ocean.

12. During his voyage of 1831, Charles Darwin visited the Galápagos Islands and gathered evidence to support his (famous, famously) theory of natural selection.

13. Today, the islands are still the (perfect, perfectly) place for scientists to conduct research.

14. Ecotourists, too, are drawn to the (spectacular, spectacularly) scenery and (fabulous, fabulously) animals.

15. If we tread very (gentle, gently) on this fragile ecosystem, we might preserve it for future generations.

EXPLORING ONLINE

Using Google or your favorite search engine, look up "Galápagos, animals, birds" or "Galápagos, Darwin's voyage" to see pictures and learn more about these islands.

PRACTICE 5

On paper or on a computer, write sentences using the following adjectives and adverbs: *quick/quickly, bad/badly, glad/gladly, real/really, easy/easily.*

> **EXAMPLES:** (cheerful) *You are cheerful this morning.*
>
> (cheerfully) *You make breakfast cheerfully.*

B. A Troublesome Pair: GOOD/WELL

Unlike most adjectives, *good* does not add *-ly* to become an adverb; it changes to *well*.

> (1) **Adjective:** Peter is a *good* student.
>
> (2) **Adverb:** He writes *well*.

- In sentence (1), the adjective *good* describes or modifies *student*.
- In sentence (2), the adverb *well* describes or modifies *writes*.

Note, however, that *well* can be used as an adjective to mean *in good health*—for example, *He felt well after his long vacation.*

PRACTICE 6

Write either *good* or *well* in each blank.

> **EXAMPLE:** Charles plays ball very _____*well*_____.

1. Lorelle is a _____ pilot.

2. She handles a plane _____.

3. How _____ do you understand virtual reality?

4. Tovah knows my bad habits very _____.

5. It is a _____ thing we ran into each other.

6. Brian works _____ with other people.

7. How _____ or how badly did you do at the tryouts?

8. Were the cherry tarts _____ or tasteless?

9. Denzel Washington is not just a _____ actor; he's a great one.

10. These plants don't grow very _____ in the sunlight.

11. Carole doesn't look as though she takes _____ care of herself.

12. He asked _____ questions at the meeting, and she answered
    them _____.

C. Writing Comparatives

> (1) John is *tall*.
>
> (2) John is *taller* than Mike.

- Sentence (1) describes John with the adjective *tall*, but sentence (2) *compares*
  John and Mike in terms of how tall they are: John is the *taller* of the two.

Taller **is called the** *comparative* **of** *tall*.

Use the comparative when you want to compare two people or things.

<table>
<tr><td colspan="2" align="center">**To Form Comparatives**</td></tr>
<tr><td colspan="2">Add *-er* to adjectives and adverbs that have *one syllable*:*</td></tr>
<tr><td>short</td><td>shorter</td></tr>
<tr><td>fast</td><td>faster</td></tr>
<tr><td>thin</td><td>thinner</td></tr>
<tr><td colspan="2">Place the word *more* before adjectives and adverbs that have *two or more syllables*:</td></tr>
<tr><td>foolish</td><td>more foolish</td></tr>
<tr><td>rotten</td><td>more rotten</td></tr>
<tr><td>happily</td><td>more happily</td></tr>
</table>

Use either *more* **or** *-er* **to show a comparison—never both.**

Example: Your voice is *louder* **than mine. (**not *more louder***)**

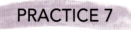

PRACTICE 7   Write the comparative form of each word. Either add *-er* to the word or write *more* before
it. Never add both *-er* and *more*!

EXAMPLES: _____ fresh *er* _____

_____ *more* willing _____

1. _____ fast _____   3. _____ thick _____

2. _____ interesting _____   4. _____ modern _____

_____

* For questions about spelling, see Chapter 35, Part D.

5. _____ hopeful _____   7. _____ valuable _____

6. _____ sweet _____   8. _____ cold _____

Here is one important exception to the rule that two-syllable words use *more* to form the comparative:

> To show the comparative of two-syllable adjectives ending in *-y*, change the *y* to *i* and add *-er*.*
>
> | cloudy | cloudier |
> | sunny | sunnier |

PRACTICE 8

Write the comparative form of each adjective.

EXAMPLE: happy _____*happier*_____

1. shiny _____   5. fancy _____
2. friendly _____   6. lucky _____
3. lazy _____   7. lively _____
4. easy _____   8. crazy _____

PRACTICE 9

The following incorrect sentences use both *more* and *-er*. Decide which one is correct and write your revised sentences on the lines provided.

REMEMBER: Write comparatives with either *more* or *-er*—not both!

EXAMPLES: Halle is more younger than her brother.
Halle is younger than her brother.

I feel more comfortabler in this chair than on the couch.
I feel more comfortable in this chair than on the couch.

1. Her new boss is more fussier than her previous one.

_____

2. The trail was more rockier than we expected.

_____

3. The people in my new neighborhood are more friendlier than those in my old one.

_____

4. Magda has a more cheerfuler personality than her sister.

_____

5. I have never seen a more duller TV program than this one.

_____

* For questions about spelling, see Chapter 35, Part G.

6. The audience at this theater is more noisier than usual.

   _____

7. His jacket is more newer than Rudy's.

   _____

8. If today is more warmer than yesterday, we'll picnic on the lawn.

   _____

PRACTICE 10   On paper or on a computer, write sentences using the comparative form of the following adjectives or adverbs: *dark, cloudy, fortunate, slowly, wet.*

   EXAMPLE: (funny) *This play is funnier than the one we saw last week.*

D. Writing Superlatives

> (1) Niko is the *tallest* player on the team.
>
> (2) Juan was voted the *most useful* player.

- In sentence (1), Niko is not just *tall* or *taller than* someone else; he is the *tallest* of all the players on the team.
- In sentence (2), Juan was voted the *most useful* of all the players.

Tallest **and** *most useful* **are called** *superlatives*.

Use the superlative when you wish to compare more than two people or things.

To Form Superlatives
Add *-est* to adjectives and adverbs of *one syllable*:   short   shortest
Place the word *most* before adjectives and adverbs that have *two or more syllables*:   foolish   most foolish
Exception: With two-syllable adjectives ending in *-y*, change the *y* to *i* and add *-est*.*   happy   happiest

Use either *most* **or** *-est* **to compare three or more things—never both.**

Example: Jaden is the most creative web designer. (not *most creativest***)**

---

* For questions about spelling, see Chapter 35, Part G.

PRACTICE 11   Write the superlative form of each word. Either add *-est* to the word or write *most* before it; do not do both.

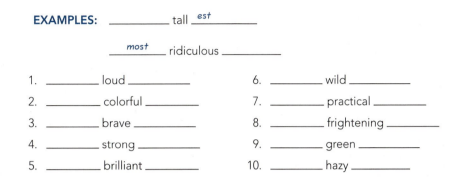

EXAMPLES: _____ tall _est_____

__most___ ridiculous _____

1. _____ loud _____   6. _____ wild _____
2. _____ colorful _____   7. _____ practical _____
3. _____ brave _____   8. _____ frightening _____
4. _____ strong _____   9. _____ green _____
5. _____ brilliant _____   10. _____ hazy _____

PRACTICE 12   The following incorrect sentences use both *most* and *-est*. Decide which one is correct and write your revised sentences on the lines provided.
REMEMBER: Write superlatives with either *most* or *-est*—not both!

EXAMPLES: Emmy is the most youngest of my three children.
Emmy is the youngest of my three children.

He is the most skillfulest guitarist in the band.
He is the most skillful guitarist in the band.

1. My nephew is the most thoughtfulest teenager I know.

   _____

2. Mercury is the most closest planet to the sun.

   _____

3. This baby makes the most oddest gurgling noises we have ever heard.

   _____

4. Jackie always makes us laugh, but she is most funniest when she hasn't had enough sleep.

   _____

5. When I finally started college, I was the most eagerest student on campus.

   _____

6. Ms. Dross raises the most strangest reptiles in her basement.

   _____

7. This peach is the most ripest in the basket.

   _____

8. He thinks that the most successfulest people are just lucky.

   _____

E. Troublesome Comparatives and Superlatives

These comparatives and superlatives are some of the trickiest you will learn:

		Comparative	Superlative
Adjective:	good	better	best
Adverb:	well	better	best
Adjective:	bad	worse	worst
Adverb:	badly	worse	worst

PRACTICE 13   Fill in the correct comparative or superlative form of the word in parentheses.
    REMEMBER: *Better* and *worse* compare *two* persons or things. *Best* and *worst* compare three or more persons or things.

EXAMPLES: Is this report _____*better*_____ (good) than my last one?
(Here two reports are compared.)

It was the _____*worst*_____ (bad) movie I have ever seen.
(Of *all* movies, it was the *most* awful.)

1. He likes jogging _____ (well) than running.

2. I like country and western music _____ (well) of all.

3. Bob's motorcycle rides _____ (bad) now than it did last week.

4. That is the _____ (bad) joke Molly has ever told!

5. The volleyball team played _____ (badly) than it did last year.

6. He plays the piano _____ (well) than he plays the guitar.

7. The traffic is _____ (bad) on Fridays than on Mondays.

8. That was the _____ (bad) cold I have had in years.

9. Sales are _____ (good) this year than last.

10. Do you take this person for _____ (good) or for _____ (bad)?

F. Demonstrative Adjectives: THIS/THAT and THESE/THOSE

This, that, these, and *those* are called **demonstrative adjectives** because they point out, or demonstrate, which noun is meant.

> (1) I don't trust *that* wobbly front wheel.
>
> (2) *Those* toys are not as safe as their makers claim.

- In sentence (1), *that* points to a particular wheel, the wobbly front one.

- In sentence (2), *those* points to a particular group of toys.

Demonstrative adjectives are the only adjectives that change to show singular and plural:

Singular	**Plural**
this book	these books
that book	those books

This and *that* are used before singular nouns; *these* and *those* are used before plural nouns.

PRACTICE 14

In each sentence, circle the correct form of the demonstrative adjective in parentheses.

1. (This, These) corn flakes taste like cardboard.

2. Mr. Lathorpe is sure (this, these) address is correct.

3. You can find (that, those) maps in the reference room.

4. Can you catch (that, those) waiter's eye?

5. I can't imagine what (that, those) gadgets are for.

6. We prefer (this, these) tennis court to (that, those) one.

7. The learning center is in (that, those) gray building.

8. (These, This) biography tells the story of Charles Curtis, the first Native American elected to the Senate.

Chapter Highlights

- **Most adverbs are formed by adding *-ly* to an adjective:**

    quick/quickly   *bright/brightly*   but *good/well*

- **Comparative adjectives and adverbs compare two persons or things:**

    I think that Don is *happier* than his brother.

    Laura can balance a checkbook *more quickly* than I can.

- **Superlative adjectives and adverbs compare more than two persons or things:**

    Last night, Ingrid had the *worst* headache of her life.

    That was the *most carefully* prepared speech I have ever heard.

- **The adjectives *good* and *bad* and the adverbs *well* and *badly* require special care in the comparative and the superlative:**

    good/better/best
    bad/worse/worst

    well/better/best
    badly/worse/worst

- **Demonstrative adjectives can be singular or plural:**

    this/that (chair)

    these/those (chairs)

PROOFREADING STRATEGY

To help you proofread for *adjective* and *adverb* errors, use two highlighters to code the text. Read slowly, and **mark every adjective purple and every adverb gray** (or colors of your choice), like these sentences below from one student's paper.

Next check every purple and gray word, one by one. **Ask yourself what word each one describes.** For example, *What word do gold and <u>purple</u> describe? (Gold and purple describe jersey, a noun. Thus, the adjectives gold and purple are correct.) What does the word <u>proudly</u> describe? (Proudly describes wears, a verb. Thus, the adverb proudly is correct.)*

My son wears his gold and purple jersey proudly. He longs to be ~~real~~ *really* tall, like his favorite players. He tells me he will have the ~~most amazingest~~ *most amazing* jump shot in the NBA.

WRITING AND PROOFREADING ASSIGNMENT

Sports figures and entertainers can be excellent role models. Sometimes, though, they teach the wrong lessons. For example, an athlete or entertainer might take drugs, have affairs, or get in trouble with the law; another might set a bad example through lifestyle or even dress.

Assume that you are concerned that your child or young sibling is being negatively influenced by one of these figures. Write a "fan letter" to this person, explaining the bad influence he or she is having on young people—in particular, on your child or sibling. Convince him or her that being in the spotlight is a serious responsibility and that a positive change in behavior could help young fans.

Brainstorm, freewrite, or cluster to generate ideas and examples to support your concern. After you revise your letter, take time to proofread: color code your adjectives and adverbs. Then check the word each one refers to and make sure your choices are correct.

CHAPTER REVIEW

Proofread these paragraphs for adjective and adverb errors. Cross out the errors and correct them above the lines.

A.   (1) The Hubble Space Telescope is the world's famousest telescope and one of the most important in history. (2) Launched into space in 1990, it orbits regular around the Earth and takes incredibly photographs. (3) Named for astronomer Dr. Edwin Hubble, it carries real sensitive equipment that captures more better and sharp images than Earth-based telescopes do. (4) This extreme detailed pictures of planets, galaxies, nebulas, and black holes have helped scientists solve age-old riddles, such as the age of the universe. (5) Hubble has helped find new galaxies and the most old planet known—3 billion years.

(6) Many people log on to the Hubble website every day just to gaze at beautiful close-ups of Mars or brilliantly gas towers rising from a nebula. (7) For them, viewing the universe through Hubble's eyes is inspirational, even spiritually. (8) Soon, NASA plans to let the Hubble telescope burn up in Earth's atmosphere. (9) Some say that its demise won't be the baddest thing that could happen because plans to launch an even more big telescope in 2018 are already under way.

EXPLORING ONLINE

hubblesite.org

Go to the Hubble website, click on Gallery, and take notes as you look at the images. Why do you think so many people log on to gaze? Why do some call the pictures "spiritual"?

B.   (1) One of the real inspirational stories of recent years is that of Malala Yousafzai. (2) In 2009, when Malala was 12 years old, the terrorist Taliban organization took over her hometown in Pakistan and demanded that the schools stop educating girls. (3) Putting herself in grave danger, Malala heroic refused to stop reading and learning. (4) Instead, she spoke out strong for women's education, criticizing the Taliban's actions on television, at protests, and in her blog. (5) In revenge, Taliban assassins attempted to silence the courageously girl, but they achieved the opposite.

Malala, the youngest Nobel Peace Prize winner, says "I am the 66 million girls deprived of education."

(6) On October 9, 2012, when Malala was 15, Taliban assassins stormed her school bus, shooting her in the head and neck. (7) Critical wounded, she was rushed to a Pakistan hospital. (8) Later, transferred to a British hospital, she endured months of treatment and many surgeries. (9) The attack sparked worldwide media coverage, outrage, and admiration for this teenager's courage. (10) Malala survived, becoming an even more louder and more clear voice for girls' education around the world.

(11) Pakistan awarded her its first National Youth Peace Prize. (12) *CNN.com* readers voted her one of 2012's most intriguingest people. (13) Incredibly, in 2014, 17-year-old Malala became the most young person in history to receive the Nobel Peace Prize. (14) The most best result, though, has been the "Malala effect," a new interest in providing educationally opportunities for the 32 million girls who have never attended school. (15) Despite the Taliban's continued threats against her life, Malala continues her fight for girls' right to get an education.

EXPLORING ONLINE

owl.english.purdue.edu/exercises/2/2/8
Choose the correct adjective or adverb. Click "Go to Answers" to grade yourself.

www.dailygrammar.com/Lesson-67-Adverbs.htm
Practice using *good* and *well*.

grammar.ccc.commnet.edu/grammar/quiz2/quizzes-to-fix/adjectives_quiz.html
Have you mastered comparatives and superlatives?
Test yourself; click "Submit" for the verdict.

Visit **MindTap** for *Grassroots* to access this chapter's ebook, flashcards, additional practice and quizzes, and more!

CHAPTER 26

Prepositions

A: Defining and Working with Prepositional Phrases

B: Troublesome Prepositions: IN, ON, and LIKE

C: Prepositions in Common Expressions

A. Defining and Working with Prepositional Phrases

A **preposition** is a word like *at*, *beside*, *from*, *of*, or *with* that shows the *relationship* between other words in a sentence. Prepositions usually show *location*, *direction*, or *time*. Here are a few examples:

Prepositions of location	above, against, around, behind, beside, between, beyond, in, under
Prepositions of direction	across, down, through, to, toward, up
Prepositions of time	after, before, during, until

Because there are so many prepositions in English, these words can be confusing, especially to nonnative speakers. Here is a partial list of common prepositions.*

<table>
<tr><th colspan="4">Common Prepositions</th></tr>
<tr><td>about</td><td>beneath</td><td>inside</td><td>through</td></tr>
<tr><td>above</td><td>beside</td><td>into</td><td>throughout</td></tr>
<tr><td>across</td><td>between</td><td>like</td><td>to</td></tr>
<tr><td>after</td><td>beyond</td><td>near</td><td>toward</td></tr>
<tr><td>against</td><td>by</td><td>of</td><td>under</td></tr>
<tr><td>along</td><td>despite</td><td>off</td><td>underneath</td></tr>
<tr><td>among</td><td>down</td><td>on</td><td>until</td></tr>
<tr><td>around</td><td>during</td><td>onto</td><td>up</td></tr>
<tr><td>at</td><td>except</td><td>out</td><td>upon</td></tr>
<tr><td>before</td><td>for</td><td>outside</td><td>with</td></tr>
<tr><td>behind</td><td>from</td><td>over</td><td>within</td></tr>
<tr><td>below</td><td>in</td><td>past</td><td>without</td></tr>
</table>

---

* For more work on prepositions, see Chapter 10, Part C.

A preposition is usually followed by a noun or pronoun. The noun or pronoun is called the **object** of the preposition. Together, the preposition and its object are called a **prepositional phrase**.

Here are some prepositional phrases:

Prepositional Phrase	=	Preposition	+	Object
after the movie		after		the movie
at Kean College		at		Kean College
beside them		beside		them
between you and me		between		you and me

The preposition shows a relationship between the object of the preposition and some other word in the sentence. Below are some sentences with prepositional phrases:

(1) Ms. Kringell arrived *at noon*.

(2) A man *in a gray suit* bought 30 lottery tickets.

(3) The huge moving van sped *through the tunnel*.

● In sentence (1), the prepositional phrase *at noon* tells when Ms. Kringell arrived. It describes *arrived*.

● In sentence (2), the prepositional phrase *in a gray suit* describes how the man was dressed. It describes *man*.

● What is the prepositional phrase in sentence (3)? _____

   Which word does it describe? _____

PRACTICE 1   Underline the prepositional phrases in the following sentences.

1. Bill collected some interesting facts about human biology.

2. Human eyesight is sharpest at midday.

3. In extreme cold, shivering produces heat, which can save lives.

4. A pound of body weight equals 3,500 calories.

5. Each of us has a distinguishing odor.

6. Fingernails grow fastest in summer.

7. One of every ten people is left-handed.

8. The human body contains approximately ten pints of blood.

9. Beards grow more rapidly than any other hair on the human body.

10. Most people with an extra rib are men.

PRACTICE 2   **CRITICAL VIEWING AND WRITING**

Closely examine this photograph, if possible in pairs or a small group. Describe the scene in detail, by writing at least ten sentences using prepositional phrases.

EXAMPLES: She holds *onto a rope.*
The blue sea lies *beneath her.*

© Ben Meyer/cultura/CORBIS

B.   Troublesome Prepositions: IN, ON, and LIKE

IN/ON for Time

Use *in* before seasons of the year, before months not followed by specific dates, and before years that do not include specific dates.

(1)   *In the summer,* some of us like to lie around in the sun.

(2)   No classes will meet *in January*.

(3)   Rona was a student at Centerville Business School *in 2004*.

Use *on* before days of the week, before holidays, and before months if a date follows.

> (4) *On Thursday*, the gym was closed for renovations.
>
> (5) The city looked deserted *on Christmas Eve*.
>
> (6) We hope to arrive in Burlington *on October 3*.

IN/ON for Place

In means *inside of.*

> (1) My grandmother slept *in the spare bedroom*.
>
> (2) The exchange student spent the summer *in Sweden*.

On means *on top of* or *at a particular place.*

> (3) The spinach pie *on the table* is for tonight's book discussion group meeting.
>
> (4) Dr. Helfman lives *on Marblehead Road*.

LIKE

Like is a preposition that means *similar to.* Therefore, it is followed by an object (usually a noun or a pronoun).

> (1) *Like you*, I prefer watching films on demand rather than going to a crowded movie theater.

Do not confuse *like* with *as* or *as if. As* and *as if* are subordinating conjunctions.* They are followed by a subject and a verb.

> (2) *As the instructions explain*, insert flap B into slit B before folding the bottom in half.
>
> (3) Robert sometimes acts *as if he has never made a mistake*.

PRACTICE 3   Fill in the correct prepositions in the following sentences. Be especially careful when using *in*, *on*, and *like*.

1. To celebrate America's one hundredth birthday, _____ July 4, 1876, the French decided to give a special statue _____ their "sister country."

---

* For more work on subordinating conjunctions, see Chapter 18.

2. Sculptor Frédéric-Auguste Bartholdi sailed _____ America, seeking

   support _____ the ambitious project.

3. Bartholdi was awed _____ America's vastness as he traveled _____ redwood

   forests, _____ prairies, and _____ mountains.

4. _____ Egypt he had seen huge monuments _____ the pyramids and

   the Sphinx, and he wanted to honor liberty _____ a structure as majestic

   as those.

5. His monument would be so big that visitors would be able to walk _____ it and

   climb _____ a staircase _____ its top.

6. Funded _____ the French, Bartholdi finally built his statue _____ a woman

   raising her torch _____ the sky.

7. _____ many delays, a newspaper urged American citizens to help pay for

   the statue's base; money poured _____ , and the base was erected _____

   Bedloe's Island _____ New York Harbor.

8. The Statue of Liberty was not shipped _____ France _____ America

   _____ 1885, and then it took six months to mount her _____ the

   foundation.

9. One million people and hundreds of ships gathered _____ the rain and fog to see

   the statue unveiled _____ October 28, 1886.

10. Today, Lady Liberty still rises 305 feet _____ the harbor, lighting the darkness

    _____ her torch and symbolizing freedom _____ the globe.

The Statue of Liberty's feet and the base of her torch arrive in New York, 1885

EXPLORING ONLINE

To learn more, look up "Statue of Liberty" on your favorite search engine. Can you answer these questions? 1. What famous person designed the metal skeleton, or scaffolding, that holds up Lady Liberty? 2. In how many pieces was the Statue of Liberty shipped from France?

C. Prepositions in Common Expressions

Prepositions often are combined with other words to form certain expressions—groups of words, or phrases, in common use. These expressions can sometimes be confusing. Below is a list of some troublesome expressions. If you are in doubt about others, consult a dictionary.

Common Expressions with Prepositions	
Expression	**Example**
acquainted with	He became *acquainted with* his duties.
addicted to	I am *addicted to* chocolate.
agree on (a plan)	They finally *agreed on* a sales strategy.
agree to (another's proposal)	Did she *agree to* their demands?
angry about or at (a thing)	The subway riders are *angry about* (or *at*) the delays.
angry with (a person)	The manager seems *angry with* Jake.
apply for (a position)	You should *apply for* this job.
approve of	Does he *approve of* the proposed budget?
consist of	The plot *consisted of* both murder and intrigue.
contrast with	The red lettering *contrasts* nicely *with* the gray stationery.
convenient for	Is Friday *convenient for* you?
correspond with (write)	My daughter *corresponds with* a pen pal in India.
deal with	How do you *deal with* friends who always want to borrow your notes?
depend on	He *depends on* your advice.
differ from (something)	A diesel engine *differs from* a gasoline engine.
differ with (a person)	On that point, I *differ with* the medical technician.
different from	His account of the accident is *different from* hers.
displeased with	She is *displeased with* all the publicity.
fond of	We are all *fond of* Sam's grandmother.
grateful for (something)	Tia was *grateful for* the two test review sessions.
grateful to (someone)	We are *grateful to* the plumber for repairing the leak on Sunday.
identical with or to	This watch is *identical with* (or *to*) hers.
interested in	George is *interested in* modern art.
interfere with	Does the party *interfere with* your study plans?

object to	She *objects to* the increase in the state sales tax.
protect against	This vaccine *protects* people *against* the flu.
reason with	Don't *reason with* a hungry pit bull.
reply to	Did the newspaper editor *reply to* your letter?
responsible for	Omar is *responsible for* marketing.
shocked at	We were *shocked at* the damage to the buildings.
similar to	That popular song is *similar to* another one I know.
specialize in	The shop *specializes in* clothing for large men.
succeed in	Gandhi *succeeded in* freeing India from British rule.
take advantage of	Let's *take advantage of* that two-for-one paperback book sale.
worry about	I no longer *worry about* my manager's moods.

PRACTICE 4   Circle the correct expressions in these sentences.

1. Most people need time to adjust to a new environment that (differs with, differs from) what is familiar and comfortable.

2. For example, entering a new college or country requires that a person (deal with, deal in) strange sights, customs, and values.

3. The difficulty of the adjustment period (depends on, depends with) the individual.

4. The process of cultural adjustment (consists in, consists of) four predictable stages.

5. During the enjoyable "honeymoon stage," a person is (interested on, interested in) the new place.

6. He or she settles in and gets (acquainted with, acquainted to) the new surroundings.

7. In the second stage, however, the excitement wears off, and the person might (worry of, worry about) not fitting in.

8. In this "conflict stage," people struggle to understand behaviors and expectations (different from, different with) those in their native country or hometown.

9. In the third, so-called critical stage, some (take advantage on, take advantage of) the opportunity and immerse themselves in the foreign culture.

10. Others feel (displeased with, displeased in) their experience and spend more time with people who share their customs.

11. During the final stage, the recovery stage, those who (deal about, deal with) their experience as an adventure usually begin to feel more at ease.

12. They (succeed on, succeed in) adapting to their new home.

Chapter Highlights

■ **Prepositions are words like** *at*, *from*, *in*, **and** *of*. **A prepositional phrase contains a preposition and its object:**

The tree *beneath my window* has lost its leaves.

■ **Be careful of the prepositions** *in*, *on*, **and** *like*:

I expect to graduate *in* June.
I expect to graduate *on* June 10.

The Packards live *in* Tacoma.
The Packards live *on* Farnsworth Avenue.

Like my father, I am a Dodgers fan.

■ **Prepositions are often combined with other words to form fixed phrases:**

convenient for, different from, reason with

PROOFREADING STRATEGY

If preposition errors are one of your error patterns, try this strategy. Using the feedback you've received from instructors and tutors who know your writing, **record the five prepositions that give you the most trouble** on your Personal Error Patterns Chart.

Carefully scan your writing for each of these five prepositions. If you are using a computer, use the *"Find"* feature to locate these words in your draft. Then **make sure that you have used each of these prepositions correctly.**

    In   *on*
~~On~~ the United States, citizens celebrate Independence Day ~~in~~ July 4 ~~with~~ parades, picnics, and fireworks.

WRITING AND PROOFREADING ASSIGNMENT

A friend or relative of yours has come to spend a holiday week in your city. He or she has never been there before and wants advice on sightseeing. In complete sentences, write directions for one day's sightseeing. Make sure to explain why you think this person would enjoy visiting each particular spot.

Organize your directions according to time order—that is, what to do first, second, and so on. Use transitional expressions like *then*, *after*, and *while* to indicate time order. Try to work in a few of the expressions listed in Part C. Proofread for your five most troublesome prepositions.

CHAPTER REVIEW

Proofread the following essay for preposition errors. Cross out the errors and correct them above the lines.

The Woman Who Loved to Count

(1) In love of numbers even as a child, Katherine Johnson counted everything: the steps to the road, the steps onto church, the number off dishes she washed. (2) She was born at West Virginia in 1918, before women could vote. (3) Despite segregation, this African-American whiz kid was a high school freshman in age 10 and graduated out college at age 18 with degrees in mathematics and French. (4) She became a teacher and wife.

(5) On 1952, Johnson applied to a position on an exciting new government agency, now called NASA, the National Aeronautics and Space Administration. (6) NASA was gathering a group of smart African-American women who specialized of fast, accurate counting. (7) In those days before widespread use from computers, Johnson's job title was "computer," and she excelled. (8) As space exploration became a priority on the United States, Johnson played a key role. (9) She was responsible in keeping spaceships in orbit and astronauts alive. (10) Her calculations contributed to America's first human spaceflight in 1961. (11) Astronaut John Glenn was so impressed of Johnson's brilliant mind that he would not fire the rockets for his famous orbit among the Earth until she checked all the equations used to plan his space voyage.

(12) At age 98, with many honorary doctorates and awards, Johnson was celebrated on the hit film *Hidden Figures*. (13) Surprisingly, Taraji Henson, who plays the scheming Cookie inside the TV series *Empire*, was cast to portray a very different woman—the hardworking, humble, elegant math star, Katherine Johnson.

EXPLORING ONLINE

web2.uvcs.uvic.ca/courses/elc/studyzone/200/grammar/prepo1.htm
Test your preposition intuition with this quick exercise.

owl.english.purdue.edu/exercises/2/14/35/
If your error patterns include prepositions of direction—
to, toward, on, into—this one's for you.

grammar.ccc.commnet.edu/grammar/quizzes/cross/cross_prep3.htm
Crossword puzzle: Have you mastered prepositions?

Visit **MindTap** for *Grassroots* to access this chapter's ebook, flashcards, additional practice and quizzes, and more!

Writing Assignments

As you complete each writing assignment, remember to perform these steps:

- Write a clear, complete topic sentence.

- Use freewriting, brainstorming, or clustering to generate ideas for the body of your paragraph, essay, or speech.

- Arrange your best ideas in a plan.

- Revise for support, unity, coherence, and exact language.

- Proofread for grammar, punctuation, and spelling errors.

WRITING ASSIGNMENT 1 *Imagine yourself going global.* Have you ever imagined leaving your familiar culture in the United States to study, work, or volunteer abroad? If you could live for one year anywhere in the world, where would you go and to what task or cause would you devote yourself? Would you want to focus on doing humanitarian work or on developing your knowledge, career, or language skills? Describe your dream destination and the work you would want to do there. Proofread for the correct use of nouns, pronouns, adjectives, adverbs, and prepositions.

WRITING ASSIGNMENT 2 *Explain your job.* Explain what you do—your duties and responsibilities—to someone who knows nothing about your kind of work but is interested in it. In your first sentence, sum up the work you do. Then name the equipment you use and tell how you spend an average working day. Explain the rewards and drawbacks of your job. Finally, proofread for the correct use of nouns, pronouns, adjectives, adverbs, and prepositions.

WRITING ASSIGNMENT 3 *Give an award.* When we think of awards, we generally think of awards for the most home runs or the highest grade point average. Write a speech for an awards dinner in honor of someone who deserves a different kind of recognition—for someone who kept showing up and was there for you, another person, or a cause, no matter what. Perhaps your parents deserve the award, or your spouse, or the law enforcement officer in your neighborhood. Be specific in explaining why this person deserves the award. You might try a humorous approach. Proofread your speech for the correct use of nouns, pronouns, adjectives, adverbs, and prepositions.

WRITING ASSIGNMENT 4 *Discuss your future.* Imagine yourself 10 years from now; how will your life be different? Pick one major way in which you expect it will have changed. You may want to choose a difference in your income, your marital status, your idea of success, or anything else that is important to you. Your first sentence should state this expected change. Then explain why this change will be important to you. Proofread for the correct use of nouns, pronouns, adjectives, adverbs, and prepositions.

Review

Proofreading

Proofread the following essay for the incorrect use of nouns, pronouns, adjectives, adverbs, and prepositions. Cross out errors and correct them above the lines. (You should find 28 errors.)

The Last Frontier

(1) When the government of Brazil opened the Amazon rainforest for settlement on the 1970s, they created the last frontier on Earth. (2) Many concerned man and woman everywhere now fear that the move has been a disasters for the land and for the people.

(3) The most large rainforest in the world, the Amazon rainforest has been hit real hard. (4) The government built highways to make it more easy for poor people to get to the land, but the roads also made investors interested to the forest. (5) Lumber companies chopped down millions of tree. (6) Ranchers and settlers theirselves

In a new effort to save the rainforest, school children in the Amazon are given outdoor classes about the value of rainforest trees.

Andre Penner/AP Images

burned the forest to make room for cattle and crops. (7) All this activities have taken their toll: 230,000 square miles of rainforest, an area almost as big as Texas, have already been destroyed. (8) Many kinds of plants and animals have been lost forever.

(9) As the rainforest itself, the Indians who live there are threatened by these wholesale destruction. (10) Ranchers, miners, loggers, and settlers have moved onto Indian lands. (11) Contact with the outside world has changed the Indians' traditional way of life. (12) A few Indian tribe have made economic and political gains; many tribes have totally disappeared, however.

(13) Many of the settler are not doing very good either. (14) People have poured into the region too rapid, and the government is unable to provide the needed services. (15) Small villages have become crowded cities, diseases (especially malaria) have spread, and lawlessness is common. (16) Worse of all, the soil beneath the rainforest is not fertile. (17) After a few years, the settlers' land, it is worthless. (18) As the settlers go into debt, businesses take advantage for the situation by buying land quick and exploiting it bad.

(19) Can the situation in the rainforest improve? (20) Although the Brazilian government has been trying to preserve those forest, thousands of fires are still set every year to clear land for cattle grazing, planting, and building. (21) On the more hopeful side, however, scientists have discovered fruits in the rainforest that are extreme high in vitamins and proteins. (22) Those fruits would be much better crops for the rainforest than the corn, rice, and beans that farmers are growing there now. (23) In new outdoor course, schools teach children of the Amazon that the rainforest is worth more alive than dead. (24) The world watches nervous. (25) Will the Earth's preciousest rainforest survive?

Transforming

This challenging exercise will test your skills. Change the subject of this paragraph from singular (*a drone*) to plural (*drones*), changing every *it* to *they* or *them*, and so forth. Make all necessary verb and other changes. Write your revisions above the lines.

(1) A drone is a flying robot, controlled remotely by a human on the ground. (2) Now any consumer can purchase a drone to play with like a toy, using a controller to keep the device circling above. (3) The drone is no toy, however. (4) Its use by the military has fueled angry ethical debates. (5) Now companies like Amazon, Walmart, and Airbus want to use it to deliver packages, take videos, find structural damage, or spray crops. (6) Businesses foresee large profits, but current air safety rules were written for airplanes, not a sky full of moving vehicles. (7) Thus, this little flying machine raises big safety and security problems. (8) In 2016, the Federal Aviation Administration ruled that a drone over 55 pounds must be registered, but even a drone under 55 pounds could be a dangerous object. (9) Many airline pilots oppose the commercial drone, which could bring down a plane. (10) Celebrities like Miley Cyrus and numerous everyday people have filed complaints about a drone hovering near their homes taking pictures. (11) Fun and profitable or dangerous: What do you think?

A Lufthansa jumbo jet nearly collided with a drone over Los Angeles in 2016. Such near-misses raise safety concerns about drones.

Jag_cz/Shutterstock.com

Writers' Workshop

Tell How Someone Changed Your Life

Strong writing flows clearly from point to point so that a reader can follow easily. In your class or group, read this essay, aloud if possible. As you read, pay special attention to organization.

Stephanie

(1) There are many people who are important to me. However, the most important person is Stephanie. Stephanie is my daughter. She has changed my life completely. She has changed my life in a positive way.

(2) Stephanie is only five years old, but she has taught me the value of education. When I found out that I was pregnant, my life changed in a positive way. Before I got pregnant, I didn't like school. I went to school just to please my mom, but I wasn't learning anything. When I found out that I was pregnant, I changed my mind about education. I wanted to give my baby the best of this world. I knew that without a good education, I wasn't going anywhere, so I decided to get my life together.

(3) Stephanie taught me not to give up. I remember when she was trying to walk, and she fell down. She didn't stop but kept on going until she learned how to walk.

(4) In conclusion, you can learn a lot from babies. I learned not to give up. Stephanie is the most important person in the whole world to me. She has changed me in the past, and she will continue to change me in the future.

Claudia Huezo, student

1. How effective is this essay?

_____ Clear thesis statement?   _____ Good support?

_____ Logical organization?   _____ Effective conclusion?

2. Claudia Huezo has organized her essay very well: introduction and thesis statement, two supporting paragraphs, conclusion. Is the main idea of each supporting paragraph clear? Does each have a good topic sentence?

3. Is each supporting paragraph developed with enough facts and details? If not, what advice would you give the writer for revising, especially for reworking paragraph (3)?

4. This student has picked a wonderful subject and writes clearly—two excellent qualities. However, did you find any places where short, choppy, or repetitious sentences could be improved?

    If so, point out one or two places where Huezo might cross out or rewrite repetitious language (where she says the same thing twice in the same words). Point out one or two places where she might combine short sentences for variety.

5. Proofread for grammar and spelling. Do you spot any error patterns this student should watch out for?

Writing and Revising Ideas

1. Tell how someone changed your life.

2. Discuss two reasons why education is (is not) important.

Before you write, plan or outline your paragraph or essay so that it will be clearly organized (see Chapter 3, Part E, and Chapter 4, Part A). As you revise, pay special attention to the order of ideas and to clear, concise writing without needless repetition (see Chapter 4, Part B).

Revising for Consistency and Parallelism

This unit will teach you some easy but effective ways to add style to your writing. In this unit, you will

- Follow the MAP to better reading and writing

- Make sure your verbs and pronouns are consistent

- Use a secret weapon of many writers—parallel structure

- Vary the lengths and types of your sentences

- Learn proofreading strategies to find and correct your own errors

REUTERS/Edgard Garrido

Follow the MAP to Better Reading and Writing

MODEL

This writer uses balanced words and phrases to describe a popular celebration in her culture. If possible, read the paragraph aloud.

Quinceañeras are coming-of-age ceremonies for Latina girls when they turn fifteen (*quince años*, thus, "quinceañera"). They can be highly <u>elaborate</u> and <u>ritualized</u>. Many start with a mass that is kind of like a wedding without the groom. The girl is traditionally dressed in a pink gown, white being reserved for brides. She is blessed by the priest, who also blesses certain symbolic objects: the quinceañera's first <u>set of heels</u>, her <u>crown</u>, her "<u>last doll</u>." These symbolic objects open the party part of the celebration in which her father changes her shoes from flats to heels, her mother crowns her, she receives a last doll from a *madrina* (godmother), and sometimes, like the bride with her bouquet, she tosses this "last doll" into a crowd of screaming little girls who will some day be quinceañeras, too. Now, as a woman, she dances her first public dance as an adult with her *papi*—traditionally, the dance is a waltz—and then a dance that is more specific to the country of origin: a *merengue* for Dominicans, a *danzón* for Cubans. Throughout this ritual she is accompanied by a "court" of 14 couples, representing her 14 years, as well as her escort, who will be handed the young lady after the men in her family (father, grandfather, brothers, sometimes a dozen uncles!) have danced with her.

Julia Alvarez, excerpted from an interview with Penguin Books.

ANALYSIS

- Describing the *quinceañera*, this writer employs two techniques you will learn in this unit. First, she uses *one verb tense consistently* all the way through.
- She also uses *balanced pairs or series of words*: *elaborate* and *ritualized* (underlined) are both adjectives. The next underlined words are all nouns: *set of heels*, *crown*, *doll*.
- Can you find any other balanced pairs or series of words?

PRACTICE

- Write about a ritual or custom you know well.
- Write about an aspect of your cultural heritage that you value (or that your parents valued).

CHAPTER 27

Consistent Tense

Consistent tense means using the same verb tense whenever possible within a sentence or paragraph. As you write and revise, avoid shifting from one tense to another—for example, from present to past—without a good reason for doing so.

(1) **Inconsistent tense:**	We *were* seven miles from shore. Suddenly, the sky *turns* dark.
(2) **Consistent tense:**	We *were* seven miles from shore. Suddenly, the sky *turned* dark.
(3) **Consistent tense:**	We *are* seven miles from shore. Suddenly, the sky *turns* dark.

- The sentences in (1) begin in the past tense with the verb *were* but then shift into the present tense with the verb *turns*. The tenses are inconsistent because both actions are occurring at the same time.

- The sentences in (2) are consistent. Both verbs, *were* and *turned*, are in the past tense.

- The sentences in (3) are also consistent. Both verbs, *are* and *turns*, are in the present tense.

Of course, you should use different verb tenses in a sentence or paragraph if they convey the meaning you want to express.

(4) Two years ago, I *wanted* to be a chef, but now I *am studying* forestry.

- The verbs in sentence (4) accurately show the time relationship: In the past, I *wanted* to be a chef, but now I *am studying* forestry.

As you proofread your papers for tense consistency, ask yourself: Have I unthinkingly moved from one tense to another, from past to present, or from present to past?

PRACTICE 1 Underline the verbs in these sentences. Then correct any tense inconsistencies above the line.

>   *got*
> EXAMPLE: As soon as I get out of bed, I did 50 push-ups.
>
> **or**   *do*
>
> As soon as I get out of bed, I did 50 push-ups.

1. We were walking near the lake when a large moose appears just ahead.

2. When Bill asks the time, the cab driver told him it was after six.

3. The woman on the red bicycle was delivering newspapers while she is enjoying the morning sunshine.

4. Dr. Choi smiled and welcomes the next patient.

5. The Oklahoma prairie stretches for miles, flat and rusty red. Here and there, an oil rig broke the monotony.

6. They were strolling down Main Street when the lights go out.

7. My cousins questioned me for hours about my trip. I describe the flight, my impressions of Paris, and every meal I ate.

8. We started cheering as he approaches the finish line.

9. If Zahra takes short naps during the day, she didn't feel tired in the evening.

10. Yesterday, we find the book we need online. We ordered it immediately.

11. Whenever I attempt the tango, I am looking goofy, not sexy.

12. My roommate saves money for three years and then took the trip of a lifetime to Vietnam and Cambodia.

13. An afternoon protein shake can provide an energy boost and kept a person from overeating later in the day.

14. As Cal opens the door, we all broke into song.

Chapter Highlights

- **In general, use the same verb tense within a sentence or a paragraph:**

   She *sings* beautifully, and the audience *listens* intently.

                      or

   She *sang* beautifully, and the audience *listened* intently.

- **However, at times different verb tenses are required because of meaning:**

   He *is* not *working* now, but he *spent* 60 hours behind the counter last week.

PROOFREADING STRATEGY

To proofread for inconsistent tense (confusing tense changes), go through your draft and **underline or highlight every verb.**

Identify the tense of every verb. Whenever the tense *changes*, is there a good reason for the change? Here is an example:

PAST-CORRECT

In 2017, Sophia completed her two-year degree in culinary arts. After

PAST-CORRECT   PRESENT-WRONG

graduating, she got a job as a chef in a Jacksonville restaurant. She decides

PRESENT-CORRECT

to open her own restaurant in 2009 and now owns two popular downtown

eateries.

In this example, the past tense works well because the writer is describing past events. The last sentence, however, should shift from past tense (*decided* in 2009) to present tense (now *owns* two restaurants).

WRITING AND PROOFREADING ASSIGNMENT

Suppose that you have been asked for written advice on what makes a successful family. Your adult child, an inexperienced friend, or a sibling has asked you to write down some words of wisdom on what makes a family work. Using your own family as an example, write your suggestions for making family life as nurturing, cooperative, and joyful as possible. You may draw on your family's experience to give examples of pitfalls to avoid or of positive behaviors and attitudes. Revise for consistent tense.

CHAPTER REVIEW

Read each of these paragraphs for consistent tense. Correct any inconsistencies by changing the tense of the verbs. Write your corrections above the lines.

A.   (1) It was 1954. (2) Eight-year-old Jack Horner discovered his first dinosaur fossil as he roams the dry hills near Shelby, Montana. (3) His discovery sparks a lifelong passion for dinosaurs and science. (4) Horner struggled with schoolwork and only later learns that he had dyslexia, yet he earns a degree in paleontology, the study of prehistoric life forms. (5) Horner and his team overturned many theories about dinosaurs. (6) For instance, he finds clusters of dinosaur nests and realizes that dinosaur mothers were fierce protectors of their young. (7) He located the largest *Tyrannosaurus rex* on record. (8) When his team dug up a whole group of *T. rex* skeletons, he concludes that the *T. rex* isn't the dreaded solitary killer of popular imagination but rather a scavenger roaming in packs. (9) Dr. Horner's fame grew. (10) He advises director Steven Spielberg on all three *Jurassic Park* films. (11) In 2009, Horner announces plans to grow a live dinosaur from DNA, a real-life Jurassic Park idea that critics called dangerous and unethical. (12) Today, by visiting schools and hosting a television science show, Horner hoped to inspire other children to question, explore, and love science.

B.   (1) Self-confidence is vital to success both in childhood and in adulthood. (2) With self-confidence, children knew that they are worthwhile and that they have important goals. (3) Parents can teach their children self-confidence in several ways. (4) First, children needed praise. (5) When they drew, for example, parents can tell them how beautiful their drawings are. (6) The praise lets them know they had talents that other people admire. (7) Second, children required exposure to many different experiences. (8) They soon found that they need not be afraid to try new things. (9) They realized that they can succeed as well at chess as they do at basketball. (10) They discovered that a trip to a museum to examine medieval armor is fascinating or that they enjoy taking a class in pottery. (11) Finally, it was very important to treat children individually. (12) Sensitive parents did not compare their children's successes or failures with those of their brothers or sisters, relatives, or friends. (13) Of course, parents should inform children if their behavior or performance in school needs improvement. (14) Parents helped children do better, however, by showing them how much they have accomplished so far and by suggesting how much they can and will accomplish in the future.

C.   (1) Like many ancient Greek myths, the story of Narcissus provided psychological insight and vocabulary still relevant today. (2) Although Narcissus was a mere mortal, this conceited young man believes himself to be as handsome as the gods. (3) Many young women fall in love with him, including a pretty nymph[1] named Echo. (4) When Narcissus rejected her affections, Echo sinks into heartbreak. (5) She faded into the landscape until the only thing left is the echo of her voice. (6) The youth's outrageous vanity infuriated the goddess Nemesis.[2] (7) She decides to teach Narcissus a lesson and dooms him to

---

1. nymph: a minor nature goddess
2. Nemesis: goddess of divine vengeance and retribution

Narcissus, 1597–1599, as imagined by the painter Caravaggio. Oil on canvas, 110 × 92 cm.

What would a twenty-first-century Narcissus look like?

fall in love with his own image. (8) As he passed by Echo's pond, he glimpses himself in the water and falls in love with his own reflection. (9) For days, Narcissus lay lovesick on the bank, pining hopelessly for his own eyes, lips, and curls, until he dies. (10) From the ashes of his funeral pyre grows a white flower now known as the narcissus. (11) The story of this arrogant young man also gave modern psychology the term *narcissist*, a person so admiring of himself that he cannot love others.

EXPLORING ONLINE

owl.english.purdue.edu/owl/resource/601/04

Good review of tense consistency.

owl.english.purdue.edu/exercises/2/22/51

Read this passage from *Roots* by Alex Haley, write down the correct tense form for each verb in brackets, and check your answers.

webapps.towson.edu/ows/exercises/VerbTenseConsistency%20-%20Exercise03.aspx

Interactive quiz. This one is difficult. Test yourself.

Visit **MindTap** for *Grassroots* to access this chapter's ebook, flashcards, additional practice and quizzes, and more!

CHAPTER 28

Consistent Person

Consistent person means using the same person or personal pronoun throughout a sentence or a paragraph. As you write and revise, avoid confusing shifts from one person to another. For example, don't shift from *first person (I, we)* or *third person (he, she, it, they)* to *second person (you).**

(1) **Inconsistent person:**	College *students* soon see that *you* are on *your* own.
(2) **Consistent person:**	College *students* soon see that *they* are on *their* own.
(3) **Consistent person:**	In college, *you* soon see that *you* are on *your* own.

- Sentence (1) shifts from the third person plural *students* to the second person *you* and *your*.

- Sentence (2) uses the third person plural consistently. *They* and *their* now clearly refer to *students*.

- Sentence (3) is also consistent, using the second person *you* and *your* throughout.

PRACTICE 1

Correct any inconsistencies of person in these sentences. If necessary, change the verbs to make them agree with any new subjects. Make your corrections above the lines.

his or her
EXAMPLE: Each hiker should bring ~~your~~ own lunch.

1. Touria treats me like family when I visit her. She always makes you feel at home.

2. I love to go dancing. You can exercise, work off tension, and have fun, all at the same time.

3. If a person has gone to a large high school, you may find a small college a welcome change.

4. When Lee and I drive to work at 6 A.M., you see the city waking up.

5. Every mechanic should make sure they have a good set of tools.

---

* For more work on pronouns, see Chapter 24.

6. People who want to buy cars today are often stopped by high prices. You aren't sure how to get the most for your money.

7. Do each of you have his or her own e-mail address?

8. Many people mistakenly think that your vote doesn't really count.

9. A teacher's attitude affects the performance of their students.

10. It took me three years to decide to enroll in college; in many ways, you really didn't know what you wanted to do when you finished high school.

11. Each person should seek a type of exercise that you enjoy.

12. The students in my CSI class were problem solvers; he loved a challenge.

13. If that is your heart's desire, she should pursue it.

Chapter Highlights

■ **Use the same personal pronoun throughout a sentence or a paragraph:**

When *you* apply for a driver's license, *you* may have to take a written test and a driving test.

When a *person* applies for a driver's license, *he or she* may have to take a written test and a driving test.

PROOFREADING STRATEGY

You, your, they, and *their* are probably the most misused personal pronouns. If pronoun agreement is one of your error patterns, **color code *you, your, they,* and *their* in your draft**. If you are using a computer, use the "*Find*" feature to locate these words.

Every time you spot one of these pronouns in your writing, **draw an arrow to its antecedent**. If the **antecedent is plural**, make sure the **pronoun is plural**. If the **antecedent is singular**, make sure the **pronoun is singular**. Here is an example:

they

Job seekers must create an excellent résumé if you want a potential employer to

them   *his or her*

call you for an interview. Each candidate must highlight their special strengths.

WRITING AND PROOFREADING ASSIGNMENT

In small groups, write as many endings as you can think of for this sentence: "You can (cannot) tell much about a person by . . ." You might write, "the way he or she dresses," "the way he or she styles his or her hair," or "the place he or she is from." Each group member should write down every sentence.

Then let each group member choose one sentence and write a short paragraph supporting it. Use people in the news or friends as examples to prove your point. When you finish drafting, proofread to make sure you have used the first, second, or third person correctly. When everyone is finished, exchange papers, locate all *you* and *they* pronouns, and check each other's work for consistent person.

CHAPTER REVIEW

Correct the inconsistencies of person in these paragraphs. Then make any other necessary changes. Write your corrections above the lines.

A.   (1) When exam time comes, do you become anxious because you aren't sure how to study for tests? (2) They may have done all the work for their courses, but you still don't feel prepared. (3) Fortunately, he can do some things to make taking tests easier. (4) They can look through the textbook and review the material one has underlined. (5) You might read the notes you have taken in class and highlight or underline the main points. (6) A person can think about some questions the professor may ask and then try writing answers. (7) Sometimes, they can find other people from your class and form a study group to compare class notes. (8) The night before a test, they shouldn't drink too much coffee. (9) They should get a good night's sleep so that your mind will be as sharp for the exam as your pencil.

B.   (1) Nearly 331 million people gathered his or her families and hit the road to enjoy America's parks and recreation areas in 2016, the year that the National Park Service turned 100. (2) Although the United States has 417 parks and recreation areas, some vacationers have no trouble choosing their destinations. (3) He or she wants to hike the Grand Canyon or fish in the Everglades; others long to drive the Blue Ridge Parkway, admiring colorful fall foliage from the comfort of his or her own car. (4) Those who cannot decide might consider maximizing your time by visiting Utah's "Mighty 5" parks, where ancient erosion through different rock types has created shapes, colors, and landscapes seen nowhere else.

(5) These five stunning parks lie so close together, it can be seen in one trip. (6) Visitors can view unearthly hoodoos (tall, sculpted rock towers) at Bryce Canyon

Hoodoo rock towers at Bryce Canyon National Park, Utah

National Park, or you can marvel at the ancient rock carvings (petroglyphs) in Capitol Reef National Park. (7) Beautiful Zion National Park offers more daring visitors 2,000-foot sandstone cliffs that he or she can climb. (8) Vacationers will proudly display one's photographs of the natural rock bridges at Arches National Park, but only expert whitewater rafters would tempt death in the Class V rapids at Canyonlands National Park. (9) If Utah doesn't fit your plans, travelers can visit **findyourpark.com** to explore the possibilities.

EXPLORING ONLINE

www.powa.org/edit/six-problem-areas.html?showall=&start=5
Review and then complete Activity 4.16: Rewrite the paragraph in consistent first person (*I* or *we*) and then in third person (*he/she* or *they*).

grammar.ccc.commnet.edu/grammar/quiz2/quizzes-to-fix/consistency_quiz.html
Interactive quiz: Test your pronoun and verb tense IQ.

Visit **MindTap** for *Grassroots* to access this chapter's ebook, flashcards, additional practice and quizzes, and more!

CHAPTER 29

Parallelism

A: Writing Parallel Constructions

B: Using Parallelism for Special Effects

A. Writing Parallel Constructions

This chapter will show you an excellent way to add clarity and smoothness to your writing. Which sentence in each pair sounds better to you?

> (1) Jennie is an artist and flies planes also.
> (2) Jennie is *an artist* and *a pilot*.
>
> (3) He slowed down and came sliding. The winning run was scored.
> (4) He *slowed* down, *slid*, and *scored* the winning run.

- Do sentences (2) and (4) sound smoother and clearer than sentences (1) and (3)?

- Sentences (2) and (4) balance similar words or phrases to show similar ideas.

This technique is called *parallelism* **or** *parallel structure*. **The italicized parts of (2) and (4) are** *parallel*. **When you use** *parallelism*, **you repeat similar parts of speech or phrases to express similar ideas.**

Jennie is	an artist . . . a pilot
He	slowed . . . slid . . . scored

- Can you see how *an artist* and *a pilot* are parallel? Both words in the pair are singular nouns.

- Can you see how *slowed, slid,* and *scored* are parallel? All three words in the series are verbs in the past tense.

Now let's look at two more pairs of sentences. Note which sentence in each pair contains parallelism.

(5) The car was big, had beauty, and it cost a lot.

(6) The car was *big, beautiful,* and *expensive.*

(7) They raced across the roof, and the fire escape is where they came down.

(8) They raced *across the roof* and *down the fire escape.*

- In sentence (6), how are *big, beautiful,* and *expensive* parallel words?

_____

- In sentence (8), how are *across the roof* and *down the fire escape* parallel phrases?

_____

Try This   Try this parallelism test: Does each word or phrase complete the sentence in the same balanced way, with the same part of speech? If so, it is parallel. Test sentence: *The car was big, beautiful, and a Chevy Tahoe.*

The car was *big.*

The car was *beautiful.*

The car was *a Chevy Tahoe.*

Certain special constructions require parallel structure:

(9) The room is *both* light *and* cheery.

(10) You *either* love geometry *or* hate it.

(11) Aricelli *not only* plays the guitar *but also* sings.

(12) Richard would *rather* fight *than* quit.

- Each of these constructions has two parts:

     both . . . and   not only . . . but also

     (n)either . . . (n)or   rather . . . than

- The words, phrases, or clauses following each part must be parallel:

     light . . . cheery   plays . . . sings

     love . . . hate   fight . . . quit

Parallelism is an excellent way to add smoothness and power to your writing. Use it in pairs or in a series of ideas, balancing a noun with a noun, an *-ing* verb with an *-ing* verb, a prepositional phrase with a prepositional phrase, and so on.

PRACTICE 1   Circle the element that is *not* parallel in each list.

EXAMPLE: blue

          red

          (colored like rust)

          purple

1. rowing
   jogging
   runner
   lifting weights

2. my four dogs
   out the door
   across the yard
   under the fence

3. painting the kitchen
   cans of paint
   several brushes
   one roller

4. persistent
   strong-willed
   work
   optimistic

5. opening his mouth to speak
   toward the audience
   smiling with anticipation
   leaning against the table

6. music shops
   clothing stores
   buying a birthday present
   electronics shops

7. dressed for the office
   laptop computer
   leather briefcase
   cellular phone

8. We shop for fruits at the market.
   We buy enough food to last a week.
   We are baking a cake tonight.
   We cook healthy meals often.

PRACTICE 2

Rewrite each sentence, using parallelism to accent the similar ideas.

EXAMPLE: Do you believe that gratitude and feeling happy are related?

Rewrite: _Do you believe that gratitude and happiness are related?_

1. Many people believe that they will be happy once they have money, they are famous, married to a spouse, or working at a good job.

   Rewrite: _____

   _____

2. Psychologist Martin Seligman found that gratitude is a key ingredient of happiness, and the "gratitude visit" was his invention.

   Rewrite: _____

   _____

3. First, you think of a person who was truly helpful to you, and then a "gratitude letter" is written by you to that person.

   Rewrite: _____

   _____

4. In this letter, explain sincerely and with specifics why you are grateful.

   Rewrite: _____

   _____

5. Then visit this person and reading your letter aloud.

   Rewrite: _____

   _____

6. According to Seligman, the ritual is moving, powerful, and there is a lot of emotion.

   Rewrite: _____

   _____

7. Seligman says people feel happier if they focus on the positive aspects of the past rather than being negative.

   Rewrite: _____

   _____

8. Gratitude visits, he believes, increase how intense, length, and frequency of positive memories.

   Rewrite: _____

   _____

9. In addition, they tend to inspire the receivers of thanks to become giving of thanks.

   Rewrite: _____

   _____

10. One gratitude visit leads to another, creating a chain of appreciation and also to make everyone feel more content.

    Rewrite: _____

    _____

PRACTICE 3 Fill in the blanks in each sentence with parallel words or phrases of your own. Be creative. Take care that your sentences make sense and that your parallels are truly parallel.

EXAMPLE: I feel _____ *rested* _____ and _____ *happy* _____.

1. Ethan's favorite colors are _____ and

   _____.

2. The day of the storm, we _____, and they

   _____.

3. Her attitude was strange. She acted as if _____

   and as if _____.

4. I like people who _____ and who

_____.

5. Some married couples _____, whereas

others _____.

6. Harold _____, but I just

_____.

7. To finish this project, work _____ and

_____.

8. _____ and _____

relax me.

9. We found _____, _____, and _____

on the beach.

10. They might want to _____ or to

_____.

B. Using Parallelism for Special Effects

By rearranging the order of a parallel series, you can sometimes add a little drama or humor to your sentences. Which of these two sentences is more dramatic?

> (1) Bharati is a wife, a mother, and a black belt in karate.
>
> (2) Bharati is a wife, a black belt in karate, and a mother.

- If you chose sentence (1), you are right. Sentence (1) saves the most surprising item—*a black belt in karate*—for last.

- Sentence (2), on the other hand, does not build suspense but gives away the surprise in the middle.

You can also use parallelism to set up your readers' expectations and then surprise them with humor.

> (3) Mike Hardware was the kind of private eye who didn't know the meaning of the word *fear*, who could laugh in the face of danger and spit in the eye of death—in short, a moron with suicidal tendencies.

- Clever use of parallelism made this sentence a winner in the Bulwer-Lytton Contest. Every year, contestants make each other laugh by inventing the first sentence of a bad novel.

PRACTICE 4

Write five sentences of your own, using parallel structure. In one or two of your sentences, arrange the parallel elements to build toward a dramatic or humorous conclusion. For ideas, look at Practice 3, but create your own sentences.

Chapter Highlights

■ **Parallelism balances similar words or phrases to express similar ideas:**

He left the gym *tired, sweaty,* and *satisfied.*

Tami not only *finished the exam in record time* but also *answered the question for extra credit.*

To celebrate his success, Alejandro *took in a show, went dancing,* and *ate a late dinner.*

PROOFREADING STRATEGY

To proofread for parallelism problems, read through your draft and **find pairs, lists, or series of words, phrases, or clauses.**

Circle or highlight the items in each pair, list, or series. **Test for parallelism** by rewriting to see whether each item could complete the sentence. Here is one example:

teamwork

Being successful in this position requires attention to detail, to work on a team, and the ability to prioritize.

TEST: **Being successful in this position requires** *attention to detail*   YES
(noun)

requires *to work on a team*   NO
(infinitive)

requires *the ability to prioritize*   YES
(noun)

WRITING AND PROOFREADING ASSIGNMENT

Write a one-paragraph newspaper advertisement to rent or sell your house or apartment. Using complete sentences, let the reader know the number of rooms, their size, and their appearance, and explain why someone would be happy there. Emphasize your home's good points, such as "lots of light" or "closet space galore," but don't hide the flaws. If possible, minimize them while still being honest.

You may want to begin with a general description such as "This apartment is a plant lover's dream." Be careful, though: if you describe only the good features or exaggerate, readers may think, "It's too good to be true." Use parallel structure to help your sentences read more smoothly. As you proofread, test for correct parallelism.

CHAPTER REVIEW

This essay contains both correct and faulty parallel constructions. Revise the faulty parallelism. Write your corrections above the lines. You should make 10 corrections.

Chinese Medicine in the United States

(1) When diplomatic relations between the United States and mainland China were restored in 1972, acupuncture was one import that sparked America's imagination and made people interested. (2) In the United States today, the most popular form of Chinese medicine is acupuncture.

(3) Acupuncture involves the insertion of thin, sterile, made of stainless-steel needles at specific points on the body. (4) Chinese medical science believes that the *chi*, or life force, can be redirected by inserting and by the manipulation of these needles. (5) They are inserted to just below the skin and are either removed quickly or leave them in for up to 40 minutes. (6) In addition, the acupuncturist can twirl them, heat them, or charging them with a mild electrical current. (7) Acupuncture can reduce pain and suffering from allergies, arthritis, backache, with migraines, and many infections. (8) It also has helped in cases of chronic substance abuse, anxiety, and for depressed people.

(9) Chinese medicine has grown in popularity and become important in the West. (10) Over 50 American schools now teach Chinese acupuncture, and more than 1,300 physician acupuncturists practice here. (11) Several studies have demonstrated acupuncture's effectiveness and how reliable it is but not the reason it works. (12) Although many medical doctors still resist acupuncture, the increasing number of practitioners and people who are patients shows how many people benefit from this centuries-old practice.

EXPLORING ONLINE

owl.english.purdue.edu/owl/resource/623/01
Review parallelism on the famous Purdue OWL website.

webapps.towson.edu/ows/selfteachingunits/Sentence%20Parallel%20Structure%20-%20Exercise01.aspx
Rewrite each sentence to correct the faulty parallelism.
Then click to check your answers.

grammar.ccc.commnet.edu/grammar/quizzes/niu/niu10.htm
Interactive quiz: Which sentence in each group has parallelism errors?

Visit **MindTap** for *Grassroots* to access this chapter's ebook, flashcards, additional practice and quizzes, and more!

Writing Assignments

As you complete each writing assignment, remember to perform these steps:

- Write a clear, complete topic sentence.

- Use freewriting, brainstorming, or clustering to generate ideas for the body of your paragraph, essay, or speech.

- Arrange your best ideas in a plan.

- Revise for support, unity, coherence, and exact language.

- Proofread for grammar, punctuation, and spelling errors.

WRITING ASSIGNMENT 1 *Pay a gratitude visit.* Experts like psychologist Martin Seligman claim that people who let themselves feel and express gratitude are happier than people who do not (see Practice 2 in this chapter). Do your own research. 1. Pick a person who has been kind or helpful to you but whom you have never properly thanked. 2. Write a letter to this person, discussing specifically, in concrete terms, why you feel grateful to him or her. 3. Arrange a visit to the object of your gratitude and—in person—read your letter aloud. 4. Then write a one-paragraph report on how the two of you felt about the experience. Are the experts right? Revise for consistent tense and person; use parallelism to make your sentences read smoothly.

WRITING ASSIGNMENT 2 *Send an e-mail of praise or complaint to a company.* What recent purchase either pleased or disappointed you? Use a search engine to find the website of this product's manufacturer. Locate the Contact Us or Customer Support page of the website, and write an e-mail that explains specifically what you like or dislike about the product. Before you click Send, proofread for the correct use of nouns, pronouns, adjectives, adverbs, and prepositions. Be sure to print a copy or send one to your instructor.

WRITING ASSIGNMENT 3 *Write about a celebration.* Reread Julia Alvarez's paragraph about the quinceañera at the beginning of this unit. Notice how the author uses parallelism as she describes the steps in this ceremony and their meaning. Plan and write a paragraph or short essay about a ceremony or celebration from your cultural tradition. Brainstorm for rich details so that your reader can visualize the steps in this ceremony. Select the best details, arrange them, and write for a diverse audience. Take a break before you revise, looking for opportunities to use parallelism to underscore pairs or series of actions or steps. Be sure you use one consistent verb tense, either past or present.

WRITING ASSIGNMENT 4 *Review a restaurant.* You have been asked to review the food, service, and atmosphere at a local restaurant. Your review will appear in a local newspaper and will have an impact on the success or failure of this eating establishment. Tell what you ordered, how it tasted, and why you would or would not recommend this dish. Note the service: was it slow, efficient, courteous, rude, or generally satisfactory? Is the restaurant one in which customers can easily carry on a conversation, or is there too much noise? Is the lighting good or poor? Include as much specific detail as you can. Revise for consistent tense and person.

Review

Proofreading

A. This composition contains inconsistent tense errors and faulty parallelism. Proofread for these errors, and correct them above the lines. (You should find 13 errors.)

A New Beginning

(1) Martha Andrews was a good student in high school. (2) After graduation, she finds a job as a bank teller to save money for college. (3) At the bank, she enjoyed knowing her regular customers and to handle their business. (4) When she was 19, she falls in love and married Patrick Kelvin, another teller. (5) By the time she was 22, she is the mother of three children. (6) Martha's plans for college faded.

(7) As her fortieth birthday approached, Martha begins thinking about going to college to study accounting; however, she has many fears. (8) Would she remember how to study after so many years? (9) Would she be as smart as the younger students? (10) Would she feel out of place among them? (11) Worst of all, her husband worried that Martha would neglect him. (12) He also fears that Martha would be more successful than he.

(13) Martha's son Lucas, who was in college himself, gave her both advice and he encouraged her. (14) With his help, Martha gets the courage to visit Middleton College. (15) An advisor in the admissions office tells her that older students were valued at Middleton. (16) Older students often enriched classes because they brought a wealth of experiences with them. (17) Martha also learns that the college had a special program to help older students adjust to school.

(18) Martha enrolls in college the next fall. (19) To their credit, she and her husband soon realize that they had made the right decision.

B. Proofread the following essay for inconsistent person and faulty parallelism. Correct the errors above the lines. (You should find 13 errors.)

True Colors

(1) One day in 1992, the life of Californian John Box changed radically for the second time. (2) That day John drove four hours to buy a new wheelchair that would allow you to play tennis. (3) Years before, a motorcycle accident had left both his legs paralyzed, but John refused to surrender his love of sports. (4) Instead, he turned anger into being determined. (5) Now a weekend wheelchair athlete, John wanted a better, lighter chair, and one that was faster. (6) When he arrived at the wheelchair manufacturer, however, the salespeople ignored him as if his disability made him invisible.

(7) Back home, furious and feeling frustration, John and his brother Mike decided to design one's own sports wheelchair. (8) The result inspired them to start

Wheelchair athletes Zach Tapec and Bobby Rohan play Quad Rugby, an extremely competitive contact sport.

a company and name her Colours. (9) Colours Wheelchair sells high-performance chairs with edgy names like Hammer, Avenger, Swoosh, and one is called Boing. (10) John Box, the company's president, hires other "wheelers," and he or she often contribute new product ideas. (11) The company also sponsors 75 wheelchair athletes. (12) In fact, Aaron Fotheringham, a wheelchair skateboarder, became the first human to perform a somersault flip in a wheelchair when he was just 14 years old.

(13) Today John Box and his brother not only want to expand his or her successful company but also in educating the public about disability. (14) "A person doesn't lose their personality by becoming disabled," declares John. (15) The disabled, he says, can be funny, brilliance, pregnant, competing, sexy, or none of the above, just like everyone else.

CRITICAL VIEWING AND WRITING

In a group with several classmates if possible, study the photograph of wheelchair athletes. Note that each man is shown twice, collage style. List at least three important details about each man. What message do you think this picture sends about disability? Does that message change or intensify when you learn that both men represent Team Colours and play wheelchair rugby, a contact sport so competitive that insiders call it "murderball"? Take notes as you think about the answers to these questions, and be prepared to report your thoughts.

JOURNAL ASSIGNMENT: Imagine that a newly disabled person has just discovered the Colours Wheelchair website, **colourswheelchair.com**. What effects might the photos and information have on this person's state of mind and view of the future?

Writers' Workshop

Shift Your Audience and Purpose

Playing with the idea of audience and purpose can produce some interesting writing—such as writing to your car to persuade it to keep running until finals are over. Likewise, writing as if you are someone else can be a learning experience. In your class or group, read this unusual essay, aloud if possible.

A Fly's-Eye View of My Apartment

(1) Hey, are you guys ready? Today is Armageddon!* When you enter this door, remember, you're not getting out alive. She's a pretty tough lady. Oh, and don't forget to eat all you can. The kids are always dropping crumbs. You can make it through the night if you stay on the ceilings. Whatever you do, stay out of the peach room that is always humid. Once the door is shut, you're trapped. Try not to be noticed on the cabinets in the room where the smells come from. There is nothing interesting in the room with the big screen, but the room with the large bed can be rather stimulating if you stay on the walls.

(2) She won't get tired of us until about 6 P.M.; that is usually around dinnertime. She switches around, using different swatters, so you never really know what to look for. When you hear the gospel music, start looking out. She gets an enormous amount of energy from this music, and her swats are accurate, which means they're deadly. It kills me how she becomes so baffled about how we get in since she has screens on the windows. Little does she know that it's every time she opens the front door.

(3) Well, I think she's ready to leave for work. I hear the lock. To a good life, fellows. See you in heaven—and remember to give her hell!

Tanya Peck, Student

---

* Armageddon: a final battle between forces of good and evil

1. How effective is Tanya Peck's essay?

   _____ Interesting subject?   _____ Good supporting details?

   _____ Logical organization?   _____ Effective conclusion?

2. This writer cleverly plays with the notions of speaker, audience, and purpose. Who is Peck pretending to be as she writes? Whom is she addressing and for what purpose?

3. The writer/speaker refers to the "pretty tough lady" of the house. Who is that lady? How do you know?

4. Peck divides her essay into two main paragraphs and a brief conclusion. Because of her unusual subject, the paragraphs do not have topic sentences. However, does each paragraph have a clear main idea? What is the main idea of paragraph (1)? Of paragraph (2)?

5. Underline any details or sentences that you especially liked—for example, in paragraph (2), the clever idea that the fly realizes that gospel music (for some mysterious reason) energizes the woman with the swatter. Can you identify the rooms described in paragraph (1)?

6. The essay concludes by playing with the terms *heaven* and *hell*. Do you find this effective—or offensive? Are these words connected to *Armageddon* in the introduction? How?

7. Proofread for any grammar or spelling errors.

Writing and Revising Ideas

1. Write a _____'s-eye view (dog, cat, flea, canary, goldfish, ant, roach) of your home.

2. Describe an important moment in history as if you were there.

Before you write, read about audience and purpose in Chapter 1, Part B. Prewrite and plan to get an engaging subject. As you revise, pay special attention to keeping a consistent point of view; really try to imagine what that person (or other creature) would say in those circumstances.

Mastering Mechanics

Even the best ideas may lose their impact if the writer doesn't know how to capitalize and punctuate correctly. In this unit, you will

- Follow the MAP to better reading and writing
- Learn when—and when not—to capitalize
- Recognize when—and when not—to use commas
- Find out how to use apostrophes
- Learn how to quote the words of others in your writing
- Learn proofreading strategies to find and correct your own errors

Follow the MAP to Better Reading and Writing

MODEL

In this humorous paragraph on a serious subject, the writer correctly uses capital letters, commas, apostrophes, and quotation marks. As you will learn in this unit, knowing these rules will add clarity to your writing and improve your grades. Read this paragraph aloud.

My daughter, Olivia, who just turned three, has an imaginary friend whose name is Charlie Ravioli. Olivia is growing up in Manhattan, and so Charlie Ravioli has a lot of local traits: he lives in an apartment "on Madison and Lexington," he dines on grilled chicken, fruit, and water, and having reached the age of seven and a half, he feels, or is thought, "old." But the most peculiarly local thing about Olivia's imaginary playmate is this: he is always too busy to play with her. She holds her toy cell phone up to her ear, and we hear her talk into it. "Ravioli? It's Olivia . . . It's Olivia. Come and play? OK. Call me. Bye." Then she snaps it shut and shakes her head. "I always get his machine," she says. Or she will say, "I spoke to Ravioli today." "Did you have fun?" my wife and I ask. "No. He was busy working. On a television" (leaving it up in the air if he repairs electronic devices or has his own talk show).

Adam Gopnik, "Bumping into Mr. Ravioli," *The New Yorker*

ANALYSIS

- This writer describes his daughter's imaginary playmate as someone too busy to play! Why do you think Olivia has invented a playmate like Ravioli? Where did she learn about cell conversations, phone machines, and busyness?

- Does this paragraph point out a modern problem? If so, is it a big-city problem or a problem that exists in many places? What is the solution?

PRACTICE

- Write about the importance of taking time to play.

- Write about a time when "child's play" taught you something important.

CHAPTER 30

Capitalization

Here are the basic rules of capitalization: Always capitalize the first word of a sentence, the pronoun *I*, and all specific (or proper) nouns or adjectives. BUT do not capitalize common nouns or adjectives.

1. nationality, race, language, religion → *Capitalize* → American, African American, French, Latino, Protestant, Jewish, Catholic, Muslim, Buddhist, and so forth

• This group is *always capitalized*.

2. names of persons, countries, states, cities, places, streets, bodies of water, and so forth

Capitalize → Bill Morse, New Zealand, Texas, Denver, Golden Gate Bridge, Jones Street, Pacific Ocean, and so forth

but not → a person, a country, a large state, a city, a bridge, an ocean, and so forth

• If you name a specific person, state, city, street, or body of water, *capitalize*; if you don't, use small letters.

3. buildings, organizations, institutions

Capitalize → Art Institute of Chicago, Apollo Theater, National Hispanic Institute, Johnson City Library, Smithson University, and so forth

but not → a museum, a famous theater, an activist group, a library, an old school, and so forth

• If you name a specific building, group, or institution, *capitalize*; if you don't, use small letters.

4. 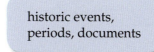 historic events, periods, documents

Capitalize → the Spanish-American War, the Renaissance, the Constitution, and so forth

but not → a terrible war, a new charter, and so forth

- If you name a specific historical event, period, or document, *capitalize;* if you don't, use small letters.

5. 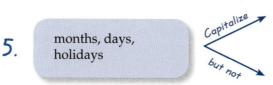 months, days, holidays

Capitalize → June, Monday, the Fourth of July, and so forth

but not → summer, fall, winter, spring

- *Always capitalize* months, days, and holidays; use small letters for the seasons.

6. 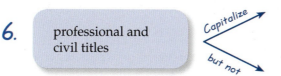 professional and civil titles

Capitalize → Dr. Smith, Professor Greenstein, Judge Alvarez, and so forth

but not → the doctor, the professor, the judge, and so forth

- If you name the doctor, judge, and so forth, *capitalize;* if you don't, use small letters.

7. 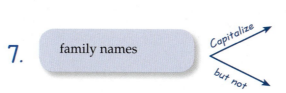 family names

Capitalize → Uncle Xavier, Grandmother Stein, Cousin Emma, Mother, Grandfather, and so forth

but not → an uncle, the grandmother, our cousin, my mother, and so forth

- If you name a relative or use *Mother, Father, Grandmother,* or *Grandfather* as a name, *capitalize;* however, if one of these words is preceded by the word *a, an,* or *the,* a possessive pronoun, or an adjective, use a small letter.

8. brand names

Capitalize → Greaso hair oil, Quick drafting ink, and so forth

- *Capitalize* the brand name but not the type of product.

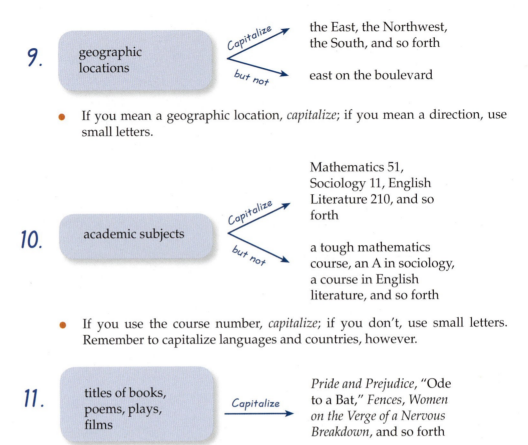

9. geographic locations

Capitalize → the East, the Northwest, the South, and so forth

but not → east on the boulevard

- If you mean a geographic location, *capitalize*; if you mean a direction, use small letters.

10. academic subjects

Capitalize → Mathematics 51, Sociology 11, English Literature 210, and so forth

but not → a tough mathematics course, an A in sociology, a course in English literature, and so forth

- If you use the course number, *capitalize*; if you don't, use small letters. Remember to capitalize languages and countries, however.

11. titles of books, poems, plays, films

Capitalize → *Pride and Prejudice,* "Ode to a Bat," *Fences, Women on the Verge of a Nervous Breakdown,* and so forth

- *Capitalize* the first letter of words in titles except for *a, an,* and *the;* prepositions; and coordinating conjunctions. However, always capitalize the first letter of the *first* and *last* words of the title.

PRACTICE 1

Capitalize where necessary.

> **EXAMPLE:** The most popular ^Bbroadway musical of all time is about a ^Ccaribbean immigrant who rose to advise ^Ggeneral ^Ggeorge ^Wwashington.

1. Alexander hamilton and the revolutionary war don't make most people think of hip-hop music.

2. Yet when a talented rapper and playwright read ron chernow's biography of hamilton, he was surprised to learn that the famous patriot was born out of wedlock in the west indies.

3. The rapper, lin-manuel miranda, read that hamilton was a brilliant idealist who dreamed of helping george washington defeat the british and build a new democracy.

4. As early american history sprang to life on the pages, miranda imagined the american revolution as a hip-hop musical, opening with hamilton's immigration to new york and ending with a deadly pistol duel.

Jesse D. Garrabrant/NBAE via Getty Images

The blockbuster musical *Hamilton* by Lin-Manuel Miranda (far right) tells the story of America's birth.

5. Lin-manuel miranda, himself a puerto rican born in washington heights, new york, felt a kinship with hamilton.

6. At age seven, miranda saw his first musical on broadway, *les misérables*,* and was astonished to see french history come alive onstage.

7. As a sophomore at wesleyan university, miranda wrote songs that would become his first musical, *in the heights*, about the hispanic neighborhood of his childhood.

8. When *in the heights* finally opened on broadway in 2008, miranda took a vacation to mexico and happened to read chernow's book.

9. He was transfixed by the rise of the orphaned hamilton, who later signed the united states constitution but whose competitive friendship with aaron burr was his undoing.

10. To miranda, hamilton's story echoed rappers like tupac shakur and the notorious b.i.g., both shot while in their prime.

11. To write the 46 musical numbers in *hamilton*, miranda borrowed from many american musical traditions including jazz, rap, hip-hop, r&b, and, of course, broadway show tunes.

12. Lines from the bill of rights, the constitution, and even the federalist papers made their way into the fast-moving vocals.

13. Miranda decided to cast racially diverse actors as the founding fathers, so everyone in the audience could identify with the immigrant story about the birth of the united states.

14. The musical went on to win many tony and grammy awards, as well as the pulitzer prize for drama.

15. Even more important, *hamilton* makes history thrilling for all ages and inspires even children to memorize every high-speed, rhyming word of every song.

**Les Misérables: The Wretched Poor*, important French novel by Victor Hugo, made into a hit musical.

Chapter Highlights

- **Capitalize nationalities, languages, races, and religions:**

    Asian, French, Caucasian, Baptist

- **Capitalize specific countries, states, cities, organizations, and buildings:**

    Belgium, Utah, Akron, United Nations, the White House

- **Capitalize months, days, and holidays, but not seasons:**

    November, Friday, Labor Day, summer

- **Capitalize professional titles only when a person is named:**

    Mayor Gomez, the mayor, Superintendent Alicia Morgan

- **Capitalize brand names, but not the type of product:**

    Dawn dishwashing detergent

- **Capitalize geographic locations, but not directions:**

    the West, west of the city

- **Capitalize academic subjects only when they are followed by a course number:**

    History 583, psychology

- **Capitalize titles of books, poems, plays, and films:**

    The House on Mango Street, "The Raven," *Rent, The Perfect Storm*

PROOFREADING STRATEGY

Incorrect use of capital and lowercase letters can confuse your readers. If capitalization is one of your error patterns, try this:

1. Proofread your entire draft once, **searching for any proper nouns** (names of specific people, places, or things). Circle or color code every proper noun and capitalized word.

2. Now check to **make sure that you have correctly capitalized** each one. This student coded his proper nouns yellow:

    In August, I will begin attending Northern Virginia community college, *Community College*

    where I will take classes in Math, English, and psychology. *math,*

"Community College" is part of the college's name and must be capitalized, whereas "math" is not a *specific* math course, so it needs no capital.

WRITING AND PROOFREADING ASSIGNMENT

Is your vacation usually a disaster or a success? Describe a particularly memorable vacation—either bad or good—in which you learned something about how to plan or enjoy a vacation.

In your first sentence, tell what you learned. Explain what went right and what went wrong. Be sure to name the places you visited and the sights you saw. You will probably want to arrange events in time order. Proofread for correct capitalization.

CHAPTER REVIEW

Proofread the following essay for errors in capitalization; correct the errors above the lines.

The Strange Career of Deborah Sampson

(1) Few Soldiers have had a stranger army career than Deborah Sampson. (2) Sampson disguised herself as a man so that she could fight in the revolutionary war. (3) Born on december 17, 1760, she spent her early years in a Town near plymouth, massachusetts. (4) Her Father left his large family, and went to sea when Sampson was seven years old. (5) After living with a Cousin and then with the widow of a Minister, sampson became a servant in a wealthy family.

(6) Household tasks and hard outdoor work built up her physical strength. (7) She was taller than the average Man and more muscular than the average Woman. (8) Therefore, she was able to disguise herself successfully. (9) Sampson enlisted in the continental army on may 20, 1782, under the name of robert shurtleff.

(10) Sampson fought in several Battles and was wounded at least twice. (11) One story says that she took a bullet out of her own leg with a penknife to avoid seeing a Doctor. (12) However, after the surrender of the british, Sampson's regiment was sent to philadelphia, where she was hospitalized with a high fever and lost consciousness. (13) At the Hospital, dr. Barnabas Binney made the discovery that ended Sampson's army life. (14) She was honorably discharged by general henry knox at west point on october 28, 1783.

(15) Officially female again, Sampson returned to Massachusetts and eventually married a Farmer named benjamin gannett. (16) The story of Sampson's adventures spread; in 1797 a book titled *the female review* was published about her. (17) When Sampson decided to earn money by telling her own story, she became the first american woman to be paid as a

Public Speaker. (18) She gave her first talk at the federal street theatre in boston in march 1802 and toured until september. (19) Her health was poor, however, and she could not continue her appearances.

(20) In 1804, paul revere, who was a neighbor of the gannetts, wrote to a member of the united states congress. (21) He asked for a pension for this Soldier who had never been paid and was still suffering from her war wounds. (22) Congress granted deborah sampson gannett a pension of four dollars a month.

(23) Deborah Sampson died in sharon, Massachusetts, in april 1827. (24) Her story inspired the People of her own time and continues to inspire People today. (25) Two plays have been written about her: *she was there* and *portrait of deborah*. (26) On veterans day in 1989, a life-size bronze statue was dedicated in front of the sharon public library to honor her.

EXPLORING ONLINE

owl.english.purdue.edu/engagement/2/1/42/
Review the rules of capitalization, and then scroll down to take the quiz. Click to check your answers.

a4esl.org/q/j/ck/ed-caps.html
Proofread these sentences for "caps" errors and correct them, then electronically check your work.

Visit **MindTap** for *Grassroots* to access this chapter's ebook, flashcards, additional practice and quizzes, and more!

Commas

The comma is a pause. It gives your reader a chance to stop for a moment to think about where your sentence has been and where it is going, and to prepare to read on.

Although this chapter covers basic uses of the comma, always keep this generalization in mind: If there is no reason for a comma, leave it out!

A. Commas after Items in a Series

(1) I like apples, oranges, and pears.

- What three things do I like? _____, _____, and _____

Use commas to separate three or more items in a series.

(2) We will walk through the park, take in a film, and visit a friend.

- What three things will we do? _____, _____, and _____

(3) She loves to explore new cultures sample different foods and learn foreign languages.

- In sentence (3), what are the items in the series? _____, _____, and _____
- Punctuate sentence (3).

However, if you want to join three or more items with *and* **or** *or* **between the items, do not use commas.**

(4) She plays tennis *and* golf *and* softball.

- Note that commas are not used in sentence (4).

PRACTICE 1 Punctuate these sentences correctly.

1. I can't find my shoes my socks or my hat!
2. Sylvia Eric and Jagger have just completed a course in welding.
3. Over lunch, they discussed new accounts marketing strategy and motherhood.
4. Frank is in Florida Bob is in Brazil and I am in the bathtub.
5. On Sunday, we repaired the porch cleaned the basement and shingled the roof.
6. The exhibit will include photographs diaries and love letters.
7. Spinning kickboxing and tai chi have become very popular recently.
8. Katya hung her coat on the hook Oscar draped his jacket over her coat and Ruby threw her scarf on top of the pile.

PRACTICE 2 On paper or on a computer, write three sentences, each containing three or more items in a series. Punctuate them correctly.

B. Commas after Introductory Phrases

(1) By the end of the season, our local basketball team will have won 30 games straight.

- *By the end of the season* introduces the sentence.

An introductory phrase is usually followed by a comma.

(2) On Thursday we left for Hawaii.

However, a very short introductory phrase, like the one in sentence (2), need not be followed by a comma.

PRACTICE 3   Punctuate these sentences correctly. One sentence is already punctuated correctly.

1. During the rainstorm we huddled in a doorway.
2. Every Saturday at 9 P.M. she carries her telescope to the roof.
3. After their last trip Fred and Nita decided on separate vacations.
4. The first woman was appointed to the U.S. Supreme Court in 1981.
5. By the light of the moon we could make out a dim figure.
6. During the coffee break George reviewed his psychology homework.
7. In the deep end of the pool he found three silver dollars.
8. In almost no time they had changed the tire.

PRACTICE 4   On paper or on a computer, write three sentences using introductory phrases. Punctuate them correctly.

C. Commas for Direct Address

> (1) Bob, you must leave now.
>
> (2) You must, Bob, leave now.
>
> (3) You must leave now, Bob.
>
> (4) Don't be surprised, old buddy, if I pay you a visit very soon.

- In sentences (1), (2), and (3), *Bob* is the person spoken to; he is being *addressed directly*.
- In sentence (4), *old buddy* is being *addressed directly*.

The person addressed directly is set off by commas wherever the direct address appears in the sentence.

PRACTICE 5   Circle the person or persons directly addressed, and punctuate the sentences correctly.

1. I am happy to inform you Mr. Forbes that you are the father of twins.
2. We expect to return on Monday Miguel.
3. It appears my friend that you have won two tickets to the opera.
4. Get out of my roast you mangy old dog.
5. Tom it's probably best that you sell the old car at a loss.
6. If I were you Hilda I would wait to make the phone call until we are off the highway.
7. Max it's time you learned to operate the lawn mower!
8. I am pleased to announce ladies and gentlemen that Beyoncé is our surprise guest tonight.

PRACTICE 6   On paper or on a computer, write three sentences using direct address. Punctuate them correctly.

D. Commas to Set Off Appositives

(1) The Rialto, a new theater, is on Tenth Street.

- *A new theater* describes *the Rialto*.

(2) An elderly man, my grandfather walks a mile every day.

- What group of words describes *my grandfather*?

_____

(3) They bought a new painting, a rather beautiful landscape.

- What group of words describes *a new painting*?

_____

- *A new theater*, *an elderly man*, and *a rather beautiful landscape* are called *appositives*.

An *appositive* is a group of words that renames a noun or pronoun and gives more information about it. The appositive can appear at the beginning, middle, or end of a sentence. An appositive is usually set off by commas.

PRACTICE 7   Circle the appositive, and punctuate the sentences correctly.

1. That door the one with the X on it leads backstage.

2. A short man he decided not to pick a fight with the basketball player.

3. Hassim my friend from Morocco will be staying with me this week.

4. My nephew wants to go to Mama's Indoor Arcade a very noisy place.

5. George Eliot a nineteenth-century novelist was a woman named Mary Ann Evans.

6. A very close race the election for mayor wasn't decided until 2 A.M.

7. On the Fourth of July my favorite holiday my high school friends get together for an all-day barbecue.

8. Dr. Bawa a specialist in tribal music always travels with a digital recorder.

PRACTICE 8   On paper or on a computer, write three sentences using appositives. Punctuate them correctly.

E. Commas for Parenthetical Expressions

(1) By the way, I think that you're beautiful.

(2) I think, by the way, that you're beautiful.

(3) I think that you're beautiful, by the way.

- *By the way* modifies or qualifies the entire sentence or idea.
- It is called a **parenthetical expression** because it is a side remark, something that could be placed in parentheses: *(By the way) I think that you're beautiful.*

Set off a parenthetical expression with commas.

Here is a partial list of parenthetical expressions:

as a matter of fact	in fact
believe me	it seems to me
I am sure	it would seem
I assure you	to tell the truth

PRACTICE 9   Circle the parenthetical expressions in the sentences below; then punctuate them correctly.

1. Believe me Felice has studied hard for her law boards.

2. He possesses it would seem an uncanny gift for gab.

3. It was I assure you an accident.

4. To tell the truth I just put a treadmill in your basement.

5. Her supervisor by the way will never admit when he is wrong.

6. A well-prepared résumé as a matter of fact can help you get a job.

7. He is in fact a black belt.

8. To begin with you need a new carburetor.

PRACTICE 10   On paper or on a computer, write three sentences using parenthetical expressions. Punctuate them correctly.

F. Commas for Dates

(1) I arrived on Monday, March 20, 2016, and found that I was in the wrong city.

- Note that commas separate the different parts of the date.
- Note that a comma follows the last item in the date.

> (2) She saw him on Wednesday and spoke with him.

However, a one-word date (*Wednesday* or *1995*) preceded by a preposition (*in*, *on*, *near*, or *from*, for example) is not followed by a comma unless there is some other reason for it.

PRACTICE 11   Punctuate these sentences correctly. Not every sentence requires additional punctuation.

1. By Tuesday October 6 he had outlined the whole history text.

2. Thursday May 8 is Hereford's birthday.

3. She was born on January 9, 1985 in a small Iowa town.

4. He was born on July 4 1976 the two-hundredth anniversary of the Declaration of Independence.

5. Do you think we will have finished the yearbook by May?

6. On January 24 1848 James Wilson Marshall found gold in California.

7. My aunt is staying with us from Tuesday to Friday.

8. Charles Schulz's final *Peanuts* comic strip was scheduled for February 13 2000 the day on which he died.

PRACTICE 12   On paper or on a computer, write three sentences using dates. Punctuate them correctly.

G. Commas for Addresses

> (1) We just moved from 11 Landow Street, Wilton, Connecticut, to 73 James Street, Charleston, West Virginia.

- Commas separate different parts of an address.
- A comma generally follows the last item in an address, usually a state (*Connecticut*).

> (2) Julio Perez *from* Queens was made district sales manager.

However, a one-word address preceded by a preposition (*in*, *on*, *at*, *near*, or *from*, for example) is not followed by a comma unless there is another reason for it.

> (3) Julio Perez, Queens, was made district sales manager.

Commas are required to set off a one-word address if the preposition before the address is omitted.

PRACTICE 13   Punctuate these sentences correctly. Not every sentence requires additional punctuation.

1. Their address is 6 Great Ormond Street London England.

2. Seattle Washington faces the Cascade Mountains.

3. That package must be sent to 30 West Overland Street Phoenix Arizona.

4. We parked on Marble Lane, across the street from the bowling alley.

5. His father now lives in Waco Texas but his sister has never left Vermont.

6. How far is Kansas City Kansas from Independence Missouri?

7. The old watch factory at 43 North Oak Street Scranton Pennsylvania has been condemned by the building inspector.

8. Foster's Stationery 483 Heebers Street Plainview sells special calligraphy pens.

PRACTICE 14   On paper or on a computer, write three sentences using addresses. Punctuate them correctly.

H. Commas for Coordination and Subordination

Chapters 17 and 18 cover the use of commas with coordinating and subordinating conjunctions. This is a brief review.

> (1) Enzio enjoys most kinds of music, but heavy metal gives him a headache.
> (2) Although the weather bureau had predicted rain, the day turned out bright and sunny.
> (3) The day turned out bright and sunny although the weather bureau had predicted rain.

- In sentence (1), a comma precedes the coordinating conjunction *but*, which joins two independent ideas.
- In sentence (2), a comma follows the dependent idea because it precedes the independent idea.
- Sentence (3) does not require a comma because the independent idea precedes the subordinate one.

Use a comma before coordinating conjunctions—*and*, *but*, *for*, *nor*, *or*, *so*, or *yet*—that join two independent ideas.

Use a comma after a dependent idea only when the dependent idea precedes the independent one; do not use a comma if the dependent idea follows the independent one.

PRACTICE 15   Punctuate correctly. Not every sentence requires additional punctuation.

EXAMPLE: Because scrapped cars create millions of tons of ~~waste~~ *waste,* recycling auto parts has become an important issue.

1. Today new cars are made from many old parts and manufacturers are trying to increase the use of recycled materials from old cars.

2. Scrapped cars can be easily recycled because they consist mostly of metals.

3. After these cars are crushed magnets draw the metals out of them.

4. However, the big problem in recycling cars is the plastic they contain.

5. Although plastic can be recycled the average car contains about 20 kinds of plastic.

6. Separating the different types of plastic takes much time but companies are developing ways to speed up the process.

7. Still, new cars need to be made differently before recycling can truly succeed.

8. Their parts should detach easily and they should be made of plastics and metals that can be separated from each other.

9. As we develop more markets for the recycled auto parts new cars may soon be 90 percent recycled and recyclable.

10. Our environment will benefit and brand-new cars will really be more than 50 years old!

PRACTICE 16 On paper or on a computer, write three sentences, one with a coordinating conjunction, one beginning with a subordinating conjunction, and one with the subordinating conjunction in the middle.

Chapter Highlights

- **Commas separate three or more items in a series:**

  He bought a ball, a bat, and a fielder's glove.

- **Unless it is very short, an introductory phrase is followed by a comma:**

  By the end of January, I'll be in Australia.

- **Commas set off the name of a person directly addressed:**

  I think, Aunt Betty, that your latest novel is a winner.

- **Commas set off appositives:**

  My boss, the last person in line in the cafeteria, often forgets to eat lunch.

- **Commas set off parenthetical expressions:**

  My wife, by the way, went to school with your sister.

- **Commas separate the parts of a date or an address, except for a one-word date or an address preceded by a preposition:**

  On April 1, 1997, I was in a terrible blizzard.

  I live at 48 Trent Street, Randolph, Michigan.

  She works in Tucson as a plumber.

- **A comma precedes a coordinating conjunction that joins two independent ideas:**

  We had planned to see a movie together, but we couldn't agree on one.

- **If a dependent idea precedes the independent idea, it is followed by a comma; if the independent idea comes first, it is not followed by a comma:**

  Although I still have work to do, my project will be ready on time.

  My project will be ready on time although I still have work to do.

PROOFREADING STRATEGY

Armed with the eight comma rules, you can proofread effectively for comma errors.

1. **Circle or highlight every comma** in your draft. This forces your eye and brain to focus on every one of them. If you are writing on a computer, use the *"Find"* feature to locate all your commas.

2. For every comma, ask, ***Does one of the eight comma rules explain why this comma needs to be here?*** If you aren't sure, review the rules in the Chapter Highlights. Make any needed corrections, like this:

C (introductory phrase)

Unlike our planet's Northern Hemisphere, the Southern Hemisphere

X (not a series—remove comma)   C (series)

contains fewer land masses, and more water. The South Pacific Ocean,

C (series)   C (series)

South Atlantic Ocean, Indian Ocean, and various seas cover almost

81 percent of Earth's southern half.

WRITING AND PROOFREADING ASSIGNMENT

We live in what is often called "the age of invention" because of rapid advances in technology, communication, and medicine. Which modern invention has meant the most to *you*, and why? You might choose something as common as disposable diapers or as sophisticated as a special feature of a personal computer.

In the first sentence, name the invention. Then, as specifically as possible, discuss why it means so much to you. Proofread for the correct use of commas.

CHAPTER REVIEW

Proofread the following essay for comma errors—either missing commas or commas used incorrectly. Correct the errors above the lines.

Warrior Champion

(1) On April 13, 2004 when platoon leader Melissa Stockwell woke up in an Iraqi hospital she realized she had lost her left leg. (2) On a routine convoy, her Humvee had been hit by a roadside bomb. (3) Sent to Walter Reed Hospital in Bethesda Maryland she received a Purple Heart a Bronze Star, and the powerful awareness that she was one of the lucky ones still with one leg two arms, and a clear mind. (4) She started rehabilitation, promising to live her life for all the soldiers, who never made it back.

(5) Stockwell a lifelong athlete and diver in high school swam as part of her physical therapy. (6) Despite multiple surgeries infections and setbacks, she took her first steps on a new prosthetic leg two months after the explosion. (7) With help from the Wounded

Sandra Mu/Getty Images

Veteran and
Paralympian
Melissa Stockwell.

Warriors, she skied down a mountain on one leg in, Breckenridge Colorado. (8) The

Challenged Athletes Foundation helped her compete in a triathlon building her confidence.

(9) In 2005, John Register, a visitor to Walter Reed told the veterans about the Paralympics

the second biggest athletic event in the world after the Olympics. (10) In these games,

disabled veterans represent their country, and show the world what they can do.

(11) Stockwell began training hard for the 2008 Paralympics in Beijing China. (12) The first

Iraq war veteran to qualify for the Paralympics, she competed in the 100-meter freestyle the

400-meter freestyle and the 100-meter butterfly. (13) When she turned to competing in

paratriathlons she found her sport. (14) Since 2010 Stockwell has been named

Paratriathlon Champion three times and, she won a Bronze Medal at the 2016 games in

Rio de Janeiro Brazil.

(15) This inspiring woman became a prosthetist measuring and fitting other amputees with artificial limbs. (16) In addition she is a wife, mother and the proud founder of the Dare2tri Paratriathlon Club which supports disabled people of all ages, and all skill levels.

EXPLORING ONLINE

owl.english.purdue.edu/exercises/3/5/15

Quiz with answers: Where have all the commas gone?

chompchomp.com/hotpotatoes/commas01.htm

Interactive quiz: Put those comma rules into action at Grammar Bytes.

grammar.ccc.commnet.edu/grammar/quizzes/comma_quiz.htm

Interactive quiz: Add commas to this essay about basketball and score!

Visit **MindTap** for *Grassroots* to access this chapter's ebook, flashcards, additional practice and quizzes, and more!

CHAPTER 32

Apostrophes

A: Using the Apostrophe for Contractions

B: Defining the Possessive

C: Using the Apostrophe to Show Possession (in Words That Do Not Already End in -*S*)

D: Using the Apostrophe to Show Possession (in Words That Already End in -*S*)

The apostrophe is a small mark that greatly confuses many people. The apostrophe has just two important uses, and this chapter will help you master both of them.

A. Using the Apostrophe for Contractions

A contraction combines two words into one.

> do + not = don't
> should + not = shouldn't
> I + have = I've

● Note that an apostrophe (') replaces the omitted letters: "o" in *don't* and *shouldn't* and "ha" in *I've*.

  BE CAREFUL: *Won't* is an odd contraction because it cannot be broken into parts in the same way the previous contractions can.

> will + not = won't

PRACTICE 1   Write these words as contractions.

1. you + are = _____

2. who + is = _____

3. was + not = _____

4. she + will = _____

5. can + not = _____

6. it + is = _____

7. I + am = _____

8. will + not = _____

PRACTICE 2   Proofread this paragraph for incorrect or missing apostrophes in contractions. Write each corrected contraction above the lines.

(1) For musicians and music lovers in the twenty-first century, its a small world. (2) Musicians whove grown up in Asia, for instance, arent influenced only by Asian musical traditions anymore. (3) Hip-hop is a perfect example of musical globalization. (4) Its inspired musicians all over the world, something the first American rappers couldnt have foreseen. (5) Many hip-hop artists in other countries, however, dont like the focus on money and sex in American hip-hop. (6) For example, many hip-hop stars from New Zealand are Pacific Islanders or Maori tribal people whove developed world-class skills and fight prejudice with music. (7) In Senegal, rappers are politically active; Sister Fa, whose Senegalese, raps in French about arranged marriages and the oppression of women. (8) Some South American hip-hop stars have embraced a lifestyle thats committed to social justice. (9) Brazilian rappers, for example, do'nt perform just music; they also perform community service, teaching youth wholl spread the word about social change. (10) As a child, Afghani rapper Sonita Alizadeh was almost sold into marriage—twice. (11) She does'nt blame her family but became an activist against selling child brides. (12) Through luck and talent, shes now attending high school in Utah on a scholarship and writing rap songs.

Afghani rapper
Sonita Alizadeh

Fred Hayes/Getty Images

EXPLORING ONLINE

www.youtube.com/watch?v=n65w1DU8cGU

Teenaged Afghani rapper Sonita Alizadeh raps powerfully
against the sale of child brides in Afghanistan.

soundsandcolours.com/articles/brazil/criolo-convoque-seu-buda-26805

For a sample of global hip hop, you might watch this video by Brazilian rapper Criolo,
who mixes samba and other local music with rap to tell the story of the streets.

PRACTICE 3 On paper or a computer, write five sentences using an apostrophe in a contraction.

B. Defining the Possessive

A *possessive* is a word that shows that someone or something owns someone or
something else.

PRACTICE 4 In the following phrases, who owns what?

EXAMPLE: "The hat of the man" means ___the man owns the hat___.

1. "The camera of Judson" means _____.

2. "The hopes of the people" means _____.

3. "The thought of the woman" means _____.

4. "The trophies of the home team" means _____.

5. "The ideas of that man" means _____.

C. Using the Apostrophe to Show Possession (in Words That Do Not Already End in -S)

| (1) the hands of my father | becomes | (2) my father's hands |

- In phrase (1), who owns what? _____
- In phrase (1), what is the *owner word*? _____
- How does the owner word show possession in phrase (2)?

  _____

- Note that what is owned, *hands*, follows the owner word.

  If the *owner word* (possessive) does not end in -s, add an apostrophe and an -s to show possession.

PRACTICE 5 Change these phrases into possessives with an apostrophe and an -s. (Note that the
owner words do not already end in -s.)

EXAMPLE: the friend of my cousin = ___my cousin's friend___

1. the eyes of Rona = _____

2. the voice of the coach = _____

3. the ark of Noah = _____

4. the technology of tomorrow = _____

5. the jacket of someone = _____

PRACTICE 6 Add an apostrophe and an *-s* to show possession in these phrases.

1. Judy briefcase   6. everyone dreams

2. the diver tanks   7. your daughter sandwich

3. Murphy Law   8. last month prices

4. Brock decision   9. that woman talent

5. somebody umbrella   10. anyone guess

PRACTICE 7 On paper or on a computer, write five sentences. In each, use an apostrophe and an *-s* to show ownership. Use owner words that do not already end in *-s*.

D. Using the Apostrophe to Show Possession (in Words That Already End in *-S*)

| (1) the uniforms of the pilots | becomes | (2) the pilots' uniforms |

- In phrase (1), who owns what? _____
- In phrase (1), what is the *owner word*? _____
- How does the owner word show possession in phrase (2)?

  _____

- Note that what is owned, *uniforms*, follows the owner word.

  If the *owner word* (possessive) ends in *-s*, add an apostrophe after the *-s* to show possession.*

PRACTICE 8 Change these phrases into possessives with an apostrophe. (Note that the owner words already end in *-s*.)

EXAMPLE: the helmets of the players = *the players' helmets*

1. the farm of my grandparents = _____

2. the kindness of my neighbors = _____

3. the dunk shots of the basketball players = _____

4. the music of Alicia Keys = _____

5. the trainer of the horses = _____

———

* Some writers add an *'s* to one-syllable proper names that end in *-s*: *James's book.*

PRACTICE 9 Add either 's or ' to show possession in these phrases. BE CAREFUL: Some of the owner words end in -s and some do not.

1. the models faces
2. the model face
3. the captain safety record
4. the children room
5. the runner time
6. Boris radio

7. my niece two iPads
8. your parents anniversary
9. the men locker room
10. three students exams
11. several contestants answers
12. Mr. Jones band

PRACTICE 10 Rewrite each of the following pairs of short sentences as *one* sentence by using a possessive.

EXAMPLE: Joan has a friend. The friend comes from Chile.

Joan's friend comes from Chile.

1. Rusty has a motorcycle. The motorcycle needs new brakes.

   _____

2. The nurses had evidence. The evidence proved that the doctor was not careless.

   _____

3. Ahmad has a salary. The salary barely keeps him in peanut butter.

   _____

4. Lee has a job. His job in the Complaint Department keeps him on his toes.

   _____

5. Bruno has a bad cold. It makes it hard for him to sleep.

   _____

6. Jessie told a joke. The joke did not make us laugh.

   _____

7. John Adams had a son. His son was the first president's son to also become president of the United States.

   _____

   _____

8. My sisters have a daycare center. The daycare center is open seven days a week.

   _____

9. The twins have a goal. Their goal is to learn synchronized swimming.

   _____

10. Darren has a thank-you note. The thank-you note says it all.

    _____

PRACTICE 11   Proofread this paragraph. Above the lines, correct any missing or incorrectly used apostrophes in possessives. BE CAREFUL: some owner words end in -*s* and some do not.

(1) Apple Computers' founder, Steve Jobs, was one of the industrys greatest innovators—and survivors. (2) Jobs first position, in the 1970s, was designing computer games for Atari. (3) Then he saw a friends' home-built computer. (4) Jobs convinced this friend, Steve Wozniak, to go into business with him. (5) At first, the partners built computers in the Jobs familys garage. (6) Their companys name came from the story of Isaac Newton, who supposedly formulated his great theory of gravity when he watched an apple fall from a tree. (7) The mens' small computers were a huge success. (8) In 1984, they launched the Macintosh, which simplified peoples interactions with their computers by replacing typed commands with clicks. (9) But then, Job's luck changed. (10) After some poor management decisions, he was fired by Apples' board of directors. (11) Despite public failure, he started over. (12) Ironically, his new company was bought by Apple 10 years later. (13) As Apple's leader once again, Jobs soon captured consumer's attention with his revolutionary iPod, iPhone, iPad, and more. (14) Since his death in 2011, Apple has remained one of the worlds' strongest brands. (15) This mans' success flowed not just from farsighted ideas but also from a willingness to learn failures lessons and begin again.

PRACTICE 12   On paper or on a computer, write six sentences that use an apostrophe to show ownership—three using owner words that do not end in -*s* and three using owner words that do end in -*s*.

BE CAREFUL: Apostrophes show possession by nouns. As the following chart indicates, possessive pronouns do not have apostrophes.

Possessive Pronouns	
Singular	**Plural**
<u>my</u> book, <u>mine</u>	<u>our</u> book, <u>ours</u>
<u>your</u> book, <u>yours</u>	<u>your</u> book, <u>yours</u>
<u>his</u> book, <u>his</u>	<u>their</u> book, <u>theirs</u>
<u>her</u> book, <u>hers</u>	
<u>its</u> book, <u>its</u>	

Do not confuse *its* (possessive pronoun) with *it's* (contraction for *it is* or *it has*) or *your* (possessive pronoun) with *you're* (contraction for *you are*).*

---

* See Chapter 36 for work on words that look and sound alike.

REMEMBER: Use apostrophes for contractions and possessive nouns only. Do not use apostrophes for plural nouns (*four marbles*), verbs (*he hopes*), or possessive pronouns (*his, hers, yours, its*).

Chapter Highlights

- **An apostrophe can indicate a contraction:**

  We're glad you could come.

  They *won't* be back until tomorrow.

- **A word that does not end in -s takes an 's to show possession:**

  Is that *Barbara's* coat on the sofa?

  I like *Clint Eastwood's* movies.

- **A word that ends in -s takes just an ' to show possession:**

  That store sells *ladies'* hats with feathers.

  I depend on my *friends'* advice.

PROOFREADING STRATEGY

Knowing the two main uses of apostrophes—contractions and possessives—will help you avoid the mistake of sticking apostrophes where they don't belong, for instance, into plural nouns or possessive pronouns like *hers* or *its*.

Go through your draft and **highlight every word that contains an apostrophe**. If you are using a computer, use the *"Find"* feature to locate all apostrophes in your draft.

For every apostrophe, you should be able to answer YES to one of two questions:

Is this apostrophe used to form a contraction?

Is this apostrophe used to indicate possession?

                      YES   YES   NO   YES

Example: Ronald didn't realize that the children's toy's weren't in the box.
                                                    toys

To find **missing apostrophes**, highlight all words ending in -s. If the word is a plural, leave it alone. If the word is a possessive noun, add an apostrophe.

                  coach's   OK—plural

Example: When the coachs whistle blew, the swimmers dove into the pool.

WRITING AND PROOFREADING ASSIGNMENT

Assume that you are writing to apply for a position as a teacher's aide. You want to convince the school principal that you would be a good teacher, and you decide to do this by describing a time when you taught a young child—your own child, a younger sibling, or a friend's child—to do something new.

In your topic sentence, briefly state who the child was and what you taught him or her. What made you want to teach this child? Was the experience easier or harder than you expected? How did you feel afterward? Proofread for the correct use of apostrophes.

CHAPTER REVIEW

Proofread this paragraph for apostrophe errors—missing apostrophes and apostrophes used incorrectly. Correct the errors above the lines.

The Magic Fastener

(1) Its hard to remember the world without Velcro. (2) Shoelaces had to be tied; jackets' had to be zipped and did'nt make so much noise when they were loosened. (3) We have a Swiss engineers' curiosity to thank for todays changes. (4) On a hunting trip in 1948, George de Mestral became intrigued by the seedpods that clung to his clothing. (5) He knew that they we're hitching rides to new territory by fastening onto him, but he could'nt tell how they were doing it. (6) He examined the seedpods to find that their tiny hooks were catching onto the threads of his jacket. (7) The idea of Velcro was born, but the actual product wasnt developed overnight. (8) It took eight more years' before George de Mestrals invention was ready for the market. (9) Today, Velcro is used on clothing, on space suits, and even in artificial hearts. (10) Velcro not only can help keep a skier warm but can also save a persons' life.

EXPLORING ONLINE

grammar.ccc.commnet.edu/GRAMMAR/quizzes/apostrophe_quiz2.htm
Test your expertise with this "Catastrophes of Apostrophic Proportions" Quiz.

owl.english.purdue.edu/exercises/3/3/10
Insert the necessary apostrophes and check your work when you finish.

Visit **MindTap** for *Grassroots* to access this chapter's ebook, flashcards, additional practice and quizzes, and more!

CHAPTER 33

Direct and Indirect Quotations

A: Defining Direct and Indirect Quotations

B: Punctuating Simple Direct Quotations

C: Punctuating Split Quotations

D: Ending Direct Quotations

A. Defining Direct and Indirect Quotations

> (1) John said that he was going.
>
> (2) John said, "I am going."

- Which sentence gives the *exact words* of the speaker, John?

  _____

- Why is sentence (2) called a *direct quotation*?

  _____

- Why is sentence (1) called an *indirect quotation*?

  _____

- Note that the word *that* introduces the *indirect quotation*.

PRACTICE 1   Write *D* in the blank if the sentence uses a *direct quotation*. Write *I* in the blank if the sentence uses an *indirect quotation*.

1. She said that she was thirsty.   _____

2. Malcolm asked, "Which is my laptop?"   _____

3. Ellah insisted that one turkey would feed the whole family.   _____

4. The students shouted, "Get out of the building! It's on fire!"   _____

5. "This is silly," she said, sighing.   _____

6. I suggested that Rod's future was in the catering business.   _____

B. Punctuating Simple Direct Quotations

Note the punctuation:

> (1) Rafael whispered, "I'll always love you."

- Put a comma before the direct quotation.
- Put quotation marks around the speaker's exact words.
- Capitalize the first word of the direct quotation.
- Put the period *inside* the end quotation marks.

   Of course, the direct quotation may come first in the sentence:

> (2) "I'll always love you," Rafael whispered.

- List the rules for a direct quotation written like the sentence above:

   _____

   _____

   _____

PRACTICE 2   Rewrite these simple direct quotations, punctuating them correctly.

1. He yelled answer the phone!

    Rewrite: _____

2. The usher called no more seats in front.

    Rewrite: _____

3. My back aches she repeated dejectedly.

    Rewrite: _____

4. Examining the inside cover, Pierre said this book was printed in 1879.

    Rewrite: _____

5. A bug is doing the backstroke in my soup the man said.

    Rewrite: _____

C. Punctuating Split Quotations

Sometimes one sentence of direct quotation is split into two parts:

> (1) "Because it is 2 A.M.," he said, "you had better go."

- *He said* is set off by commas.

- The second part of the quotation—*you had better go*—begins with a small letter because it is part of one directly quoted sentence.

(2) "Because it is 2 A.M. . . . you had better go."

A direct quotation can also be broken into separate sentences:

(3) "It is a long ride to San Francisco," he said. "We should leave early."

- Because the second part of the quotation is a separate sentence, it begins with a capital letter.
- Note the period after *said*.

BE CAREFUL: If you break a direct quotation into separate sentences, be sure that both parts of the quotation are complete sentences.

PRACTICE 3   Rewrite these split direct quotations, punctuating them correctly.

1. Before the guests arrive she said let's relax.

   Rewrite: _____

2. Don't drive so fast he begged I get nervous.

   Rewrite: _____

3. Although Mort is out shellfishing Fran said his hip boots are on the porch.

   Rewrite: _____

4. Being the youngest in the family she said has its advantages.

   Rewrite: _____

5. This catalog is fantastic the clerk said and you can have it for free.

   Rewrite: _____

PRACTICE 4   On paper or on a computer, write three sentences using split quotations.

D. Ending Direct Quotations

A sentence can end in any of three ways:

- with a period (.)
- with a question mark (?)
- with an exclamation point (!)

The period is *always* placed inside the end quotation marks:

(1) He said, "My car cost five thousand dollars."

The question mark and the exclamation point go before or after the quotation marks—depending on the sense of the sentence.

> (2) He asked, "Where are you?"
>
> (3) Did he say, "I am 32 years old"?
>
> (4) She yelled, "Help!"

● The question mark in sentence (2) is placed before the end quotation marks because the direct quotation is a question.

● The question mark in sentence (3) is placed after the end quotation marks because the direct quotation itself *is not a question*.

Note that sentence (2) can be reversed:

> (5) "Where are you?" he asked.

● Can you list the rules for the exclamation point used in sentence (4)?

_____

_____

Note that sentence (4) can be reversed:

> (6) "Help!" she yelled.

PRACTICE 5   Rewrite these direct quotations, punctuating them correctly.

1. Marlena asked is that your Humvee.

   Rewrite: _____

2. Did Shenoya make the team he inquired.

   Rewrite: _____

3. Be careful with that mirror she begged the movers.

   Rewrite: _____

4. The truck driver shouted give me a break.

   Rewrite: _____

5. Did she say I wouldn't give my social security number to that telemarketer?

   Rewrite: _____

   _____

Chapter Highlights

- **A direct quotation requires quotation marks:**

  Benjamin Franklin said, "There never was a good war or a bad peace."

- **Both parts of a split quotation require quotation marks:**

  "It isn't fair," she argued, "for us to lose the money for the after-school programs."

- **When a direct quotation is split into separate sentences, begin the second sentence with a capital letter:**

  "It's late," he said. "Let's leave in the morning."

- **Always place the period inside the end quotation marks:**

  He said, "Sometimes I talk too much."

- **A question mark or an exclamation point can be placed before or after the end quotation marks, depending on the meaning of the sentence:**

  She asked, "Where were you when we needed you?"

  Did she say, "Joe looks younger without his beard"?

PROOFREADING STRATEGY

If quotation marks give you trouble, use this strategy.

1. **Scan your draft** for sentences in which you give **someone's exact words**.

2. **Check these sentences** for correct use of commas, quotation marks, and capitalization.

3. For every quotation mark before the quoted words start, **make sure that you have provided the end quotation mark**.

   Gwendolyn just texted "Can ~~can~~ you meet me for coffee?"

WRITING AND PROOFREADING ASSIGNMENT

Write a note to someone with whom you have had an argument. Your goal is to get back on friendly terms with this person. In your first sentence, state this goal, asking for his or her open-minded attention. Then tell him or her why you think a misunderstanding occurred and explain how you think conflict might be avoided in the future. Refer to the original argument by using both direct and indirect quotations. When you are finished drafting, proofread for the correct use of quotation marks; be careful with *all* punctuation.

CHAPTER REVIEW

Proofread this essay for direct and indirect quotations. Punctuate the quotations correctly and make any other necessary changes above the lines.

Satchel Paige

(1) Some people say that the great pitcher Leroy Paige was called Satchel because of his big feet. (2) Paige himself said I got the nickname as a boy in Mobile before my feet grew. (3) He earned money by carrying bags, called satchels, at the railroad station. (4) I figured out a way to make more money by carrying several bags at a time on a pole he said. (5) Other boys began shouting at him that he looked like a satchel tree. (6) The name stuck.

(7) Unfortunately, for most of Paige's long pitching career, major league baseball excluded African-American players. (8) However, Satchel Paige pitched impressively in the black leagues and in tours against white teams. (9) In 1934 he won a 13-inning, one-to-nothing pitching duel against the white pitcher Dizzy Dean and a team of major league all-stars. (10) My fastball admitted Dean looks like a change of pace alongside of that little bullet old Satchel shoots up to the plate!

(11) After Jackie Robinson broke the major league color barrier in 1948, Satchel Paige took his windmill windup to the Cleveland Indians. (12) He became the oldest rookie in major league history. (13) Some people said that he was too old, but his record proved them wrong. (14) His plaque in the Baseball Hall of Fame reads he helped pitch the Cleveland Indians to the 1948 pennant.

(15) Satchel Paige pitched off and on until he was 60 years old. (16) When people asked how he stayed young, he gave them his famous rules. (17) Everyone remembers the last one. (18) Don't look back he said. (19) Something might be gaining on you.

EXPLORING ONLINE

www.dailygrammar.com/371to375.shtml
Practice with answers: Place quotation marks and capitalize correctly.

grammar.ccc.commnet.edu/grammar/quizzes/quotes_quiz.htm
Challenging interactive quiz: Think hard and punctuate.

Visit **MindTap** for *Grassroots* to access this chapter's ebook, flashcards, additional practice and quizzes, and more!

CHAPTER 34

Putting Your Proofreading Skills to Work

Proofreading is the important final step in the writing process. After you have planned and written a paragraph or an essay, you must **proofread**, carefully checking each sentence for correct grammar, punctuation, and capitalization. Proofreading means applying everything you have learned in Units 2 through 7. Is every sentence complete? Do all your verbs agree with their subjects? Have you mistakenly written any comma splices or sentence fragments?

This chapter gives you the opportunity to practice proofreading skills in real-world situations. As you proofread the paragraphs and essays that follow, you must look for any—and every—kind of error, just as you would in the real world of college or work. The first five practices tell you what kinds of errors to look for. If you have trouble, go back to the chapters listed and review the material. The final practices, however, give you no clues at all, so you must put your proofreading skills to the real-world test.

- Before you proofread, review your **Personal Error Patterns Chart** that you learned to keep in Chapter 9. Take special care to proofread for the errors you tend to make.

- Use the **proofreading strategies** that work best for you. In this book, you have practiced strategies like reading out loud as you look for errors, reading from the bottom up, and color highlighting. Apply your favorite strategies here!

- Examine the **proofreading checklist** at the end of this chapter for a quick reminder of what to look for.

- Keep a **dictionary** handy. If you are not sure of the spelling of a word, look it up.

PRACTICE 1

Proofread this paragraph, correcting any errors above the lines. (You should find 13 individual errors.) To review, see these chapters:

Chapter 14   past participle errors

Chapter 19   run-ons and comma splices

Chapter 24   pronoun errors

Chapter 26   preposition errors

Charles Sykes/AP Images

Singer-songwriter Ed Sheeran with fans

(1) Most popular singers are support by teams of people whom write their songs, play backup music, use Auto-Tune to correct there off-key vocals, and style their "looks." (2) On the world of carefully crafted superstars, British singer-songwriter Ed Sheeran is the exception, he has became a global sensation anyway. (3) Sheeran learned to sing and play guitar as a child, realizing early that his passion was writing and performing soulful solos. (4) As a teenager, he couch-surfed his way through London and Los Angeles to play gigs and make a name for hisself. (5) He built his own fan base through live performances, self-released music, and videos in YouTube, at age 20, he signed a major record deal. (6) A prolific songwriter, Sheeran has wrote or collaborated on songs with stars like Justin Bieber, One Direction, rapper Lupe Fiasco, and Taylor Swift, for who he was once the wildly popular opening act. (7) Now in his late twenties, the red-haired performer has sold millions of records worldwide a generation of fans love his raw, emotional singing. (8) Without the conventional pop-star packaging, Ed Sheeran sells out arenas all over the world.

PRACTICE 2

Proofread this paragraph, correcting any errors above the lines. (You should find 14 individual errors.) To review, see these chapters:

Chapter 11   sentence fragments
Chapter 13   past tense errors
Chapter 25   adjective and adverb errors
Chapter 29   parallelism

(1) Can exercise make us smarter? (2) Vigorous exercise tones muscles, aids weight loss, and the heart is strengthened. (3) But, according to many studies, aerobic workouts also increase brainpower. (4) In one experiment, students at the University of Illinois memorized letters. (5) Then picked those letters from a list. (6) Next, the students were divided into three groups. (7) For 30 minutes, some sat quiet, some run on a treadmill, and weight lifting was done by some. (8) After a 30-minute rest period. (9) The students taked the letter test again. (10) Every time, the group who runned on the treadmill was more quicker and more accurate than the other two groups. (11) Studies of laboratory mice in Taiwan reinforced these results. (12) Rodents who worked out strenuously on tiny treadmills performed complex mental tasks more effective than mice who run at their own pace. (13) Under a microscope, the brains of the more athletic mice showed positive changes. (14) Exciting new studies at Harvard explain why. (15) A substance that scientists call *irisin*, released in the brain during exercise. (16) Both improves brain function and new brain cells are formed. (17) Hard, aerobic exercise really does. (18) Benefit body *and* mind.

PRACTICE 3

Proofread this paragraph, correcting any errors above the lines. (You should find 18 individual errors.) To review, see these chapters:

Chapter 11	sentence fragments
Chapter 14	past participle verb errors
Chapter 19	run-ons and comma splices
Chapters 23 and 32	plural and possessive errors

(1) Christiane Amanpour is one of the most respected foreign correspondents in the world, but she calls herself an "accidental journalist." (2) Because she never intended to become one. (3) Her native Iran had no freedom of the press, journalism did not interest her. (4) Christiane attended high school in England. (5) Then the revolution in Iran brought chaos to her family, her fathers money was froze, the families fund were very tight. (6) Christianes' sister dropped out of journalism college in London, Christiane took her place for the sole reason of saving the tuition money. (7) Soon she was hook on reporting. (8) After graduating from the University of Rhode Island, she applied for a job at a new cable station. (9) Called CNN. (10) She longed to write news story's and go overseas but was

mock by her boss, who said she didn't have the right looks and that her name was difficult to pronounce. (11) Amanpour worked hard and hid her frustration with doing routine task. (12) Like bringing people coffee. (13) Every time a new job opened at CNN, she applied for it. (14) Her big break was being send to Germany and the Gulf War. (15) With gunfires and rockets around her, she reported the news with intelligence and heart. (16) Today Amanpour is global affairs anchor for ABC and chief international correspondent for CNN. (17) She is one of the few journalist followed by world leaders.

PRACTICE 4

Proofread this paragraph, correcting any errors above the lines. (You should find 20 individual errors.) To review, see these chapters:

Chapter 11   sentence fragments
Chapter 12   subject/verb agreement errors
Chapter 31   comma errors
Chapter 32   apostrophe errors

(1) Every spring and summer, storm chaser's spreads out across the midwestern part of the United States known as Tornado Alley. (2) Armed with video cameras maps and radios. (3) These lovers of violent weather follows huge weather systems called supercells, which sometimes produces tornados. (4) On a good day, a storm chaser may find a supercell. (5) And get close enough to film the brief, destructive life of a tornado. (6) Some joins the storm-chasing tours offered every summer by universities or private companies. (7) Others learn what they can from the Internet and sets off on their own to hunt tornados. (8) Storm chasing can be very dangerous. (9) A large tornado spins winds between 125 and 175 mph, tearing roofs off houses ripping limbs from trees, and overturning cars. (10) The greatest danger comes from airborne branches boards shingles and glass hurtling through the air like deadly weapons. (11) Even if a supercell don't spawn tornados. (12) It often produces winds over 50 mph, heavy rain, large hail, and intense lightning. (13) Most storm chasers avoids these risks by racing out of a tornados' path before it gets too close. (14) Despite or perhaps because of these dangers, dramatized in the 1996 movie *Twister*. (15) Storm chasing remains popular. (16) Fans claim that few things in life matches the thrill of discovering a tornado and witnessing the power of nature.

PRACTICE 5   Proofread this paragraph, correcting any errors above the lines. (You should find 14 individual errors.) To review, see these chapters:

Chapter 21   relative pronoun errors
Chapter 25   adjective and adverb errors
Chapter 30   capitalization errors
Chapter 31   comma errors

(1) A courageous child whom lost his life to cancer lives on in thousands of random acts of kindness. (2) Jayden Lamb was a happy generous first grader in michigan when he was diagnosed with a rare form of cancer. (3) During his three-year battle with the disease, he remained brave uncomplaining and upbeat. (4) Just after his death in 2012, Jayden's grieving parents were getting coffee from a Drive-through when, on a whim, they paid the tab of the driver behind them. (5) Several days later, they anonymous paid off a stranger's layaway bill at walmart. (6) These acts of giving eased their grief. (7) When they wrote about these experiences on their Facebook page, "Keep on Truckin' Team Jayden," they set off a chain reaction. (8) Inspired by Jayden's story strangers began committing random acts of kindness. (9) One waitress received a $50 tip with a note which read, "In memory of Jayden Lamb." (10) An unemployed man was told that the bicycle his son wanted for christmas had been paid for in Jayden's honor. (11) A nameless donor even dropped a $2,000 diamond ring in a red salvation army kettle, along with the words, "Paying it forward, Jayden style." (12) Tens of thousands of people have bought others' meals and gas, shoveled snow from a neighbor's drive, given to charities, and sometimes shared descriptions of their well deeds in his honor.

PRACTICE 6   Proofread this essay, correcting any errors above the lines.

Women on the Force

(1) Anyone who watches crime dramas on television would think that woman are work busily alongside men in police precincts across the country. (2) Actress Mariska Hargitay's Detective Olivia Benson in *Law & Order: Special Victims Unit* and Mary McDonnell's Commander sharon raydor in *Major Crimes* are just two examples. (3) In real life, however, things dont go this smooth.

(4) Although police departments have became much more racially diverse since 1990, law enforcement remains a stubbornly male-dominated world. (5) Women who want to enter that world often must prove oneself to male counterparts, enduring harassment, being discriminated against, and lingering doubts about there physical strength or courage. (6) Only 13 percent of police officer nationally are women. (7) Yet those who stick it out often does so for love of the job and of public service. (8) On her first morning at the police academy, Kathy Katerman suffered a broken nose in a boxing exercise with a larger male officer. (9) Instead of racing for the door, she grab some ice and continued her long day of basic training. (10) To prove her emotional and physical strenth to the other recruits, she did not go to the hospital until the workday ended. (11) Major Katerman went on to spent 28 years on the force in North miami beach, Florida, rising to became the third-highest ranked officer in the Investigative Division.

(12) Despite the obstacles, opportunitys for women in law enforcement are increasing. (13) The number of female police chiefs has rose nationwide to 220, with top cops in cities like Los Angeles, Houston, phoenix, and Columbus. (14) These promotions reflect their leadership skills and system savvy; however, the vast majority of chiefs are still men. (15) Yet research shows that female officers also bring unique skill that precincts need

Over 600 new members of the New York City Police Department (NYPD) at graduation, 2017

Drew Angerer/Getty Images

now. (16) Woman tend to defuse tense situations through communicate and critical thinking, not violence. (17) They are better at community outreach. (18) They draw they're guns less and very rarely use excessive force. (19) These are the very abilities that many police departments seek now as they work to improving community relations and trust. (20) Women who are tough, fitness, smart, and cool in a crisis might consider this career even though they wont solve crimes in an hour and always look glamorous.

PRACTICE 7

Proofread this essay, correcting any errors above the lines.

Quiet, Please!

(1) America is loud. (2) Horns and sirens pierces the air, car stereos pump out loud music. (3) Cell phones rings, shriek, or trumpets the owner's noise of choice. (4) Construction equipments, lawnmowers, and leaf blowers buzz and roar into the public space. (5) Restaurant and movie theater manager's often seem to link loudness with cultural cool. (6) Sounds are measured in decibels, with the human voice measuring about 60 decibels, the sound of a car is about 80 decibels. (7) According to the U.S. Environmental Protection Agency, 70 decibels is a safe daily average. (8) Here is the problem: the level of noise that many of us hear every day are far above this.

(9) The sound of a food blender, for example, measures 90 decibels. (10) MP3 players can blast 100 to 107 decibels, and a jet taking off is 120 decibels of ear-splitting noise. (11) All of this racket are taking it's toll on us both physically and in psychological ways. (12) According to the American Speech-Language-Hearing Association (ASHA), 28 million U.S. citizens have already suffer hearing loss from too much noise, and one in five teens has already lost hearing, just from listening to music. (13) Furthermore, loud noise raises blood pressure increases stress hormone levels, and deprives us of sleep. (14) Noise pollution also increases aggression and even violence and harms concentration and learning. (15) One study found that New york children in classrooms that faced the train tracks were almost a year behind children taught in more quieter parts of the same school.

(16) In Europe, noise pollution has been taken serious for years. (17) Now in the United States, organizations like the Noise Pollution Clearinghouse is trying to raise awareness of the problem and promote solutions. (18) Members of this organization believes that just as smoke or toxins in the air are not acceptable, neither is loud noise. (19) They are working for new laws. (20) To enforce our right to peace and quiet.

Chapter Highlights

- **Know your error patterns.** In Chapter 9, you learned how to recognize and chart your **personal error patterns**, the mistakes—such as sentence fragments or apostrophes—you tend to make. Before you proofread, review your **Personal Error Patterns Chart**. Take special care to proofread for these errors.

- **Use the proofreading strategies that work best for _you_.** In Chapter 9 and throughout the book, you have learned and practiced many strategies—like reading out loud, reading from the bottom up, and color highlighting. Put your favorite strategies to work.

- **Know where to find help.** If you need more help with recognizing and eliminating your personal error patterns, consult print sources, such as this book; online resources, such as the Exploring Online websites listed at the end of each chapter, or the OWLs you have bookmarked; and expert people, such as the staff of your college's writing lab.

PROOFREADING STRATEGY

A proofreading checklist like the one below can be an effective tool for remembering what to look for when reviewing your writing.

Proofreading Checklist

- ☐ Check for sentence fragments, comma splices, and run-on sentences.
- ☐ Check for verb errors: present tense -_s_ endings (verb agreement), past tense -_ed_ endings, past participles, and tense consistency.
- ☐ Check for incorrect singular and plural nouns, incorrect pronouns, confused adjectives and adverbs, and incorrect prepositions.
- ☐ Check all punctuation: commas, apostrophes, semicolons, quotations marks.
- ☐ Check all capitalization.
- ☐ Check spelling and look-alikes/sound-alikes.

☐ Check for omitted words and typos.

☐ Check layout, format, titles, dates, and spacing.

☐ Check for all personal error patterns.

WRITING AND PROOFREADING ASSIGNMENT

How have you strengthened your writing skills by taking this course? If possible, look back at a paper you wrote early in the term, and reflect on how you have developed as a writer. Write one or more paragraphs in which you describe the concepts and skills you have learned that have improved your writing the most.

Apply what you have learned throughout this course to produce an error-free paper. Use this opportunity to practice consulting your Personal Error Patterns Chart, applying your favorite proofreading strategies, and using a proofreading checklist to find and rid your writing of mistakes.

EXPLORING ONLINE

owl.english.purdue.edu/owl/resource/561/01

Proofreading guide.

a4esl.org/q/j/vm/mc-stockmarket.html

Interactive quiz: Correct a mix of errors and learn about the stock exchange.

journalism.uoregon.edu/~russial/grammar/grambo.html

Test of the Emergency Grammar System. Challenge yourself and have fun.

Visit **MindTap** for *Grassroots* to access this chapter's ebook, flashcards, additional practice and quizzes, and more!

Writing Assignments

As you complete each writing assignment, remember to perform these steps:

- Write a clear, complete topic sentence.

- Use freewriting, brainstorming, or clustering to generate ideas for the body of your paragraph, essay, letter, or commercial.

- Arrange your best ideas in a plan.

- Revise for support, unity, coherence, and exact language.

- Proofread for grammar, punctuation, and spelling errors.

WRITING ASSIGNMENT 1 *Write an online review to compliment or to complain.* Write a review and post it to a website such as Yelp or TripAdvisor to praise an especially helpful salesperson or a particularly good restaurant. If you are not feeling complimentary, write the opposite: a letter of complaint about a place of business. State your compliment or complaint, describing what occurred and explaining why you are pleased or displeased. Remember, how well your post is written will contribute to the impression you make. Proofread carefully for the correct use of capitals, commas, apostrophes, and quotation marks.

WRITING ASSIGNMENT 2 *Explore a social problem.* Choose a social problem that matters to you and take a stand. Think of an issue about which you are passionate—school loan debt, equal pay, crowded prisons, and so on. For help in finding an issue, scroll a site like **www.isidewith.com/polls**. Express your opinion in your topic sentence and develop your paragraph or short essay with at least three reasons that support your stand. Proofread carefully for the correct use of capitals, commas, apostrophes, and quotation marks.

WRITING ASSIGNMENT 3 *Create a print ad.* You and several classmates considering careers in advertising have been asked to create a print ad for a magazine, newspaper, or billboard. You must sell one product or idea of your choice—anything from a brand of jeans to a cell phone to a good cause, like recycling or becoming a foster parent. Your goal is to capture people's attention with a strong picture and then persuade them with a few well-chosen words. Sketch and draft your ad; don't let punctuation errors get in the way of your message. For ideas, visit this website: **adbusters.org/spoofads**.

WRITING ASSIGNMENT 4 *Discuss an unusual friendship.* Have you ever had or witnessed a truly unusual friendship—for instance, between two people many years apart in age, between people from different social worlds who bonded because of a shared hobby or problem, or between a human being and an animal? Select one such unusual friendship and capture its essence in writing. How did the friendship start? What do you think bonded the two friends? Be as specific as possible so that the reader will understand this special relationship. Proofread carefully for correct use of capitals, commas, apostrophes, and quotation marks.

Review

Proofreading

A. Proofread the following e-mailed cover letter for incorrect or missing capitals, commas, apostrophes, and quotation marks. Correct all errors above the lines. (You should find 25 individual errors.)

To: teresa.willingham@easternvalleyhospital.com

From: kayla.johnston@easternvalley.edu

Subject: certified nursing assistant Position

Dear Ms. Willingham:

I read your advertisement for a Certified Nursing Assistant position on LinkedIn.com, and i would like to apply for the job. I have all of the qualifications youre seeking.

For the past year and a half I have worked as a part-time CNA for Baxter Home Health care in lincolnton. My duties have included assisting clients with personal care (bathing, dressing, and grooming), monitoring and assisting with medications, checking vital signs making and serving meals, and documenting all of my actions and observations. I graduated from Valley View high school in 2015 with a 3.4 GPA. On may 11 2016 I earned my CNA certification at eastern valley community college. Since then, I have continued to attend classes as a pre-nursing major. Im dependable punctual, and detail oriented. In my last evaluation, my supervisor wrote, "kayla is one of our most caring and conscientious employees.

It would be a "pleasure" to have the opportunity to discuss the position and answer any questions you may have, I hope that you will call me at (801) 555-1616 to schedule an interview.

Sincerely your's,

Kayla Johnston

B. Proofread the following essay for incorrect or missing capitals, commas, apostrophes, and quotation marks. Correct the errors above the lines. (You should find 34 individual errors.)

Winning On and Off the Court

(1) Few basketball players have achieved the combination of on-court excellence and off-court generosity embodied by kevin Durant, superstar forward for the Golden state warriors. (2) Durant was named the NBAs most valuable player and starred on the winning Olympic teams of 2012, and 2016.

(3) Born in 1988, he was largely raised by his grandmother in Maryland, she was his rock, insisting that Durants' height of six feet, nine inches was a blessing. (4) Soon his on-court skills proved him to be a basketball prodigy. (5) He could dunk dribble like a guard and share the ball with his teammates. (6) After one successful year at the University of Texas, Durant was drafted second overall in 2007 by the Seattle supersonics. (7) He became Rookie of the Year in 2008, just before the SuperSonics moved to Oklahoma City and were renamed the thunder. (8) For the next nine years Durant electrified fans with his brilliant play winning four league-scoring titles and other elite awards. (9) In 2016, he became a free agent. (10) Despite deep roots in oklahoma city, he joined the golden state warriors hoping to win a championship.

(11) Off the court, Kevin Durants generous community efforts are also exceptional. (12) When a tornado devastated Oklahoma in 2013 he quickly donated one million dollars, a figure matched both by nike his sponsor, and by the Thunder his Kevin Durant charity Foundation helps homeless and foster care youth and their family members. (13) One program Positive Tomorrows provides books educational supplies, and household items for families transitioning from homelessness to more settled lives. (14) As former Texas head coach rick barnes said of Durant Hes a once-in-a-lifetime guy.

Writers' Workshop

Explain a Cause or an Effect

Examining causes and effects is a useful skill, both in college and at work. This student's thoughtful essay looks at the effects of school pressure to "speak like an American." In your group or class, read it aloud if possible. As you read, pay attention to the causes and effects he describes.

In America, Speak Like an American

(1) Many teachers tell immigrant students to lose their accents and "speak like an American." They mean well. They want the children to succeed. However, this can also encourage children to be ashamed of who they are and give up their heritage.

(2) When I was in fourth grade, I was sent to a class for "speech imperfections." Apparently, I had a Spanish accent. The class wasn't so bad, it taught us to say "chair" instead of "shair" and "school" instead of "eschool." It was so important for me to please the teacher, I did practically everything she asked. She told us things like "The bums on the street have accents, that's why they're not working." I abandoned my roots and my culture and embraced "America." I learned about Stonewall Jackson and William Shakespeare. Soon Ponce de León and Pedro Calderón de la Barca were just memories at the back of my mind. I listened to country music and rock because this was "American."

(3) I can't remember when it happened, but suddenly I found myself listening to Spanish love songs. They were great! They were so sincere, the lyrics were beautiful. While turning the radio dial one day, I stopped at a Hispanic radio station. It was playing salsa. "Holy smokes," I thought to myself. All the instruments were synchronized so tightly. The horn section kept accenting the singer's lines. All of a sudden, my hips started swaying, my feet started tapping,

and I stood up. And then the horror. I couldn't dance to this music, I had never learned how. There I was, a Puerto Rican boy, listening to Puerto Rican music but unable to dance the typical Puerto Rican way.

(4) Anger flared through me as I remembered my fourth-grade teacher. I was also upset with my parents, in their zeal to have me excel, they kept me from my roots as a first-generation Hispanic American. But that was years ago. I have searched for my Latin heritage. I've found beautiful music, wonderful literature, and great foods. I now associate with "my people" as well as with everyone else, and I am learning the joys of being Sam Rodriguez, Puerto Rican.

Sam Rodriguez, Student

1. How effective is Sam Rodriguez's essay?

   _____ Clear main idea?   _____ Good supporting details?

   _____ Logical organization?   _____ Effective conclusion?

2. Does the essay have a *thesis statement*, one sentence that states the main idea of the entire essay? Which sentence is it?

3. In paragraph (2), the writer says that he "abandoned [his] roots." In his view, what caused him to do this?

4. Underline the lines and ideas you find especially effective and share them with your group or class. Try to understand exactly why you like a word or sentence. For example, in paragraph (3), we can almost experience the first time the writer really *hears* salsa—the instruments, the horns accenting the singer's lines, his tapping feet and swaying hips.

5. As the writer gets older, he realizes he has lost too much of his heritage. At first he is angry (short-term effect), but what long-term effect does this new understanding have on him?

6. What order does this writer follow throughout the essay?

7. This fine essay is finished and ready to go, but the student makes the same punctuation error five times. Can you spot and correct the error pattern that he needs to watch out for?

Writing and Revising Ideas

1. What does it mean to "become American"?

2. Write about something important that you gave up and explain why you did so.

Plan carefully, outlining your paragraph or essay before you write. State your main idea clearly and plan your supporting ideas or paragraphs. As you revise, pay special attention to clear organization and convincing, detailed support.

Improving Your Spelling

Some people are naturally better spellers than others, but anyone can become a better speller. In this unit, you will

- Follow the MAP to better reading and writing

- Master six basic spelling rules

- Learn to avoid common look-alike/sound-alike errors

- Learn proofreading strategies to find and correct your own errors

Follow the MAP to Better Reading and Writing

MODEL

Read this paragraph aloud if possible. Do you know why each underlined word is spelled correctly?

The current trend to sexualize female news anchors may help some networks <u>seize</u> higher ratings, but it has negative <u>effects</u> as well. According to a recent study from Indiana University, male viewers have more trouble understanding the news when it is delivered by a sexy TV anchor. In the study, researchers Maria Elizabeth Grabe and Lelia Samson showed two news clips to 400 test subjects. In both clips, the same journalist reported the same <u>stories</u>, but in one she wore a tightly <u>fitting</u> suit that accentuated her waist, red lipstick, and jewelry. In the other clip, she wore a shapeless suit, no make-up, and no jewelry. The ability of male <u>viewers</u> to recall the information in her report dropped when they watched the more sexualized anchor. Even more <u>surprising</u> was <u>their</u> assessment that the sexy anchor was less competent to report on serious topics like war and politics though the quality of reporting was identical in both clips. <u>Interestingly</u>, the anchor's appearance had no effect on whether female viewers thought she was a competent professional. Because TV executives are still <u>largely</u> male, the researchers warn that sexualizing female anchors may increase network ratings, but it <u>professionally</u> damages the <u>women</u> themselves.

Dr. Karen Cox, "Sexy Anchors Distract Men from the News" (unpublished article)

ANALYSIS

- Through her choice and arrangement of words, this writer exposes a worrisome trend in TV news. She also avoids common spelling errors that many college students make. If you can't explain why every underlined word is correct, this unit is for you.

PRACTICE

- Give examples of anchors' clothing from one network and write about the message that these looks send.

- Write about the message sent by someone's style of dress: a rapper, athlete, Goth, nerd, banker, hipster, and so on.

CHAPTER 35

Spelling

A. Suggestions for Improving Your Spelling

One important ingredient of good writing is accurate spelling. No matter how interesting your ideas are, your writing will not be effective if your spelling is incorrect.

Tips for Improving Your Spelling

1. **Look closely at the words on the page.** Use any tricks you can to remember the right spelling. For example, "Argument has no *e* because I lost the *e* during an argument" or "*Believe* has a *lie* in it."

2. **Use a dictionary.** Even professional writers frequently check spelling in a dictionary. As you write, underline the words you are not sure of and look them up when you write your final draft. If locating words in the dictionary is a real problem for you, consider a "poor speller's dictionary." Ask your professor to recommend one.

3. **Use a spell checker.** If you write on a computer, make a habit of using the spell checker. See Part B for tips and cautions about spell checkers.

4. **Keep a list of the words you misspell.** Look over your list whenever you can and keep it handy as you write.

5. **Look over corrected papers for misspelled words** (often marked *sp*). Add these words to your list. Practice writing each word three or four times.

6. **Test yourself.** Have a friend dictate words from your list or from this chapter or use flashcards; computerized flashcards can be helpful.

7. **Review the basic spelling rules explained in this chapter.** Take time to learn the material; don't rush through the entire chapter all at once.

8. **Study the spelling list in Part I,** and test yourself on those words.

9. **Read through Chapter 36, "Look-Alikes/Sound-Alikes,"** for commonly confused words (*their*, *there*, and *they're*, for instance). The practices in that chapter will help you eliminate some common spelling errors from your writing.

B. Computer Spell Checkers

If you write on a computer, always run the spell checker as part of your proofreading process. A spell checker picks up certain spelling errors and gives you alternatives for correcting them. Your program might also highlight misspelled words as you write.

What a spell checker cannot do is *think*. If you have written one correctly spelled word instead of another—*if* for *it*, for example—the spell checker cannot bring that error to your attention. If you have written *then* for *than*, the spell checker cannot help.* To find such errors, you must always proofread your paper *after* running the spell checker.

PRACTICE 1

In a small group, read this poem, which "passed" spell check. Above the lines, correct the errors that the spell checker missed.

My righting is soup eerier

Too yore pay purr this thyme.

Iran my SA threw spell check,

Each sill able an rime.

Two bad, ewe awe full righters,

Fore ewe probe lee en vee me.

My verb all cents muss bee immense,

four aye right sew quick lee.

Eye donut kneed a textbook.

I through it inn the lake.

The pro fey sore rote big read Marx.

Their muss bee sum miss take!

C. Spotting Vowels and Consonants

To learn some basic spelling rules, you must know the difference between vowels and consonants. Refer to the following chart.

The **vowels** are *a*, *e*, *i*, *o*, and *u*.
The **consonants** are *b*, *c*, *d*, *f*, *g*, *h*, *j*, *k*, *l*, *m*, *n*, *p*, *q*, *r*, *s*, *t*, *v*, *w*, *x*, and *z*.
The letter *y* can be either a vowel or a consonant, depending on its sound:
       happy   shy
       young   yawn

---

* For questions about words that sound the same but are spelled differently, check Chapter 36, "Look-Alikes/Sound-Alikes."

- In both *happy* and *shy*, *y* is a vowel because it has a vowel sound: an *ee* sound in *happy* and an *i* sound in *shy*.

- In both *young* and *yawn*, *y* is a consonant because it has the consonant sound of *y*.

PRACTICE 2　　Write *V* for vowel or *C* for consonant in the space over each letter. Be careful of the *y*.

EXAMPLE:

C	C	V	C	C	V
s	t	a	r	r	y

1.

t	h	e	r	e

2.

j	u	m	p

3.

r	e	l	y

4.

y	a	m	s

5.

h	i	d	d	e	n

6.

s	i	l	v	e	r

D. Doubling the Final Consonant (in Words of One Syllable)

When you add a suffix, or ending, that begins with a vowel (like *-ed*, *-ing*, *-er*, *-est*) to a word of one syllable, double the final consonant *if* the last three letters of the word are consonant-vowel-consonant, or *cvc*.

> mop + ed = mopped　　　　swim + ing = swimming
>
> burn + er = burner　　　　thin + est = thinnest

- *Mop*, *swim*, and *thin* all end in *cvc*; therefore, the final consonants are doubled.
- *Burn* does not end in *cvc*; therefore, the final consonant is not doubled.

PRACTICE 3　　Which of the following words double the final consonant? Check to see whether the word ends in *cvc*. Double the final consonant if necessary; then add the suffixes *-ed* and *-ing*.

	Word	Last Three Letters	-ed	-ing
EXAMPLES:	drop	cvc	dropped	dropping
	boil	vvc	boiled	boiling
1.	plan			
2.	brag			
3.	dip			
4.	sail			
5.	stop			

PRACTICE 4　　Which of the following words double the final consonant? Check for *cvc*. Then add the suffixes *-er* or *-est*.

	Word	Last Three Letters	-er	-est
EXAMPLES:	hot	cvc	hotter	hottest
	cool	vvc	cooler	coolest

1. tall _____   _____   _____
2. short _____   _____   _____
3. fat _____   _____   _____
4. slim _____   _____   _____
5. wet _____   _____   _____
6. quick _____   _____   _____

E. Doubling the Final Consonant (in Words of More Than One Syllable)

When you add a suffix that begins with a vowel to a word of more than one syllable, double the final consonant *if*

(1) the last three letters of the word are *cvc, and*

(2) the accent or stress is on the *last* syllable.

> begin + ing = beginning
>
> patrol + ed = patrolled

- *Begin* and *patrol* both end in *cvc.*
- In both words, the stress is on the last syllable: *be-gin´, pa-trol´.* (Pronounce the words aloud and listen for the correct stress.)
- Therefore, *beginning* and *patrolled* double the final consonant.

> gossip + ing = gossiping
>
> visit + ed = visited

- *Gossip* and *visit* both end in *cvc.*
- However, the stress is **not** on the last syllable: *gos´-sip, vis´-it.*
- Therefore, *gossiping* and *visited* do not double the final consonant.

PRACTICE 5

Which of the following words double the final consonant? First, check for *cvc*. Then check for the final stress and add the suffixes *-ed* and *-ing.*

	Word	Last Three Letters	-ed	-ing
EXAMPLES:	repel	*cvc*	*repelled*	*repelling*
	enlist	*vcc*	*enlisted*	*enlisting*
1.	occur	_____	_____	_____
2.	happen	_____	_____	_____
3.	polish	_____	_____	_____
4.	commit	_____	_____	_____
5.	offer	_____	_____	_____
6.	prefer	_____	_____	_____
7.	exit	_____	_____	_____

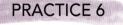

8.	travel	_____	_____	_____
9.	wonder	_____	_____	_____
10.	omit	_____	_____	_____

PRACTICE 6

Which words in parentheses double the final consonant? First, check for *cvc*. Then add the suffixes *-ed* and *-ing*. In words of two or more syllables, check for the final stress.

Hayao Miyazaki, Movie Magician

(1) Many Americans are just _____ to learn about Hayao Miyazaki, one of the
$$\text{(begin + ing)}$$

world's greatest animators. (2) Born in Tokyo in 1941, Miyazaki _____ college just as
$$\text{(attend + ed)}$$

the arts of *manga* (Japanese comics) and *anime* (animated movies) were _____ in
$$\text{(bud + ing)}$$

Japan. (3) After _____ his degree, he was _____ a job in an
$$\text{(get + ing)}$$ $$\text{(offer + ed)}$$

animation studio. (4) With his _____ ability to draw and his creative mind,
$$\text{(stun + ing)}$$

Miyazaki _____ the work.
$$\text{(enjoy + ed)}$$

Princess Mononoke, raised by wolves, is one of Miyazaki's strong girl heroines.

(5) Soon he was not only _____ animes but also _____,
(draw + ing)   (invent + ing)

_____, and _____ them. (6) With director Isao Takahata, he _____ a
(plan + ing)   (direct + ing)   (open + ed)

new film studio, Studio Ghibli. (7) By _____ his own company, he could realize
(run + ing)

his vision, _____ the anime in new directions.
(shift + ing)

(8) Above all, Miyazaki is _____ to _____ with children in mind.
(commit + ed)   (film + ing)

(9) With clear colors and imaginative plots, his movies are _____ in _____,
(root + ed)   (feel + ing)

not logic. (10) Films like *My Neighbor Totoro, Princess Mononoke,* and *Ponyo* have

_____ themes such as courage, environmental awareness, and the bonds
(explore + ed)

of love. (11) The idea for his film *Spirited Away* _____ to Miyazaki when
(occur + ed)

he had _____ _____ for a while and _____ with
(stop + ed)   (work + ing)   (stay + ed)

a friend who had a 10-year-old daughter. (12) The filmmaker _____ to make a
(vow + ed)

movie that _____ to little girls. (13) In fact, his heroines are often strong girls,
(appeal + ed)

some _____ superpowers and some not.
(possess + ing)

(14) To make a film, Miyazaki begins without even _____ the story, which then
(know + ing)

develops through the drawings. (15) The results have _____ him to the top ranks
(propel + ed)

of animated filmmakers, _____ him many awards and millions of fans, first in
(win + ing)

Japan and then the world over.

F.   Dropping or Keeping the Final *E*

When you add a suffix that begins with a vowel (like *-able*, *-ence*, and *-ing*), drop the final *e*.

When you add a suffix that begins with a consonant (like *-less*, *-ment*, and *-ly*), keep the final *e*.

> write + ing = writing   pure + ity = purity

- *Writing* and *purity* both drop the final *e* because the suffixes *-ing* and *-ity* begin with vowels.

> hope + less = hopeless   advertise + ment = advertisement

- *Hopeless* and *advertisement* keep the final *e* because the suffixes *-less* and *-ment* begin with consonants.

Here are some exceptions to memorize:

argument	courageous	knowledgeable	simply
awful	judgment	manageable	truly

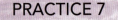 **PRACTICE 7** Add the suffix shown to each word.

EXAMPLES: come + ing = _____*coming*_____

rude + ness = _____*rudeness*_____

1. blame + less = _____
2. guide + ance = _____
3. debate + ing = _____
4. motive + ation = _____
5. sincere + ly = _____
6. desire + able = _____
7. argue + ment = _____
8. home + less = _____

9. response + ible = _____
10. rejoice + ing = _____
11. awe + ful = _____
12. manage + er = _____
13. judge + ment = _____
14. fame + ous = _____
15. grieve + ance = _____
16. arrange + ing = _____

G. Changing or Keeping the Final Y

When you add a suffix to a word that ends in -*y*, change the *y* to *i* if the letter before the *y* is a consonant.
Keep the final *y* if the letter before the *y* is a vowel.

> happy + ness = happiness   delay + ed = delayed

- The *y* in *happiness* is changed to *i* because the letter before the *y* is a consonant, *p*.
- However, the *y* in *delayed* is not changed to *i* because the letter before it is a vowel, *a*.

When you add -*ing* to words ending in *y*, always keep the *y*.

> copy + ing = copying   delay + ing = delaying

Here are some exceptions to memorize:

day + ly = daily   pay + ed = paid

lay + ed = laid   say + ed = said

When the final *y* is changed to *i*, add -*es* instead of -*s*.

> fly + es = flies   candy + es = candies
>
> marry + es = marries   story + es = stories

PRACTICE 8 Add the suffix shown to each of the following words.

EXAMPLES: vary + ed = _____*varied*_____

buy + er = _____*buyer*_____

1. cry + ed =   _____
2. mercy + ful =   _____
3. worry + ing =   _____
4. say + ed =   _____
5. juicy + er =   _____

6. enjoy + able =   _____
7. clumsy + ness =   _____
8. wealthy + est =   _____
9. day + ly =   _____
10. merry + ly =   _____

PRACTICE 9

Add the suffixes in parentheses to each word.

1. lively   (er)   _____
       (est)   _____
       (ness)   _____

2. beauty   (fy)   _____
       (ful)   _____
       (es)   _____

3. healthy   (er)   _____
       (est)   _____
       (ly)   _____

4. study   (es)   _____
       (ous)   _____
       (ing)   _____

5. busy   (ness)   _____
       (er)   _____
       (est)   _____

6. try   (es)   _____
       (ed)   _____
       (al)   _____

PRACTICE 10

Add the suffix shown to each word in parentheses. Write the correctly spelled word in each blank.

Winter Blues

(1) Although Kim _____ to ignore her feelings, she always felt _____,
                 (try + ed)   (hungry + er)

_____, _____, and _____ during the winter months. (2) As part of
(sleepy + er)   (angry + er)   (lonely + er)

her _____, she went about her _____ as usual, but she knew that she no
    (deny + al)   (busy + ness)

longer found life as _____ as before.
                  (pleasure + able)

(3) Then one day she read a _____ magazine article about a medical
                              (fascinate + ing)

condition called *seasonal affective disorder*, or *SAD*. (4) Kim _____ saw
                                         (immediate + ly)

the _____ between her yearly mood changes and the symptoms that people
      (similarity + es)

with SAD _____. (5) She learned that winter SAD is a kind of depression
        (display + ed)

triggered _____ by lack of _____ to light—by insufficient sunshine,
         (primary + ly)   (expose + ure)

inadequate indoor light at home or work, or even by _____ cloudy weather.
                                              (mercy + lessly)

(6) _____, Kim discovered that three or four kinds of treatment are
    (Happy + ly)

available. (7) The most severe cases—people who sleep more than 14 hours a day and

still feel _____, for example—are usually cured by light therapy given in
       (fatigue + ed)

a clinic or at home under a doctor's care. (8) Taking medication, _____,
(exercise + ing)

or _____ one's diet often brings _____ relief. (9) Kim did
(change + ing)   (notice + able)

some research on the Web and found a list of SAD clinics, _____, and
(guide + ance)

support. (10) Attending a light-therapy clinic near her home, she soon experienced her

_____ winter in years.
(healthy + est)

H. Choosing *IE* or *EI*

Write *i* before *e*, except after *c*, or in any *ay* sound like *neighbor*:

> niece, believe, conceive, weigh

- *Niece* and *believe* are spelled *ie*.
- *Conceive* is spelled *ei* because of the preceding *c*.
- *Weigh* is spelled *ei* because of its *ay* sound.

    However, words with a *shen* sound are spelled with an *ie* after the *c*: *ancient*, *conscience*, *efficient*, *sufficient*.

    Here are some exceptions to memorize:

either	height	seize	their
foreign	neither	society	weird

PRACTICE 11

Pronounce each word out loud. Then fill in the blanks with either ie or ei.

1. f __ __ ld
2. w __ __ ght
3. n __ __ ther
4. w __ __ rd
5. ch __ __ f
6. s __ __ ze
7. rec __ __ ve
8. br __ __ f
9. h __ __ ght
10. ach __ __ ve
11. effic __ __ nt
12. v __ __ n
13. th __ __ r
14. for __ __ gn
15. cash __ __ r

I. Commonly Misspelled Words

Below is a list of commonly misspelled words. They are words that you probably use daily in speaking and writing. Each word has a trouble spot, the part of the word that is often spelled incorrectly. The trouble spot is in bold type.

    Two tricks to help you learn these words are (1) to copy each word twice, underlining the trouble spot, and (2) to copy the words on flashcards and have someone else test you. If possible, consult this list while or after you write.

1. a**cross**
2. ad**d**ress
3. answ**er**
4. arg**u**ment
5. ath**le**te
6. beginn**ing**
7. behav**ior**
8. cal**en**dar
9. car**ee**r
10. cons**cience**
11. crow**ded**
12. defin**ite**
13. de**s**cribe
14. des**perate**
15. diff**er**ent
16. dis**app**oint
17. dis**app**rove
18. doesn**'t**
19. eigh**th**
20. embar**rass**
21. environ**ment**
22. exa**gg**erate
23. famili**ar**
24. finall**y**

25. government	38. maintain	51. possible	64. speech
26. grammar	39. mathematics	52. prefer	65. strength
27. height	40. meant	53. prejudice	66. success
28. illegal	41. necessary	54. privilege	67. surprise
29. immediately	42. nervous	55. probably	68. taught
30. important	43. occasion	56. psychology	69. temperature
31. integration	44. opinion	57. pursue	70. thorough
32. intelligent	45. optimist	58. reference	71. thought
33. interest	46. particular	59. rhythm	72. tired
34. interfere	47. perform	60. ridiculous	73. until
35. jewelry	48. perhaps	61. separate	74. weight
36. judgment	49. personnel	62. similar	75. written
37. knowledge	50. possess	63. since	

Personal Spelling List

In your notebook, keep a list of words that *you* misspell. Add words to your list from corrected papers and from the exercises in this chapter. First, copy each word as you misspelled it, underlining the trouble spot; then write the word correctly. Use the following form. Study your list often.

	As I Wrote It	**Correct Spelling**
1.	*disappointed*	*disappointed*
2.		
3.		

Chapter Highlights

- **Double the final consonant in one-syllable words that end in** *cvc*:

  hop/hopped   tan/tanning

- **Double the final consonant in words of more than one syllable if they end in** *cvc* **and if the stress is on the last syllable:**

  begin/beginning   prefer/preferred

- **Drop the final** *e* **when adding a suffix that begins with a vowel:**

  hope/hoping   time/timer

- **Keep the final** *e* **when adding a suffix that begins with a consonant:**

  hope/hopeful   time/timely

- **Change the** *y* **to** *i* **when adding a suffix if the letter before the** *y* **is a consonant:**

  snappy/snappiest   pity/pitiful

- **Keep the final** *y* **when adding a suffix if the letter before the** *y* **is a vowel:**

  buy/buying   delay/delayed

- **Write** *i* **before** *e,* **except after** *c,* **or in any** *ay* **sound like** *neighbor*:

  believe, niece, *but* receive, weigh

- **Remember that there are exceptions to all of these rules. Check a dictionary whenever you are uncertain.**

PROOFREADING STRATEGY

If poor spelling is one of your error patterns, keep your Personal Spelling List of errors and a dictionary beside you as you write.

1. Use the **bottom-up proofreading technique**. Read your draft sentence by sentence from the last sentence to the first. This will help you see possible misspellings and typos more easily.

2. Ask **someone who is a good speller** to read your draft and help you spot any misspellings and typos. Then correct these yourself; this will help you learn correct spellings. Tutors in your college's writing lab or classmates who have a good eye for errors can be excellent sources of help.

WRITING AND PROOFREADING ASSIGNMENT

Success can be defined in many ways. In a small group, discuss what the term *success* means to you. Is it a rewarding career, a happy family life, lots of money?

Now pick the definition that most appeals to you and write a paragraph explaining what success is. You may wish to mention people in the news or friends to support your main idea. Proofread your work for accurate spelling, especially the words covered in this chapter. Finally, exchange papers and read each other's work. Did your partner catch any spelling errors that you missed?

CHAPTER REVIEW

Proofread this essay for spelling errors. Correct the errors above the lines.

A Precious Resource

(1) Many people have pleasant memorys of recieving their first library card or chooseing books for the first time at a local public library. (2) Widely recognized as a priceless resource, the public library is defined just as you might expect: a collection of books and other materials supported by the public for public use.

(3) Several New England towns claim the honor of contributeing the first public money for a library. (4) However, the first such library of meaningful size and influence—the first fameous public library—originated in Boston, Massachusetts, in 1854. (5) The Boston Public Library, with its useful refrence collection and its policy of circulateing popular books, set the pattern for all public librarys subsequently created in the United States and Canada. (6) By the end of the nineteenth century, many state goverments were begining to raise taxes to support libraries. (7) They beleived that public libraries had an extremely important role to play in helping people pursue knowlege and continue thier education. (8) Although public libaries today have much the same goal, they now offer a truely admireable number

The beautiful Library of Congress in Washington, D.C., offers the public an array of services and resources. Explore online at **loc.gov**.

of resources and services. (9) These include story hours for children, book discussion clubs for adults, intresting lectures, art exhibits, literacy classes, and most recently, computer training and guideance.

(10) Technology, of course, has transformed the management of the public library as well as the way the library is used. (11) The bigest changes—today's computerized catalogs, searchable databases, and Internet access—would definately have gone beyond the wildest dreams of even the most commited early public libary supporters.

EXPLORING ONLINE

grammar.ccc.commnet.edu/grammar/quiz2/quizzes-to-fix/spelling_quiz3.htm

Interactive quiz: Add endings to these words.

grammar.ccc.commnet.edu/grammar/quiz2/quizzes-to-fix/spelling_add4.htm

Select the pair of words that correctly complete each sentence. Click "submit" to get your score.

Visit **MindTap** for *Grassroots* to access this chapter's ebook, flashcards, additional practice and quizzes, and more!

CHAPTER 36

Look-Alikes/ Sound-Alikes

The pairs or sets of words in this chapter might look or sound alike, but they have different meanings. Review this chart, studying any words that confuse you (for instance *your* and *you're* or *their* and *there*). Add these to your Personal Error Patterns Chart and be sure to do the practice exercises in this chapter.

Commonly Confused Words

Word	Meaning	Examples
a	Used before a word beginning with a consonant or a consonant sound	*a* story *a* lake *a* user (here *u* sounds like the consonant *y*)
an	Used before a word beginning with a vowel (*a, e, i, o, u*) or silent *h*	*an* address *an* onion *an* honor (*h* in *honor* is silent)
and	Joins words or ideas	He owns a car *and* a motorcycle.
accept except	To receive Other than; excluding	Chris *accepted* the job offer. The library is open every day *except* Sunday.
affect effect	To have an influence on; to change (noun) The result of a cause or an influence (verb) To cause	Her love of cooking *affected* her decision to become a chef. Forming a study group had a positive *effect* on Anna's grades. The new law will *effect* tax rate increases.
been	Past participle form of *to be*; usually used after the helping verb *have, has,* or *had*	Mario has never *been* to Portugal.
being	The *-ing* form of *to be*; usually used after the helping verb *is, are, am, was,* or *were*	She was *being* honest.

buy	To purchase	I *buy* my books online.
by	Near; by means of; before	The time flew *by*.
fine	Good or well; a penalty	On a *fine* day like today, we like to be outside.
		The *fine* for the overdue book was $1.50.
find	To locate	We must *find* another apartment.
it's	Contraction of *it is* or *it has*	*It's* still snowing.
its	A possessive that shows ownership	The company just redesigned *its* website.
know	To have knowledge or understanding	Do you *know* Judge Meriwether?
knew	Past tense of the verb *know*	She *knew* the correct answer.
no	A negative	*No*, I don't speak French.
new	Recent, fresh, unused	The *new* manager has made many changes.
lose	To misplace; not to win	You will *lose* weight if you diet and exercise.
loose	Too large; not restrained	The dog was running *loose* in the neighborhood.
mine	A possessive that shows ownership	He gave me his e-mail address, and I gave him *mine*.
mind	Intelligence; to object; to pay attention to	Have you changed your *mind*?
		I didn't *mind* waiting.
past	That which has already occurred; it is over with	We can't change the *past*, but we can learn from it.
passed	The past tense of the verb *to pass*	I *passed* the test.
quiet	Silent, still	He is usually very *quiet* and shy.
quit	To give up; to stop doing something	Donna *quit* smoking three months ago.
quite	Very; exactly	Her new hairstyle made *quite* a change to her appearance.
rise	To get up by one's own power	My grandfather always *rises* at dawn.
raise	To lift an object; to grow or increase	Emil *raises* horses.
sit	To seat oneself	Let's *sit* on the porch.
set	To place or put something down	Please *set* the bucket down.
suppose	To assume or guess	I *suppose* they broke up.
supposed	Ought to or should (it is followed by *to*)	That film is *supposed* to be excellent.

their	A possessive that shows ownership	The children have washed *their* hands.
there	Indicates a direction or a place; also a way of introducing a thought	He left *there* in a hurry. *There* is a solution to this problem.
they're	A contraction: *they* + *are* = *they're*	*They're* too busy to break for lunch.
then	Afterward; at that time	She stretched for ten minutes *then* set off on her run.
than	Used in a comparison	Ken is taller *than* Jorge.
through	In one side and out the other; finished; by means of	If you look *through* this telescope, you'll see Jupiter. *Through* hard work and dedication, she became #1.
though	Although (used with *as*, *though* means *as if*)	*Though* she's not wealthy, she's happy. You look *as though* you've seen a ghost.
to	Toward	They love going *to* the beach.
	To can also be combined with a verb to form an infinitive	We plan *to* practice every day.
too	Also; very	Amir is handsome and smart, *too*.
two	The number 2	The new semester begins in *two* weeks.
use	To make use of	*Use* your time wisely.
used	In the habit of; accustomed to (it is followed by *to*)	I *used* to jog two miles a day.
weather	Refers to atmospheric conditions	Bad *weather* forced the party indoors.
whether	Indicates a question	He's not sure *whether* he can be there.
where	Indicates place or location	*Where* did you go on vacation?
were	The past tense of *are*	The dogs *were* wet and muddy.
we're	A contraction: *we* + *are* = *we're*	*We're* going to be late for our appointment.
whose	Indicates ownership and possession	*Whose* cell phone is ringing?
who's	A contraction of *who is* or *who has*	*Who's* winning?
your	A possessive that shows ownership	*Your* speech was very interesting.
you're	A contraction: *you* + *are* = *you're*	*You're* so lucky!

Personal Look-Alikes/Sound-Alikes List

In your Personal Error Patterns Chart or your notebook, keep a list of look-alikes and sound-alikes that you have trouble with. Add words to your list from corrected papers and from the exercises in this chapter; consider also such pairs as *advice/advise*, *break/brake*, *principle/principal*, *patience/patients*, and so forth.

First, write the word you used incorrectly; then write its meaning or use it correctly in a sentence, whichever best helps you remember. Now do the same with the word you meant to use.

	Word	**Meaning**
1.	you're	contraction of you are
	your	You left your key in the lock.
2.	_____	_____
	_____	_____
3.	_____	_____
	_____	_____
4.	_____	_____
	_____	_____

PRACTICE 1

Three sets of these words are confused and misused more than any others: *their/they're/there*, *your/you're*, and *its/it's*. To check your mastery, circle each correct word in parentheses. If you have trouble, refer to the chart.

1. If (your, you're) a parent, what happens at an amazing middle school in Brooklyn, NY, just might change (your, you're) child's life.

2. IS 318 in Brooklyn has become famous for (it's, its) chess program, but unlike most schools with top chess teams, (its, it's) in a high-poverty, high-crime area.

3. The school and (its, it's) brilliant young players shatter stereotypes; (their, they're, there) chess team has won 26 national championships in the last 10 years.

4. "(Your, You're) not good at chess because of the color of your skin or how much money your parents make," says one student. "(Your, You're) good because of mental discipline, passion, and hard work."

5. A documentary film about the school's chess students and (their, they're, there) teachers, *Brooklyn Castle*, takes (its, it's) name from the royal names of chess pieces, like queen, king, knight, rook.

6. For the young men and one young woman in the movie, IS 318 is (their, they're, there) castle, and (their, they're, there) building successful lives along with learning chess.

7. If (your, you're) child has ADD, you might be interested in Patrick Johnston, one student in the film who struggles with this problem.

8. (Your, You're) going to see Patrick's concentration and self-esteem rise as he struggles to learn chess and win his first tournament games.

9. (Their, They're, There) is evidence that students who study and play chess for just four months will see (their, they're, there) IQ test scores rise.

10. If you meet the kids and teachers in *Brooklyn Castle*, (your, you're) going to see why.

PRACTICE 2

Read each sentence carefully and then circle the correct word or words. If you aren't sure, refer to the chart.

1. In the (passed, past), books on *etiquette*—polite and respectful behavior in social situations—(were, where) best sellers.

2. (Its, It's) different today, when rudeness and even bullying are common, (weather, whether) one is at school, in traffic, or online.

3. In "wired" countries around the world, one negative (affect, effect) of social media seems (too, to) be a lack of concern for the feelings of others.

4. South Korea is one of the first countries that has (passed, past) laws to make sure (its, it's) children practice netiquette.

5. *Netiquette* refers (to, two) the rules of polite and respectful behavior on the Internet.

6. South Korean second graders study textbooks (who's, whose) lessons include netiquette.

7. They (set, sit) at (their, there) desks and learn not to be cyber bullies; they are taught the signs of computer addiction.

8. As they go (through, though) school, 15 of (they're, their) textbooks will discuss netiquette.

9. As the result of (a, an) 2007 law, any South Korean who posts online is (supposed, suppose) to submit his or her real name and address.

10. Although some argue this hurts free speech, most people say it effectively reduces cruel (an, and) anonymous comments.

PRACTICE 3

The following paragraphs contain 22 look-alike/sound-alike errors. Proofread for these errors, writing the correct word choice above the line.

What Happened to the Honeybees?

(1) Since the 1980s, about 90 percent of wild honeybees in the United States have disappeared. (2) Beehives that use to be healthy and buzzing have become quite. (3) In 2016 alone, 44 percent of commercial honeybee colonies died out, according to the United States Department of Agriculture. (4) Its a problem that urgently needs to be solved because honeybees play a critical role in natural cycles. (5) Bees pollinate many of the fruits, vegetables, and other crops that we eat or feed to farm animals. (6) Without bees, the price of many foods would raise so much that only the very wealthy could afford too by them.

(7) In the passed few years, scientists have found two main causes of bee colony collapse. (8) New pesticides called neonics have toxic affects on bees, who might fly threw the spray or land on plants covered with these chemicals. (9) Despite there harm

to bees, these pesticides are still been used. (10) A second danger to bees is a tiny parasitic mite that attacks an kills bees. (10) Once their weakened by pesticides, bees our even more vulnerable to the mites. (11) Than there entire hive, which use to be clean and safe, becomes infested, and all it's bees die. (12) Scientists urge both commercial be keepers and individuals with one or too small hives to inspect frequently for mights and than treat the problem fast.

Chapter Highlights

Some words look and sound alike. Below are a few of them:

- **it's/its**

   It's the neatest room I ever saw.

   Everything is in *its* place.

- **their/they're/there**

   They found *their* work easy.

   They're the best actors I have ever seen.

   Put the lumber down *there*.

- **then/than**

   I was a heavyweight boxer *then*.

   He is a better cook *than* I.

- **to/too/two**

   We are going *to* the stadium.

   No one is *too* old to learn.

   I bought *two* hats yesterday.

- **whose/who's**

   Whose Italian dictionary is this?

   I'm not sure *who's* leaving early.

- **your/you're**

   Is *your* aunt the famous mystery writer?

   You're due for a promotion and a big raise.

PROOFREADING STRATEGY

If you tend to confuse the *look-alikes/sound-alikes*, **keep your Personal Error Patterns Chart updated** with the specific words you misuse, such as *their* and *there*, *affect* and *effect*, and *your* and *you're*.

Every time you proofread, **search your draft for every one of these words**. If you are using a computer, use the *"Find"* feature to locate them. Then double-check the meaning of the sentence to make sure that you've used and spelled the word correctly.

WRITING AND PROOFREADING ASSIGNMENT

Look back through this chapter and make a list of the look-alikes that most confuse you. List at least five pairs or clusters of words. Then use them all correctly in a paper about a problem on your campus or in your neighborhood (such as a lack of public parks or playgrounds, too much drug or alcohol use, or a gulf between computer haves and have-nots). Try to use every word on your look-alikes list and proofread to make sure you have spelled everything correctly.

CHAPTER REVIEW

Proofread this essay for look-alike/sound-alike errors. Write your corrections above the lines.

D'Wayne Edwards: Just for Kicks

(1) If your a fan of stylish shoes, you might no the work of D'Wayne Edwards. (2) He not only designs the world's top athletic shoes, but he also created Pensole Academy, were talented young designers can break into the elite world of shoe design for companies like Nike and Adidas. (3) Edwards's rapid raise from a talented kid who loved "kicks" (sneakers) too a creative force is inspiring.

(4) At age 11, Edwards drew his first shoe and new he wanted to be a footwear designer. (5) Later, he shared his career goal with a high school guidance counselor in Inglewood, California, but she said he was been unrealistic and should join the military. (6) The affect of her negativity, he now says, was strong motivation to prove her wrong. (7) At age 17, Edwards won the national Reebok design contest and knew he would never quiet designing.

(8) After he graduated from high school, Edwards's mother couldn't fine the money for design school, so he worked as an file clerk for footwear company L.A. Gear. (9) Each department had a suggestion box. (10) Every day, D'Wayne dropped a sketch of a new shoe into that box, along with the suggestion that the company hire him as a shoe designer. (11) Six months and 180 sketches later, L.A. Gear offered him a design job. (12) He poured

NOAH DAVIS

D'Wayne Edwards (third from right) teaching the next generation of sneaker designers

his heart and mine into the work. (13) By age 23, he was head designer. (14) By 28, he had his own brand. (15) In 2000, he got a job at Nike, where his Goadome 2 became the best-selling boot in Nike history. (16) Than he got the chance to design the Air Jordan 2.

(17) Yet Edwards's crowning achievement might be Pensole Academy, we're lucky students learn by doing, creating shoe designs and prototypes all by hand. (18) His academy welcomes minorities, women, and working-class artists—groups often missing from the world of shoe design. (19) "Its the education you wish you'd had in school," says one student. (20) The academy is abuzz with energy, colorful materials, and futuristic shoes by designers who's stylish kicks you just might be wearing next year.

PRACTICE 4   CRITICAL THINKING AND WRITING

If possible, in a group with four or five classmates, discuss the personal qualities or actions that helped D'Wayne Edwards get his first design job and, later, many promotions. Are there any lessons you can learn for yourself from the story of Edwards's career? Take notes for a composition.

EXPLORING ONLINE

grammar.ccc.commnet.edu/grammar/quizzes/affect_except_options.htm

Practice these tricky pairs: *effect, affect* and *except, accept.*

grammar.ccc.commnet.edu/grammar/quiz2/quizzes-to-fix/confusibles.htm

Can you tell these look-alikes apart? For help, check your dictionary!

a4esl.org/q/h/lb/ho1.html

Practice sound-alikes, like *night/knight*, that may confuse ESL
students. Pick easy, medium, or difficult, and test yourself.

Visit **MindTap** for *Grassroots* to access this chapter's ebook, flashcards, additional practice and
quizzes, and more!

Writing Assignments

As you complete each writing assignment, remember to perform these steps:

- Write a clear, complete topic sentence.

- Use freewriting, brainstorming, or clustering to generate ideas for the body of your paragraph, essay, letter, or review.

- Arrange your best ideas in a plan.

- Revise for support, unity, coherence, and exact language.

- Proofread for grammar, punctuation, and spelling errors.

WRITING ASSIGNMENT 1 *Express your opinion.* Write a letter or e-mail to either a newspaper editor or an elected official (a mayor, governor, or senator, for example) in which you suggest one solution to a particular problem, such as educational budget cuts or gun control. For topic ideas and information, visit the United Nations List of Human Rights Issues at **www.ohchr.org/EN/Issues/Pages/ ListofIssues.aspx**. State your opinion in your topic sentence or thesis statement, and present at least three reasons in support of your opinion. Consider actually mailing your letter to the recipient, but not before you proofread for spelling errors that would weaken your writing.

WRITING ASSIGNMENT 2 *Solve a problem.* You have identified what you consider to be a problem in your place of employment. When you go to your supervisor, you are asked to write up your concerns and to suggest a solution. Begin first by describing the problem, and then give background information, including what you suspect are the causes of the problem. Then offer suggestions for solving it. End with some guidelines for evaluating the success of the changes. In your concluding sentence, thank your supervisor for his or her consideration of your letter. Don't let typos or mistaken look-alikes/sound-alikes detract from your ideas. Proofread for accurate spelling!

WRITING ASSIGNMENT 3 *Review a movie.* Your college newspaper has asked you to review a movie. Pick a popular film that you especially liked or disliked. In your first sentence, name the film and state whether or not you recommend it. Explain your evaluation by discussing two or three specific reasons for your reactions to the movie. Describe as much of the film as is necessary to make your point, but do not retell the plot. Proofread for accurate spelling. Consider posting your review at **www.movievine.com** or **www.franksreelreviews.com**.

WRITING ASSIGNMENT 4 *Describe a family custom.* Most families have customs that they perform together. These customs often help strengthen the bond that the members of the family feel toward each other. A custom might be eating Sunday dinner together, going to religious services, celebrating holidays in a special way, or even holding a family council to discuss difficulties and concerns. Write about a custom in your family that is especially meaningful. Of what value has this custom been to you or other members of the family? Proofread for accurate spelling.

Review

Proofreading

The following essay contains a number of spelling and look-alike/sound-alike errors. First, underline the misspelled or misused words. Then write each correctly spelled word above the line. (You should find 38 errors.)

Everyday Angel

(1) On January 2, 2007, construction worker Wesley Autry and his too young daugters were standing on a New York City subway platform waiting for the train. (2) Suddenly, a 20-year-old student standing nearby suffered a siezure and tumbled onto the subway tracks. (3) Autry saw the headlights of an approaching train and realized that the young men was about to be run over right in front of the children. (4) Leapping onto the rails, Autry pulled the strugling student down into the shallow drainage ditch between the tracks and pined him their while one train and than another rumbled over them with about two inchs to spare. (5) The next day, national and international headlines proclaimed Autry to be an "angle," a "superman," a "hero," and "one in a million." (6) Autry explained simply, "I just tryed to do the right thing."

(7) But his action began a nationel arguement about how far one should go to help others. (8) People couldn't help wondering if they themselfs would make a similer split-second decision to risk they're own lives for a total stranger. (9) Was Autry's act truely a one-in-a-million occurence? (10) After all, pychologists and sociologists point out that people quiet often fail to act in a emergancy because of the "bystander effect." (11) The bystander effect is the tendency to do nothing in a crisis because one assumes that someone else will take any nesessary action.

(12) On the other hand, Autry's bravery inspirred people worldwide. (13) CNN reconized him as an "everyday hero," and in 2007, *Time* magazine named him one of 100 poeple "whose power, talent or moral example is transforming the world." (14) Some went so far as to honor his selfless behavor buy giving him awards, scholarships for his children, cash, and free trips. (15) Others gained new confidence in they're own ability to peform a dareing rescue. (16) In one poll, most New Yorkers beleived that they would probly jump off a ferry boat to save a child who had fallen overboard, try to stop a mugger from steeling an elderly women's money, and even run into a burning building to save someone traped inside.

EXPLORING ONLINE

www.cnn.com/specials/cnn-heroes

Visit the CNN Heroes website and read about the difference everyday individuals have made around the world. Whom would you nominate to be a hero in your community? Write down three reasons to support your choice.

Writers' Workshop

Examine Positive (or Negative) Values

One good way to develop a paragraph or essay is by supporting the topic sentence or the thesis statement with three points. A student uses this approach in the following essay. In your group or class, read her work, aloud if possible.

Villa Avenue

(1) The values I learned growing up on Villa Avenue in the Bronx have guided me through 35 years and three children. Villa Avenue taught me the importance of having a friendly environment, playing together, and helping people.

(2) Villa Avenue was a three-block, friendly environment. I grew up on the middle block. The other ones were called "up the block" and "down the block." Mary's Candy Store was up the block. It had a candy counter and soda fountain on the left and on the right a jukebox that played three songs for 25 cents. My friends and I would buy candy, hang out, and listen to the Beatles and other music of the sixties. A little down from Mary's on the corner was Joey's Deli. When you walked into Joey's, different aromas would welcome you to a world of Italian delicacies. Fresh mozzarella in water always sat on the counter, with salami, pepperoni, and imported provolone cheese hanging above. On Sundays at Joey's, my father would buy us a black-and-white cookie for a weekly treat.

(3) On Villa Avenue, everyone helped everyone else. Everybody's doors were open, so if I had to go to the bathroom or needed a drink of water, I could go to a dozen different apartments. If my parents had to go somewhere, they would leave me with a friend. When people on the block got sick, others went to the store for them, cleaned for them, watched their kids, and made sure they had food to eat. If someone died, everyone mourned and pitched in

to help with arrangements. When I reflect on those days, I realize that the way the mothers looked out for each other's children is like your modern-day play group. The difference is that our play area was "the block."

(4) The whole street was our playground. We would play curb ball at the intersection. One corner was home plate, and the other ones were the bases. Down the block where the street was wide, we would play Johnny on the Pony with 10 to 15 kids. On summer nights, it was kick the can or hide and seek. Summer days we spent under an open fire hydrant. Everyone would be in the water, including moms and dads. Sometimes the teenagers would go to my Uncle Angelo's house and get a wine barrel to put over the hydrant. With the top and bottom of the barrel off, the water would shoot 20 to 30 feet in the air and come down on us like a waterfall.

Loretta M. Carney, Student

1. How effective is Loretta Carney's essay?

    _____ Clear main idea?   _____ Good supporting details?

    _____ Logical organization?   _____ Effective conclusion?

2. What is the main idea of the essay? Can you find the thesis statement, one sentence that states this main idea?

3. The writer states that Villa Avenue taught her three values. What are they? Are these clearly explained in paragraphs 2, 3, and 4? Are they discussed in the same order in which the thesis statement presents them? If not, what change would you suggest?

4. Does this essay *conclude* or just stop? What suggestions would you make to the writer for a more effective conclusion?

5. Proofread Carney's essay. Do you see any error patterns that she should watch out for?

Writing and Revising Ideas

1. Describe a place or person that taught you positive (or negative) values.

2. Do places like Villa Avenue exist anymore? Explain why you do or do not think so.

See Chapters 5, 6, and 7 for help with planning and writing. You might wish to present your topic with three supporting points, the way Loretta Carney does. As you revise, pay close attention to writing a good thesis sentence and supporting paragraphs that contain clear, detailed explanations.

Reading Selections

Reading Tools for Writers

Active Reading

Reading Strategies for Writers

Annotated Model Essay: Diane Sawyer, "Daring to Dream Big"

Connecting Your Reading and Writing

Checklist for the Reader & Checklist for the Writer

Reading Selections

Sherman Alexie, "Superman and Me"

Esther Cepeda, "Tamales and Other Holiday Foods"

Beve Stevenson, RN, BN, "A Day in the Life of an Emergency Room Nurse"

John Quiñones, "Heroes Everywhere"

James Campbell, "Are We Losing Our Connection to Nature?"

Leonard Pitts, "Putting the Brakes on Driving While Texting"

Rebecca Sutton, "The Art of Sharing Secrets"

Christine Porath, "No Time to Be Nice at Work"

Andrew Lam, "Waste More, Want More"

Kunal Nayyar, "Garbage, Man"

Constance Staley, "Zoom In and Focus"

Maya Angelou, "Mrs. Flowers"

Karen Castellucci Cox, "World of Skillcraft: The Unexpected Benefits of Gaming"

Liza Gross, "The Hidden Life of Bottled Water"

Angela Johnston, "Charming Robotic Seal Raises Ethical Concerns"

Susan Cain, "Introverts Run the World—Quietly"

MP Dunleavy, "Buy Yourself Less Stuff"

Daniel Goleman, "Emotional Intelligence"

Reading Tools for Writers

The professional reading selections in this unit were chosen to interest you, make you think, and inspire you. Many deal with issues you face at college, at work, or at home. Others explore provocative contemporary themes and problems. Your instructor may ask you to read a selection and be prepared to discuss it in class or to write a composition or journal entry about it. The more carefully and actively you read these selections, the better you will be able to think, talk, and write about them.

Active Reading

If you read something for fun or something that isn't very important—like a magazine article about a celebrity breakup or a retail mailer advertising a sale—you'll probably read it once and set it aside. But in college and the workplace, reading assignments are more demanding. You will be asked to read and understand new, challenging information; you will be expected to learn how to perform intellectual tasks that may feel new or even uncomfortable at first. So to master textbook chapters and college assignments, you'll need to become an **active reader**.

An *active reader* doesn't just passively read to the bottom of the page or screen, but uses **strategies** to help him or her understand and retain the written material—highlighting, jotting notes, pausing to think, asking questions, and so on.

You have already practiced active reading every time you worked through a chapter or lesson in this book. The MAP approach to learning that you learned about in Chapter 1, Part A, has guided you to read a short MODEL (a sentence or paragraph), then helped you ANALYZE what you read by answering questions, and finally, given you opportunities to PRACTICE what you just learned, usually by writing. This process is active reading. In this unit, however, you will read longer written models, analyze them, and write about them.

Here are specific *strategies* that will help you become a more active and effective reader.

Reading Strategies for Writers

1. Focus.   First, find a quiet, pleasant place to read and write—for instance, in the library or a private spot at home. Mute and put away all your electronic devices (unless you are reading on one). Research shows that the key to successfully completing any assignment is **mental focus**—something that many people today can't or won't achieve. Why? Because they are using their smartphones or other devices while trying to read or write! Remember: the biggest obstacle to college and work success is distraction, so unplug and focus.*

2. Preview the reading selection.   This strategy is especially important for longer, more difficult reading assignments like textbook chapters and literature. Before you begin to read, scan the chapter or article to get a sense of the author's main idea and supporting points. Notice the title, which should indicate what the author will be writing about. Scan the headnote and any subtitles (often in boldface type); next, quickly read the first and last paragraphs. Finally, skim the

---

* For more on this strategy, see "Zoom In and Focus" by college textbook author Constance Staley in the readings that follow.

whole selection, looking for the main supporting ideas. **Previewing** will increase your understanding and enjoyment as you read.

3. Annotate.

Now read the piece through, thinking about its meaning and **annotating**—that is, marking the print book with pencil or pen or marking an online reading selection in ways that will help you understand it, learn, and remember. If you are reading online, learn to how to comment, highlight, and so on. Ask yourself what main point the author is making. What details support this main idea? What is his or her attitude? Does the author use one or more of the nine paragraph and essay patterns you learned about in Chapters 5, 6, and 7? As you read, think, and question, *annotate*. Just be selective, however, in what you mark. *Too much* annotation can be confusing when you discuss the selection in class or write about it. Following are some ways in which good readers annotate.

- **Underline or highlight important ideas.** Underlining or highlighting what you consider the main ideas or most striking points will help you later to remember and discuss what you have read. Some students number the main points in order to understand the development of the author's ideas.

- **Jot your reactions in the margins.** If you strongly agree or disagree with an idea, write *yes* or *no* next to it. Record other questions and comments, as if you were having a conversation with the author. If you are working online, use the *comment* or *sticky note* feature. Writing assignments will often ask you to respond to a particular idea or situation in a selection. Having already noted your reactions and ideas will help you focus your thinking and your writing.

- **Ask questions.** You will occasionally come across material that raises questions for you. Reread the passage. If you still have questions, place a question mark or note in the margin, reminding yourself to ask a classmate or the instructor for an explanation.

- **Note effective or powerful writing.** If a particular line strikes you as important, moving, or memorably written, underline or highlight it. You may wish later to quote it in your written assignment. Notice too any interesting devices a writer uses and how he or she has organized the piece. Do you see good examples of the writing patterns you learned in Chapters 5, 6, and 7? Let yourself be inspired. For instance, if you read a narrative that starts with the punchline and then loops back to the beginning of the story, you might want to try that technique yourself.

4. Build your vocabulary.

Reading is an excellent way to build vocabulary. As you annotate, always have a print or online dictionary handy. If you come across a new word that makes it difficult to follow what the author is saying, look it up immediately, jot the definition in the margin (or an online comment), and resume reading. If, however, you can sense the meaning from the **context**—how the word fits the sentence—just highlight it and, when you have finished the selection, check a dictionary. If you aren't sure how the word *sounds*, search the word and "pronunciation" online to hear it said correctly in English. Then say the word aloud and speak it in a sentence. Keep a list of great new words you learn, and try them out when you write.

5. Reread.   If you expect to discuss or write about a selection, reading it through only once is usually not enough. Don't procrastinate. Budget your time so you will be able to focus on a second or third reading. You might be surprised at how much more you understand the second time. Perhaps you will understand ideas that were unclear the first time around or notice interesting new points and details. You might change your mind about things you originally agreed or disagreed with or suddenly hear the rhythms of first-rate writing.

6. Review and Retell.   Before discussing, writing about, or being tested on written material, **review**: skim the piece and read your annotations—especially your underlinings, reactions, and questions. Read important sections aloud if possible, as you look at the words on the page. Then, **retell** out loud in your own words the main ideas and summarize what the selection is about. Reviewing and retelling will refresh your understanding, "lock it in," and prepare you to share your ideas.

Annotated Model Essay

The following professional essay has been annotated by a student. Your own responses to this essay would, of course, be different. Examining how this essay was marked may help you annotate other selections in this book and read more actively in your other courses and at work.

Daring to Dream Big
Diane Sawyer

I see her on TV—she's a top journalist.

A beauty contest?

I like this comparison—my dad is my island.

Wow, this is interesting. Being a beauty queen is not enough.

Main idea? DREAM BIG. Many of my friends don't set high goals for themselves. Do I?

Aspired = aimed

Good question: How would I answer it? Should I dream bigger?

I was seventeen years old, a high school senior in Louisville, Kentucky, representing my state in the 1963 America's Junior Miss competition in Mobile, Alabama. In the midst of it all, there was one person who stood at the center—at least my psychological center—someone I viewed as an island in an ocean of anxiety. She was one of the judges, a well-known writer, a woman whose sea-gray eyes fixed on you with laser penetration. Her name was Catherine Marshall.

During the rehearsal on the last day of the pageant, the afternoon before it would all end, several of us were waiting backstage when a pageant official said Catherine Marshall wanted to speak with us. We gathered around. Most of us were expecting a last-minute pep talk, but we were surprised.

She fixed her eyes upon us. "You have set goals for yourselves. I have heard some of them. But I don't think you have set them high enough. You have talent and intelligence and a chance. I think you should take those goals and expand them. Think of the most you could do with your lives. Make what you do matter. Above all, dream big."

It was not so much an instruction as a dare. I felt stunned. This woman I admired so much was disappointed in us—not by what we were but by how little we aspired to be.

I won the America's Junior Miss contest that year. I graduated in 1967 with a BA degree in English and a complete lack of inspiration about what I should do with it. I went to my father. "What is it that you enjoy doing most?" he asked.

"Writing," I replied slowly. "And working with people. And being in touch with what's happening in the world."

He thought for a moment. "Did you ever consider television?"

At that time there were few if any women journalists on television. The idea of being a pioneer in the field sounded like dreaming big. That's how I came to get up my nerve and go out to convince the news director at Louisville's WLKY-TV to let me have a chance.

He gave it to me. For the next two and a half years I worked as a combination weather and news reporter. Eventually, though, I began to feel restless. I'd wait for the (revelation,) the sign pointing in the direction of the Big Dream. What I didn't realize is what Catherine Marshall undoubtedly knew all along—that the dream is not the destination but the journey.

Today I'm coeditor of CBS's *Sixty Minutes*. I keep a suitcase packed at all times so that I can fly out on assignment at a moment's notice. When I go out into the world, I can almost hear a wonderful woman prodding me with her fiery challenge to stretch farther and, no matter how big the dream, to dream a little bigger still. God, she seems to be saying, can forgive failure, but not failing to try.

Marshall's speech really motivated Sawyer to act.

revelation = discovery

I never thought of it this way.

This story makes me think of the importance of good role models—a good writing topic?

I'm inspired! Should I go for it and be a dentist instead of a dental assistant?

PRACTICE

Read the following excerpt from a news article, and practice active reading.

The job market's most sought-after skills can be tough to spot on a résumé. Companies across the U.S. say it is becoming increasingly difficult to find applicants who can communicate clearly, take initiative, problem-solve and get along with co-workers. Those traits, often called soft skills, can make the difference between a standout employee and one who just gets by.

While such skills have always appealed to employers, decades-long shifts in the economy have made them especially crucial now. Companies have automated or outsourced many routine tasks, and the jobs that remain often require workers to take on broader responsibilities that demand critical thinking, empathy or other abilities that computers can't easily simulate. As the labor market tightens, competition has heated up for workers with the right mix of soft skills, which vary by industry and across the pay spectrum—from making small talk with a customer at the checkout counter, to coordinating a project across several departments on a tight deadline.

"Employers Find 'Soft Skills' Like Critical Thinking in Short Supply" by Kate Davidson. Wall Street Journal, *Aug. 30, 2016.*

1. Underline or highlight the sentence that best states the main idea.

2. Underline or highlight important ideas.

3. Circle unfamiliar words that you will look up later.

4. Find something that raises a question for you and write that question in the margin.

5. Restate, out loud in your own words, what news this article is reporting.

Connecting Your Reading and Writing

By now you know how interconnected reading and writing are. As a writer, you can learn a great deal from reading the work of excellent writers. You can get ideas for great topics to write about or be inspired by a clever title, see how an introduction sets up what follows or how a pro organizes his or her ideas with the same patterns you learned in Chapters 5, 6, and 7. For example, in the reading selections that follow, TV anchor John Quiñones uses *illustration* to bring bullying and courage to life, professor and concerned mother Karen Castellucci Cox uses *classification* to take a fresh look at video games, and Beve Stevenson accurately but hilariously describes the *process* of her day as an ER nurse. You'll be challenged to think and maybe inspired to write by the ideas all these writers share about their most important experiences, their passions, and their life's work.

As an active reader, you will see that all the parts of a paragraph or essay that you've learned in this and other English courses are also essential parts of most every professional essay, book chapter, or article. Now when you read, you are a bit of an insider. You've begun to learn the basics, techniques, and tricks that good writers know. Of course, a research article will have a serious title and tone, a clear style, and good factual evidence, whereas a personal essay might be more emotional, vividly detailed, and even funny. This chart will help you visualize the reading and writing connection.

Checklist for the Reader	**Checklist for the Writer**
What does the title tell me?	Is my title clear and catchy?
What are the subject, audience, and purpose of this reading selection?	Are my subject, audience, and purpose clear?
How does the introduction lead to or reveal the main idea? What is the main idea? Is it stated in one sentence?	Is my introduction engaging and my main idea stated as a topic or thesis sentence?
With what evidence, details, and examples does the author support the main idea? Do topic sentences state important points? Do subheads point to key ideas?	Are my topic sentences clear? Do I support each one with evidence—facts, details, examples, perhaps anecdotes?
How did the author organize this piece? Is he or she contrasting two things? Telling a story? Trying to persuade me? Examining causes or effects?	Is my writing well organized by time, space, or importance? Or did I use one of the nine patterns of organization (e.g., illustration, comparison-contrast, persuasion)?
Can I follow from point to point? Does this writer use helpful transitions?	Do transitional words and phrases guide my reader?
What tone and language are used (serious, funny, formal, casual)? What sentences or sections strike me as most powerfully written?	Does my writing use exact, detailed, factual language? Is my tone serious and formal or casual, in line with my subject?
How does the author conclude—with a final thought or challenge?	Does my paper conclude strongly, not just leave off?
On second reading of this work, do I agree or disagree? Did it move me, make me angry, make me think? How would I rate this selection and why?	Reading my paper like a kindly stranger, do I find any unclear, undeveloped, or dull parts? Is my paper free of errors? Is this my best work?

Think of everything you read as a chance to learn something new. Participate in class discussions about what you've read even if you feel shy. You will gain confidence in yourself and your ideas by expressing them. Enjoy reading.

Superman and Me

Sherman Alexie

"Superman and Me" by Sherman Alexie, from *The Most Wonderful Books*, published by Milkweed Press, 1998. Reprinted by permission of Nancy Stauffer Associates. Copyright © 1997 Sherman Alexie. All rights reserved.

Growing up on the Spokane Indian Reservation, Sherman Alexie and his classmates were "expected to fail." This article tells the story of how the author refused to fail and instead found his true calling as a writer and poet. In 2010, Alexie's *War Dances* won the Pen/Faulkner Fiction Award, and his movie *Smoke Signals* has become a classic.

1   I learned to read with a Superman comic book. Simple enough, I suppose. I cannot recall which particular Superman comic book I read, nor can I remember which villain he fought in that issue. I cannot remember the plot, nor the means by which I obtained the comic book. What I can remember is this: I was three years old, a Spokane Indian boy living with his family on the Spokane Indian Reservation in eastern Washington State. We were poor by most standards, but one of my parents usually managed to find some minimum-wage job or another, which made us middle-class by reservation standards. I had a brother and three sisters. We lived on a combination of irregular paychecks, hope, fear and government surplus food.

2   My father, who is one of the few Indians who went to Catholic school on purpose, was an avid[1] reader of westerns, spy thrillers, murder mysteries, gangster epics, basketball player biographies and anything else he could find. He bought his books by the pound at Dutch's Pawn Shop, Goodwill, Salvation Army, and Value Village. When he had extra money, he bought new novels at supermarkets, convenience stores and hospital gift shops. Our house was filled with books. They were stacked in crazy piles in the bathroom, bedrooms and living room. In a fit of unemployment-inspired creative energy, my father built a set of bookshelves and soon filled them with a random assortment of books about the Kennedy assassination, Watergate, the Vietnam War and the entire twenty-three-book series of the Apache westerns. My father loved books, and since I loved my father with an aching devotion, I decided to love books as well.

3   I can remember picking up my father's books before I could read. The words themselves were mostly foreign, but I still remember the exact moment when I first understood, with a sudden clarity[2], the purpose of a paragraph. I didn't have the vocabulary to say "paragraph," but I realized that a paragraph was a fence that held words. The words inside a paragraph worked together for a common purpose. They had some specific reason for being inside the same fence. This knowledge delighted me. I began to think of everything in terms of paragraphs. Our reservation was a small paragraph within the United States. My family's house was a paragraph, distinct from the other paragraphs of the LeBrets to the north, the Fords to our south and the Tribal School to the west. Inside our house, each family member existed as a separate

---

1. avid: enthusiastic and eager
2. clarity: clear understanding

paragraph but still had genetics[3] and common experiences to link us. Now, using this logic, I can see my changed family as an essay of seven paragraphs: mother, father, older brother, the deceased sister, my younger twin sisters and our adopted little brother.

At the same time I was seeing the world in paragraphs, I also picked up 4 that Superman comic book. Each panel, complete with picture, dialogue and narrative was a three-dimensional paragraph. In one panel, Superman breaks through a door. His suit is red, blue and yellow. The brown door shatters into many pieces. I look at the narrative above the picture. I cannot read the words, but I assume it tells me that "Superman is breaking down the door." Aloud, I pretend to read the words and say, "Superman is breaking down the door." Words, dialogue, also float out of Superman's mouth. Because he is breaking down the door, I assume he says, "I am breaking down the door." Once again, I pretend to read the words and say aloud, "I am breaking down the door." In this way, I learned to read.

This might be an interesting story all by itself. A little Indian boy teaches 5 himself to read at an early age and advances quickly. He reads "Grapes of Wrath"[4] in kindergarten when other children are struggling through "Dick and Jane." If he'd been anything but an Indian boy living on the reservation, he might have been called a prodigy[5]. But he is an Indian boy living on the reservation and is simply an oddity[6]. He grows into a man who often speaks of his childhood in the third-person, as if it will somehow dull the pain and make him sound more modest about his talents.

A smart Indian is a dangerous person, widely feared and ridiculed by 6 Indians and non-Indians alike. I fought with my classmates on a daily basis. They wanted me to stay quiet when the non-Indian teacher asked

"A smart Indian is a dangerous person."

Author Sherman Alexie taught himself to read with Superman comics.

---

3. genetics: characteristics and traits passed from parents to their children
4. *Grapes of Wrath*: John Steinbeck's novel about the Great Depression
5. prodigy: a child genius, one with exceptional talents
6. oddity: an unusual person or thing

Helene Rogers/Art Directors & TRIP/Alamy Stock Photo

for answers, for volunteers, for help. We were Indian children who were expected to be stupid. Most lived up to those expectations inside the classroom but subverted[7] them on the outside. They struggled with basic reading in school but could remember how to sing a few dozen powwow[8] songs. They were monosyllabic[9] in front of their non-Indian teachers but could tell complicated stories and jokes at the dinner table. They submissively[10] ducked their heads when confronted by a non-Indian adult but would slug it out with the Indian bully who was ten years older. As Indian children, we were expected to fail in the non-Indian world. Those who failed were ceremonially accepted by other Indians and appropriately pitied by non-Indians.

I refused to fail. I was smart. I was arrogant. I was lucky. I read books late into the night, until I could barely keep my eyes open. I read books at recess, then during lunch, and in the few minutes left after I had finished my classroom assignments. I read books in the car when my family traveled to powwows or basketball games. In shopping malls, I ran to the bookstores and read bits and pieces of as many books as I could. I read the books my father brought home from the pawnshops and secondhand. I read the books I borrowed from the library. I read the backs of cereal boxes. I read the newspaper. I read the bulletins posted on the walls of the school, the clinic, the tribal offices, the post office. I read junk mail. I read auto-repair manuals. I read magazines. I read anything that had words and paragraphs. I read with equal parts joy and desperation. I loved those books, but I also knew that love had only one purpose. I was trying to save my life.

Despite all the books I read, I am still surprised I became a writer. I was going to be a pediatrician[11]. These days, I write novels, short stories and poems. I visit schools and teach creative writing to Indian kids. In all my years in the reservation school system, I was never taught how to write poetry, short stories or novels. I was certainly never taught that Indians wrote poetry, short stories and novels. Writing was something beyond Indians. I cannot recall a single time that a guest teacher visited the reservation. There must have been visiting teachers. Who were they? Where are they now? Do they exist? I visit the schools as often as possible. The Indian kids crowd the classroom. Many are writing their own poems, short stories and novels. They have read my books. They have read many other books. They look at me with bright eyes and arrogant wonder. They are trying to save their lives. Then there are the sullen[12] and already defeated Indian kids who sit in the back rows and ignore me with theatrical precision. The pages of their notebooks are empty. They carry neither pencil nor pen. They stare out the window. They refuse and resist. "Books," I say to them. "Books," I say. I throw my weight against their locked doors. The door holds. I am smart. I am arrogant. I am lucky. I am trying to save our lives.

7

8

_____

7. subverted: undercut, defied
8. powwow: an Indian social gathering
9. monosyllabic: speaking only in one-syllable words
10. submissively: without resistance; obediently
11. pediatrician: a doctor who treats children
12. sullen: moody and silent

LANGUAGE AWARENESS QUESTIONS

1. In paragraph 3, the author describes learning that "a paragraph was a fence that held words." Does this metaphor help you understand what a paragraph does? How would *you* define a paragraph?

2. Alexie taught himself to read as a preschooler. "If he'd been anything but an Indian boy living on the reservation, he might have been called a prodigy," the author writes of himself (paragraph 5). Explain what he means and what emotion comes through these words.

DISCUSSION AND WRITING QUESTIONS

1. Why would a smart Indian be a "dangerous person, widely feared and ridiculed" (paragraph 6)? Why would non-Indians adopt this opinion? Why would Indian children adopt this self-defeating idea?

2. What does the author mean when he writes in paragraph 7, "I was trying to save my life"? What point is he making about reading books and educating oneself? Where else does he mention this idea of saving lives?

3. Based on Alexie's story, what outward support and/or inner characteristics does a person need to break free of stereotypes and dead ends and forge a path to success? For example, what role did Alexie's father play in his development?

WRITING ASSIGNMENTS

1. Sherman Alexie writes about an activity—reading—that gave him strength and hope during a very painful time in his life. Write a composition describing an activity, tool, or person that has given you strength and hope for your future.

2. Has there ever been a time in your life when someone *expected* you to fail? If so, who was it, what happened, and how did you react?

3. Have you ever been rejected or even ridiculed by your peers for making an unpopular decision or taking an unpopular action? Why did you defy the group's wishes and choose to go your own way?

Tamales and Other Holiday Foods

Esther Cepeda

Reprinted with permission from The Washington Post Writers Group.

Do all members of an ethnic group have the same tastes, eat the same foods, and enjoy the same music? Esther Cepeda, a nationally syndicated columnist with *The Washington Post* and self-described "picky eater," uses herself as an example as she discusses holiday foods, cultural identity, and the American melting pot.

I t was like an object lesson from a training film about cultural competency[1]: a fluffy rug in my classroom surrounded by 20 native Spanish-speaking first-graders. I'd just read aloud the English version of "Too Many Tamales," Gary Soto's children's story about mischievous Maria's secret angst[2] after having lost her mother's diamond ring in a batch of corn dough.   1

------

1. cultural competency: ability to interact with people of different cultural backgrounds
2. angst: anxiety, dread

"Did you ever lose your ring when making the Christmas tamales, Ms. Cepeda?" asked one of my students. **2**

"No, I don't eat tamales," I responded. "But I did lose my wedding ring in the broccoli bin at the grocery store once." **3**

Mic drop. **4**

"You don't eat tamales?" the children asked incredulously[3]. **5**

"Nope. Don't make them, don't eat them—I don't like them. Not everyone does, you know," I told the gawking[4] crowd of youngsters. **6**

I almost added my other fun cultural/culinary fact—that I've never eaten a burrito—but I figured I'd blown their minds enough for one day. I went on to explain that I grew up with my father's family from Ecuador and in our house, for the Christmas meal, the assembly lines of women were dedicated to making empanadas, the deep-fried turnovers that are filled with savory or sweet fillings. **7**

"Pumpkin pie tamales? Bleccchhh, I don't even like pumpkin pie much less a consumer-driven cultural mash-up"

This warm memory of teaching first generation immigrants that even in Hispanic communities there is diversity in how we celebrate and eat recently came to mind when I got the following pitch from a public relations firm: **8**

"The holidays are the perfect time for friends and family to gather and celebrate the festive season, but cooking for a crowd can often be difficult. This year, skip the hassle and prepare tamales for all of your guests using an IMUSA Tamale Steamer! . . . With recipes like George Duran's Pumpkin Pie Tamales, Aaron Sanchez's Tamales de Mole Amarillo[5], and Cheesy Sun-Dried Tomato Tamales, your guests are sure to find a flavorful option to enjoy." **9**

Pumpkin pie tamales? Bleccchhh, I don't even like actual pumpkin pie much less such a consumer-driven cultural mash-up (but I'm a picky eater—my white husband would absolutely adore pumpkin pie tamales just as he loves each dish in its original form). **10**

Several years ago I would have tsk-tsked at the insularity[6] of a PR firm assuming that because I have a Hispanic-sounding name, I would naturally be interested in helping shill[7] "tamale steamers." But in our ethnic foodie culture such thinking is backward—blatant[8] commercialization of ethnic dishes and flavors is not only the norm, but a welcome and tasty way that the American melting pot works its magic. **11**

These days not only can you find countless recipes for tamales in variations from authentic (in traditional pork, chicken and sweet corn permutations[9]) to gourmet (vegan spinach zucchini or mushroom and roasted garlic) but also "Americanized" versions, such as the recipe for "Tamale Pie" I found on Martha Stewart's website ("Tamale pie is a holdover from America's first flush of romance with Mexican cuisine. The love affair hasn't let up—not with the lure of cornbread, cheese, and chili, even when made with turkey.") **12**

Not only that, but you can make "homemade" tamales even if you're too busy to go through the hours-long rigmarole[10] of mixing corn flour with lard, letting it rest, etc. Last week while I was at an Albertson's grocery store way outside the city, near the Wisconsin border, I saw pre-mixed dough for tamales **13**

---

3. incredulously: in disbelief
4. gawking: staring
5. Tamales de Mole Amarillo: spicy, yellow sauce for chicken and meats
6. insularity: ignorance of other cultures besides one's own
7. shill: to sell something you pretend to love (but someone has paid you to do so)
8. blatant: very obvious
9. permutations: variations
10. rigmarole: fuss, hassle

("Gluten Free"!) in four holiday flavors: Original, Chile Pepper, Pineapple and Strawberry.

If your local supermarket isn't quite as cosmopolitan as this, never fear, the good folks at Chicago-based food distributor La Guadalupana ("La Casa de la Masa") will mail you two 5 lb. buckets of dough for under $20. La Guadalupana's website says that Pedro and Lucy Castro arrived from Mexico in 1945 and set up shop. In 1992 their son Rogelio moved production to a USDA approved plant and started expanding.   14

How's that for achieving the American dream? I wonder if Pedro and Lucy ever imagined a world where tamales are so mainstream that their ready-to-wrap dough sits next to frozen apple pies and scalloped potatoes for holiday revelers[11] to take and make.   15

Alas, even ease of preparation cannot sway me to the charms of the tamale. My sons' Christmases have involved the toil of making sugar cookie dough from scratch and stamping out festive shapes—someday we may even graduate to empanadas.   16

LANGUAGE AWARENESS QUESTIONS

1. This article opens in a classroom of Spanish-speaking first-graders. What words and phrases reveal the students' shock at learning that their teacher doesn't like tamales (paragraphs 3–6)?
2. Cepeda introduces this cozy scene by comparing it to "a lesson from a training film about cultural competency" (paragraph 1). Review the definition of the term *cultural competency*. What cultural lesson did the children learn that day?

DISCUSSION AND WRITING QUESTIONS

1. In paragraphs 11 and 12, Cepeda says her attitude about our "ethnic foodie culture" has changed. She now sees pumpkin pie and strawberry tamales as the "American melting pot working its magic." Do you agree or disagree? Give examples of other ethnic foods and traditions that have entered the American mainstream.
2. Pedro and Lucy's food distribution company, La Guadalupana, is presented as an example of the American dream (paragraphs 14, 15). Is it? Do you believe the American dream is alive and well? Give an example from your life or observations.
3. Do most Americans possess cultural competency—the ability to get along with and understand other cultures? Explain your answer. Is cultural competency a good thing to possess?

WRITING ASSIGNMENTS

1. Choose one holiday and write a short composition that describes your family's holiday traditions. You might want to devote one paragraph to special foods for that holiday and another paragraph to other rituals and traditions your family cherishes. Include specific details, and as you write, use senses: hearing, sight, smell, taste, touch.
2. Define the American dream as you understand it. Does it still exist? Write your personal definition of this term and develop your definition with examples from your own life or the life of someone you know well.
3. Is America a melting pot of cultures (beyond having diverse foods in many of its markets)? Do different cultures blend together into something good and new here, or do they remain separated from each other?

---

11. revelers: people celebrating in a lively way

A Day in the Life of an Emergency Room Nurse

Beve Stevenson, RN, BN

Beve Stevenson, "A Day in the Life of an ER Nurse," *Alberta RN*. Adapted by permission of the author. https://beeproductions.ca/about/

Beve Stevenson is a veteran emergency nurse who has worked in emergency rooms in Calgary, Alberta, Canada, and in a trauma helicopter. She is also a stand-up comedian, writer, and motivational speaker who believes that comedy is the perfect antidote to a high-stress job. Here she describes her workday in a busy urban hospital.

1   As I enter the hospital through the ER entrance, I assess the overall mood of the waiting room. Is everyone patient and quiet, or is the frustration palpable?[1] I change into my comfy scrubs and secure my stethoscope around my neck as I mentally prepare for my day.

2   I survey the work environment that only an ER nurse could consider normal: patients of all shapes, sizes, and colors in various states of undress, illness, and lucidity[2]. There is a cacophony[3] of loud voices, crying children, gurneys[4] and people darting about in a frantic dance. Continuing through the ER hallway, I can easily hear conversations of physicians behind the curtains with their patients. "You did this . . . how?" "How long have your teeth been itchy?" "With a fork?"

3   "What brings you to hospital?"

4   "A cab."

5   I am relieved not to be assigned to triage[5] today. Increased patient volumes and acuity[6], bed and nursing shortages, not to mention agonizingly long waiting times, have made triage the bane[7] of the ER nurse's existence. The triage nurse, otherwise known as "The Bag in the Bubble," assumes the brunt[8] of waiting room abuse and acts as detective, counselor, organizer, diplomat, gatekeeper, interpreter, and sometimes magician too. No one taught us any of this in nursing school.

6   "Why do you want to see the doctor today?"

7   "None of your *?&% business!"

8   For twelve hours, I will be responsible for everything that happens in my six-bed area. I will assess and treat twenty-five patients with seemingly every kind of illness or trauma. Two will go to the OR, one will lose her baby, and another will go to heaven. I will witness the effects of domestic abuse. I will calm a frightened child and his parents, then dodge a few punches and the occasional poorly aimed spitball. I will peel off socks that haven't been removed for a year and not be surprised by what is beneath. I will start dozens of IVs, produce mounds of paperwork, and fix at least one computer problem. I will give multiple medications, initiate a blood transfusion, assist with a fracture reduction, then arrange for Home Care. For thirty minutes, a man will insist,

> "What brings you to hospital?"
> "A cab."

---

1. palpable: obvious
2. lucidity: state of mental clarity
3. cacophony: harsh mixture of sounds
4. gurneys: rolling carts for patient transport
5. triage: process of determining and prioritizing patients' medical needs
6. acuity: the level of severity of illness
7. bane: something that brings misery or difficulty
8. brunt: the main impact

with almost religious fervor[9], that he is unconscious. I will tidy up after a herd of messy medical students. I will print labels, wipe brows and bums, collect blood samples, and educate new immigrants on the proper use of Tylenol. I will convince a teenager that her horoscope is not an effective method of birth control. I will constantly reassess my patients' conditions, making sure to alert the physician if someone deteriorates. Somehow, I will find time to ease my patients' fears by telling a few jokes. I will encourage the use of helmets, teach crutch walking and proper wound care. And that is just *today*.

9   Having *ER*[10] on television has helped in one way; I can now communicate great thirst after work by ordering a STAT[11] margarita. But often patients confuse TV for reality. Haven't they noticed that there aren't any wildly good-looking doctors like George Clooney or Noah Wyle working here? No physicians smooch with gorgeous nurses in the bedpan room. I've never seen a doctor rush out to the ambulance bay—that is, except to get a Coke out of the machine. And no patient's problem can be fixed in just one hour, ever.

10   On a short break, several nurses meet in the staff room for some "Vitamin C." I take mine black. Here we are free to discuss typical ER subjects like festering[12] wounds while we eat. There's almost always a plate of old, greasy "share food" that could easily double as a food-poisoning lab. Why do health-care professionals eat this stuff?

11   Often the shift's most difficult skill is not the tough IV start, but plain old communication. Blend several languages, cultural and generational differences; mix in anxiety, fear, missing teeth, intoxication, speech impediments[13], dementia, ignorance, and embarrassment. Add a dash of medical jargon[14], and soon everyone is confused beyond belief. Imagine the loud assessment of the severely hearing-impaired patient; everyone within earshot cannot help but learn much more than they wanted to, including the play-by-play of a rectal examination.

12   By shift's end, I'm totally exhausted, my hands raw from washing, my voice hoarse, and my feet screaming in agony. When I stop at the grocery store on my way home, I notice how a woman's ankles literally *flow* over the sides of her shoes. I know that her Lasix[15] dose is sub-therapeutic, just as I know the man behind me is an asthmatic who still smokes. I cannot seem to turn off this constant assessment of everyone around me.

13   At a party in the evening, gore-curious guests who work "normal" jobs and whose trauma experience is likely limited to occasional mishaps with the office stapler, interrogate me about my work. I cannot divulge[16] what truly transpired, nor do they really want to know even if they think they do. One guest launches into the gory details of her recent surgical procedure, even offering to show me her abscess[17]. I decline.

14   Despite all of this, I am proud to be an Emergency Nurse. Now, where is my STAT margarita?

---

9. fervor: emotional intensity
10. *ER*: a television drama about an emergency room
11. STAT: medical expression meaning "immediately, without delay"
12. festering: infected
13. impediments: difficulties
14. jargon: words used in a specific profession
15. Lasix: medication for water retention
16. divulge: reveal
17. abscess: area of infected tissue and pus

LANGUAGE AWARENESS QUESTIONS

1. What does the author mean when she says that her work environment is one that "only an ER nurse could consider normal" (paragraph 2)?
2. In paragraph 5, she uses *parallelism* to describe the triage nurse as "detective, counselor, organizer, diplomat, gatekeeper, interpreter, and sometimes magician too." What part of speech is repeated? Why do you think she ends her series with "magician"?

DISCUSSION AND WRITING QUESTIONS

1. Did any specifics about this nurse's day surprise you? What details did you find most effective?
2. If you went to the emergency room where the author works, would you want her to be your nurse? Why or why not? In your opinion, what are the qualities of a good nurse? How important is sense of humor in this and other careers?
3. Reread paragraph 8, aloud if possible, underlining examples of *parallelism*. What effect does the author's use of parallel words have on her description of her many daily tasks?

WRITING ASSIGNMENTS

1. Write your own *Day in the Life . . .* composition. Complete the title as you wish (for example, *of a Single Mother*, *a Soldier in Afghanistan*, *a Fast-Food Worker*, *a Game Designer*, and so on). Use time order, present tense verbs, and many specific details to show the reader exactly what that day is like.
2. What are your main sources of stress at work, at home, or at school? How do you cope with these stresses? Use humor if you wish.
3. The author writes in paragraph 9 that "patients often confuse TV for reality." Give examples of television shows that lead viewers to form misconceptions about certain professions, such as law enforcement, medicine, or teaching. How do the characters in the show differ from the real professionals?

Heroes Everywhere

John Quiñones

pp. 1–5 from HEROES AMONG US by JOHN QUINONES. COPYRIGHT © 2009 BY JOHN QUIÑONES. Reprinted by permission of HarperCollins Publishers.

If you saw someone being treated unfairly, would you speak up? ABC News anchor John Quiñones has been filming bullies and bystanders[1] for his TV show *What Would You Do?* He believes that if just one person dares to speak, others will follow. In this powerful chapter from his book *Heroes Among Us: Ordinary People, Extraordinary Choices*, Quiñones describes everyday heroes captured in action by his hidden cameras.

On a Saturday morning, at a bakery near Waco, Texas, I found a display of bigotry[2] as fresh as the coffee and pastries people stopped in to buy. A young Muslim woman dressed in a traditional headscarf ordered a pastry from the man behind the counter.   1

---

1. bystanders: those who watch an event but don't get involved
2. bigotry: prejudice, intolerance

Matthew Eisman/Getty Images

Author John Quiñones on the set of his TV show *What Would You Do?*

"You'll have to leave," he told her.   2

"What do you mean?" the woman asked politely.   3

"We don't serve camel jockeys in here," he said.   4

Several customers milled about the store, looking uncomfortable, trying   5
not to pay attention. I was watching all this on TV monitors in a room in the
back of the bakery. Both the Muslim woman and the man behind the counter
were actors and hidden cameras were rolling. It was all part of the TV show I
host for ABC News called *What Would You Do?*

"You won't serve me?" asked the woman, seemingly dumbfounded.   6

"How do I know you don't have a bomb in that bag?" the man behind the   7
counter retorted.

"This is outrageous," said the woman playing the part of a Muslim.   8

I watched in astonishment what happened next. An older man approached   9
and gave our man behind the counter an emphatic thumbs-up. "Good job,"
he said. "I like the way you dealt with her." Then he took his bag of donuts
and left.

It was a scene I was ashamed to have witnessed.   10

Moments later, in the parking lot with a camera crew in tow, I caught up   11
with this man as he climbed into his pickup truck.

"Excuse me, sir," I said. "My name is John Quiñones."   12

But before I could ask him a single question, he jumped out of his truck,   13
jabbed his finger in my face and snapped: "You're not an American."

That hit me hard.   14

I'm a native, sixth-generation American. But it's true I grew up in   15
segregation, in the barrio. I'd known where "my place" was, and that was
on the west side of San Antonio. The north side of the city, which was mostly
white, was pretty much forbidden to someone who looked like me. These
were the unspoken rules of my childhood, and now I was hearing them loud
and clear.

After a short break, we reset the scene. 16

On cue, our Muslim actress approached the counter and asked to buy 17
a sweet roll. Again, the actor playing the bigoted man behind the counter
refused to serve her.

"How do I know you're not a terrorist?" he taunted her. "You're dressed 18
like one."

"Excuse me?" said the actress playing our Muslim. 19

"Look, take your jihad[3] back out to the parking lot. I've got to protect my 20
customers," the clerk said.

This time we noticed two young women customers—one of whom 21
later turned out to be Muslim, although her typical Texas clothing gave no
indication of this—who stopped in their tracks. They were staring, their
mouths wide open, incredulous[4]. Finally, one of them mustered the courage
to speak up.

"You're really offensive," she practically shouted at the clerk. 22

Her friend joined in: "You're disgusting." 23

They stood their ground and demanded to speak to the clerk's manager. 24
Even though they'd never met the woman who was being abused, her cause
was theirs.

Watching these women stand up for what they believed in made me 25
proud to live in a country where people are willing to risk getting into a
fight, or worse, to defend a stranger being bullied. The millions of viewers
who tune in to watch *What Would You Do?* each week get a thrill from seeing
everyday heroes like these women in action. And, as the anchor of the show,
I get the same thrill.

The confrontation in Waco wouldn't be my last encounter with intolerance 26
and bigotry.

A year later, at a delicatessen in New Jersey, I myself jumped into the 27
fray. As customers looked on I pretended to be a Mexican day laborer and,
speaking in broken English, tried to order a sandwich. Again, the man behind
the counter was an actor.

"Speak English or take your pesos down the road," he snapped. 28

"Por favor," I pleaded. "Café con un sandwich." 29

"We're building a wall to keep you people out," he shouted. "We don't 30
serve illegals here."

Even though I knew it was all an act, the words cut through me like a knife. 31
I asked the other customers for help. But each one turned away, giving me the
cold shoulder.

"I don't speak Mexican," they said time and again. One customer not only 32
agreed with our racist man behind the counter, but also told me if I didn't
leave, he would throw me out of the deli himself or call the cops.

But then, just when I thought no one would step up against racism, the 33
tide turned. All it took were the words of one compassionate customer: "He's
a human being just like you and me," she said.

Immediately, the crowd joined in, angrily berating the racist proprietor. 34
"This is America! We're a melting pot. Maybe you're the one who should leave!"

"I found a display of bigotry as fresh as the coffee and pastries."

---

3. jihad: Muslim war or holy war
4. incredulous: disbelieving

Finally, people with the courage to face down bigotry. It was as though 35
someone had pulled the knife out.

If you ask me, that's what heroism is all about. Most people think it 36
involves dramatic events and near superhuman feats of courage. I have
found that this is not the case at all. There are so many problems and
challenges in the world today and, as a TV journalist, I see more than my
share. But lately, I find myself seeking out everyday heroes, people looking
to make the world a better place. I think we're all searching for them, in
some way or another.

And I find them wherever I go. 37

LANGUAGE AWARENESS QUESTIONS

1. Explain what the author is saying with his title, "Heroes Everywhere." What is his definition of *heroism* and *heroes* (paragraph 36)?
2. Quiñones quotes people from his TV show *What Would You Do?* using the words *American* and *America* three different times (paragraphs 13, 15, and 34). How does the meaning change each time?

DISCUSSION AND WRITING QUESTIONS

1. Quiñones narrates the story of the Muslim woman being verbally abused before he reveals that the scene is a setup for his TV program *What Would You Do?* (paragraphs 1–5). How does delaying this information make the introduction more powerful?
2. When Quiñones poses as a Mexican day laborer in a deli, he says the actor's racist words "cut through me like a knife" (paragraph 31). Why do these words hurt so much even though Quiñones knows this is an act? Does his experience reveal something about the power of hateful words?
3. In that scene, most customers first remain silent, but the "tide turned" after one customer spoke up (paragraph 33). Read about the definition of "bystander effect" Chapter 7, Part A. How does the bystander effect relate to this scene and others Quiñones describes? What is the antidote[5] for bystander effect?

WRITING ASSIGNMENTS

1. If you have watched the program *What Would You Do?*, describe your most memorable episode and what made it stand out. If you haven't seen the program, write about an episode that you think Quiñones should produce and explain why.
2. Write about an everyday hero you know. Is it a specific act of courage that makes this person stand out? Or does this person model a lifestyle that you find heroic? Support your main idea with details and specifics.
3. Experts say that prejudice is often rooted in ignorance or fear of a particular group of people. What is the best way to promote tolerance and respect for people who are different from ourselves? For ideas, you might explore **www.tolerance.org/** or **www.stopbullying.gov/**.

---

5. antidote: remedy or cure

Are We Losing Our Connection to Nature?

James Campbell

From the *Los Angeles Times*. Op-Ed, July 29, 2016. Reprinted with permission from James Campbell.

The amount of time that Americans spend outdoors has fallen surprisingly since the 1980s. In this opinion piece from the *Los Angeles Times*, James Campbell draws on factual evidence and his wilderness experience as he looks at this major shift in our relationship to nature. He is the author of *Braving It: A Father, a Daughter, and an Unforgettable Journey into the Alaskan Wild* and *The Final Frontiersman: Heimo Korth and His Family, Alone in Alaska's Wilderness.*

1   The childhood I had wandering through the woods and fields near my home unsupervised from morning until dark today seems like a lost world. Many children now spend less than 30 minutes *per week* playing outside.

2   It's not just kids and their preoccupation with iPads and video games, or busy streets and "stranger danger" that is fueling the disinclination[1] to get outdoors. It's a widespread phenomenon. Grown-ups fare little better. Statistics from the Environmental Protection Agency suggest that adults, too, spend 93% of their lives inside buildings or vehicles, living under what nature writer Richard Louv calls "protective house arrest."

3   Are we as Americans actually losing our connection to the outdoors? Conservation ecologist[2] Patricia Zaradic of the Environmental Leadership Program and conservation[3] biologist Oliver Pergams of the University of Illinois at Chicago have documented a disturbing trend of declining per-capita[4] visits to national parks and forests, drops in hunting and fishing licenses, and other sliding indicators of nature recreation since the late 1980s. They see at work a fundamental cultural shift away from nature.

4   Other researchers and environmental psychologists think these trends are, in some cases, even rising to the level of an unreasonable phobia[5]. A growing number of Americans, they say, are suffering from "biophobia," a "prejudice against nature," or what the Diagnostic and Statistical Manual of Mental Disorders categorizes as "natural environment phobia."

5   Biophobia research traditionally focused on specific categories of fears—such as darkness, heights or animals, especially snakes and spiders. Recently, however, researchers whose findings were published in the *Journal of Environmental Psychology* discovered that modern-day fears of the natural world have no such locus[6]. In children especially, anxiety can be evoked by the most unexceptional circumstances: a flock of noisy birds or a strong wind.

6   Ashley Inslee, a biologist at Bosque del Apache Refuge in New Mexico, has observed this firsthand. "We're seeing more kids sheltered and afraid," she said in an interview. "Even college kids interested in conservation haven't been out hunting, fishing, hiking."

7   Humans are "biologically prepared" through natural selection to be fearful of objects and situations that can threaten our survival. And those certainly do

"How did parents who freely wandered outside become so anxious about their kids doing the same?"

---

1. disinclination: reluctance, lack of enthusiasm
2. conservation ecologist: preservation and management of natural resources
3. conservation: an expert in preserving diverse plant and animal species
4. per capita: for each person
5. phobia: extreme irrational fear
6. locus: particular place or position

William Haefeli/Conde Nast/Newscom

"Which trail has the best cell-phone reception?"

exist in the wild. Two summers ago, when my daughter and I backpacked over Alaska's Brooks Range and canoed out to the Arctic Ocean, we were scared sometimes. In 20 million acres of wilderness, far from anything resembling help, we encountered grizzlies and one bold polar bear, Class III+ rapids[7,] and the kind of weather that, if one is not prepared, can kill. But those fears had real and concrete causes. This spreading indiscriminate[8] aversion[9] to nature in general is something new. . . .

8   How did we get to the point where reasonable fears—say about a mountain lion seen near a running trail—blow up into generalized phobias about nature? How did parents who freely wandered outside become so anxious about their kids doing the same? Surely, we as parents are complicit[10] in our kids' giving the wonder of the outdoors the cold shoulder.

9   One of the great American conservationists, Aldo Leopold, knew something about getting his children outside. The Leopolds kept a "shack," a rebuilt chicken coop, on land along the Wisconsin River. I recently took a guided tour of Leopold's simple shack and noted that this was a location for family getaways. It's one of the things that distinguished him from the solitary Henry David Thoreau[11]. Leopold and his wife, Estella, and their five kids fished, hunted, explored, tended a garden, cut firewood, restored native prairie and planted trees—together. Leopold and Estella certainly had never heard of natural environment phobia, but they did notice that when their children returned from their

---

7. Class III+ rapids: intermediate degree of difficulty for river rafters
8. indiscriminate: not careful or selective
9. aversion: strong dislike
10. complicit: partly to blame
11. Henry David Thoreau: nineteenth-century American writer and naturalist who lived alone at Walden Pond for more than two years

outings, they were physically and emotionally renewed by their contact with the outside world. They were happier.

A growing body of evidence corroborates[12] the Leopolds' observation that daily "green exercise" can produce rapid improvements in mental well-being and self-esteem; boost problem-solving skills, cooperation, focus and self-discipline; and reduce aggression. **10**

In our family, my wife and I have witnessed the benefits of nature firsthand. We've tried to make the outdoors central to our daughters' lives. It wasn't always easy. Often, especially when they were young, they'd grumble about going for a hike. But when we returned home, they had a bounce in their step. The combination of fresh air and the sense of accomplishment had performed its mood-enhancing magic. **11**

Perhaps more parents should take a lesson from the Leopolds. Though most of us do not have our own riverfront land, we can find a nearby park or a trail. Getting outside and breaking the stranglehold of electronics—on ourselves as much as our kids—requires a concerted[13] effort. And yet it's worth it to make room for nature in our lives, especially as parents. By spending time in nature with our children, we teach them that we value two things: being with them and the natural world. **12**

LANGUAGE AWARENESS QUESTIONS

1. How is a phobia different from a fear that has a factual cause (like fear of falling on an icy sidewalk)? What is *biophobia* in the context of this article?
2. Going outdoors and breaking the "stranglehold of electronics" requires effort, Campbell writes. What does he mean by the *stranglehold of electronics*?

WRITING AND DISCUSSION QUESTIONS

1. The author uses his own and the Leopolds' experience, as well as research, to support his main idea that we are losing our connection with nature. What evidence did you find most powerful? How serious a problem is it that many people stay indoors nearly all day?
2. Do you or your friends relish time outdoors or in the wild or do you avoid or feel anxious about nature? Why do you think this is? Campbell says "green exercise" has many positive effects on our attitudes and behavior (paragraph 10). Why, then, do people resist it?
3. Discuss the Leopolds' house on the river and their adventures there. Would you like to create regular experiences like this for your family or friends? Why or why not? Describe your dream destination. Where would you go and with whom? What things would you do there?

WRITING ASSIGNMENTS

1. The place children grow up (farm, mountains, desert, city, suburbs) can greatly influence their loves, fears, skills, and ideas. Did you grow up spending time in nature or not? Did you hunt, fish, or do chores outside, go to parks? How did the place you grew up shape you, your abilities, and your current relationship to the natural world?
2. Imagine you teach at a middle school, and the teachers worry that at recess, the children sit with their phones and don't go out. The principal wants you to design a program—activities, course changes, field trips, whatever you want—that will motivate students to appreciate nature and try activities such as gardening, playing ball, camping, cycling, and more. What would you do?

---

12. corroborates: confirms
13. concerted: planned or undertaken together

3. If we humans really are losing our connection to nature, what could be some effects or consequences of this? What happens when we spend time walking in beautiful places, kayaking a lake, feeling awe at a canyon or a sunset? What would losing these things mean (to individuals and to society)?

Put the Brakes on Driving While Texting

Leonard Pitts

Have you ever texted while driving even though you know it's dangerous? Made a phone call? Eaten a burger? In this column for the *Miami Herald*, nationally syndicated columnist Leonard Pitts examines the national problem of otherwise sensible people taking tremendous risks while driving. Pitts won the Pulitzer Prize for insightful commentary on American society in 2004.

1   The amazing thing about the debate over the need for laws to ban texting while driving is that there is a debate over the need for laws to ban texting while driving.

2   In the first place, you'd think you wouldn't need a law, that simple common sense would be enough to tell us it's unsafe to divert attention to a tiny keyboard and screen while simultaneously piloting two tons of metal, rubber, glass and, let us not forget, flesh, at freeway speeds—or even street speeds. In the second place, if common sense were insufficient, you'd think lawmakers would have rushed to back it up with tough laws.

3   Think again.

4   The issue has been moved to the front burner recently by a confluence[1] of events. In late July, a study by the Virginia Tech Transportation Institute quantified[2] the blatantly[3] obvious: Texting while driving is dangerous. Researchers found that the person who does so is the functional equivalent of a drunken driver, a whopping 23 times more likely to be involved in an accident or near-collision. Actually, according to a study in *Car and Driver* magazine, the texter is a significantly greater threat than a mere drunk.

5   About the same time the VTTI study was released, four senators introduced legislation that would require states to pass laws banning drivers from texting or risk losing federal highway funds. According to the *Los Angeles Times*, only 16 states and Washington, D.C., already have such laws on the books.[4]

6   And last week, Transportation Secretary Ray LaHood announced a summit in which lawmakers, law enforcement, academics, safety experts, and other stakeholders will study texting and other driving distractions. You want my response to this flurry of attention and activity? I can give it to you in a syllable: Duh.

_____

1. confluence: coming together
2. quantified: expressed in a number or quantity
3. blatantly: glaringly, extremely
4. As of June 2017, 47 states and the District of Columbia had banned texting while driving, but behavior and rising death tolls continue.

"The texter is a significantly greater threat than a mere drunk."

What else is there to study? What more is there to say? The danger is all too self-evident. And if it were not, it has been quite aptly[5] illustrated in episodes like last year's commuter train crash in California in which the operator was texting and 25 people died.   7

Enough. Ban texting while driving. And cell phone use, too. Because what researchers tell us is that it's not the physical difficulty of juggling the devices that endangers us. It is the distraction: a driver so wrapped up in communicating with a person who isn't there that he is drawn away from his primary duty of keeping the car between the lines. The brain doesn't have sufficient bandwidth for both.   8

So yeah, there ought to be a law. And it ought to have some teeth in it. On the second offense, maybe a hefty fine, or brief loss of driving privileges. On the third, maybe you earn a free stay of a couple days and nights at the lovely graybar hotel.   9

If you sense here the zeal of the newly converted, congratulations on your perception. I stopped using my cell behind the wheel (I was never dumb enough to text) two weeks ago. Had myself an epiphany[6], I did: Was reviewing last night's game with my son really worth dying for? I decided it was not. So I no longer make or take calls while driving.   10

If it's an emergency, I told my family, dial me again and I'll call you back. But the calls are hardly ever urgent, are they? That's not what this epidemic is about. Rather, it's about this idea—new within the last 15 years or so of our hyper-connected, hyper-productive culture—that it's never OK to be out of touch or unreachable.   11

Whither[7] solitude? Whither the moment just spent communing with your own thoughts? Do you really have that much to say? I'll save you the trouble: You don't.   12

Phoning while driving, texting while driving . . . here's a novel idea. How about driving while driving? And for those truly urgent messages that just can't wait, I propose a simple solution: 13

Pull over.   14

LANGUAGE AWARENESS QUESTIONS

1. Do Pitts's first three paragraphs capture your attention as a reader? Were any words or sentences especially effective? How does Pitts seem to feel about this topic?
2. The author describes his *epiphany*, a word often used to mean a spiritual breakthrough (paragraph 10). Why does he use such a strong word in the context of distracted driving?

DISCUSSION AND WRITING QUESTIONS

1. Pitts argues that common sense alone should keep drivers from texting while driving, but it seems not to (paragraph 2). Why do you think so many drivers text anyway? What beliefs might keep them from using common sense?
2. Studies prove that driving while texting is even more dangerous than driving while drunk. Do the statistics that the author cites in paragraph 4 surprise you? Why is "distracted driving" so dangerous? Should states also ban all cell phone use as well as eating in the car?

---

5. aptly: appropriately, perfectly
6. epiphany: sudden deeply meaningful realization
7. Whither: old-fashioned word for "Where?" "What happened to . . . ?"

3. Look up the current statistics on texting and driving. Can anything be done to change the behavior of millions of drivers, especially teenagers? Read Pitts's ideas in paragraph 9. Then, in a small group if possible, design a program to convince people not to text and drive. What approach might really work?

WRITING ASSIGNMENTS

1. Pitts wonders if the real reason we spend so much time talking and texting on our cell phones is that we no longer know how to be alone, in solitude (paragraphs 11 and 12). Do you agree or disagree? Do you and your friends take time to do things alone, or must you feel constantly connected?
2. Because research shows that distracted driving is as dangerous as drunk driving, some states are considering a ban on all cell phone use while driving, even if the driver uses a hands-free device. Would you support such a law? Discuss why or why not.
3. Review this short video, created to stop young people from texting and driving. Do you think it will achieve its purpose? Why or why not? How many of these texters do you think might really stop texting while driving after this meeting? Which of their words and expressions led you to your conclusions? **www.youtube.com/watch?v=E9swS1VI6Ok**

The Art of Sharing Secrets

Rebecca Sutton

From arts.gov/art-works/2016, National Endowment for the Arts.

Secrets have incredible power, whether kept inside us or told. The creator of *PostSecret.com* found a way to tap into that power through a mix of old-fashioned postcards and an Internet blog. As a result, people from all over the world have been inspired to visit or share their deepest secrets with strangers. Rebecca Sutton wrote this intriguing article for *arts.gov*, National Endowment for the Arts.

Secrets are typically meant for hiding: in diaries, in hearts, in deep, dark corners of closets. But as part of PostSecret, the wildly popular community art project, anonymous[1] senders write their secrets nakedly on postcards, without even an envelope to veil them. As the postcards make their way to the home of PostSecret founder Frank Warren, these secrets are exposed to the postal workers who collect, sort, and deliver the mail, and if chosen for the PostSecret blog, to millions of readers around the world.

"I think in the DNA of PostSecret is the trust of strangers and the intimacy[2] that can come from that," said Warren in a recent phone interview. "There's something about the power that comes from these vulnerable secrets, and the courage that strangers show in trusting people they'll never meet with their deepest, most personal stories."

The project began in 2004, when Warren handed out 3,000 self-addressed postcards on the streets of Washington, DC, and asked people to write down and mail a secret they had never shared before. "I got back just a handful, but I scanned them, put them on the web, and the website went viral," said Warren.

---

1. anonymous: name unknown
2. intimacy: deep closeness

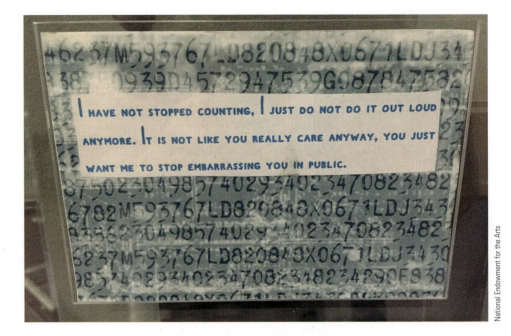

A postcard on display at the National Postal Museum's PostSecret exhibit

"That's when people around the world started to buy their own postcards. They started arriving with postmarks not just from Washington, DC, but from California and Texas and Beijing and Warsaw and Auckland and Iraq and Dublin."

Since then, the website has received 500 million hits, and Warren has received over a million postcards by mail. More than 500 of these are currently on exhibit at the National Postal Museum, a 2016 Blue Star Museums participant. Wedged between Plexiglass, the secrets shown in *PostSecret: The Power of a Postcard* are by turn disturbing and shocking, funny and heartbreaking, hopeful and remorseful[3]. They are short, poetic confessions fit into 4.25 by 6 inches, and often made more affecting[4] through carefully wrought[5] illustrations, collage[6], and typography[7]. They can serve as reminders that you are not alone in your painful feelings or experiences, and just as often make you realize how lucky you are that those painful feelings or experiences are not your own. A selection of secrets on exhibit includes: **4**

I told my family that I had a business trip and took a vacation by myself. **5**
I steal flowers from gravestones and put them in a vase on my kitchen table. **6**
My grandmother's cooking sucks! **7**
Imagine my surprise when you loved me back. **8**
I know he doesn't love me anymore. **9**
I'm afraid my unborn children will not be as beautiful as my sister's kids. **10**
I leave poetry in library books. **11**

Although Warren said that PostSecret has its roots in mail art, he believes the nature of the project has "created a special community that goes beyond that," he said. "It's amazing the stories I've heard from people who have been **12**

---

3. remorseful: full of guilt or regret
4. affecting: touching, moving
5. wrought: made with care and thought
6. collage: an artwork made of mixed materials glued to a background
7. typography: the style and look of printed material

"I told my family that I had a business trip and took a vacation by myself."

motivated to change their lives by an anonymous secret shared by someone they'll never meet."

It's also motivated people to change the lives of others. Warren noted that over a million dollars have been raised for suicide prevention, and the site has raised awareness about eating disorders and other mental health issues. **13**

There have also been touching individual stories. Warren spoke about a postcard he received that read, "I wish Santa Claus was real so I wouldn't have to see the look of disappointment on my son's face when I told him that his mother had lost her job and there wouldn't be any Christmas presents this year." The response was so great when the secret was posted that Warren was able to connect the original sender with well-wishers, and hundreds of dollars were raised for the woman and her child. Warren said that the mother later wrote him an e-mail saying that "through that experience, the real gift and grace of Santa Claus became true." **14**

This type of outreach and fundraising is yet another example of how PostSecret has leveraged[8] the relationship between the postal system and the Internet. Although the Internet is what has allowed PostSecret to become as well-known as it is today, the project's insistence on postcards—tangible[9], hand-decorated, and highly personal—quite literally gives the secrets more weight and depth than e-mail can offer. **15**

"I think that PostSecret would not have been possible except at this point," said Warren, noting the interplay between traditional and digital forms of communication. "Connecting that too is a real cultural movement we're having right now because of the web, where young people especially are sharing more of themselves, are sharing parts of who they are that their parents' generation and earlier generations would never talk about. So PostSecret caught that confessional wave." **16**

In today's automated, impersonal world, it's somehow comforting to walk between the display cases at the National Postal Museum, surrounded by secrets, and know that we can trust strangers—from our postal workers to museum visitors to blog readers—to safeguard and embrace us at our most vulnerable and exposed. **17**

LANGUAGE AWARENESS QUESTIONS

1. What is a secret? Why does it have power?
2. According to its founder Warren, *PostSecret* has created a "special community" (paragraph 12). Why is it special?

DISCUSSION AND WRITING QUESTIONS

1. *PostSecret* depends on anonymity, offering privacy to the secret-teller. Why is it so important that the senders of these postcards can remain anonymous, unidentified (paragraph 1)? Is it still a secret if it's shared anonymously?
2. Did it surprise you that an unemployed mother was tracked, connected with "well-wishers," and given money (paragraph 14)? Does this story, however heartwarming, undercut the safety of an anonymous blog?
3. Why do you think so many people visit *PostSecret* to read the handmade postcards (paragraph 4)? Contrast *PostSecret* and social media as places to share personal information. What human need is each one answering? Are they filling the same or very different needs?

---

8. leveraged: used to maximum advantage
9. tangible: touchable, physical

WRITING ASSIGNMENTS

1. What makes a person keep a secret? What makes a person want or need to share a secret? What are the consequences of keeping and of telling?
2. In paragraph 15, the author writes that poetic, hand-decorated postcards "quite literally gives the secrets more weight and depth than e-mail can offer." Is she right? Or can e-mailed secrets have as much power?
3. Tell a meaningful, true story (or, if you choose, a personal secret) on a plain postcard or a 4.25-by-6-inch piece of paper. Before you create your card, visit PostSecret.com or search "postsecret cards, images" to see the ways people combine words and images. Notice how the small size affects your topic, what you tell, and how you present it visually.

No Time to Be Nice at Work

Christine Porath

Like Internet bullying, bad behavior in the workplace has been increasing in recent years. "How we treat one another at work matters," declares researcher and author Christine Porath. In this article, she discusses the causes of rudeness and disrespect at work, their negative effects on people and earnings, and the simple changes that create a positive workplace.

"Why is respect— or lack of it—so potent?"

Mean bosses could have killed my father. I vividly recall walking into a hospital room outside of Cleveland to see my strong, athletic dad lying with electrodes strapped to his bare chest. What put him there? I believe it was work-related stress. For years he endured two uncivil[1] bosses. 1

Rudeness and bad behavior have all grown over the last decades, particularly at work. For nearly 20 years I've been studying, consulting and collaborating with organizations around the world to learn more about the costs of this incivility[2]. How we treat one another at work matters. Insensitive interactions have a way of whittling away at people's health, performance and souls. 2

Bosses produce demoralized[3] employees through a string of actions: walking away from a conversation because they lose interest; answering calls in the middle of meetings without leaving the room; openly mocking people by pointing out their flaws or personality quirks[4] in front of others; reminding their subordinates[5] of their "role" in the organization and "title"; taking credit for wins, but pointing the finger at others when problems arise. Employees who are harmed by this behavior, instead of sharing ideas or asking for help, hold back. 3

I've surveyed hundreds of people across organizations spanning more than 17 industries, and asked people why they behaved uncivilly. Over half of them claim it is because they are overloaded, and more than 40 percent say 4

1. uncivil: rude, disrespectful
2. incivility: rude, disrespectful speech or behavior
3. demoralized: having lost hope or confidence
4. quirks: peculiar habits
5. subordinates: people in lower positions

they have no time to be nice. But respect doesn't necessarily require extra time. It's about how something is conveyed; tone and nonverbal manner are crucial.

* * * * *

INCIVILITY also hijacks[6] workplace focus. According to a survey of more than 4,500 doctors, nurses and other hospital personnel, 71 percent tied disruptive behavior, such as abusive, condescending[7] or insulting personal conduct, to medical errors, and 27 percent tied such behavior to patient deaths. My studies with Amir Erez, a management professor at the University of Florida, show that people working in an environment characterized by incivility miss information that is right in front of them. They are no longer able to process it as well or as efficiently as they would otherwise.   **5**

In one study, the experimenter belittled[8] the peer group of the participants, who then . . . came up with 39 percent fewer creative ideas during a brainstorming task focused on how they might use a brick. In our second study, a stranger—a "busy professor" encountered en route to the experiment— was rude to participants by admonishing[9] them for bothering her. Their performance was 61 percent worse on word puzzles, and they produced 58 percent fewer ideas in the brick task than those who had not been treated rudely. We found the same pattern for those who merely witnessed incivility: They performed 22 percent worse on word puzzles and produced 28 percent fewer ideas in the brainstorming task.   **6**

Incivility shuts people down in other ways, too. Employees contribute less and lose their conviction, whether because of a boss saying, "If I wanted to know what you thought, I'd ask you," or screaming at an employee who overlooks a typo in an internal memo.   **7**

Many are skeptical about the returns of civility. A quarter believe that they will be less leader-like, and nearly 40 percent are afraid that they'll be taken advantage of if they are nice at work. Nearly half think that it is better to flex one's muscles to garner[10] power. They are jockeying[11] for position in a competitive workplace and don't want to put themselves at a disadvantage.   **8**

Why is respect—or lack of it—so potent? Charles Horton Cooley's 1902 notion of the "looking glass[12] self" explains that we use others' expressions (smiles), behaviors (acknowledging us) and reactions (listening to us or insulting us) to define ourselves. How we believe others see us shapes who we are. We ride a wave of pride or get swallowed in a sea of embarrassment based on brief interactions that signal respect or disrespect. Individuals feel valued and powerful when respected. Civility lifts people. Incivility holds people down. It makes people feel small.   **9**

* * * * * *

Leaders can use simple rules to win the hearts and minds of their people— with huge returns. Making small adjustments such as listening, smiling, sharing and thanking others more often can have a huge impact. In one   **10**

---

6. hijacks: seizes and forces something to go in a different direction
7. condescending: superior, looking down on
8. belittle: make someone or something seem unimportant
9. admonishing: criticizing
10. garner: get
11. jockeying: struggling in every way possible to gain something
12. looking glass: a mirror

unpublished experiment I conducted, a smile and simple thanks (as compared with not doing this) resulted in people being viewed as 27 percent warmer, 13 percent more competent and 22 percent more civil.

Civil gestures can spread. Ochsner Health System, a large Louisiana health care provider, implemented what it calls the "10/5 way." Employees are encouraged to make eye contact if they're within 10 feet of someone, and say hello if they're within five feet. Ochsner reports improvements on patient satisfaction and patient referrals. **11**

* * * *

Civility[13] pays dividends[14]. J. Gary Hastings, a retired judge in Los Angeles, told me that when he informally polled juries about what determined their favor, he found that respect—and how attorneys behaved—was crucial. Juries were swayed based on thin slices of civil or arrogant behavior. **12**

Across many decisions—whom to hire, who will be most effective in teams, who will be able to be influential—civility affects judgments and may shift the balance toward those who are respectful. **13**

Given the enormous cost of incivility, it should not be ignored. We all need to reconsider our behavior. You are always in front of some jury. In every interaction, you have a choice: Do you want to lift people up or hold them down? **14**

LANGUAGE AWARENESS QUESTIONS

1. The author says that a key reason people are so upset by disrespect at work (or elsewhere) is that we all have a *looking-glass self* (paragraph 9). What is the *looking-glass self*?
2. "Insensitive interactions have a way of whittling away at people's health, performance, and souls" (paragraph 2). In the context of this article, what does it mean to have your soul whittled away?

DISCUSSION AND WRITING QUESTIONS

1. Incivility and disrespect don't happen only at work. Share examples you have witnessed of rude, discourteous behavior at school, in stores, or other public places. Why do people behave like this? Why is it getting worse?
2. The author gives many examples of the most demoralizing boss behaviors and, later, of uplifting behaviors at work (paragraphs 3, 10, and 11). With classmates, make a list of what you consider the worst boss behaviors and another list of the behaviors that make you want to do a great job.
3. Porath provides a lot of research and evidence to prove her important points (paragraphs 5, 6, 7). What evidence did you find most persuasive? Why?

WRITING ASSIGNMENTS

1. Choose a person who lifted you up in life. Write a composition that details what this person did or said and the effects of those actions and words. How did this person make you feel? Did your life path or behavior change as a result of this relationship?
2. Create a one-paragraph word portrait of your own looking-glass self as a college student; that is, how do you imagine your professors or other students see you at school? In your second paragraph, analyze your self-portrait. Do you think this mirror self is accurate or not? Is it holding you down or lifting you up?

---

13. civility: courteous, respectful speech and behavior
14. dividends: rewards or returns

3. Porath's conclusion asks the reader a direct question. Did the conclusion make you want to examine your own behavior—to be more civil, friendly, or kind at work, in your family, or elsewhere?

Waste More, Want More

Andrew Lam

From Perfume Dreams: Reflections on the Vietnamese Diaspora. Reprinted with permission of the author.

As a child, writer Andrew Lam fled Vietnam with his family and landed in San Francisco. Like many immigrants, they arrived poor but determined to build a new life. Although the Lams later worked their way to middle-class American comfort, they survived at first by scavenging for food. The author brings his unique perspective to this selection from his book *Perfume Dreams*.

1   When I was young, I used to eat food taken from a supermarket's garbage bin. We first came to America from Vietnam in the mid-'70s as refugees, and my eldest brother got a job working in a supermarket across from our crowded, ramshackle[1] apartment. Among his many chores he found one particularly distasteful: throwing expired food into the garbage bin nightly, then pouring Clorox on top to discourage scavengers[2] and the poor. So without fail he would call friends and relatives to come over in the dark of night and salvage whatever we wanted before he poured the chemical over perfectly preserved bags of cookies, frozen dinner trays, cans of tuna, bags of flour and a myriad[3] of other edible goods.

2   After a while the supermarket manager caught on to this scheme and had a new trash bin installed with a padlock. My brother was soon thereafter out of a job.

3   Not much has changed since then, as far as being wasteful goes. In fact, it's gotten worse. Sure, we recycle, we talk green, and we want to save the polar bears. But Americans still remain as wasteful as ever.

4   A study by the Natural Resources Defense Council released recently found that Americans "waste 10 times as much food as someone in Southeast Asia, up 50 percent from Americans in the 1970s." We are throwing away up to 40 percent of our food, the research finds. That is estimated to be around $165 billion in wasted food each year. And even if we suffer from a long-drawn recession[4], the average family of four winds up throwing away the equivalent of up to $2,200 in food a year.

5   But then there are the side effects: garbage production in the United States has doubled in the last 30 years. In *Gone Tomorrow: The Hidden Life of Garbage*, Heather Rogers reported that approximately 80 percent of U.S. products are used once, then thrown away, while 95 percent of all plastic, two-thirds of all glass containers, and 50 percent of all aluminum beverage cans are never recycled,

"Garbage has become the legacy of our era."

---

1. ramshackle: seeming ready to collapse
2. scavengers: people who search for things others throw away
3. myriad: many
4. recession: period of lowered economic activity

Athit Perawongmetha/Reuters

This child and her parents, like many others, live on the Siem Reap dumpsite in Cambodia.

but instead get burned or buried. Indeed, the average American discards[5] almost seven pounds of trash per day. Of all people on earth we produce the most waste.

The United States has less than 5 percent of the world's population, yet it consumes more than 30 percent of the world's energy resources, and generates 70 percent of total global toxic waste. "If everyone on the planet consumed at U.S. rates, we would need 3 to 5 planets to support our consumption[6]!" notes Global Alliance for Incinerator Alternatives.

6

Not long ago, frugality[7] was a virtue. Now, two-thirds of our economy is based on consumption. In the age of melting glaciers and rising sea levels, in an age where polar bears drown and frogs die en masse and coral reefs disappear and biodiversity dwindles along with forestland—in the age, that is, of global warming, where hurricanes ravage cities and towns—our way of life has become unsustainable[8]. It has created an unprecedented[9] crisis on a planetary scale.

7

"When consumption becomes the very reason economies exist, we never ask, 'How much is enough?' 'Why do we need all this stuff?' and 'Are we any happier?'" writes David Suzuki, author of *The Sacred Balance: Rediscovering Our Place in Nature*.

8

"Our personal consumer choices have ecological, social, and spiritual consequences," Suzuki writes. "It is time to re-examine some of our deeply held notions that underlie our lifestyles."

9

More Americans are beginning to ask these same questions after Katrina. But materialism[10] is a powerful force, and when elevated into a concept called consumerism[11], refined by the genius of advertising and given the title "American Dream," few can resist. Consumer spending makes up more than

10

---

5. discard: get rid of
6. consumption: buying and using things up
7. frugality: thriftiness, habit of wasting little
8. unsustainable: not able to be continued
9. unprecedented: never done before
10. materialism: valuing money and physical things above intellectual or spiritual things
11. consumerism: belief in the value of buying things

70 percent of our economy. We know we need to change, but like many an overweight person who wants to diet and exercise, we, as a nation, haven't found the will to break the habit. And it doesn't help that we're told all the time that consumption is good for the American economy.

As it is, garbage has become the legacy[12] of our era. The largest man-made structure? It used to be the Great Wall of China. Today's largest man-caused structure is now by far the Eastern Great Garbage[13] Patch—swirling plastics that gather in gyrating[14] movements of ocean currents—between California and Hawaii that some scientists believe to be the size of Texas.

Back in the '70s when my brother worked in the supermarket and we were impoverished, I remember hauling some of the supermarket's expired food home to my family with giddiness. What Americans threw away was sustenance[15] back home in Vietnam, where children scavenged through piles of garbage for anything salvageable[16] and people canvassed[17] the neighborhoods buying old papers and magazines to recycle or begged for slop to feed their pigs.

My own family and relatives, too, have moved on from our humble beginnings as refugees in America to become middle-class Americans whose motto, at times, seems to be "shop 'til you drop." The latest technology, the latest trend in fashion, the newest cars, the best laptop, the latest iPads and iPhones—we've got to have them all. And yes, though I try to be frugal, I am part of that equation. I have thrown away good food after a dinner party, have bought more than I can eat. I own the latest technology. I am, too, part of the statistics.

Alas, I am not alone. Even as Americans are beginning to wonder if our way of life has a direct consequence on the weather, everyone else wants to become us. From China to Bombay, from Cape Town to Rio de Janeiro—everyone wants a piece of the good life a la American style, and our collective[18] desires are putting more pressure on ecosystems already on the brink.

A while back, walking home, I saw two old Chinese ladies looking for aluminum cans and plastic bottles in a garbage bin behind a restaurant near my home. One of the workers came out and yelled at the old ladies to stop.

As I watched the two old ladies scurrying away into the shadows, I thought of my own humble past. But I fear that, with the way things go, with global warming threatening to undermine our civilization, those two old scavengers may well represent our own retro-future[19].

LANGUAGE AWARENESS QUESTIONS

1. The title of this essay plays on the old saying, "Waste not, want not"—that is, if you don't waste things, you will have enough. How does Lam's title flip the meaning?
2. Lam writes in paragraph 7 that "not long ago, frugality was a virtue." Define frugality as you have observed it in someone you know. What happened to frugality in our culture?

---

12. legacy: inheritance, what is left behind after death
13. Eastern Great Garbage Patch: a huge floating island of garbage in the Pacific Ocean
14. gyrating: turning in circles
15. sustenance: enough nourishment to keep living
16. salvageable: able to be saved
17. canvassed: surveyed, searched
18. collective: shared
19. retro-future: a past that becomes the future again

DISCUSSION AND WRITING QUESTIONS

1. Did Lam's introduction effectively engage your attention? What details stood out? How do paragraphs 1 and 2 lead into his thesis, or main idea, in paragraph 3? What is that main idea? How does Lam's conclusion circle back to his introduction?

2. The author provides much factual evidence of Americans' wastefulness. For instance, what percent of their food do Americans throw away? How many pounds of trash does the average American toss out every day? What other numbers or facts do you think best support his argument?

3. Do you agree with Lam that our wastefulness—with food and things—is hurting the planet, for example, by creating huge amounts of plastic garbage? Or do you think his position is overstated?

WRITING ASSIGNMENTS

1. Advertisers want us to believe that the American dream is achieved by buying the latest watches, phones, clothes, cars. Do you believe this is true? Are there other visions or definitions of the American dream that seem better to you? Describe one of them.

2. The average family of four throws away about $2,200 of food each year. Evaluate your own food consumption habits or those of your family. In what ways do you waste food and create unnecessary trash? What actions could you realistically take to improve your food habits?

3. Are there advantages to being poor or in having to struggle to make it? What positive lessons can these experiences teach and what personality traits can they build? Develop your composition with examples.

Garbage, Man

Kunal Nayyar

Many college students have jobs, and actor Kunal Nayyar was no different. Now a star on the hit comedy series *The Big Bang Theory*, he once worked on the University of Portland's housekeeping crew while majoring in finance. Born in London, raised in India, and currently living in Los Angeles, Nayyar describes his memorable first job in his collection of humorous, autobiographical essays, *My Accent Is Real: And Some Other Things I Haven't Told You.*

1   Like every college student, I needed a job for some extra cash. Problem was, I didn't have any "job qualifications," because, to be honest, I had never worked a day in my life. So the summer after my freshman year, I decided to take a job in the university's housekeeping department (because the job description exactly matched my level of expertise). My job was to clean toilets, empty out the dumpsters, scrub the floors, move furniture, set up chairs for events, and basically do everything else that no one else in the university wanted to do.

2   Aaaaaaand I loved it. I swear. I took pride in my ability to stack and unstack chairs. Not to brag, guys, but I might actually be the fastest chair stacker this side of the equator. I figured out a superbly efficient way of folding the chair's legs in one fluid motion; it must have been muscle memory from all my years of badminton.

3   My boss, Luis, looked a bit like the villain from *God of War*. Or like the genie in *Aladdin* if he was Satan and Medusa's[1] love child. He had a very black and pointed

_____
1. Medusa: female monster with snakes for hair from Greek mythology

goatee, a sharp, hooked nose, a long, skinny tongue that he loved to show off, and a scar down the middle of his chest from triple bypass open-heart surgery. He claimed to have slept with thousands of women and seemed determined to tell us about each and every one. He also drove a red Corvette, which automatically made him very, very cool. There's cool, and then there's Luis cool.

Every morning Luis would give me a new objective for the day, such as: "A 4 professor just died. Go clean out his office." Not even twenty-four hours after this poor soul had lost his life, I was in his office, packing up his possessions, clearing out all the books and the plants and the memories, and somehow trying to squeeze his couch and table out the office door. It was my first lesson in physics, really; just *because you can get something into the room doesn't mean you can get it out*. I spent four hours cleaning that office, and another four trying to squeeze the furniture out the door. *Maybe this is what it feels like to give birth.*

Another morning Luis would say, "Empty out the dormitory dumpster!" So 5 I hopped into my little truck and drove to the dorm, and scraped the dumpster walls of gunk. Let's just say that I discovered a new appreciation for people who tie their garbage bags up tightly, because there is nothing worse than actually having to touch, see, and smell what people are throwing away. So tie up your garbage bags tightly, please!

One member of my daily cohort[2] was this guy whose name was Khrish. 6 He always smelled like fish. He secretly wanted to be a Nepalese[3] pop star and would always sing us these terrible songs about his love for mountains. Everyone teased poor Khrish about his singing, but he didn't mind. Because he didn't understand that they were laughing at him.

"Cover your ears, Khrish is at it again!" "Run for shelter, here comes the Khrish 7 train!"

Khrish would laugh and keep going. 8

"STOP THE DAMN SINGING!" 9

And Khrish would raise his voice and belt the tune as loudly as he could. 10 On top of his vocal challenges—that is, hitting a single note on key—Khrish faced an uphill battle, given that he wanted to be a Nepalese pop star who sings Nepalese songs about the Himalayas . . . in Portland.

I loved those guys. You probably imagine the housekeeping department as a 11 group of people who clean up other people's messes for money and don't really want to be there, but in my experience that wasn't true. We all had fun together. We took pride in our work. It didn't feel like a *lowly job* or a *bad job*; it just felt like a job. And it also taught me a lesson or two about cultural sensitivities[4], and how race relations can be a two-way street. One day I was joking around with a coworker named Andy, a chubby ex-marine with a soft demeanor[5]. Andy lit up when I told him my mother was coming to Portland for a visit.

"You bringing her to the company picnic?" Andy asked. 12

"I don't know if she'll get along with all the white trash," I said. 13

Andy didn't say much later that afternoon. Or the next few days. At the time I 14 didn't really understand the full connotations[6] behind "white trash," and I didn't know it was derogatory[7]. I suppose, in hindsight, a phrase that uses the word *trash* can't really be seen as a compliment, but I thought I was just making a joke. A few days later Andy still wasn't talking to me, so I asked him if something was wrong.

---

2. cohort: group
3. Nepalese: from Nepal
4. cultural sensitivities: different ways that people of various cultures are offended or pleased
5. demeanor: outward behavior
6. connotations: shades of a word's meaning besides the literal meaning
7. derogatory: insulting

"Kunal, don't you know that I'm white trash, too? Why would you call us that?" **15**

"I'm sorry," I said, meaning it. "I didn't really know what it meant." And that **16** was the truth. I sincerely didn't know that *white trash* was a horrible term. I explained this in great detail to Andy, and he realized that I didn't have any negative feelings about him, or about our coworkers, or about white people in general, and soon we were back to being chums again. But it reminded me that words can be hurtful.

Lunch was every day's highlight. We had an hour break and everyone **17** shared their food on a big communal[8] table, usually while laughing at the sheer volume of hygiene products we'd found in the morning's trash; or Khrish's latest song; or details from Cool Luis's disgusting orgies[9].

Someone always brought fish, others pasta, some brought chicken salad; **18** I always brought peanut butter and jelly sandwiches because it was the only thing I knew how to make.

As the summer drew to a close, on one of my last days on the job, I had to **19** drive the mini-truck to the computer lab, where I was told to pick up a desk. Easy enough. I drove the truck up a long ramp, parked it on the landing in the front of the building, and went inside to help the guys lift the desk.

Then I heard screaming. **20**

I ran outside. **21**

The mini-truck was rolling backward. Down the ramp. With no one in it. **22** At the bottom of this ramp is the main university lawn, the kind of picnic area that they show in every college brochure where students are reading and playing Frisbee and sunbathing. The truck careened[10] straight toward this lawn, and before I could make a move, the truck hit the bottom of the ramp, toppled upside down in the picnic area, and flipped on its belly.

Oh man. **23**

In my hurry to grab the desk I had forgotten to set the emergency brake, **24** and the truck simply glided back down the ramp.

Out of nowhere—somehow within seconds—a man came sprinting toward **25** the scene, barking into a walkie-talkie. A short, stocky guy. Looked like a God of War villain. It was Luis. My boss.

"Is anyone hurt?" Luis asked. **26**

"No." **27**

"Any damage?" **28**

No damage. Luis immediately took command of the scene. He set the place **29** in order and right there I saw why my boss was *the* boss.

In that moment, of course, I was worried about the truck and anyone on **30** the lawn who might be hurt, but later, when the guilt began to creep into the pit of my stomach, I worried this would cause problems with the university and/or jeopardize[11] my scholarship. What if this incident cost me everything that my family had invested? Life doesn't just mess you over on a Saturday night when you're blackout drunk; it can just as easily mess you over on a Tuesday afternoon when you're going to lift a desk.

But Luis took the fall. He wouldn't tell the department which one of his **31** guys had made the mistake, and, as a result, he was suspended for two weeks without pay.

"That's not right," I said. "It should be my punishment." **32**

> *"It didn't feel like a lowly job or a bad job; it just felt like a job."*

---

8. communal: shared
9. orgies: wild parties, usually sexual in nature
10. careened: moved quickly in an uncontrolled way
11. jeopardize: to put something or someone into danger

Luis wouldn't listen to me.   33

I felt awful. "Please. It's my fault. Fire me. I'll fire myself. I'm fired." I still   34
feel awful. I pleaded for him to let me take the blame, but no matter what I
said, he wouldn't budge. He insisted on being my fall guy.

I suppose we all had each other's backs. We all screwed around and we   35
told dirty jokes and we laughed at each other's expense, and maybe we all
came from different walks of life and places of origin—immigrants, marines,
Nepal, Texas, India—but at the end of the day it didn't matter. At the end of
the day we stuck together. We had an unspoken bond; together we were safe.

Many years later, my wife and I endowed a scholarship at the University   36
of Portland. For the inauguration[12] of the fund I came to the school auditorium
to give a little speech to the students. There were about three hundred people
in the room.

In the back of the auditorium, someone raised his hand. An older guy.   37

"You won't remember me, but we worked together once," the man said. It   38
was Khrish.

We ran toward each other with open arms. It felt like the movies. We   39
hugged in the center of the stage as the crowd erupted in applause.

Later that night we met for beers and swapped life stories. Nothing much   40
had changed in his life. Except for one thing.

He had a new song.   41

And you know what?   42

It wasn't bad. It was actually, dare I say it, decent.   43

And this time no one laughed.   44

LANGUAGE AWARENESS QUESTIONS

1. How effective is the title of this essay? Two meanings of it are possible, but which meaning is the author's preference, based on his punctuation?
2. Do you assume from this essay that the author comes from a poor, middle class, or wealthy family? What words or sentences provide evidence for your opinion?

DISCUSSION AND WRITING QUESTIONS

1. Nayyar makes a point of saying that he and his coworkers did not find their jobs "cleaning up other people's messes" demeaning but actually liked them. Why do you think they enjoyed their work (paragraph 11)?
2. Contrast the author's impression of his boss, Luis, before and after the truck incident (paragraphs 3 and 25 to 34). "I saw why my boss was my boss," he writes (paragraph 29). What did Nayyar see in Luis's words and behavior that day that increased his respect for the man? Why did Luis take the fall for Nayyar? Was this the right thing to do?
3. In paragraph 30, Nayyar writes, "Life doesn't just mess you over on a Saturday night when you're blackout drunk; it can just as easily mess you over on a Tuesday afternoon when you're going to lift a desk." What point is he making here? Describe a time you were "messed over on a Tuesday afternoon." How did you react?

WRITING ASSIGNMENTS

1. Have you had a boss, teacher, or friend for whom your admiration grew (or diminished) after you watched him or her respond to a particular incident? Explain how you felt about this person before, what happened, and how your feelings or judgment changed.

---

12. inauguration: ceremony to celebrate the beginning of something

2. Nayyar has become one of the highest paid actors on television. At the end of the essay, he endows a scholarship at his alma mater. If you have financial success, will you help others? Why or why not? What or whom would you donate to and why?

3. The college cleaning staff came from many cultural and linguistic backgrounds: native-born Americans and immigrants, college students and uneducated workers, Hispanic people and Indian people. Yet they were all close. Draw on your experiences to explain why some workplaces stay segregated and others promote getting along and real teamwork. Include three reasons or factors if you can.

Zoom In and Focus

Constance Staley

Adapted from Constance Staley, *Focus on College Success* (Cengage Learning)

Many people think they are clever multitaskers, deftly shifting back and forth between activities—studying, texting, cooking dinner, taking calls. But college success expert Constance Staley warns that this habit we are so proud of is one of the single biggest obstacles to achievement in college. Read on to learn the number one habit of successful students and employees.

In college, the ability to zoom in on your academic work is critical. Learning new material, solving problems, and writing all require that you zoom in, focus on one task at a time, and pay attention. This ability is sometimes called *single tasking*, and it may be an endangered skill. 1

According to experts, zooming in is harder than ever. They go so far as to say that as a society we're losing the ability to reflect or contemplate[1]—to think deeply. We're on our phones, doing all kinds of things, for roughly five hours per day. Not only are we interrupted by technology's distractions, but we now have a much greater capacity to distract ourselves. In the past, we used our down time to think about solutions to problems in our lives or to mull[2] over important decisions, whereas now, we turn to our phones immediately, as if to say, "I'm bored; amuse me" or "I'd better keep up!" No wonder some call this the Age of Distraction. 2

So You Think You Can Multitask?

It's not that technology is "the bad guy." In fact, technology has tremendous advantages, but what's needed is the discipline to turn it on when needed—and turn it off when a task calls for focus. For many students, one of the biggest challenges to succeeding in college can be summed up in one word—multitasking. Multitasking is task-switching, or trying to do two, three, or more things at once. You might get a phone call while answering one of the 205 billion e-mails sent each day in the U.S. or sending one of 500 million Tweets, and at the same time be conducting online research for a class (Clark, 2016; Internet live stats). If you're impressed with your own multitasking skills (*ahem*) and that's how you're planning to handle the college workload, your grades and career plans will almost certainly suffer. 3

The odd thing about the so-called ability to multitask is that it makes people feel productive, powerful, and prolific[3]. Think about it: We work too 4

---

1. contemplate: think about over time, meditate upon
2. mull: think about deeply
3. prolific: very productive

Rodin's famous sculpture, *The Thinker*, is one of the most revered artworks on the planet. Why do you suppose this is so?

many hours, crowd our lives with obligations, and rush from one thing to the next. We assume we're good at multitasking. We can surf the internet, crank up Pandora, binge watch *Grey's Anatomy*, and read this chapter—all at the same time, right? Not so fast.

The more you try to switch between tasks, the more you end up sacrificing the self-discipline required for in-depth study. Recent research indicates that multitasking actually hurts your brain's ability to learn, and that it's harder to retain what you're trying to learn while you're distracted (Khawand, 2009). According to one study, when you're distracted by e-mail, texts, or phone calls, your IQ drops by 10 or more points, partly because of "attention residue[4]"—you've moved on to a new task, but you're still thinking about the previous one (Giang, 2016). Would you want a brain surgeon to stop your operation to check her Facebook "likes" or answer texts from her kids every so often? Probably not. Her ability to stay focused on your surgery is all-important for a good result.   5

"No wonder some call this the Age of Distraction."

Not only do interruptions break our focus, but they also increase the number of mistakes we make, and often actually *cost*—rather than *save*—time. Picture yourself working on a complex math homework problem and getting close to a solution, but suddenly stopping to check a text ping or see who's e-mailed. When you get back to the math problem, you have to reconstruct[5] what you had figured out before you "left." That could take a little time or a great deal of time—and if you bounce back and forth constantly while working on all of your assignments, you might never finish any of them. At the very least, it might take you twice as long.   6

The workplace is also a hotbed of multitasking, which some employers mistakenly encourage. American workers on average are interrupted or switch between tasks every three minutes and five seconds. Research demonstrates that it takes them an average of 23 minutes and 15 seconds just to "reboot" and get back to their original tasks. Without even trying, it's possible to waste as much as six   7

---

4. residue: small amount that remains
5. reconstruct: re-create, build again

hours a day on the job! (Schulte, 2015) "Americans are working longer and harder hours than ever before, but accomplishing less. Eighty-three percent of workers say they're stressed about their jobs, and nearly 50 percent say work-related stress is interfering with their sleep" (Gregoire, 2016). Yet all this multitasking and stress are costing businesses millions of dollars a year in lost productivity.

Unplug and Seek the Alone Zone

Students and employees who can zoom in and single-task make greater, faster gains and are more successful. But technology's stimulation gives the brain a squirt of dopamine[6], which can be addictive. The addictive call of technology means that, for serious assignments, you must actively resist the seductive[7] ping and flash of your devices. Unplug them for now, put them out of sight, and find a quiet work space. As Jason Fried and David Heinemeier Hansson, the authors of *Rework* (2010), wisely claim, "Interruption is the enemy of productivity. Instead, you should get in the alone zone. Long stretches of alone time are when you're most productive. When you don't have to mind-shift between various tasks, you get a boatload done" (pp. 25–26). **8**

In college, one of your greatest keys to success will be resisting the powerful temptation to multitask. Zoom in on one assignment at a time, quiet your mind, and stick to one thing until you're finished—or until you've gone as far as you can. Then move on to the next assignment or project. **9**

References

Clark, D. (2016, March 7). Actually, you should check email first thing in the morning. *Harvard Business Review*. Retrieved from https://hbr.org/2016/03/actually-you-shouldcheck-email-first-thing-in-the-morning

Fried, J., & Hanson, D. (2010). *Rework*. New York: Crown Business, pp. 25–26.

Giang, V. (2016, March 1). These are the long-term results of multitasking. *Fast Company*. Retrieved from http://www.fastcompany.com/3057192/how-to-be-asuccess-at-everything/these-are-the-long-term-effects-of-multitasking

Gregoire, C. (2016, January 20). The American workplace is broken. Here's how we can start fixing it. *Huffington Post*. Retrieved from http://www.huffingtonpost.com/entry/american-workplace-broken-stress_us_566b3152e4b011b83a6b42bd

Internet live stats. Retrieved from http://www.internetlivestats.com/twitter-statistics/

Khawand, P. (2009). *The accomplishing more with less workbook*. On the Go Technologies, LLC.

Schulte, B. (2015, June 1). Work interruptions can cost you 6 hours a day: An efficiency expert explains how to avoid them. *The Washington Post*. Retrieved from https://www.washingtonpost.com/news/inspired-life/wp/2015/06/01/interruptions-at-work-can-cost-you-up-to-6-hours-a-day-heres-how-to-avoid-them/

LANGUAGE AWARENESS QUESTIONS

1. What is *attention residue* (paragraph 5)? Can you describe a time you experienced attention residue after interrupting an unfinished assignment to do something else?
2. The author urges the reader to "actively resist the seductive ping and flash of your devices" when a task needs focus (paragraph 8). *Seductive* is a word that often describes a flirtatious, sexy man or woman. What do those pings and flashes tempt us to do?

---

6. dopamine: brain chemical related to feelings of pleasure and reward
7. seductive: tempting

DISCUSSION AND WRITING QUESTIONS

1. Staley writes that zooming in—single tasking—is becoming an "endangered skill" (paragraph 1). What does she mean by this, and why does it matter?
2. The problem, the author writes, is not technology but that many people lack the discipline to "turn if off when a task calls for focus" (paragraph 3). Later she calls technology addictive (paragraph 8). Do you see evidence in yourself and others that smartphones and other devices are addictive (paragraph 8)? Explain.
3. "Interruption is the enemy of productivity" (paragraph 8). Make a list of things that interrupt your concentration on schoolwork and other important tasks. If completion of an assignment is the goal, why do people let themselves be distracted from the task at hand?

WRITING ASSIGNMENTS

1. Zooming in, focusing, single tasking, being in the zone—these are all terms for single-minded concentration. Although concentration takes discipline, people who achieve it talk about the pleasure of being "in the zone." Describe a time when you had such an experience. Give specific details of the setting, the goal you were working toward, and your feelings.
2. For five days, follow Staley's advice whenever you do any school or work assignment requiring focus. Unplug and seek the "alone zone." Work on one task at a time until you finish it. Then take and break and move to task two. Keep notes and write about your experience. How did working this way make you feel? Could you resist the pings and flashes? Were you able to zoom in and focus?
3. Review this 11-step presentation on how to stop multitasking: **www.wikihow.com/Avoid-Multi-Tasking**. Write a review of this advice, briefly summarizing it and expressing your opinion about whether it would really help a person who cannot concentrate to stop multitasking, zoom in, and focus.

Mrs. Flowers
Maya Angelou

Maya Angelou (born Marguerite Johnson) is one of America's best-loved poets and the author of *I Know Why the Caged Bird Sings*. In this book, her life story, she tells of being raped when she was eight years old. Her response to the traumatic experience was to stop speaking. In this selection, Angelou describes the woman who eventually threw her a "life line."

For nearly a year, I sopped around the house, the Store, the school and the church, like an old biscuit, dirty and inedible. Then I met, or rather got to know, the lady who threw me my first life line. 1

Mrs. Bertha Flowers was the aristocrat of Black Stamps. She had the grace of control to appear warm in the coldest weather, and on the Arkansas summer days it seemed she had a private breeze which swirled around, cooling her. She was thin without the taut[1] look of wiry people, and her printed voile[2] 2

1. taut: tight, tense
2. voile: a light, semi-sheer fabric

dresses and flowered hats were as right for her as denim overalls for a farmer. She was our side's answer to the richest white woman in town.

Her skin was a rich black that would have peeled like a plum if snagged, but then no one would have thought of getting close enough to Mrs. Flowers to ruffle her dress, let alone snag her skin. She didn't encourage familiarity. She wore gloves too. 3

I don't think I ever saw Mrs. Flowers laugh, but she smiled often. A slow widening of her thin black lips to show even, small white teeth, then the slow effortless closing. When she chose to smile on me, I always wanted to thank her. The action was so graceful and inclusively benign[3]. 4

She was one of the few gentlewomen I have ever known and has remained throughout my life the measure of what a human being can be . . . 5

One summer afternoon, sweet-milk fresh in my memory, she stopped at the Store to buy provisions. Another Negro woman of her health and age would have been expected to carry the paper sacks home in one hand, but Momma said, "Sister Flowers, I'll send Bailey up to your house with these things." 6

She smiled that slow dragging smile. "Thank you, Mrs. Henderson. I'd prefer Marguerite though." My name was beautiful when she said it. "I've been meaning to talk to her, anyway." They gave each other age-group looks. 7

Momma said, "Well, that's all right then. Sister, go and change your dress. You going to Sister Flowers's." . . . 8

There was a little path beside the rocky road, and Mrs. Flowers walked in front swinging her arms and picking her way over the stones. 9

She said, without turning her head, to me, "I hear you're doing very good school work, Marguerite, but that it's all written. The teachers report that they have trouble getting you to talk in class." We passed the triangular farm on our left, and the path widened to allow us to walk together. I hung back in the separate unasked and unanswerable questions. 10

"Come and walk along with me, Marguerite." I couldn't have refused even if I wanted to. She pronounced my name so nicely. Or more correctly, she spoke each word with such clarity that I was certain a foreigner who didn't understand English could have understood her. 11

"Now no one is going to make you talk—possibly no one can. But bear in mind, language is man's way of communicating with his fellow man and it is language alone which separates him from the lower animals." That was a totally new idea to me, and I would need time to think about it. 12

"Your grandmother says you read a lot. Every chance you get. That's good, but not good enough. Words mean more than what is set down on paper. It takes the human voice to infuse[4] them with the shades of deeper meaning." 13

I memorized the part about the human voice infusing words. It seemed so valid and poetic. 14

She said she was going to give me some books and that I not only must read them. I must read them aloud. She suggested that I try to make a sentence sound in as many different ways as possible. 15

"I'll accept no excuse if you return a book to me that has been badly handled." My imagination boggled at the punishment I would deserve 16

_____
3. benign: kind, gentle
4. infuse: to fill or penetrate

if in fact I did abuse a book of Mrs. Flowers's. Death would be too kind and brief.

The odors in the house surprised me. Somehow I had never connected Mrs. Flowers with food or eating or any other common experience of common people. There must have been an outhouse, too, but my mind never recorded it.   17

The sweet scent of vanilla met us as she opened the door.   18

"I made tea cookies this morning. You see, I had planned to invite you for cookies and lemonade so we could have this little chat. The lemonade is in the icebox."   19

It followed that Mrs. Flowers would have ice on an ordinary day, when most families in our town bought ice late on Saturdays only a few times during the summer to be used in the wooden ice-cream freezers.   20

She took the bags from me and disappeared through the kitchen door. I looked around the room that I had never in my wildest fantasies imagined I would see. Browned photographs leered or threatened from the walls and the white, freshly done curtains pushed against themselves and against the wind. I wanted to gobble up the room entire and take it to Bailey, who would help me analyze and enjoy it.   21

"Have a seat, Marguerite. Over there by the table." She carried a platter covered with a tea towel. Although she warned that she hadn't tried her hand at baking sweets for some time, I was certain that like everything else about her the cookies would be perfect.   22

They were flat round wafers, slightly browned on the edges and butter-yellow in the center. With the cold lemonade they were sufficient for childhood's lifelong diet. Remembering my manners, I took nice little lady-like bites off the edges. She said she had made them expressly for me and that she had a few in the kitchen that I could take home to my brother. So I jammed one whole cake in my mouth and the rough crumbs scratched the insides of my jaws, and if I hadn't had to swallow, it would have been a dream come true.   23

As I ate she began the first of what we later called "my lessons in living." She said that I must always be intolerant of ignorance but understanding of illiteracy. That some people, unable to go to school, were more educated and even more intelligent than college professors. She encouraged me to listen carefully to what country people called mother wit. That in those homely sayings was couched the collective[5] wisdom of generations.   24

When I finished the cookies she brushed off the table and brought a thick, small book from the bookcase. I had read *A Tale of Two Cities* and found it up to my standards as a romantic novel. She opened the first page and I heard poetry for the first time in my life.   25

"It was the best of times and the worst of times . . ." Her voice slid in and curved down through and over the words. She was nearly singing. I wanted to look at the pages. Were they the same that I had read? Or were there notes, music, lined on the pages, as in a hymn book? Her sounds began cascading[6] gently. I knew from listening to a thousand preachers that she was nearing the end of her reading, and I hadn't really heard, heard to understand, a single word.   26

---

5. collective: gathered from a group
6. cascading: falling like a waterfall

"I was liked, and what a difference it made. I was respected not as Mrs. Henderson's grandchild or Bailey's sister but for just being Marguerite Johnson."

"How do you like that?" 27

It occurred to me that she expected a response. The sweet vanilla flavor 28
was still on my tongue and her reading was a wonder in my ears. I had to
speak.

I said, "Yes ma'am." It was the least I could do, but it was the most also. 29

"There's one more thing. Take this book of poems and memorize one for 30
me. Next time you pay me a visit, I want you to recite."

I have tried often to search behind the sophistication of years for the 31
enchantment I so easily found in those gifts. The essence escapes but its aura[7]
remains. To be allowed, no, invited, into the private lives of strangers, and
to share their joys and fears, was a chance to exchange the Southern bitter
wormwood[8] for . . . a hot cup of tea and milk with Oliver Twist.[9]

I was liked, and what a difference it made. I was respected not as Mrs. 32
Henderson's grandchild or Bailey's sister but for just being Marguerite
Johnson.

Childhood's logic never asks to be proved (all conclusions are absolute). I 33
didn't question why Mrs. Flowers had singled me out for attention, nor did it
occur to me that Momma might have asked her to give me a little talking to.
All I cared about was that she had made tea cookies for *me* and read to *me* from
her favorite book. It was enough to prove that she liked me.

LANGUAGE AWARENESS QUESTIONS

1. In her first paragraph, Angelou describes her young self with a *simile*: she "sopped
   around . . . like an old biscuit, dirty and inedible." What does this say about her feelings
   as a sexual assault survivor?
2. Mrs. Flowers describes the power of reading words aloud, and her demonstration has a
   profound effect on Marguerite (paragraphs 13, 25, and 26). Describe that effect.

DISCUSSION AND WRITING QUESTIONS

1. Angelou vividly describes Mrs. Flowers's appearance and style (paragraphs 2–5). What
   kind of woman is Mrs. Flowers? What words and details convey this impression?
2. What strategies does Mrs. Flowers use to reach out to Marguerite? What gifts does
   Mrs. Flowers give her?
3. What does Marguerite's first "lesson in living" include (paragraph 24)? Do you think such
   a lesson could really help a young person live better or differently?

WRITING ASSIGNMENTS

1. Has anyone ever thrown you a lifeline when you were in trouble? Describe the problem
   or hurt facing you and just what this person did to reach out. What "gifts" did he or she
   offer you (attention, advice, and so forth)? Were you able to receive them?

   If you prefer, write about a time when you helped someone else. What seemed to
   be weighing this person down? How were you able to help?
2. Mrs. Flowers read aloud so musically that Marguerite "heard poetry for the first time
   in [her] life." Has someone ever shared a love—of a sport, gardening, or history, for
   example—so strongly that you were changed? What happened and how were you
   changed?

---

7. aura: a special quality or air around something or someone
8. wormwood: something harsh or embittering
9. Oliver Twist: a character from a novel by Charles Dickens

3. Many people have trouble speaking up—in class, at social gatherings, even to one other person. Can you express your thoughts and feelings as freely as you would like in most situations? What opens you up, and what shuts you up?

World of Skillcraft: The Unexpected Benefits of Gaming

Karen Castellucci Cox

The $100 billion video game industry attracts players of all ages, but especially teenagers. Their hours spent with controller in hand worry both parents and teachers, who question the value of these games. Here, Professor Karen Cox instead explores what benefits may be gained when young people play digital games (and hopes that her children's obsession with *Minecraft* might yield something useful after all).

Using games to enhance learning is not a new idea. Preschool teachers use such strategies every time their small charges play games like "I Spy" to learn colors or "Simon Says" to practice motor control[1]. The rise of digital technology has included some video games for educators. One of the earliest offerings, *Oregon Trail*, helped students imagine what it would have been like to outfit a covered wagon in the 1800s and creep across the Rockies during a brutal winter. Newer digital tools help students learn math facts, practice grammar, or memorize the periodic table. But these aren't the games that students rush to play when they get home from school. And they aren't the games parents complain about when they can't pry Jared or Jayla away from the screen for a family dinner.

The commercial video game industry has been built around games that look very different from the educational games young people might play at school. With motion-picture quality graphics and sound, the best-selling games are often dismissed by parents and teachers as empty entertainment at best or needlessly violent and sexualized at worst. However, a small but growing field of research suggests that playing certain video games can teach valuable skills, knowledge, or behaviors. These skills can be divided into four types: physical, social/emotional, intellectual, and creative.

The first category, physical skills, is vital for children as they acquire balance and physical coordination through active play, such as jumping rope or shooting baskets. On the surface, playing video games seems the opposite of such physical activity. Yet the newest generation of video games includes body sensor devices that allow players to swing a virtual golf club, balance on an imaginary snowboard, or boogie to a popular tune. And the benefits of getting up and moving are not limited to be-bopping children. Studies of the elderly and those with degenerative[2] diseases who play *Dance Dance Revolution* show very real increases in mobility, balance, and muscle strength. Other research has shown that surgeons who played commercial games, especially "first-person shooter" games, made fewer operating room

1. motor control: control of body movements
2. degenerative: marked by progressive loss of function

errors. In one study that followed surgeons at Beth Israel Medical Center in New York, doctors who had played video games at some point in their lives made 37 percent fewer errors than their non-playing counterparts. A similar study at University of Rome used games on the Nintendo Wii to improve the accuracy of laparoscopic[3] surgeons. So gaming can measurably increase physical skills such as eye-hand coordination and accuracy.

4   The second type of skills fostered by some video games includes social and emotional abilities vital to the development of successful adults. Social games that encourage team activities build social aptitude[4] and emotional maturity. *League of Legends*, for example, is a multiplayer online game in which players join teams to navigate a fantasy world, defying dragons and monsters while competing in arena battles. Successful *LoL* gamers exhibit positive behaviors online that make them attractive team members. In fact, the game developers have introduced a code of behavior that rewards players who "provide constructive feedback, build relationships, and help new players." The most popular multiplayer game, *World of Warcraft*, encourages similar teamwork skills, but adds intricate rules for developing one's avatar[5]—an online character to represent oneself. Avatars such as a mage[6], warrior, or priest let players try on new selves that possess personal strengths they already have or ones they wish to embody. When team battle games become heated, as they frequently do, gamers practice skills to stay calm under intense pressure, compete in a healthy way, and manage disappointment when defeated. Far from being socially isolating, multiplayer games encourage the emotional growth that will help these gamers thrive as adults in their social and work lives.

"Parents and teachers often dismiss best-selling games as empty entertainment at best or needlessly violent and sexualized at worst."

Gamers try out *Legend of Zelda: Breath of the Wild* at a gaming convention, L.A., 2016.

Kevork Djansezian/Getty Images

———
3. laparoscopic: using small incisions and instruments
4. aptitude: ability
5. avatar: a digital character that represents a human player
6. mage: magician

Intellectual skills are the third type and the ones most often measured in schools. This constellation[7] of skills includes thinking critically, solving problems, and analyzing experiences. Intriguingly, action-adventure games challenge players in these very areas. *The Legend of Zelda: Breath of the Wild* immerses[8] gamers in a fantastical kingdom whose secrets must be unlocked as the player's avatar walks, climbs, or paraglides through lush scenery. Even basic challenges like staving off hunger require trial-and-error as the player discovers edible plants and learns to make elixirs[9] for strength. Action-adventure games like *Zelda* foster persistence, a quality linked to success, since problems become easier to solve as the gamer uncovers hidden clues. Likewise, problem-solving is reinforced positively because the stakes are low. If his or her avatar fails, the gamer just boots back up and tries again. Developing a penchant[10] for solving puzzles gives gamers an edge later in life when they solve on-the-job problems with complex solutions or must critically assess information and its sources.

Finally, certain video games promote creativity, considered by some to be the highest form of human expression. Creative learners tend to seek outlets for their imaginative expression, which may explain why *Minecraft* is the most popular game in the world. At its most basic, *Minecraft* is an online building game, a kind of digital Legos. But like action-adventure games, it requires players to uncover secrets and solve problems if they are to survive. Gamers may play individually or team up by the dozens in wiki-like[11] collaborations to create intricate[12] cathedrals, desert temples, and whole villages. In a rare crossover[13] from commercial play to the classroom, some teachers are developing courses around *Minecraft* in which students replicate[14] famous structures like the Roman Colosseum or re-create stage performances of Shakespeare.

Parents and gamers alike should embrace the discovery that some commercial video games offer concrete skill-building in the four major learning areas. The present ESRB rating system for video games shows only the level of violence and sexual content in a game—useful to parents but sadly incomplete. Why not rate each game for educational value as well? Such a move would be welcomed by parents and teachers and perhaps promote more crossover. Shifting the focus to types of skills promoted by a game would also give parents peace of mind that time spent gaming is not necessarily wasted but may even help young people acquire skills valuable for school and life.

LANGUAGE AWARENESS QUESTIONS

1. Action-adventure games foster *persistence*, according to the author (paragraph 5). What is that quality and why is it often associated with success in school and career?
2. The author suggests that video games are not as "socially isolating" as parents and teachers fear (paragraph 4). What does that phrase mean?

---

7. constellation: cluster of related things
8. immerses: involves deeply
9. elixirs: magical potions
10. penchant: an attraction/liking
11. wiki-like: collaborative
12. intricate: detailed
13. crossover: a move from one field or style to another
14. replicate: make a copy

DISCUSSION AND WRITING QUESTIONS

1. How are games like "Simon Says" or basketball similar to or different from video games? Is one type of activity better than another? Is there a generational gap involved here?
2. First-person shooter games are often criticized for promoting violence. What is surprising then about the research studies presented in paragraph 3? Do the benefits described outweigh the potential negative impact of violent games?
3. The author argues that the team-building skills learned in multiplayer video games will help players thrive in their future work lives (paragraph 4). Consider the games you may have played with friends or online. Can you point to specific skills you have gained that might translate into daily life?

WRITING ASSIGNMENTS

1. Design your ideal avatar (paragraph 4). What would s/he look like? What special talents, skills, or superpowers would s/he have? In your second paragraph, discuss whether this avatar represents qualities you already have or ones you would like to have.
2. In her last paragraph, the author proposes a rating system that includes the educational value of games. Look up the present rating system developed by the Entertainment Software Rating Board (esrb.org). What are the content ratings and guidelines for each category? Now develop guidelines and ratings for a new category called skill-building or educational value.
3. Multiplayer games like League of Legends were developed with team play in mind. But how do you account for the group efforts that take place in Minecraft? Go online and learn about Greenfield, the largest city ever built in Minecraft. A team of supervisors and architects has spent several years developing this virtual city. Explain what makes this effort attractive to its participants.

The Hidden Life of Bottled Water

Liza Gross

"The Hidden Life of Bottled Water," by Liza Gross, as appeared in *Sierra*. Reprinted by permission of the author.

Consumers buy more bottled water than ever, believing that they are satisfying their thirst with something healthy. In fact, they might be better off just turning on the tap, according to this writer for *Sierra*, a magazine devoted to conservation and the environment.

1   Americans used to turn on their faucets when they craved a drink of clear, cool water. Today, concerned about the safety of water supplies, they're turning to the bottle. Consumers spent more than $11.8 billion on bottled water last year, establishing the fount[1] of all life as a certifiably hot commodity. But is bottled really better?

2   You might think a mountain stream on the label offers some clue to the contents. But sometimes, to paraphrase Freud, a bottle is just a bottle. "Mountain water could be anything," warns Connie Crawley, a health and nutrition specialist at the University of Georgia. "Unless the label says it comes

---

1. fount: source

from a specific source, when the manufacturer says 'bottled at the source,' the source could be the tap."

"Consumers spent more than $11.8 billion on bottled water last year, but is bottled really better?"

Yosemite brand water comes not from a bucolic[2] mountain spring but from deep wells in the undeniably less picturesque Los Angeles suburbs, and Everest sells water drawn from a municipal source in Corpus Christi, Texas—a far cry from the pristine[3] glacial peaks suggested by its name. As long as producers meet the FDA's[4] standards for "distilled" or "purified" water, they don't have to disclose the source.   3

Even if the water does come from a spring, what's in that portable potable[5] may be *less* safe than what comes out of your tap. Bottled water must meet the same safety standards as municipal-system water. But while the EPA[6] mandates daily monitoring of public drinking water for many chemical contaminants, the FDA requires less comprehensive testing only once a year for bottled water. Beyond that, says Crawley, the FDA "usually inspects only if there's a complaint. Yet sources of bottled water are just as vulnerable to surface contamination as sources of tap water. If the spring is near a cattle farm, it's going to be contaminated."   4

Let's assume your store-bought water meets all the safety standards. What about the bottle? Because containers that sit for weeks or months at room temperature are ideal breeding grounds for bacteria, a bottle that met federal safety standards when it left the plant might have unsafe bacteria levels by the time you buy it. And because manufacturers aren't required to put expiration dates on bottles, there's no telling how long they've spent on a loading dock or on store shelves. (Bacteria also thrive on the wet, warm rim of an unrefrigerated bottle, so avoid letting a bottle sit around for too long.) But even more troubling is what may be leaching[7] from the plastic containers. Scientists at the FDA found traces of bisphenol A—an endocrine[8] disruptor that can alter the reproductive development of animals—after 39 weeks in water held at room temperature in large polycarbonate containers (like that carboy[9] atop your office water cooler).   5

Wherever you get your water, *caveat emptor*[10] should be the watchword. If you're simply worried about chlorine or can't abide its taste, fill an uncapped container with tap water and leave it in the refrigerator overnight; most of the chlorine will vaporize. If you know your municipal water is contaminated, bottled water can provide a safe alternative. But shop around. The National Sanitation Foundation (NSF) independently tests bottled water and certifies producers that meet FDA regulations and pass unannounced plant, source, and container inspections. And opt for glass bottles—they don't impart the taste and risks of chemical agents and they aren't made from petrochemicals[11].   6

To get information on bottled-water standards—or to find out what's in the water you buy—contact the Food and Drug Administration, (888) INFO-FDA, **www.fda.gov**. For information on your tap water, call the EPA's Safe Drinking Water Hotline, (800) 426-4791, **www.epa.gov/safewater**.   7

----

2. bucolic: rural
3. pristine: pure
4. FDA's: Food and Drug Administration's
5. potable: a beverage that is safe to drink
6. EPA: Environmental Protection Agency
7. leaching: dissolving, draining away
8. endocrine: hormonal
9. carboy: oversized bottle
10. *caveat emptor*: a warning in Latin meaning "buyer beware"
11. petrochemicals: compounds derived from petroleum or natural gas

LANGUAGE AWARENESS QUESTIONS

1. What does the corporation want you to believe when its water bottle shows an icy mountain stream and the words "bottled at the source"? What do the image and words *really* tell you as an educated consumer?
2. The author uses the Latin expression *caveat emptor* in relation to the bottled water industry (paragraph 6). What is she saying?

DISCUSSION AND WRITING QUESTIONS

1. Why might tap water be safer than bottled water?
2. Even if bottled water meets all safety standards, what other problems can affect its quality?
3. What is the author suggesting about the American public and its obsession with bottled water? What is she trying to accomplish by writing this article? Does she succeed?

WRITING ASSIGNMENTS

1. Check a campus or nearby location that sells bottled water (vending machine, cafeteria, campus store). Which brand of bottled water is sold? Contact the Food and Drug Administration (see Gross's last paragraph) to find out what information the federal government has collected on that brand. Is it spring water? Tap water from another location? Safe to drink? What ingredients does it contain? Have any problems been associated with it? Report your findings in a letter to the campus newspaper.
2. Study the contents label of one of your favorite snacks. What are the ingredients? Consult a dictionary to "translate" those ingredients. Does your appetite diminish as a result? Describe the snack, including what you thought its ingredients were and what the ingredients really are. Conclude with a recommendation for other consumers.
3. Gross suggests that perhaps the public has been fooled by the bottled-water industry. What other products do people buy despite evidence that they are useless or even harmful? Find an ad for one such product and describe how it works—how it creates a need where there is none. Attach the ad to your description.

Charming Robotic Seal Raises Ethical Concerns

Angela Johnston

Angela Johnston, "Robotic seals comfort dementia patients but raise ethical concerns," KALW, August 17, 2015. Reprinted with permission of KALW.

Living with robots is rapidly becoming a reality. Think robotic vacuums, self-driving cars, drones. Now robots designed to offer comfort or companionship are being used in some medical settings. Angela Johnston reports on one adorable baby bot that exposes difficult issues that caretakers will face increasingly in the future. This report aired on *Crosscurrents*, KALW Public Radio.

At the Livermore Veteran's Hospital there are a few animals residents can see: wild turkeys that run around the grounds, rattlesnakes that hide out in the dry grass, and therapy dogs that make weekly visits. But there's one animal in particular that Bryce Lee is always happy to see: a baby harp seal.

This seal isn't alive. It's a robot called Paro that was invented in Japan, but Lee doesn't necessarily know that as he pets it while it coos and purrs. He and the other senior patients here have dementia[1] or similar loss of cognitive function, caused by stroke or traumatic brain injury, and Paro the seal was designed to comfort them. It's a type of tool known by scientists as a "carebot[2]." 2

Lee interacts with Paro under the supervision of Cassandra Stevenson, a recreation therapist here at the V.A. hospital. Because of his condition, Lee doesn't normally speak much, but Stevenson gets him to talk by asking him questions about the seal, questions like what he thinks it eats, and if it catches the fish by itself. 3

Cute but Complex

Paro is pretty adorable. It has big black eyes that open, close, and follow your movements. It's about the size of a large cat, and when you pick it up, it's heavier than you'd expect. It weighs exactly six pounds, so it feels like you are holding a newborn baby. It charges by sucking on an electric pacifier. Inside its fuzzy, white exterior, the seal has sensors that detect touch, sound, light, heat, and movement, and it reacts in different ways. It can recognize its own name. 4

"We started using it with the residents and a lot of them think it's real," says Kathy Craig, another therapist at the V.A. "They'll bark at it, they'll pet it, they'll sing to it. We find it works better with people with dementia because if the residents are aware that it's not real, we find that sometimes they don't engage with it as much." 5

Craig thinks it's a useful tool for residents who are antisocial[3], agitated[4], or sad. "We'll bring out the Paro robot and set it down and they'll start talking to the Paro, they'll talk to other people, it'll brighten their mood. And if they're maybe at risk of wandering and getting lost, instead of that happening, they might sit down with Paro for a while and spend some time with it." 6

Craig says they're even doing a study on whether seal time can replace anti-anxiety[5] medication. Nursing and therapy staff have noticed Paro also brings out a sense of nurturing and caring in patients. The veterans smile as they stroke Paro's fur. They ask questions about it, call it baby names, and even flirt with it. 7

Real Dog vs. Robot Seal

In addition to Paro, live dog therapy is also available for the residents at the V.A. A few times a month, volunteers come with their dogs and let the veterans play with them. Their interactions are very similar to when they play with Paro. In fact, the little white dog, Bailey, that visits frequently is the same size and color as Paro the seal. 8

"There's a pretty large body of evidence to show that interacting with animals can help things like lower blood pressure, reduce depression, reduce subjective[6] pain, decrease the time it takes to recover from chronic[7] ailments," says Dr. Geoffrey Lane, the psychologist who brought Paro to the 9

"What happens to our moral character when we increasingly transfer our responsibilities for caring to robots?"

---

1. dementia: decline of mental processes caused by brain disease or injury
2. carebots: robots used in the care of humans
3. antisocial: not wanting other people's company
4. agitated: upset
5. anxiety: fear and worry
6. subjective: based on personal feeling or opinion
7. chronic: long-lasting, ongoing

Livermore hospital three years ago. He says watching a particularly difficult patient interact with live therapy dogs was the reason he brought the robot to the hospital in the first place.

"She was screaming and yelling a heck of a lot, most of the time medications weren't working, and all the other things that staff were doing weren't working," says Lane. "But one thing I did notice is that when the dogs were brought into the room, that's when she stopped."   **10**

As useful as they are, Lane says live dogs present some problems: they are unpredictable, they can transmit disease, and most importantly, they go home at the end of the day. "So I thought to myself, 'Is there some way we could bring animals into her room and just kind of leave them there?' For practical reasons we can't do that, so I went to the computer and . . . found an article on a blog about the Paro."   **11**

Dr. Lane thinks there isn't much of a difference if a resident plays with Bailey or Paro. He says humans are wired for connection.   **12**

"People are able to connect with this robot. It's designed to behave in a way and interact with the person so that you want to touch it, you want to pet it, you want to interact with it. They have the same reaction that they do to any other cute animal or cute baby."   **13**

Moral and Ethical Questions

However, not everyone is on the same page as Dr. Lane. Shannon Vallor is a virtue ethicist[8] and philosophy professor at Santa Clara University. She studies the ways our habits influence the development of our moral character, and she thinks there are a few ethical issues to worry about when using carebots.   **14**

Paro, the robotic baby seal, charging

8. virtue ethicist: expert who studies moral choices, stressing individual goodness and character

"People have demonstrated a remarkable ability to transfer their 15
psychological expectations of other people's thoughts, emotions, and feelings
to robots," Vallor says.

Nurses and therapists at the Livermore V.A. don't explicitly[9] tell the 16
patients Paro the seal is a robot. They play along with questions about where
it lives and what type of fish it eats. Vallor says with dementia patients, the line
between reality and imagination can already be blurred, but that "we should
worry about it with people who are in the facility for other reasons, who are
lonely and who want to feel like somebody cares about them."

And there's another problem. It has to do with us, the people who are actually 17
doing the caring. "My question is what happens to us, what happens to our moral
character and our virtues in a world where we increasingly have more and more
opportunities to transfer our responsibilities for caring for others, to robots?"
Vallor asks. "And where the quality of those robots increasingly encourages us
to feel more comfortable with doing this, to feel less guilty about it, to feel in fact
maybe like that's the best way that we can care for our loved ones?"

She says that caring is really hard, even for the most well-meaning human 18
beings. "At a certain point we just run out of emotional resources, and at that
point both the human caregiver and the person they are caring for is at risk.
The robots are reliable, the robots are trustworthy, we don't have to worry that
the robots are going to get burned out, stressed out, that they are going to lose
their patience, and we have to worry about that with human caregivers."

So Vallor says she doesn't deny the potential usefulness of carebots, but 19
thinks we should be wary[10] of our intentions when we design them. "Not
'How could we replace you?' but 'How could we help you become a better
caregiver?'" That means making robots that might challenge us, ones that
make us work to form a relationship, and encourage conversation with others.

Back at the Livermore V.A., Bryce Lee is talking to therapist Cassandra 20
Stevenson about Paro. "She's a pretty domesticated[11] seal, right?" says Stevenson.

"Yeah, she is," Lee laughs and responds. 21

Paro could be an example of the middle ground that ethicist Shannon 22
Vallor speaks of. It's helping therapists like Stevenson do her job better. It's
getting patients like Lee outside of his room, helping him socialize. But
by not getting in the way of human-to-human interaction, it could help us
develop our caring responsibilities rather than deplete[12] them.

LANGUAGE AWARENESS QUESTIONS

1. What is a *carebot* (paragraph 2)? Do you think we will see more carebots in the near future?
2. Johnston vividly describes Paro in paragraph 4. What phrases and details help you "see and experience" Paro?

DISCUSSION AND WRITING QUESTIONS

1. Were you surprised at the way patients at Livermore responded to Paro? Why do you think live dogs and this robotic seal both make patients feel better, less anxious, more talkative? What are the pros and cons of using Paro versus a dog?

---

9. explicitly: clearly
10. wary: cautious
11. domesticated: tamed
12. deplete: use up, drain

2. The writer examines her subject from many angles, quoting therapists, doctors, and patients. What are the strongest arguments for using Paro with dementia patients? Why is Dr. Vallor, the ethicist, more cautious about carebots (paragraphs 16–17)? What does she fear might happen in the future?

3. Imagine a future in which humans use robots in many emergency, medical, and other situations. Give examples of wise uses of robots, for instance, in dangerous rescues, deadly epidemics, and so forth. Name some unwise uses.

WRITING ASSIGNMENTS

1. Have you ever been a caregiver to a person or a loved animal? Capture this experience in words for the reader. What were the satisfactions, even joys, of caregiving? What were the burdens, frustrations, the cost to you personally? Share any important lessons you learned.

2. If your friend or loved one were in a nursing home or hospital long-term, would you want him or her to spend time with Paro? Why or why not? If this person liked Paro, would that sometimes make you feel you didn't have to visit as often? Discuss.

3. What characteristics and actions make a person moral and good, in your view? Imagine that you find yourself in a group of people saying and doing things you would never say or do on your own—for instance, on Facebook when friends start posting hurtful comments about a person, at work where your co-workers are stealing small items, or even in an angry crowd on the street. Choose one situation. What forces would support and/or prevent you from doing what you consider to be "the right thing"? What would you do?

Introverts Run the World—Quietly

Susan Cain

When you come home from a large party, do you feel energized or exhausted? Do you prefer one-on-one conversations or group activities? Would you rather work alone or on a team? The answers to such questions reveal where you fall on an important personality scale. Susan Cain explores fascinating differences between introverts and extroverts; she is the author of *Quiet: The Power of Introverts in a World That Can't Stop Talking*.

1   The theory of evolution[1]. The theory of relativity[2]. The *Cat in the Hat*. All were brought to you by introverts[3]. Our culture is biased against quiet and reserved people, but introverts are responsible for some of humanity's greatest achievements—from Steve Wozniak's invention of the Apple computer to J. K. Rowling's Harry Potter. And these introverts did what they did not in spite of their temperaments[4]—but because of them.

2   Introverts make up a third to a half of the population. That's one out of every two or three people you know. Yet our most important institutions—our schools and our workplaces—are designed for extroverts. And we're living

---

1. evolution: the process by which all living things gradually develop
2. theory of relativity: Albert Einstein's revolutionary theory of space and time
3. introverts: people who are energized by solitude or one-on-one conversation, not large groups
4. temperaments: personalities, ways of acting and reacting

with a value system that I call the New Groupthink, where we believe that all creativity and productivity comes from an oddly gregarious[5] place.

Picture the typical classroom. When I was a kid, we sat in rows of desks, and we did most of our work autonomously[6]. But nowadays many students sit in "pods" of desks with four or five students facing each other, and they work on countless group projects—even in subjects like math and creative writing. Kids who prefer to work by themselves don't fit, and research by educational psychology professor Charles Meisgeier found that the majority of teachers believe the ideal student is an extrovert[7]—even though introverts tend to get higher grades, according to psychologist Adrian Furnham.

3

The same thing happens at work. Many of us now work in offices without walls, with no respite from the noise and gaze of co-workers. And introverts are routinely passed over for leadership positions, even though the latest research by the management professor Adam Grant at Wharton shows that introverted leaders often deliver better results. They're better at letting proactive[8] employees run with their creative ideas, while extroverts can unwittingly put their own stamp on things and not realize that other people's ideas aren't being heard.

4

Of course, we all fall at different points along the introvert-extrovert spectrum. Even Carl Jung[9], who popularized these terms in the first place, said there was no such thing as a pure introvert or a pure extrovert—that "such a man would be in a lunatic asylum." There's also a term, ambivert, for people who fall smack in the middle of the spectrum.

5

But many of us recognize ourselves as one or the other. And culturally we need a better balance between the two types. In fact, we often seek out this balance instinctively. That's why we see so many introvert-extrovert couples (I'm an introvert happily married to an extrovert) and the most effective work teams have been found to be a mix of the two types.

6

The need for balance is especially important when it comes to creativity and productivity. When psychologists look at the lives of the most creative people, they almost always find a serious streak of introversion because solitude is a crucial ingredient for creativity.

7

Charles Darwin[10] took long walks alone in the woods and emphatically turned down dinner party invitations. Theodore Geisel, better known as Dr. Seuss, dreamed up his creations in a private bell tower in the back of his house in La Jolla. Steve Wozniak invented the first Apple computer alone in his cubicle at Hewlett Packard.

8

Of course, this doesn't mean that we should stop collaborating with each other—witness Wozniak teaming up with Steve Jobs to form Apple. But it does mean that solitude matters. And for some people it's the air they breathe. In fact, we've known about the transcendent[11] power of solitude for centuries; it's only recently that we've forgotten it. Our major religions all tell the story of seekers—Moses, Jesus, Mohammed, Buddha—who go off alone, to the wilderness, and bring profound revelations back to the community. No wilderness, no revelations.

9

"There's zero correlation between good ideas and being a good talker."

---

5. gregarious: sociable
6. autonomously: independently
7. extrovert: person who is outgoing, social, energized by large groups
8. proactive: likely to jump in and take action
9. Carl Jung: influential psychologist of the twentieth century
10. Charles Darwin: man who proposed the theory of evolution
11. transcendent: beyond ordinary experience, spiritual

This is no surprise, if you listen to the insights of contemporary psychology.   10 It turns out that you can't be in a group without instinctively mimicking others' opinions—even about personal, visceral[12] things like who you're physically attracted to. We ape other people's beliefs without even realizing we're doing it.

Groups also tend to follow the most dominant person in the room even   11 though there's zero correlation between good ideas and being a good talker. The best talker might have the best ideas, but she might not. So it's much better to send people off to generate ideas by themselves, freed from the distortion of group dynamics, and only then come together as a team.

I'm not saying that social skills are unimportant, or that we should abolish[13]   12 teamwork. The same religions that send their sages off to lonely mountaintops also teach us love and trust. And the problems we face today in fields like economics and science are more complex than ever, and need armies of people to solve them. But I am saying that we all need alone time. And that the more freedom we give introverts to be themselves, the more they'll dream up their own unique solutions to the problems that bedevil us.

LANGUAGE AWARENESS QUESTIONS

1. What does Cain mean by the New Groupthink (paragraph 2)?
2. "Solitude is a crucial ingredient for creativity," she writes, and then gives some famous examples (paragraphs 7–9). What does she mean, "No wilderness, no revelations"?

DISCUSSION AND WRITING QUESTIONS

1. After reading this article, do you consider yourself an introvert or an extrovert? Share some specifics or an incident that reveals your personality. To take Cain's 20-question quiz, go here and scroll down: **www.npr.org/2012/01/30/145930229/quiet-please-unleashing-the-power-of-introverts**.
2. Do you agree that our society favors extroverts? Was your grade school set up for introverts or extroverts (paragraph 3)? How about the physical arrangement of your present college classes or your workplace (paragraph 4)? Explain.
3. People in groups, says Cain, tend to follow the most dominant talker in the room rather than the one with the best ideas (paragraph 11). Have you ever experienced this dynamic? Plan a creative way to manage a classroom or workplace discussion so that everyone gets a chance to speak. How would it work?

WRITING ASSIGNMENTS

1. Why might an introvert-extrovert pair make the most effective marriage or work partners (paragraph 6)? Describe a pair you know well that illustrates this claim. Does one person dominate, or have they found a way to balance their strengths and personalities? Explain.
2. State one career goal you are considering, and explain two to three ways in which this job will be a good match for your personality. First, state whether you are an introvert, extrovert, or a bit of both. Then show how two or three of your traits are suited to this job. For example, "As an extrovert, I love to keep moving. As a drug company representative, traveling and meeting new people constantly will be good for me."
3. In the past decade, the "open office" (with glass or no walls between desks) has come to dominate most American workplaces. Your company's president is planning a new office building, and your boss has asked you to do some research on "open offices and productivity" and to write up your findings on the pros and cons of open versus private offices. Write a report that weighs both the positive and negative effects of working in an open office.

_____

12. visceral: gut-level
13. abolish: do away with

Buy Yourself Less Stuff

MP Dunleavey

From Dunleavey, MP, *Money Can Buy Happiness: How to Spend to Get the Life You Want*. Reprinted by permission of the author.

The secret to happiness may not be having more money but knowing how to spend the money you've got. According to personal finance expert and author MP Dunleavey, we can learn to better manage our money and our happiness. But first we need to understand what forces influence our spending decisions and what we really want.

"No wonder Americans are experiencing an epidemic of debt and bankruptcy."

1   Nearly forty years ago, Richard Easterlin, now an economist at the University of Southern California, began examining people's material desires and how they felt once they achieved those goals. Easterlin reviewed surveys of thousands of Americans, who said they believed the good life consisted of owning certain things—like having a nice car, pool, vacation home, and so on. While they themselves had only 1.7 of the desired items, they felt that owning 4.4. (on average) would constitute a satisfactory life.

2   That seems reasonable. You don't quite have all the things you want, but you're sure that when you acquire them, you'll be satisfied. But when Easterlin then studied people's responses to the same questions many years later, he found that although on average people now owned 3.1 of the desired goods, now they believed they wouldn't achieve the so-called good life until they owned 5.6 of them.

3   You can see how the underlying itch to acquire more (and more) turns into a never-ending treadmill of consumption[1]—not because the things we want are bad, but because we attach to them an impossible outcome: that certain possessions can and will increase our happiness.

4   The confounding[2] factor is that owning and buying stuff actually is fun. It's a normal, natural part of life—one of the perks of having to spend your allotted time on planet earth. But a problem unfolds when the momentary kick fades, and your natural instinct is to want to achieve that feel-good state again somehow.

5   So you strive for the next thing, in the belief that maybe if you get more bang for your buck, this time it will last. Unfortunately, a buck can buy only so much bang, and very quickly you're caught on what researchers have dubbed the "hedonic[3] treadmill," the ceaseless quest for *moremoremore* that drives our lives, dominates our thoughts, and erodes our quality of life.

The Grass Is Always Greener

6   Why? Because people have an astonishing ability to adapt to almost any circumstance, positive or negative, with little change in our overall sense of well-being. Even studies of cancer patients and paraplegics[4] have shown that people whom most of us would imagine to be depressed or suffering actually report being about as happy as healthy folks—because they've adapted to

---

1. consumption: buying and using things up
2. confounding: confusing
3. hedonic: pleasure-seeking
4. paraplegics: people paralyzed from the waist down

their lives. To be sure, a calamity like a sudden death, divorce, or job loss can be traumatic and isn't something you adjust to quickly at all. But the bulk of human experiences, *especially when it comes to most monetary or material gains*, have a surprisingly short-lived effect on how happy you are.

Materialism and Your Neighbor

We are all vulnerable to the financial and material influences of the environment in which we live—never mind the pervasive power of media and advertising. But as much as you want to believe you're in charge of your own behavior, it pays to be aware of the impact that others' behavior may have on your own "investment" decisions, whether you know it or not.   7

This was captured in an article I read about the phenomenon of automaticity[5]—the fascinating and depressing human tendency to imitate what's going on around us. One study found that when people were told to complete a task next to an experimenter who, for example, often rubbed her face, subjects likewise tended to rub their faces, even though afterward they had no idea that the experimenter's fidgeting had been "contagious." Another study found that when people were merely shown a series of words associated with being elderly, they behaved in a more elderly manner (i.e., walked slower, were more forgetful), again, without realizing they had succumbed to a series of covert directions, if you will.   8

It's not hard to imagine, then, the impact on your own financial desires when a friend spends twenty minutes relating her latest shopping extravaganza, describing her new Bose stereo, or has you take a spin in her cute new customized, fully loaded Mini Cooper.   9

Inflation of Our Expectations

So although it may seem obvious that buying less stuff will provide you with extra resources to invest in a happier way of life, every day you have to fend off a series of stealth[6] assaults on your financial sanity—including the steady inflation of your own expectations for what a so-called "normal" or "average" life consists of.   10

Witness the average size of a new single-family home. In the early 1970s, it was 1,500 square feet. As of early 2005 the average home size had grown to 2,400 square feet—and with it, people's expectations of how big an "average" home should be as well as which amenities should come with it, says Gopal Ahluwalia, vice president of research for the National Association of Home Builders.   11

What was once considered upscale is now the "new normal" for homeowners today, Ahluwalia says, from his and hers walk-in closets in the master bedroom to kitchen islands with cooktops to three-car garages. (People don't want a three-car garage because they have three cars, he added, but because they want to make sure they have enough storage for all their excess stuff.)   12

Nor have home sizes increased because people have bigger families. In the last thirty-five years, Ahluwalia says, the average family size declined to 2.11 people from 3.58.   13

---

5. automaticity: the unconscious impulse to copy the behavior of those near us
6. stealth: secret, hidden

That hasn't stopped people from spending a lot more money for an 14 expanded way of life—whether or not they can afford it. No wonder Americans are experiencing an epidemic of debt and bankruptcy, the likes of which has never been seen before.

If Only Bigger Was Always Better

How do you combat the multitude of forces that influence how you spend 15 your money and live your life? The first step is to become better acquainted with the joys of "inconspicuous consumption."

Inconspicuous consumption[7] doesn't get a lot of airtime. You can't get it 16 on sale at Kmart: Walmart doesn't carry big tubs of it at a discount. The less-tangible[8] pleasures in life rarely have the same wow power as things, even though they are more deeply satisfying. The core assets [of happiness][9] are all based on inconspicuous consumption—spending less on stuff and more on life.

LANGUAGE AWARENESS QUESTIONS

1. The title of this persuasive article flatly states the author's position. Did the title make you want to read on, or not? If not, what title would you create for this article?
2. Dunleavy urges readers to pay more attention to *inconspicuous consumption* (paragraphs 15-16). What does this term mean? Give an example of a way you can spend time or just a little money and get great pleasure in return.

DISCUSSION AND WRITING QUESTIONS

1. Dunleavey says that the problem with the things we want is not the things themselves but our belief that they will bring us happiness (paragraph 3). Is she right? Have you ever wanted something badly and then gotten it? Did it make you happy? For how long?
2. In paragraphs 8 and 9, Dunleavey describes "automaticity," the human impulse to copy what we see around us. Does this explain why people buy fad products or follow the crowd? Do you see examples of such copying behavior in the lives of your peers, friends, or relatives? In your own life?
3. What does Dunleavey mean by "spending less on stuff and more on life" and by "core assets of happiness" (paragraph 16 and footnote)? List as many examples as you can of your and your loved ones' core assets of happiness.

WRITING ASSIGNMENTS

1. Define happiness for you and/or your family. Give detailed examples. Do you think your idea of happiness is too connected to the "never-ending treadmill" of buying or wanting stuff? Or do other kinds of low-cost or no-cost experiences bring you happiness?
2. In her books and blogs about the "Not So Big House," Sarah Susanka argues we should downsize American homes. Families are happier living in smaller spaces, she says, because small rooms feel cozier, children learn to share, and adults and children

---

7. Inconspicuous consumption: ways of spending our time and money that increase happiness, as opposed to conspicuous or "show-off" spending
8. tangible: touchable, material
9. "core assets" of happiness: things that bring more lasting happiness like friends, health, fun, spending time wisely, and giving to others

communicate more often. Consider your living situation now or growing up. Do you agree or disagree with her ideas?

3. If you were offered a job earning $120,000 a year, but you got to see your family for just a few hours a week, or you could keep your current job earning $80,000 but giving you much more family time—which would you choose? Explain.

Emotional Intelligence

Daniel Goleman

How important to a person's success is IQ—that is, his or her score on an intelligence test? According to a widely read book, other personality traits and skills are even more important than IQ. The author, Daniel Goleman, calls these traits and skills *emotional intelligence*. How would you rate your emotional IQ?

"How could someone of obvious intelligence do something so irrational?"

1   It was a steamy afternoon in New York City, the kind of day that makes people sullen[1] with discomfort. I was heading to my hotel, and as I stepped onto a bus, I was greeted by the driver, a middle-aged man with an enthusiastic smile.

2   "Hi! How're you doing?" he said. He greeted each rider in the same way.

3   As the bus crawled uptown through gridlocked traffic, the driver gave a lively commentary: there was a terrific sale at that store . . . a wonderful exhibit at this museum . . . had we heard about the movie that just opened down the block? By the time people got off, they had shaken off their sullen shells. When the driver called out, "So long, have a great day!" each of us gave a smiling response.

4   That memory has stayed with me for close to twenty years. I consider the bus driver a man who was truly successful at what he did.

5   Contrast him with Jason, a straight-A student at a Florida high school who was fixated[2] on getting into Harvard Medical School. When a physics teacher gave Jason an 80 on a quiz, the boy believed his dream was in jeopardy[3]. He took a butcher knife to school, and in a struggle the teacher was stabbed in the collarbone.

6   How could someone of obvious intelligence do something so irrational? The answer is that high IQ does not necessarily predict who will succeed in life. Psychologists agree that IQ contributes only about 20 percent of the factors that determine success. A full 80 percent comes from other factors, including what I call *emotional intelligence.*

7   Following are some of the major qualities that make up emotional intelligence, and how they can be developed:

---

1. sullen: gloomy
2. fixated: rigidly focused
3. jeopardy: danger

1. Self-awareness. The ability to recognize a feeling as it happens is the 8
keystone of emotional intelligence. People with greater certainty about their
emotions are better pilots of their lives.

Developing self-awareness requires tuning in to . . . gut feelings. Gut 9
feelings can occur without a person being consciously aware of them. For
example, when people who fear snakes are shown a picture of a snake, sensors
on their skin will detect sweat, a sign of anxiety, even though the people say
they do not feel fear. The sweat shows up even when a picture is presented so
rapidly that the subject has no conscious awareness of seeing it.

Through deliberate effort we can become more aware of our gut feelings. 10
Take someone who is annoyed by a rude encounter for hours after it occurred.
He may be oblivious[4] to his irritability and surprised when someone calls
attention to it. But if he evaluates his feelings, he can change them.

Emotional self-awareness is the building block of the next fundamental of 11
emotional intelligence: being able to shake off a bad mood.

2. Mood Management. Bad as well as good moods spice life and build 12
character. The key is balance.

We often have little control over *when* we are swept by emotion. But we 13
can have some say in *how long* that emotion will last. Psychologist Dianne Tice
of Case Western Reserve University asked more than 400 men and women
about their strategies for escaping foul moods. Her research, along with that
of other psychologists, provides valuable information on how to change a
bad mood.

Of all the moods that people want to escape, rage seems to be the hardest 14
to deal with. When someone in another car cuts you off on the highway, your
reflexive[5] thought may be, *That jerk! He could have hit me! I can't let him get
away with that!* The more you stew, the angrier you get. Such is the stuff of
hypertension and reckless driving.

What should you do to relieve rage? One myth is that ventilating[6] will 15
make you feel better. In fact, researchers have found that's one of the worst
strategies. Outbursts of rage pump up the brain's arousal system, leaving you
more angry, not less.

A more effective technique is "reframing," which means consciously 16
reinterpreting a situation in a more positive light. In the case of the driver who
cuts you off, you might tell yourself: *Maybe he had some emergency.* This is one
of the most potent ways, Tice found, to put anger to rest.

Going off alone to cool down is also an effective way to defuse anger, 17
especially if you can't think clearly. Tice found that a large proportion of men
cool down by going for a drive—a finding that inspired her to drive more
defensively. A safer alternative is exercise, such as taking a long walk. Whatever
you do, don't waste the time pursuing your train of angry thoughts. Your aim
should be to distract yourself.

The techniques of reframing and distraction can alleviate[7] depression and 18
anxiety as well as anger. Add to them such relaxation techniques as deep
breathing and meditation and you have an arsenal of weapons against bad
moods. "Praying," Dianne Tice also says, "works for all moods."

---

4. oblivious: totally unaware
5. reflexive: automatic
6. ventilating: "letting off steam," raving
7. alleviate: reduce, make better

3. Self-motivation. Positive motivation—the marshaling[8] of feelings of enthusiasm, zeal, and confidence—is paramount for achievement. Studies of Olympic athletes, world-class musicians, and chess grandmasters[9] show that their common trait is the ability to motivate themselves to pursue relentless training routines.   19

To motivate yourself for any achievement requires clear goals and an optimistic, can-do attitude. Psychologist Martin Seligman of the University of Pennsylvania advised the MetLife insurance company to hire a special group of job applicants who tested high on optimism, although they had failed the normal aptitude test. Compared with salesmen who passed the aptitude test but scored high in pessimism, this group made 21 percent more sales in their first year and 57 percent more in their second.   20

A pessimist is likely to interpret rejection as meaning *I'm a failure; I'll never make a sale.* Optimists tell themselves, *I'm using the wrong approach*, or *That customer was in a bad mood.* By blaming failure on the situation, not themselves, optimists are motivated to make that next call.   21

Your . . . positive or negative outlook may be inborn, but with effort and practice, pessimists can learn to think more hopefully. Psychologists have documented that if you can catch negative, self-defeating thoughts as they occur, you can reframe the situation in less catastrophic terms.   22

4. Impulse Control. The essence of emotional self-regulation is the ability to delay impulse in the service of a goal. The importance of this trait to success was shown in an experiment begun in the 1960s by psychologist Walter Mischel at a preschool on the Stanford University campus.   23

Children were told that they could have a single treat, such as a marshmallow, right now. However, if they would wait while the experimenter ran an errand, they could have two marshmallows. Some preschoolers grabbed the marshmallow immediately, but others were able to wait what, for them, must have seemed an endless twenty minutes. To sustain themselves in their struggle, they covered their eyes so they wouldn't see the temptation, rested their heads on their arms, talked to themselves, sang, even tried to sleep. These plucky kids got the two-marshmallow reward.   24

The interesting part of this experiment came in the follow-up. The children who as four-year-olds had been able to wait for the two marshmallows were, as adolescents, still able to delay gratification in pursuing their goals. They were more socially competent and self-assertive, and better able to cope with life's frustrations. In contrast, the kids who grabbed the one marshmallow were, as adolescents, more likely to be stubborn, indecisive, and stressed.   25

The ability to resist impulse can be developed through practice. When you're faced with an immediate temptation, remind yourself of your long-term goals—whether they be losing weight or getting a medical degree. You'll find it easier, then, to keep from settling for the single marshmallow.   26

5. People Skills. The capacity to know how another feels is important on the job, in romance and friendships, and in the family. We transmit and catch moods from each other on a subtle, almost imperceptible level. The way someone says thank you, for instance, can leave us feeling dismissed, patronized, or genuinely   27

---

8. marshaling: gathering together, using
9. chess grandmasters: experts at the game of chess

appreciated. The more adroit[10] we are at discerning the feelings behind other people's signals, the better we control the signals we send.

The importance of good interpersonal skills was demonstrated by 28 psychologists Robert Kelley of Carnegie-Mellon University and Janet Caplan in a study at Bell Labs in Naperville, Ill. The labs are staffed by engineers and scientists who are all at the apex[11] of academic IQ tests. But some still emerged as stars while others languished[12].

What accounted for the difference? The standout performers had a 29 network with a wide range of people. When a non-star encountered a technical problem, Kelley observed, "he called various technical gurus and then waited, wasting time while his calls went unreturned. Star performers rarely faced such situations because they built reliable networks *before* they needed them. So when the stars called someone, they almost always got a faster answer."

No matter what their IQ, once again it was emotional intelligence that 30 separated the stars from the average performers.

LANGUAGE AWARENESS QUESTIONS

1. Reframing is an important tool for managing our own difficult moods, like anger, depression, or anxiety (paragraph 16). How does reframing work? Give an example.
2. What is an optimist? What is a pessimist? Why are optimists often better salespeople (paragraphs 20–21)?

DISCUSSION AND WRITING QUESTIONS

1. Goleman names five qualities that contribute to emotional intelligence. What are they?
2. Describe someone you observed recently who showed a high level of emotional intelligence in a particular situation. Then describe someone who showed a low level of emotional intelligence in a particular situation. Which of the five qualities did each person display or lack?
3. In paragraphs 23 to 25, Goleman discusses a now-famous study of children and marshmallows. What was the point of this study? Why does Goleman say that the most interesting part of the study came later, when the children reached adolescence?

WRITING ASSIGNMENTS

1. Write a detailed portrait of a person whom you consider an "emotional genius." Develop your paper with specific examples of his or her skills.
2. Anger is one of the hardest emotions to deal with. Imagine a friend with an anger problem has asked you for advice. He has lost a job because of several outbursts at work. Drawing on Goleman's EQ categories, what action steps would you suggest that your friend take?
3. Goleman claims that weak emotional areas can be strengthened with practice. Choose one of the five qualities that you would like to improve in yourself. (It might help to think of a recent occasion when you wish you had displayed more self-awareness, better impulse control, and so forth.) Now brainstorm specific ways you can improve in this area, select the best ideas, and write a step-by-step paragraph plan to raise your EQ.

10. adroit: skilled
11. apex: top, topmost point
12. languished: stayed in one place

Parts of Speech Review

A knowledge of basic grammar terms will make your study of English easier. Throughout this book, these key terms are explained as needed and are accompanied by ample practice. For your convenience and reference, the following is a short review of the eight parts of speech.

Nouns

Nouns are the names of persons, places, things, animals, activities, and ideas.*

Persons:	Ms. Asfour, Dwayne, accountants
Places:	Puerto Rico, Vermont, gas station
Things:	sandwich, Amazon, eyelash
Animals:	whale, ants, Snoopy
Activities:	running, discussion, tennis
Ideas:	freedom, intelligence, humor

Pronouns

Pronouns replace or refer to nouns or other pronouns. The word that a pronoun replaces is called its *antecedent*.**

My partner succeeded; *she* built a better mousetrap!

These computers are amazing; order four of *them* for the office.

Everyone should do *his* or *her* best.

All students should do *their* best.

---

* For more work on nouns, see Chapter 23.

** For more work on pronouns, see Chapter 24.

Pronouns take different forms, depending on how they are used in a sentence. They can be the subjects of sentences (*I, you, he, she, it, we, they*) or the objects of verbs and prepositions (*me, you, him, her, it, us, them*). They also can show possession (*my, mine, your, yours, his, her, hers, its, our, ours, their, theirs*).

Subject:	*You* had better finish on time.
	Did *someone* leave a laptop on the chair?
Object of verb:	Bruno saw *her* on Thursday.
Object of preposition:	That iPad is for *her*.
Possessive:	Did Adam leave *his* sweater on the dresser?

Verbs

Verbs can be either action verbs or linking verbs. Verbs can be single words or groups of words.*

Action verbs show what action the subject of the sentence performs.

> Leila *bought* a French dictionary.
>
> Ang *has opened* the envelope.

Linking verbs link the subject of a sentence with a descriptive word or words. Common linking verbs are *be, act, appear, become, feel, get, look, remain, seem, smell, sound,* and *taste*.

> This report *seems* well organized and complete.
>
> You *have been* quiet this morning.

The **present participle** of a verb is its *-ing* form. The present participle can be combined with some form of the verb *to be* to create the progressive tenses, or it can be used as an adjective or a noun.

Alfredo *was waiting* for the report.	(*past progressive tense*)
The *waiting* taxis lined up at the curb.	(*adjective*)
Waiting for trains bores me.	(*noun*)

The **past participle** of a verb can be combined with helping verbs to create different tenses, it can be combined with forms of *to be* to create the passive voice, or it can be used as an adjective. Past participles regularly end in *-d* or *-ed*, but irregular verbs take other forms (*seen, known, taken*).

———

* For more work on verbs, see Unit 3.

> He *has edited* many articles for us.   (*present perfect tense*)
>
> This report *was edited* by the committee.   (*passive voice*)
>
> The *edited* report reads well.   (*adjective*)

Every verb can be written as an *infinitive: to* plus the *simple form* of the verb.

> She was surprised *to meet* him at the bus stop.

Adjectives

Adjectives describe or modify nouns or pronouns. Adjectives can precede or follow the words they describe.*

> *Several green* chairs arrived today.
>
> Collins Lake is *dangerous* and *deep*.

Adverbs

Adverbs describe or modify verbs, adjectives, or other adverbs.**

> Brandy reads *carefully*.   (*adverb describes verb*)
>
> She is *extremely* tired.   (*adverb describes adjective*)
>
> He wants a promotion *very* badly.   (*adverb describes adverb*)

Prepositions

A **preposition** begins a *prepositional phrase*. A **prepositional phrase** contains a preposition (a word such as *at*, *in*, *of*, or *with*), its object (a noun or pronoun), and any adjectives modifying the object.***

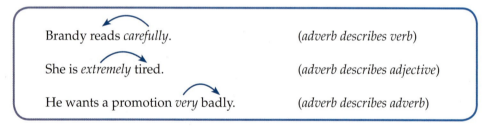

Preposition	Object
after	*work*
on	the blue *table*
under	the broken *stairs*

---

* For more work on adjectives, see Chapter 25.

** For more work on adverbs, see Chapter 25.

*** For more work on prepositions, see Chapter 26.

Conjunctions

Conjunctions are connector words.

Coordinating conjunctions (*and, but, for, nor, or, so, yet*) join two equal words or groups of words.*

> Shanara is soft-spoken *but* sharp.
>
> Ms. Chin *and* Mr. Warburton attended the technology conference.
>
> He printed out the spreadsheet, *and* Ms. Helfman faxed it immediately.
>
> She will go to Norfolk Community College, *but* she will also continue working at the shoe store.

Subordinating conjunctions (*after, because, if, since, unless*, and so on) join an independent idea with a dependent idea.

> *Whenever* Alexi comes to visit, he takes the family out to dinner.
>
> I haven't been sleeping well *because* I've been drinking too much coffee.

Interjections

Interjections are words such as *ouch* and *hooray* that express strong feeling. They are rarely used in formal writing.

If the interjection is the entire sentence, it is followed by an exclamation point. If the interjection is attached to a sentence, it is followed by a comma.

> *Hey!* You left your wallet on the counter.
>
> *Oh*, she forgot to send in her tax return.

A Reminder

REMEMBER: Sometimes the same word may be used as a different part of speech.

> Terrance *thought* about the problem. (*verb*)
>
> Your *thought* is a good one. (*noun*)

EXPLORING ONLINE

web2.uvcs.uvic.ca/elc/studyzone/330/grammar/parts.htm

This quick parts-of-speech review offers self-checking exercises.

_____

* For more work on conjunctions, see Chapters 17 and 18.

Guidelines for Students of English as a Second Language

Count and Noncount Nouns

Count nouns refer to people, places, or things that are separate units. You can often point to them, and you can always count them.

Count Noun	Sample Sentence
computer	The writing lab has ten *computers*.
dime	There are two *dimes* under your chair.
professor	All of my *professors* are at a conference today.
notebook	I carry a *notebook* in my backpack.
child	Why is your *child* jumping on the table?

Noncount nouns refer to things that are wholes. You cannot count them separately. Noncount nouns may refer to ideas, feelings, and other things that you cannot see or touch. Noncount nouns may refer to food or beverages.

Noncount Noun	Sample Sentence
courage	It takes *courage* to study a new language.
equipment	The company sells office *equipment*.
happiness	We wish the bride and groom much *happiness*.
bread	Who will slice this loaf of *bread*?
meat	Do you eat *meat*, or are you a vegetarian?
coffee	The *coffee* turned cold as we talked.

For more noncount nouns, visit **http://grammar.ccc.commnet.edu/grammar/noncount.htm**.

Plurals of Count and Noncount Nouns

Most count nouns form the plural by adding *-s* **or** *-es*. Some count nouns have irregular plurals.*

Plurals of Count Nouns	
ship/ships	video game/video games
flower/flowers	nurse/nurses
library/libraries	knife/knives
child/children	woman/women

Noncount nouns usually do not form the plural at all. It is incorrect to say *homeworks*, *equipments*, or *happinesses*.

PRACTICE 1   Write the plural for every count noun. If the noun is a noncount noun, write *no plural*.

1. mountain   _____
2. wealth   _____
3. forgiveness   _____
4. student   _____
5. generosity   _____

6. man   _____
7. assignment   _____
8. homework   _____
9. knowledge   _____
10. bravery   _____

Some nouns have both a count meaning and a noncount meaning. Usually, the count meaning is concrete and specific. Usually, the noncount meaning is abstract and general.

> *Count meaning:* All the *lights* in the classroom went out.
> *Noncount meaning:* What is the speed of *light*?

> *Count meaning:* Odd *sounds* came from the basement.
> *Noncount meaning:* The speed of *sound* is slower than the speed of light.

Food and beverages, which are usually noncount nouns, may also have a count meaning.

> *Count meaning:* This store sells *fruits*, *pies*, and *teas* from different countries.
> *Noncount meaning:* Would you like some more *fruit*, *pie*, or *tea*?

Articles with Count and Noncount Nouns

Indefinite Articles

The words *a* and *an* are **indefinite articles**. They refer to one *nonspecific* (indefinite) thing. For example, "a man" refers to *any* man, not to a specific, particular man. **The article** *a* **or** *an* **is used before a singular count noun.****

———————
* For work on singular and plural nouns, see Chapter 23.
** For when to use *an* instead of *a*, see Chapter 36.

Singular Count Noun	With Indefinite Article
question	a question
textbook	a textbook
elephant	an elephant
umbrella	an umbrella

The indefinite article *a* or *an* is never used before a noncount noun.

Noncount Noun	Sample Sentence
music	*Incorrect:* I enjoy a music.
	Correct: I enjoy music.
health	*Incorrect:* Her father is in a poor health.
	Correct: Her father is in poor health.
patience	*Incorrect:* Good teachers have a patience.
	Correct: Good teachers have patience.
freedom	*Incorrect:* We have a freedom to choose our courses.
	Correct: We have freedom to choose our courses.

PRACTICE 2   The indefinite article *a* or *an* is italicized in each sentence. Cross out *a* or *an* if it is used incorrectly. If the sentence is *correct*, write correct on the line provided.

1. My friends give me *a* help when I need it.   _____

2. The counselor gives her *an* advice about which courses to take.   _____

3. *An* honesty is the best policy.   _____

4. We have *an* answer to your question.   _____

5. They have *an* information for us.   _____

Definite Articles

The word *the* is a **definite article.** It refers to one (or more) *specific* (definite) things. For example, "the man" refers not to *any* man but to a specific, particular man. "The men" (plural) refers to specific, particular men. The article *the* also is used after the first reference to a thing (or things). For instance, "I got a new cell phone. The phone has a fabulous camera." **The article *the* is used before singular and plural count nouns.**

Definite (*The*) and Indefinite Articles (*A/An*) with Count Nouns

I saw *the* film. (singular; refers to a specific film)

I saw *the* films. (plural; refers to more than one specific film)

I saw *a* film. (refers to any film; nonspecific)

I enjoy seeing *a* good film. (refers to any good film; nonspecific)

I like *a* film that has an important message. (refers to any film that has an important message; nonspecific)

I saw *a* good film. *The* film was about the life of a Cuban singer. (refers to a specific film)

The definite article *the* is used before a noncount noun only if the noun is specifically identified.

Noncount Noun	Sample Sentence
fitness	*Incorrect:* He has *the* fitness. (not identified)
	Correct: He has *the* fitness of a person half his age. (identified)
	Incorrect: The fitness is a goal for many people. (not identified)
	Correct: Fitness is a goal for many people. (not identified, so no *the*)
art	*Incorrect:* I do not understand *the* art. (not identified)
	Correct: I do not understand *the* art in this show. (identified)
	Incorrect: The art touches our hearts and minds. (not identified)
	Correct: Art touches our hearts and minds. (not identified, so no *the*)

PRACTICE 3 The definite article *the* is italicized whenever it appears below. Cross it out if it is used incorrectly. If the sentence is correct, write *correct* on the line provided.

1. She dresses with *the* style. _____

2. *The* beauty of this building surprises me. _____

3. This building has *the* beauty of a work of art. _____

4. *The* courage is an important quality. _____

5. Mateo has *the* wealth but not *the* happiness. _____

Verb + Gerund

A **gerund** is a noun that is made up of a verb plus *-ing*. The italicized words below are gerunds.

> *Playing* solitaire on the computer helps some students relax.
>
> I enjoy *hiking* in high mountains.

In the first sentence, the gerund *playing* is the simple subject of the sentence.* In the second sentence, the gerund *hiking* is the object of the verb enjoy.** Some common verbs are often followed by gerunds.

Some Common Verbs That Can Be Followed by a Gerund	
Verb	**Sample Sentence with Gerund**
consider	Would you *consider* **taking** a course in psychology?
discuss	Let's *discuss* **buying** a scanner.
enjoy	I *enjoy* **jogging** in the morning before work.
finish	Abril *finished* **studying** for her physiology exam.
keep	*Keep* **trying** and you will succeed.
postpone	The Brookses *postponed* **visiting** their grandchildren.
quit	Three of my friends *quit* **smoking** this year.

The verbs listed above are *never* followed by an infinitive (*to* + the simple form of the verb).***

> *Incorrect:* Would you consider *to take* a course in psychology?
>
> *Incorrect:* Let's discuss *to buy* a scanner.
>
> *Incorrect:* I enjoy *to jog* in the morning before work.

PRACTICE 4

Write a gerund after each verb in the blank space provided.

1. Lucinda enjoys _____ television in the evening.

2. Have you finished _____ for tomorrow's exam?

3. T.J. is considering _____ to Mexico next month.

4. I have postponed _____ until I receive the results of the test.

5. We are discussing _____ a car.

---

* For more on simple subjects, see Chapter 10, Part A.

** For more on objects of verbs, see Chapter 24, Part F.

*** For more on infinitives, see Chapter 16, Part E.

Preposition + Gerund

A preposition* may be followed by a gerund.

> I forgive you *for **stepping*** on my toe.
>
> Elena believes *in **pushing*** herself to her limits.
>
> We made the flight *by **running*** from one terminal to another.

A preposition is *never* followed by an infinitive (*to* + the simple form of the verb).

> *Incorrect:* I forgive you *for **to step*** on my toe.
>
> *Incorrect:* Elena believes *in **to push*** herself to her limits.
>
> *Incorrect:* We made the flight *by **to run*** from one terminal to another.

PRACTICE 5   Write a gerund after the preposition in each blank space provided.

1. We have succeeded in _____ the DVD you wanted.

2. You can get there by _____ left at the next corner.

3. Thank you for _____ those striped socks for me.

4. I enjoy sports like _____ and _____ .

5. Between _____ to school and _____ , I have little time

   for _____ .

Verb + Infinitive

Many verbs are followed by the **infinitive** (*to* + the simple form of the verb).

Some Common Verbs That Can Be Followed by an Infinitive	
Verb	**Sample Sentence**
afford	Carla can *afford **to buy*** a new outfit whenever she wants.
agree	I *agree **to marry*** you a year from today.
appear	He *appears **to be*** inspired by his new job.
decide	Will they *decide **to drive*** across the country?
expect	Jamal *expects **to graduate*** next year.
forget	Please do not *forget **to cash*** the check.
hope	My nephews *hope **to visit*** Santa Fe this year.
intend	I *intend **to study*** harder this semester than I did last semester.

_____

* For more on prepositions, see Chapter 26.

mean	Did Franco *mean **to leave*** his lunch on the kitchen table?
need	Do you *need **to stop*** for a break now?
plan	Justin *plans **to go*** into advertising.
promise	Sharon has *promised **to paint*** this wall green.
offer	Did they really *offer **to babysit*** for a month?
refuse	Haim *refuses **to walk*** another step.
try	Let's *try **to set*** up this tent before dark.
wait	On the other hand, we could *wait **to camp*** out until tomorrow.

PRACTICE 6   Write an infinitive after the verb in each blank space provided.

1. The plumber promised _____ the sink today.

2. My son plans _____ a course in electrical engineering.

3. We do not want _____ late for the meeting again.

4. They refused _____ before everyone was ready.

5. I expect _____ Jorge next week.

Verb + Gerund or Infinitive

Some verbs can be followed by *either* a gerund *or* an infinitive.

Some Common Verbs That Can Be Followed by a Gerund or an Infinitive	
Verb	**Sample Sentence**
begin	They *began **to laugh**.* (infinitive)
	They *began **laughing**.* (gerund)
continue	Fran *continued **to speak**.* (infinitive)
	Fran *continued **speaking**.* (gerund)
hate	Juan *hates **to drive*** in the snow. (infinitive)
	Juan *hates **driving*** in the snow. (gerund)
like	My daughter *likes **to code**.* (infinitive)
	My daughter *likes **coding**.* (gerund)
love	Phil *loves **to watch*** soccer games. (infinitive)
	Phil *loves **watching*** soccer games. (gerund)
start	Will you *start **to write*** the paper tomorrow? (infinitive)
	Will you *start **writing*** the paper tomorrow? (gerund)

PRACTICE 7   For each pair of sentences, first write an infinitive in the space provided. Then write a gerund.

1. a. (infinitive)   Ivana hates _____ in long lines.

    b. (gerund)   Ivana hates _____ in long lines.

2. a. (infinitive)   When will we begin _____ dinner?

    b. (gerund)   When will we begin _____ dinner?

3. a. (infinitive)   Carmen loves _____ in the rain.

    b. (gerund)   Carmen loves _____ in the rain.

4. a. (infinitive)   The motor continued _____ noisily.

    b. (gerund)   The motor continued _____ noisily.

5. a. (infinitive)   Suddenly, the people started _____ .

    b. (gerund)   Suddenly, the people started _____ .

EXPLORING ONLINE

a4esl.org/q/h/grammar.html
Pick the ESL quizzes you need most, and build your English skills!

a4esl.org/q/j/km/mc-noncount.html
Practice those count and noncount nouns.

Index

Thematic Index to the Readings

These thematic clusters suggest some ways to group and discuss the reading selections in Unit 9.

Rhetorical Index to the Readings

Five Useful Ways to Join Ideas

Coordination

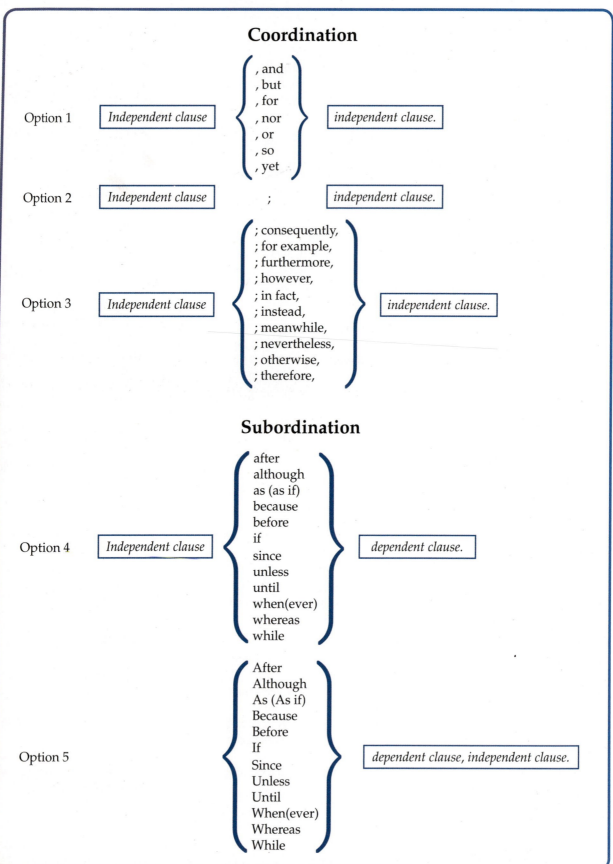

Option 1 Independent clause { , and / , but / , for / , nor / , or / , so / , yet } independent clause.

Option 2 Independent clause ; independent clause.

Option 3 Independent clause { ; consequently, / ; for example, / ; furthermore, / ; however, / ; in fact, / ; instead, / ; meanwhile, / ; nevertheless, / ; otherwise, / ; therefore, } independent clause.

Subordination

Option 4 Independent clause { after / although / as (as if) / because / before / if / since / unless / until / when(ever) / whereas / while } dependent clause.

Option 5 { After / Although / As (As if) / Because / Before / If / Since / Unless / Until / When(ever) / Whereas / While } dependent clause, independent clause.